FREEDOM TO LEARN

THIRD EDITION

CARL R. ROGERS

H. JEROME FREIBERG
UNIVERSITY OF HOUSTON

Merrill, an imprint of
Macmillan College Publishing Company
New York

Maxwell Macmillan Canada
Toronto

Maxwell Macmillan International
New York   Oxford   Singapore   Sydney

Editor: Linda A. Sullivan
Production Editor: Sheryl Glicker Langner
Text Designer: Patricia Cohan
Cover Designer: Robert Vega
Production Manager: Pamela D. Bennett
Electronic Text Management: Marilyn Wilson Phelps, Matthew Williams, Jane Lopez, Vincent A. Smith

This book was set in Bookman by Macmillan College Publishing Company and was printed and bound by R.R. Donnelley & Sons Company. The cover was printed by Phoenix Color Corp.

Macmillan College Publishing Company
866 Third Avenue
New York, NY 10022

Macmillan College Publishing Company is part of the
Maxwell Communication Group of Companies.

Maxwell Macmillan Canada, Inc.
1200 Eglinton Avenue East, Suite 200
Don Mills, Ontario M3C 3N1

Library of Congress Cataloging-in-Publication Data
Rogers, Carl R. (Carl Ransom)
      Freedom to Learn / Carl R. Rogers.—3rd ed.
          p.   cm.
      Rev. ed. of: Freedom to learn for the 80s, ©1983.
      Includes biographical references (p.) and index.
      ISBN 0-02-403121-6
      1. Learning, Psychology of. 2. Education—Experimental methods.
3. Academic freedom. 4. Educational innovations. I. Freiberg, H.
Jerome. II. Title.
LB1051.R636   1994
370.15—dc20
                                     93-34791
                                     CIP

Printing: 1 2 3 4 5 6 7 8 9   Year: 4 5 6 7

FOREWORD

◆

My father, Carl Rogers, was a quiet revolutionary. As one of the founders of humanistic psychology, he developed the client centered approach to counseling and psychotherapy which is widely used here and abroad. Unassuming in appearance and casual in dress, Carl frequently astounded people with his ability to listen—to really hear the emotional content as well as the spoken word. Above all, he valued the worth and dignity of the individual and trusted their capacity for self direction if given the proper environment. After years and years of careful research he verified the notion that a safe, supportive environment allowed each person (including children!) to journey down the path of self-discovery, self-esteem and self-directed learning. He described how to create that safe environment in detail. The basic premise is that if we are genuine, caring, empathic and congruent as teachers, parents, or counselor, we will be fostering the growth and learning capacity of others. That sounds simple. It is not. These methods and principles are expanded and clarified in this book.

Although most of Carl's work in his early years encompassed the field of psychotherapy, he and his colleagues soon realized that the psychological truths they were uncovering were applicable to education, organizational development and mediation or conflict resolution. His original edition of *Freedom to Learn* and the second edition, *Freedom to Learn for the 80's* brought a bright light into a rather dull educational field. It gave support to teachers who believed in humanistic values, and inspired innovative reform in classrooms. But sadly, during this time period, too many policymakers reverted back to prescriptive, externally designed learning rather than engaging the student in designing his or her own areas of interest. The conservative backlash rigidified the methods and the educational content in our schools.

I believe, as did Carl, that the future of our nation, indeed of the planet, depends on the nurturing of the creative life force in each and every child. As teachers and parents we hold that delicate bud of creativity in our hands. It can easily be squashed and thwarted. Often I hear statements from my own clients and students such as: "My teacher didn't like my writing, so I gave up," or, "I had to learn a bunch of stuff that had no relevance to my life, so I dropped out, intellectually." Or, "The art teacher gave me a C so I quit doing art."

We need young adults who can think and act creatively, who value human life, are able to make discerning decisions, and know how to communicate and negotiate rather than fight. It is our responsibility as guardians of these values to establish learning environments that foster freedom and responsibility.

If you are a person who loves kids, enjoys their curiosity, has faith in their ability to learn and grow no matter what their background, and want to discover new ways to foster their development, you will find this book worthwhile and enriching.

If you are a teacher, a school administrator, a parent, or young adult interested in a healthy educational system, this book will excite you. I encourage high school and college students to read this volume because it is when students demand their rights to a creative learning environment that action will be fast in forthcoming. I believe in the youth. My experience with my three daughters and my four grandchildren (Carl's great-grandchildren) constantly reminds me of the ever increasing capacity for our children and our children's children to surpass us in original, constructive, resourceful, thought and action. But it takes mentors and facilitators of person-centered learning to create the garden in which such children will blossom.

It occurs to me that you, the reader, might be interested in the kind of education Carl and Helen Rogers provided for me and my brother, David. I offer you some vignettes that illustrate my parents' valuing of what was then called "progressive education" and my own experience as a student. It may shed some light on the kind of learning experience that lasts a lifetime (1).

> ❦ *I know from experience that spontaneity and self-expression are nurtured in a loving, nonjudgmental, and stimulating environment. At Harley School in Rochester, New York, I was given such an educational opportunity. Although my parents were struggling through the depression years, their top priority was to send me and my brother, David, to a private, "progressive" school. The classes were small, with only fifteen or twenty pupils per class,*

and fostered a sense of joy in learning. Our curiosity and freedom of spirit were rewarded. Both our school and home environments gave the message that to be a conformist was a deadly path. We were encouraged to think for ourselves, to be our own authorities.

During these years at Harley School—grades one through six—art was a frequent happening. The art studio room was large, bright, airy, and equipped with a potter's wheel, painting easels, and abundant materials. We could draw, sculpt, paint, and make woodblocks or collages. Freedom reigned. I particularly remember being inspired by the apple tree bursting forth in fluffy pink and white blossoms outside the studio window. I set up the easel and enthusiastically tried to capture the scene. When I couldn't get the effect I wanted, I asked the teacher for help. She never said I was doing it wrong. She suggested ways of experimenting with mixing colors and methods that might get the desired results. First came spontaneity and my own creative burst. The technical help followed when I needed and asked for it. " Learn by doing" was the philosophy.

When I came home from school and told my neighborhood friends about my project, I was saddened by what they told me about their art classes in the public school. They sat at desks, were handed small pieces of paper, and were told what to draw and how to draw it. There seemed to be no joy in the process of making art, only the questions, "Did I do it right?" or "What will my grade be?"

When my father accepted a full professorship at Ohio State University in Columbus, my brother and I went to University School, the teacher training school on that campus. Many young, motivated student teachers were practicing their newly developed skills. Again I was in an educational setting where freedom of choice and responsibility for our own education was emphasized. The core curriculum course demanded that students choose their own area of study, make a plan to pursue it, do the necessary research as a project, and give a report to the class. We were trained to think and be self-starters, using our ingenuity and creativity at each step.

My most memorable project (one that shows my early interest in the educational process) was a research project I designed and carried out in the ninth grade. I compared the philosophies and methods of several elementary schools. The introduction to my thirty-five-page report (which I still have) posed these questions: What are the differences in the philosophies of education? What are the methods of teaching and the philosophy of traditional schools compared with the progressive schools? My intention was to get data to show which was the better method.

I visited three elementary schools that provided a sample of both traditional and progressive methods. I wrote detailed observation notes on the environment (desks that were nailed down compared to movable furniture), the behavior of the teachers (laying down strict rules and asking for conformity as compared to respecting the child by first listening and then suggesting a way). While observing the traditional school, I wrote, "It is like having puppets at the desks instead of human beings." My comments about the fourth grade in the more progressive school included: "In the afternoon the children take the responsibility of planning their own studies with the aid of the teacher. I think this is very helpful for them since it helps them to think about the world around them and its problems. If the teachers planned all their work for them I don't think they would get as interested in it as they seemed to be. Half the fun and work is to plan out how you're going to find out the things you want."

In a handwritten note to the principal of my school, my teacher wrote: "Natalie has put her youthful finger (I was thirteen years old) on some things which many adults—even students of education—frequently overlook. . . . I think this is a good case in point of the unlimited opportunity inherent in the emphasis upon self-directive learning."

In this paper I referred many times to the difference between the educational process in the German dictatorship and that of a democratic society, a clue to the fact that I was already deeply troubled about the rumblings in Europe. My political consciousness was budding at the time the Third Reich was emerging.

The philosophy and values of the educational system in which I was raised fostered creativity. In turn, I have used these values to develop similar environments for others. This philosophy includes: encouraging curiosity and experimentation, valuing individual freedom and responsibility, giving support and constructive criticism instead of judgment and grades, valuing the creative process more than the product, choosing to pursue one's own interests and goals rather than predetermined goals of the teacher, and having respect for the inner truth of each individual.

Americans tend to think that anything that has been done before is passé. But in my opinion, the truth is that those experiments in education bore out principles of learning that hold true today. Carl Rogers' methods and wisdom are urgently needed today!

When it was first suggested that *Freedom to Learn* be updated, I had my doubts that anyone could improve on Carl's work. However, Dr. Jerome Freiberg—a superb teacher and a dedicated facilitator to children and youth, (particularly those who have been underserved by the educational system)—has brought excellent fresh sources and writings, adding a new dimension to the book. This third edition will inspire teachers and administrators alike.

Jerry spent nearly three years revising *Freedom to Learn* to reflect the quarter century of practice that has evolved since Carl wrote the first edition. Traveling across the country, he talked with students in schools that are student-centered. From these discussions he found substantial reasons "Why Kids Love School." Thus, the new first chapter emerged. Interviewing teachers and administrators of schools that are built around the needs of the learner resulted in another important new chapter, "Administrators as Facilitators."

There has been a push to overly control schools in the misguided belief that this would improve them. However, controlled and over-regulated schools have led to stifled and fearful learning environments. With limited experience in democratic classrooms and schools, teachers often ask, "When you give students freedom what happens to discipline?" To answer this significant question Freiberg wrote: "Is There Discipline in Person-centered Classrooms?"

Twenty years of research on person-centered learning is summarized in the chapter "Researching Person-centered Issues in Education." Freiberg's twenty-five years of working in schools is very evident in the ideas and practical examples provided in the chapter "Ways of Building Freedom." The last two chapters: "Transforming Schools: A Person-centered Perspective," and "Some Reflections," challenge each of us to reconsider our role in supporting healthy and caring learning environments for all children.

The third edition is in keeping with Carl Rogers' values and style. I know my father would be pleased that his ideas continue to flourish and grow. At 85, he remained open to new perspectives, and new ways of perceiving and thinking. He never wanted disciples who would rigidify his ideas—he hoped people would take his learnings and develop them further. This edition of *Freedom to Learn* takes us many steps further on the pathway to reaching the goal of person-centered learning.

Natalie Rogers, Ph.D.

Author of: *Emerging Woman: A Decade of Midlife Transitions* (1980) and *The Creative Connection: Expressive Arts as Healing* (1993)
August, 1993 Santa Rosa, California

REFERENCES

1. These vignettes are excerpted from a forthcoming book: *Positive Regard: Carl Rogers and the Notables He Inspired,* edited by Melvin Suhd, Science & Behavior Books, Palo Alto, CA., forthcoming in 1994.

PREFACE

◆

*It is in fact nothing short of a miracle that the
modern methods of instruction have not yet entirely strangled the
holy curiosity of inquiry; for this delicate little plant, aside from
stimulation, stands mainly in need of freedom; without this it goes to
wrack and ruin without fail.*
Albert Einstein

Carl Rogers, the eminent psychologist and modern-day father of humanistic education, wrote the first edition of *Freedom to Learn* in 1969. The book was in response to a request from his niece, a teacher, who wanted Carl to respond to the needs of teachers to be more student-centered.

Carl's ideas about education grew from a lifetime of thought and interaction with people, both as a counselor and as a psychologist. He pioneered the modern case approach to research, drawn from people's lives and to provide meaning to a field that emphasized experimentation in the laboratory and studies of rat behaviors as a measure of everyday life. Carl Rogers broke with the highly formalized tradition of writing in the third person, prevalent in professional psychological journals in the 1940s and in many journals today. He spoke directly to the reader by using the first person, creating a sense of personal communication.

Revising a book is always a daunting experience. Revising *Freedom to Learn* has presented both unique opportunities to update an important statement about education and a challenge to keep that statement true to its original intent. *Freedom to Learn* was first revised in 1983 from its 1969 original. In the second edition Carl Rogers provided new research data about the use of a person-centered approach and current examples of how people in educational settings from elementary school through college experience person-centered learning. Carl sought the input of many researchers and educators for that revision, and I was one of the contributors. My role in the 1983 revision was to provide current examples from the research and illustrations of person-centered classrooms. I also provided feedback on the manuscript during its preparation. Carl and I were in correspondence regarding changes to be made during the writing of the text.

During the past twenty years I have dedicated my efforts to improving the environments in which teachers and students work and learn. I have been a sixth-grade teacher and team leader in an inner-city middle school in Rhode Island; a volunteer teacher in a maximum-security prison in Warwick, Rhode Island; a substitute teacher in a rural junior-senior high school in western Massachusetts; and director of Teacher Corps projects in Houston, a job that merged teaching with community. I also directed the Institute for Research on Urban Schooling at the University of Houston and the Center for Education in the Inner Cities in Houston. I have also had the pleasure to work with teachers across the nation—from Preston County, West Virginia, to Dunsmuir, California.

My research and hands-on work in schools and the previous writings I provided for the 1983 revision of *Freedom to Learn* led Natalie Rogers, Carl's daughter, and the publishers at Merrill/Macmillan to ask me to coauthor this third edition. It was from this perspective that I began the humbling project of providing a 1990s perspective to a book that contains some of the most important work in education. This third edition is a revision of earlier versions with the same title. Some chapters have been retained with few changes because they still remain timely, but almost half the book is new material that incorporates more recent experiences. In one instance an interview conducted in 1980 was repeated again at the same school in 1992 with striking results.

The challenge of maintaining the fidelity of Carl's ideas and his perspective about learning was only an iota less difficult than sustaining his first-person dialogue with the reader. It was decided by Natalie Rogers, the publisher, and myself that we would keep the first-person exchange. Several options were discussed, trying to distinguish between Carl's and my words. It was finally decided that each chapter would be identified as to its authorship in the end notes at the conclusion of the book. Maintaining fidelity to Carl's philosophy and ideals was our primary goal, and identifying authorship each time words or sentences were added would be counter to the clarity and interaction that Carl strived for in his writings.

Carl Rogers' birth in 1902 was a beginning, his death in February 1987 a destination; but the eighty-five years of his life were a remarkable journey. His memorial is a celebration of life and of the joy he provided personally and through his writings and meetings with hundreds of thousands of people. We believe the third edition of *Freedom to Learn* will continue the legacy left to us by Carl Rogers: an increased awareness of the importance of the person.

I conclude this preface with a guiding principle of Carl Rogers' life:

All individuals have within themselves the ability to guide their own lives in a manner that is both personally satisfying and socially constructive. In a particular type of helping relationship, we free . . . *the individual* to find their inner wisdom and confidence, and they will make increasingly healthier and more constructive choices. **—Carl Rogers** (1, p. xiv)

H. Jerome Frieberg

REFERENCES

1. Carl R. Rogers, "Personal Communications," in *The Carl Rogers Reader*, ed. Howard Kirschenbaum and Valerie Land Henderson (Boston: Houghton Mifflin, 1989).

ACKNOWLEDGMENTS

◆

A book that includes cases and vignettes joins together the resources and experiences of many people. This book would not be possible without the contributions of the following people. They have our special thanks:

Julie Ann Allender
David Aspy
John Barkham
Karen Voltz Bachofer
Bernice Boggess
Andrew Dunn
Bob Ferris
Dorothy Fadiman
Jeanne Ginsberg
Barbara Shiel McElveny
Tim Merrifield
Ron Miller
Michael McClellan
"Winnie Moore" (pseudonym)

Janice Nease
Diane Rabinowitz
Diana Ritenour
Flora Nell Roebuck
Natalie Rogers
William Romey
Ruth Sanford
Susan Sherwood
Betty Smith
Jim Stuckey
Gay Leah Swenson
Annette Watson
Alvin White

In addition to the above contributors, I would like to thank Gale Parker, a teacher of twenty years and a doctoral student in education at the University of Houston, who read every word written, and gave supportive and honest feedback. Thanks also to Patricia Brown who provided able assistance in the management of the permission requests for the book and Elena Vess for taking time to review the book in its latter stages.

The revision would not have been possible without Jeff Johnston and Linda Sullivan taking a personal interest in the third edition of *Freedom to Learn*. Most important was the belief by Natalie Rogers, that her father's work could be improved upon, and her faith in me, that I could make those improvements.

A special thanks goes to Linda Freiberg for her substantial intellectual and psychological support. Thanks also to my children, Oren and Ariel Freiberg. They have given my work in education a very dear and special meaning.

I want to extend my gratitude to the reviewers of the book: Neil Prokosch, National-Louis University; Nancy Lee Karlovic, Western Washington University; and Flora Roebuck, Texas Woman's University. I also want to thank David Berliner, Arizona State University; Jane Stallings, Texas A & M University; William Glasser; and Flora Roebuck for providing their perspectives on this edition of the book, and allowing us to include their comments on the back cover.

Recognition must be given to the many teachers, students, and administrators that provided access to their schools, their thoughts and feelings about conditions necessary for authentic learning. Special thanks to Sieg Mueller, Bernard Karlin, and Donald Feinstein, Chicago Public Schools, and James Lytle and Holly Perry, Philadelphia Public Schools.

Appreciation is also given to my colleagues at the University of Houston, who supported my work through a Faculty Development Leave in the Spring of 1991, which gave me the time to begin the research and conduct interviews for the book.

Finally, this text would not have been possible without the creative and notable efforts of the editorial team at Merrill/Macmillan, including Linda Sullivan, Editor; Sheryl Langner, Production Editor; Corrina Greive, Editorial Assistant; Dawn Potter, Copy Editor; and David Faherty, Senior Marketing Manager.

CONTENTS

◆

FOR THE TEACHER 149

INTRODUCTION

◆

Our educational system is failing to meet the real needs of society. Our schools constitute the most traditional, conservative, rigid, bureaucratic institution of our time. It is the institution most resistant to change. While these statements are accurate, they do not describe the whole situation. There *are* new developments: alternative schools, creative classrooms, opportunities for independent study, all kinds of adventurous enterprises being carried on by dedicated teachers, administrators, and parents. The major purpose of revising *Freedom to Learn* is to encourage these trends, these new hopes in the educational world, and to point the way to still further advances.

Another broader purpose is that we wish to aid the development of our most precious natural resource: the minds and hearts of our children and young people. It is their curiosity, their eagerness to learn, and their ability to make difficult and complex choices that will decide the future of our world. We need the help of all of our young—the despairing, alienated youth of the inner city; the aimless, affluent youth; the serious, thoughtful children; the whole great mass of our young people—if we are to preserve this fragile planet and build a future world worthy of whole persons. The only way we can be assured of that help is to assist our youth to learn deeply and broadly and, above all, to learn how to learn. No one book, no one person can achieve such an aim, but we can all do our bit. This volume is our contribution to that purpose.

This revision appears at an important time in our history. In this country during the last ten years, educators for the most part have reverted to teaching the "basics." We have lowered our expectations of what children can do and learn. This has drained away much of the creativity, the soul and essence of what our schools can be.

In response to minimal expectations for learning, many teachers have become frightened and inhibited about being creative. A ninth-grade teacher says, "I think twice about what I'm doing. Is there anything controversial in this lesson plan? If there is, I won't use it. I won't use things where a kid has to make a judgment."

How will students make judgments in the future without the opportunity to make judgments now? Ninth graders will soon be facing a world filled with controversy—political, social, international, as well as personal. They will be involved in making judgments, choices, and decisions that will affect their own lives, their families, their society. Yet to the extent that frightened attitudes prevail, as expressed by this teacher, students will have no experience in school that will prepare them for life in this difficult world. They will not engage in discussion of controversial matters, will not face new and complex problems in need of solution, will not learn how to make responsible decisions and abide by the consequences. A parent who is also a teacher sums it all up when she expresses her worries about her son: "I want him to be able to evaluate opinions and be able to think. People who can't think are ripe for dictatorship!"

This book takes a very strong stand. It believes in young people. It gives evidence that in a genuinely human climate, which the teacher can initiate, young people can find themselves respected, can make responsible choices, can experience the excitement of learning, can lay the basis for living as effective concerned citizens—well informed, competent in knowledge and skills, and confident about facing the future. A study reported in 1992 by Allan Steckler and his colleagues in the *American Journal of Health Promotion* concludes that caring and supportive climates in classrooms, schools, and districts are the best predictors for the promotion of good health care (1).

It is rather remarkable that suddenly authors, professionals, politicians, and government officials have discovered what facilitative teachers have always known—that humanity is the most important part of our schools. Articles appear daily in journals, newspapers, and magazines about teachers, schools, and students who are moving beyond the basics to richer, more rewarding learning experiences. Recently, the educational establishment seems more willing to experiment with humane elements in schools and classrooms—not perhaps out of any grounded philosophy about the roles of teacher and student, but more out of desperation and the realization that past ideas and practices have borne little fruit. The need for new ideas and opportunities for learning seem more urgent today than at any other time.

These new initiatives for opening up our schools and classrooms seem to spring up just as flowers bloom in the desert after a rainfall. The question remains: Will these initiatives, like the flowers in the desert, again fold and disappear due to a lack of substance? Or can they be sustained to create a foundation upon which we can build and grow, allowing a generation of children to flourish?

In this book you will find many examples of teachers who are real persons and who treat their students as real persons. You will discover the creative ways in which the minds of students are opened to the possibilities of reading, writing, and arithmetic, and much, much more. You will see classrooms in which teachers have provided freedom with responsibility, a freedom in which the excitement of significant learning flourishes.

When *Freedom to Learn* was first published in 1969, reports from students and teachers seemed to indicate that more significant learning took place in classrooms where there was a human climate, where attitudes and feelings could be expressed, where the student could choose from a wide range of options, where the teacher served as a facilitator of learning. But there was almost no hard evidence available at that time. Now, primarily because of years of research, we have a stronger foundation upon which to base our position. In studies involving hundreds of teachers and thousands of students from primary grades through technical schools, researchers have accumulated extensive data. The research shows that when a teacher is real, understanding, and caring, students learn more of the "basics" and, in addition, exhibit more creativity and problem-solving qualities. For the first time, the student-oriented teacher has the facts to back up his or her classroom stance. Chapter 13, which reports on the research findings, provides a foundation for the philosophy behind person-centered learning.

The following are the general aims of this book:

◆ To help teachers foster a climate of trust in the classroom so that curiosity and the natural desire to learn can be nourished and enhanced

◆ To encourage a participatory mode of decision making in all aspects of learning, a role in which students, teachers, and administrators each have a part

◆ To help students prize themselves, to build their confidence and self-esteem

◆ To uncover the excitement in intellectual and emotional discovery, which leads students to become lifelong learners

◆ To develop in teachers the attitudes that research has shown to be most effective in facilitating learning

◆ To help teachers grow as persons and find rich satisfaction in their interaction with learners

◆ To provide a support group for educators through contacts with networks, organizations, and individuals who are concerned about person-centered learning

◆ To provide a resource guide of books, materials, and publications that will extend and generate new ideas

◆ To create an awareness that for all of us, the good life is within, not something that is dependent on outside sources

Let me describe how the book is organized:

The first part, "Difficulties and Opportunities," includes three chapters. Chapter 1, "Why Do Kids Love School?" begins with what students think about school. Those interviews were conducted in schools that were identified as being student-centered. Their responses led to the title of the chapter. Chapter 2, "The Challenge of Present-day Teaching," realistically explores some of the external forces and circumstances that make the teaching profession a very difficult one today. Chapter 3, "As a Teacher, Can I Be Myself?" examines those elements within the teacher and the classroom that open up the possibility of discovering a richly interactive, growing life within the teaching profession.

The second part, "Responsible Freedom in the Classroom," includes four chapters. Chapter 4, "A Sixth-grade Teacher Experiments," and chapter 5, "A French Teacher Grows with Her Students," look at two teachers as they journey into person-centered learning. Chapter 6, "Administrators As Facilitators," describes how administrators can facilitate person-centered learning environments. Examples are given of facilitative administrators who provide a support system for students and teachers. Chapter 7, "Other Facilitators of Freedom," provides a forum for teacher-facilitators to tell their own stories of excitement, frustration, and reward as they work to humanize their classrooms.

The third part, "For the Teacher," includes five chapters: chapter 8, "The Interpersonal Relationship in the Facilitation of Learning"; chapter 9, "Becoming a Facilitator"; chapter 10, "Ways of Building Freedom"; chapter 11, "The Politics of Education"; and chapter 12, "Is There Discipline in Person-centered Classrooms?" These five chapters are intended to be of help to the teacher who wishes to take risks in innovation, who would like to move toward being a facilitator of responsible freedom. The chapters include the following questions: What is the nature of a facilitative relationship? How may it be implemented—in the teacher's own attitudes and in practical classroom management? What is involved in the education of humanistically oriented teachers? What about the issue of power, personal and institutional—the politics of education?

Chapter 13, "Researching Person-centered Issues in Education," begins with the original research of David Aspy and Flora Roebuck, which was reported in the 1970s, and then continues to the present. It provides strong support for the value of person-centered attitudes in the learning process.

The fourth part, "The Philosophical and Value Ramifications," includes three chapters: chapter 14, "A Modern Approach to the Valuing Process"; chapter 15, "Freedom and Commitment"; and chapter 16, "The Goal: The Fully Functioning Person." This section presents the philosophical stance in regard to the ever-present questions of values, the issue of free choice in a world of determinism, and the kind of person toward which we aim.

The fifth part, "A Moratorium on Schooling?" includes chapter 17, "Transforming Schools: A Person-centered Perspective." This chapter looks beyond legislative and bureaucratic mandates of school reforms to schools that have transformed themselves from within. An urgent call for a national dialogue on learning is made in this chapter.

The sixth part, "A Journey Begun," includes chapter 18, "Some Reflections." It gives a fresh summary of the advantages of a person-centered approach in the classroom. It also points to the resistance to change that is evident in our educational system and explores some of the reasons for this. It closes with a challenge to the reader.

An appendix, "Resources for Change: A Learning Community," is added to the book to provide a network of resources to assist you in the development of person-centered learning environments.

The book is so constructed that while it follows a somewhat logical progression, almost every chapter may be read separately as complete in itself. Thus, the reader may move to the chapters of greatest personal interest and find that they make sense by themselves though there may be some loss of context.

No one has as yet offered a viable solution to the gender issues in writing. In most cases the teacher is designated as *she*, given that 70 percent of teachers are female. The generic term *student* is alternated between *he* and *she*. Individual case examples reflect the gender of the author.

Case material and the experiences of others give richness to the educational philosophy of person-centered learning. A humanistic approach to education is neither the product of one person nor the result of its being implemented in only one way. As you will see, teachers of different ages, different interests, different personalities, and different subject-matter fields can all find distinctive ways of creating in their own groups, classes, courses, or departments an atmosphere of responsible freedom in which creative learning can take place.

REFERENCES

1. A. Steckler, R. Goodman, K. McLeory, S. Davis, and G. Koch, "Measuring the Diffusion of Innovative Health Promotion Programs," *American Journal of Health Promotion* 6 (1992): 214–25.

DIFFICULTIES
AND OPPORTUNITIES

CHAPTER 1

WHY DO KIDS LOVE SCHOOL?

◆

"I wish we could go to school all year round."
3d grader, Preston County, West Virginia

"My teacher really listens to me."
6th grader, Newton, Massachusetts

"They teach you by relating to you."
7th grader, Chicago

"They don't push you, they help you."
8th grader, Chicago

"They give good greetings. . . . Some even give hugs."
9th grader, Philadelphia

"They just don't teach you math, but they'll find out how you are doing."
12th grader, Houston

Freedom to Learn is about students and the people who care about their future. It is also about what we value in education: curiosity, motivation, caring, excitement, joy, and a meaningful life. It is not a cookbook for success, but a framework of realistic possibilities that can fundamentally change the way we think about schools, students, and learning.

What can we learn from students who love school? In our need to improve education, we have focused on what's wrong with education without asking what's right. Asking what's right with some of our schools does not imply a rose-colored view of the world. I have been most critical of our educational system; but I also realize that if we look for the negative, we will find it. By only looking for the pathologies in our world, we miss the opportunities to look for and learn from our successes. Do all students love or even like school? The answer is a resounding no! But there *are* youth in high school who feel punished when they are sick and need to miss school.

We shouldn't substitute tools for thinking, intellect for wisdom, bureaucracy for action. The best of us make mistakes and learn from them. A little chaos is healthy for any organization if we remember why we are here: for the person (1). These thoughts are not part of a radical manifesto but the essence of *In Search of Excellence,* a best-selling book about the importance of people and their need for creativity and autonomy in the workplace. They are also from some thoughts by Tom Peters ten years later, one of the co-authors of the book (2). Remembering why we are here—for our students—is paramount in our educational system.

What is unique about the learning environments and experiences of the students whose statements begin this chapter? How can their successful experiences help transform the way we offer students opportunities to learn? This chapter is a celebration of what is for some people (and what could be for many others) a warm, caring, creative learning environment—a learning place that has meaning and purpose, is person-centered, and creates learning communities where students are valued and everyone knows each other's name. Places that are person-centered can create the most extraordinary results in difficult surroundings. Relating, helping, and even hugs are part of a curriculum that students in public elementary, middle, and high schools experience each day in the inner cities of Chicago, Philadelphia, Houston; in Newton and Preston County; and in other communities across this nation. Love is among the strongest of human emotions. In this chapter, urban, rural, and suburban children describe, in their own words, the love they have for learning, a joy that extends to loving their teachers and the place called school.

STUDENT INTERVIEWS

During a six-month period in the early 1990s, I traveled to Philadelphia, Chicago, New Orleans, Houston, and Charleston, West Virginia, interviewing students and educators about their thoughts on school. I interviewed students in cafeterias, hallways, classrooms, and conference rooms. Some interviews were one on one, but most were in small groups of five or six students. I found the students more willing to talk when several of their peers also were involved. I tried to find students who represented a cross section of cultures and ethnicities. I visited schools that did a particularly good job of serving students who have traditionally been underserved by our educational system in the past. It was a remarkable experience. Prior to these interviews, I was extremely discouraged about our system of public education. But I saw enough optimism in the faces and words of these students for me to begin looking for meaningful solutions.

Why can't all learning experiences be as positive as the ones these students indicate? What is unique about learning environments that give students the resilience to grow in a difficult world? What lessons can we learn from these students and from those who have facilitated their learning? I found common threads that were consistent from one school to the next and from one student to another. Looking from the students' perspective, I discovered links that bound them and their facilitators into remarkable learning communities.

♦ *Students want to be trusted and respected.*   When sixth graders were asked what they wanted most from their middle school teachers, the common response was "respect." Melinda, a tenth grader in West Virginia said, "Just respect the teacher and they will respect you." A senior at the High School for the Performing and Visual Arts (HSPVA) in Houston said, "They talk to us and with us, which is, you know, a lot different than talking down to us." In Chicago, at the Montefiore School for troubled boys, Antonio, a sixth grader, said the teachers trusted the students to "begin making decisions about [how] you gonna have to learn. . . . You gonna have to do it on your own. . . . You're not gonna have no more teachers to walk you to class." A seventh grader at O'Farrell Community School in San Diego said about respect, "All my teachers show respect to all of the students in the classes, and so we show respect to them."

The entire learning environment needs to be infused with trust and respect. The current principal of HSPVA, Annette Watson, who was a teacher at the school twenty-one years ago, talked about how her own principal, Ruth Denney, trusted the teachers. Ms. Watson said, "The slogan of our school was and is 'Education Is an Adventure in Trust.' She [Denney] trusted us to do the very best job possible; in turn, we trusted the students who came to us to do the very best job possible."

♦ *Students want to be part of a family.*   In each of the interviews I conducted, the term *family* was a common thread. "They treat you like family" was the response of an eighth grader in Chicago. At the New Orleans Free School, a public school founded in 1972 as an alternative private school, near the trolley lines, some distance from the French Quarter, Termenisia, an eighth grader, said, "If I was you, I would come to this school because, well, it's like family." Christina, a senior at Houston's HSPVA said, "This is just really our home. I mean, I am here more than at home." O'Farrell Community School is built around houses and families rather than grade levels. A parent comments about her child's experience there: "I like the idea of these educational families, a very close contact with teachers and students" (3).

With 20 percent of Americans moving each year and with millions of children and youth living with only one parent, the idea of an extended family may only be captured in the school setting. A functional family provides unconditional love and support, as well as responsibility. Many of the students I met seemed to value these family characteristics and were willing to be active participants in learning communities that offered these qualities.

◆ *Students want teachers to be helpers.* Gustavo, an eleventh grader in a Houston high school with 3,400 students, said, "On a personal basis, they [the teachers] go to each individual and ask how you are doing. Some people are going to be at a different [academic] level than another individual." I asked Gustavo how a teacher could possibly meet 140 students each day. Joe, another student, interjected, "It's hard. You can tell by their faces at the end of the day." Gustavo agreed, "Like they're real tired, but they are still willing to help you out."

◆ *Students want opportunities to be responsible.* I watched students attend town meetings to decide on issues that affected the entire school, defuse conflicts that in the past led to fistfights, help each other and their teachers in class, and leave something behind when they graduated. In each case, the school, its faculty, and its staff trusted students enough to allow them to be active participants and citizens in their learning communities. A high school student at HSPVA said it best: "You have to start with the students. If you can somehow make them feel like they have a place in the world, then they would want to learn more about how to live in that world." In Philadelphia, at the Amy-6 Middle School, students meet weekly at schoolwide town meetings to discuss issues ranging from fights with other students, to gangs, to smoking in the bathrooms. At HSPVA, sixty students are elected each year to a parliament that focuses on student concerns. For example, students were leaving campus during lunch to get candy and sodas, which created security problems. To eliminate the need to leave campus, the parliament decided to request vending machines. The administration acted upon the request and the problem of students leaving campus was solved.

◆ *Students want freedom, not license.* The students in each of the schools I visited were eager to share their experiences. They also had a keen sense of the fine line between freedom and license. They talked about the importance of structure without rigidity. A senior in Houston said about his freedom during four years of high school, "I think our freedom is more freedom of expression than just being wild and having no self-control. It's like we have a purpose, and so our freedom is freedom to express ourselves."

◆ *Students want a place where people care.* Beginning teachers are often given the advice "Don't smile until Christmas." But research, in fact, supports warm, supportive environments that allow teachers and students to work collaboratively to achieve mutual goals. Schools that kids love all have caring people, and the caring comes in many forms. At HSPVA the janitor has a weekly column in the school newspaper where he provides advice to the students. A seventh grader at O'Farrell Community School said, "Most of the teachers here really care about me. They help not just with the subjects they teach, but with other subjects and personal things. It is different than other schools where they tell you to get your mind off anything that is not their subject" (4, p. 80). A sixth grader at the same school echoed those feelings when he said, "Most of the teachers want us to study and do well in school so that we can do well in life. If I dropped out of school, my teachers would be disappointed" (4, p. 195).

◆ *Students want teachers who help them succeed, not fail.* In each of the cities I visited, students expressed a common theme: "They [the teachers] don't let you fail." A ninth grader at Milby High School in Houston, a 3,600-student, mostly Latino high school, said it best: "The teachers care about your grades; they care about the whole class. They help you out a lot. . . . You can go up to them, they listen to you, they support you. They do things out of the ordinary that teachers don't have to do. . . . They just don't teach you math, they find out how you are doing. If they have an off period, you're welcome to come talk to them. Even, I mean, problems with your schoolwork or just problems like at home, they try to help." A twelve-year-old boy who could not function in any other school came to the Montefiore School in Chicago, which for many boys is a last stop before prison. He talked about the way a teacher motivates him to be successful by allowing him to keep working until he succeeds. "She'll give you a chance. When you do something wrong, she'll let you do it over again until you get it right. . . . [In] other schools you don't get a chance, they would keep yelling at you. They just tell you that you are suspended. They won't even talk to you. You know, Ms. Jones, she'll never let you give up." Another student attending the same school said, "When you are at regular schools, you do something wrong, they'd either say, 'You got detention,' or 'You have suspension,' but at this school, they try to help you out with your problems. This is a school of opportunity."

◆ *Students want to have choices.* Students need to have some say over what they learn. This may be reflected in a selection of special classes or clubs, or it might be an entire school curriculum that students select for part of the school day. In New Orleans, students talk about their selection of community service through internships. John, an eighth grader at the New Orleans Free School, said, "This school has internships as we can leave [the school] to work . . . like I work with children in the Children's Museum. . . . That's an internship. Every Thursday, I work at the museum half a day, and I come back to school to finish the rest of the day. I found it helpful. It is working with children, and I like working with children." Other students hold internships at city hall and nursing homes. Students select the type of community service they like, prepare a resume, and go for interviews.

CITIZEN OR TOURIST CLASSROOMS

Schools that kids love have teachers, principals, staff, and parents who are person-centered. Students are active, involved, and engaged citizens; they are stakeholders in their learning communities. The love that students have for learning reflects directly on what happens in classrooms. How teachers view their role is crucial. When teachers are facilitators of learning rather than mere givers of information, students are challenged to think for themselves. When teachers respect students as sources of knowledge rather than consumers, students become engaged in the learning process.

Generally, classrooms can be divided into two categories: classes in which students are consumers of information or classes in which students are producers of ideas. In the consumer classroom, students sit and listen to lectures, do worksheets—reams of worksheets—sit mostly by themselves with little or no intellectual interaction with others, and rarely cooperate. A parent recently wrote to a columnist with the following observation about her children's schooling:

> As a parent who works, I have a hard time believing that my children's success in school will translate into success in life. While they write book reports following their teacher's instructions, I have to write business reports using my own ingenuity. In the "real world" I must have the self-confidence to stand out by being me, but my children bring home good grades for being the same and doing the same as every other student in class. (5, p. 2e)

The concerns expressed by this mother, whose children are bringing home good grades, about the sameness of school and the one-size-fits-all approach to education are increasingly common among people who care about our youth and their future. Researchers have shown that during the last fifty years the pendulum between teacher-centered and student-centered learning has swung too often to the teacher-centered side. In fact, studies of classroom interaction in 1965 showed that teachers talked in secondary mathematics classrooms between 80 and 85 percent of the time. They talked in social studies classrooms during the same period from 70 to 73 percent of the time (6). Those same figures are consistent with John Goodlad's findings in 1983 after several years spent observing high school classrooms throughout the United States (7). Recent studies continue to show high levels of teacher talk in today's classrooms. All this talking *to* students creates passive observers, although some educators and researchers argue that such high levels of teacher talk or direct instruction lead to greater achievement gains. The few classrooms or school environments fostering person-centered learning that have been studied in detail (by David Aspy, Flora Roebuck, and others) show significant gains in both affective and cognitive learning. It is little wonder that in a passive environment students become bored.

Too Many Tourists in the Classroom

The perception that school is boring grows as students move through the grades. This boredom relates to the passivity some administrators, teachers, and the public expect of students in the school. Many students seem simply to be visitors or *tourists* in the classroom, moving from one idea to the next without any sense of comprehension, commitment, or involvement. This is particularly true at the secondary school level.

The idea of students as tourists emerged in my mind as I sat in a chair in Florence, Italy, observing Michelangelo's sculpture of David. The white marble sculpture towers over you, yet it has all the grace of a swan. Hordes of tour groups from around the world entered the sun-drenched hall with their guides. One guide ushered his group in and out of the hall in a matter of two minutes. In that time he explained the height of the sculpture, how long it took to carve, the type of marble used, and the detail of the hands, pointing particularly to the veins that were visible in the sculpture. The tourists barely had time to look down to verify the information (which was also in their guidebooks), look up at David, and hear their guide say, "It's time to move on, group. We have a lot of ground to cover today and many museums to see. Follow me!" As I watched them, I felt I had seen this pattern before.

Our tourists in the classroom rarely get called on by the teacher and seldom raise their hands to volunteer information. Given the opportunity, they sit in the back of the room and try to be invisible when it's time to participate. Some of the tourists constantly receive reprimands from the teacher, rarely get to work in the enrichment centers because they don't finish their work on time, and are generally social isolates in the classroom. A social pattern is created in classrooms: the "haves," who interact with the teacher and receive praise, support, and positive glances; and the "have nots," who are simply ignored. Nearly 80 percent of classroom interaction is dominated by 20 percent of the students. There almost seems to be an unwritten agreement between the teacher and these tourists: "Leave me alone and I won't bother you." Those left alone become our tourists—never involved, never excited, never chosen . . . simply here (8).

The classrooms and schools I have observed seem to encourage students to be either tourists or citizens. They fall into one of two distinct learning environments: passive or active. Kids love schools that have active learning environments. In active learning environments, students are encouraged to become engaged through cooperative learning activities, peer teaching, learning centers, field trips, projects, and classroom discourse that requires multiple levels of thinking. Students become citizens of the learning environment, taking responsibility for each other and the facility they enter each day. The schools that kids love have the qualities of active learning environments, allowing students to become shareholders in their own learning. The qualities listed in Figure 1.1 reflect differences in students whom I have observed in the two types of learning environments.

FIGURE 1.1
Passive vs. Active Classrooms

PASSIVE	ACTIVE
Students as tourists	Students as shareholders
Do low-level worksheets	Do small-group projects
Work by themselves	Work in cooperative learning groups of two or four
Work on what the teacher has provided	Create new ideas and materials through projects
Seldom write	Write every day
Rarely have their work prominently displayed	Students (self-selected) work displayed
Seldom discuss the reasons for their answers	Usually think/talk aloud about the way they derived an answer
Seldom participate in class	Take the initiative to interact with teachers and peers
View the classroom as "yours"	View the classroom as "ours"
Teacher-controlled discipline	Cooperative management
Have few friends in class	Have several friends in class
Usually late to class	Usually on time or early to class
Are more often absent from school	Have fewer absences
Feel neutral or hate school	Enjoy and involve themselves in school

H. J. Freiberg, *What to Do the First Days and Weeks of School* (Houston: Consistency Management Associates, 1992), p. 33.

At a time when our nation is at odds over the best way to educate our youth, many principals, teachers, and students seem to agree that we can, and know how to, create positive learning environments where students excel rather than just survive. Students and teachers surveyed at different times and places are in remarkable agreement about the overwhelming need to facilitate a place "where kids love school." The teachers I have met across the nation are asking to be set free from the red tape, regulations, and bureaucracy in order to create positive and caring learning environments for children and youth.

The difficulties faced by our schools are highlighted in this book's second chapter and in many reports by governmental and private commissions and publications during the past decade. Since the report *A Nation at Risk* declared in 1983 that the "state of our schools should be considered an act of war," more than three hundred commission reports have documented the failings of our educational system. The initial series of reports blamed teachers; however, more recent reports reflect a realization that placing blame on teachers is good for gaining attention but does little to solve the problem (9). Current reports have recommended that teachers (not students or, in most cases, parents) be empowered to make changes. In our world of instant everything, we tend to jump on the bandwagon of what's "hot" today. Short-term media successes are highlighted on television and in the newspapers but disappear in a few months. What has not been well documented are learning environments that give children the opportunity to grow in an atmosphere of freedom that lasts for years.

The lessons learned from interviews and case studies can be broadened to change the way a majority of students learn. We need to begin building on proactive and additive models of success rather than on individual or collective deficits. Therefore, I conclude this chapter with a few examples of schools that foster person-centered learning communities.

SCHOOLS THAT LOVE KIDS

Person-centered Learning Communities

In today's rapidly changing and trendy world, it is rare to be able to follow the development of an innovative school that has been true to its mission for more than twenty years. The High School for the Performing and Visual Arts (HSPVA) in Houston opened its doors in 1971. In 1980, students from HSPVA were interviewed for the second edition of *Freedom to Learn*. They were asked about their learning and the role that school played in their lives (10). In 1992, twenty-one years after HSPVA began, we traveled back to find out if the school is still a place where students want to go.

HSPVA in 1980. As you approach the school on Austin Street near downtown Houston, you first see a proud but weathered edifice with "Temple Beth Israel" carved into the stones above the front entrance. Since 1971 this renovated synagogue has served as HSPVA's home, a school that is part of the Houston Independent School District. In the intervening years, eight temporary buildings have been wheeled onto the grounds to accommodate the expanding enrollment, and the school must often borrow space from buildings across the street. The campus of renovated and temporary buildings houses five hundred students drawn from every part of the city and from surrounding suburban areas that lack such a facility. Students represent every ethnic group, every life-style, and every socioeconomic level. Here they spend three hours per day in their art areas (dance, drama, instrumental music, vocal music, media arts, or the visual arts) and the remaining four hours in required or elective academics.

The opening of HSPVA represented the first attempt by any public school in the nation to correlate concentrated training in the arts with the conventional academic high school curriculum. It was the first of Houston's alternative schools and has served as the model for the magnet schools that followed. The school has a full-time staff of thirty-four and several additional part-time certified teachers. In addition, the principal, Norma Lowder, points out that each year as many as forty or fifty professionals, who may not have certification as teachers but who have a wealth of expertise to share, are invited to the campus to teach special classes, to conduct workshops, and to present lectures and demonstrations.

Upon entering the campus, the visitor is drawn into its climate of informal camaraderie. There is neither the repressed silence of a custodial atmosphere nor the noise of the disengaged and idle. Instead, there is the busy hum of activity, earnest discussion, and purposeful movement.

"I look for teachers who are not rigid, who are flexible enough to recognize that geometry class may be a total loss today because the orchestra is playing in Jones Hall tonight; then, because geometry suffered through this, a [music] teacher who will say, 'You may have the kids for some of my time today to work on geometry,'" explains Ms. Lowder. Close friendships among HSPVA faculty members develop from this sense of community and mutual help, and the spin-offs include a high level of job satisfaction and a low rate of turnover. This low turnover rate, along with the frequent occasions for individualized instruction and tutorial help that faculty members offer to students, enhances the quality of teacher-student relationships.

Interestingly—and in keeping with findings reported later in this book—young people from the school consistently perform among the highest in the district academically and constitute a high proportion of the district's merit scholars. In 1979, three of the thirty nationally selected presidential scholars honored for academic achievement came from HSPVA. Numerous awards line the walls of the school's offices. Because the student body is drawn from a wide area, parents are seldom physically present at the school. For students whose ethnic ties bind their families closely to their neighborhoods, coming to HSPVA may represent their first venture beyond their cultural boundaries. Parental support is strong, however, and the community takes pride in the school and often requests performances from the student groups.

We asked a group of June 1980 graduates how they felt about their experiences at HSPVA. The following are representative responses from three graduates:

Susan   HSPVA let me be myself and let me grow pretty much on my own. I was never forced into a mold but was allowed to be an individual, allowed to do my artwork the way I felt it should be done.

John   In order to be very real you have to know all the facets of yourself and that's a process that takes a long time. Once I allowed that to sink in, it just made me feel that much easier about learning. I can learn now. I can take things, and I can actually see my development. It is a very confident feeling.

Sandra   Attending school at HSPVA can be described in one word: it is an *experience*. Although this experience may be different for each individual student, the basic foundation of creativity, growth, and learning is there for everyone. From the very first day a student walks on campus, he is exposed to creativity. Creativity at HSPVA is one thing that is never lacking—there seems to be a constant flow of it, not only within each art area, but also between them. One art area is always serving as inspiration for another. Students at HSPVA are not afraid of their creativity; instead, they are proud of it, and are free to express it in many ways, both in their individual art areas and in their academic subjects as well.

As a result of this creative freedom, the HSPVA student has the opportunity to grow to his highest potential in anything he does. He is exposed to many different philosophies and ideas, and thus is provided with a broad base from which to grow and form his own beliefs.

Much of this growth results from the student being given the opportunity to be around people involved in all the arts, and thus learning many different ways of looking at things. Because of this exposure, he becomes open to many different kinds of expression, and not only does he learn about different areas of the arts, but he also learns a great deal about life and about himself as well.

HSPVA is definitely a very exciting, special place to be.

It is a compelling experience to watch these students. Here is a setting in which their sense of promise and self-worth can flower. It is clearly a school where the teachers have become facilitators of learning.

HSPVA Today. In 1982, HSPVA moved to a new location in the heart of the arts community of Houston. It was the first high school of its kind to be built specifically for students of the performing and visual arts. The students had outgrown their old converted building, which had more temporary classrooms outside in trailers than permanent classrooms in the school. The new HSPVA is a few blocks from a main thoroughfare dotted with galleries and museums. The school is located in a neighborhood of modest one- and two-story homes built in the 1940s and 1950s. Rather than standing out from the community, the two-story school blends in. While many schools on the East Coast and in the Midwest look like their factory-era counterparts, HSPVA looks like a modern high-tech facility. The building is clean, with wonderful color and graphics, and student work is displayed throughout.

Walking from the parking area in front of the school, I was immediately attracted to the sounds of French horns. A quartet of students was sitting near the front of the school, practicing. They were one of many groups practicing music outside. Their teacher was also outside, moving from group to group, listening and giving feedback on their work. Other students with sketch pads were drawing. Their teacher was also moving around, giving encouragement and feedback to each student.

In this age of high technology, I still rely on an intuitive sense of values to decide how a school functions, driven in part by questions I ask. How does it feel when I approach the school and walk through the door? Is it a place where I would want to learn? Is it inviting? What does it sound like? Are people talking and laughing, or is there an institutional silence? You can tell much about a school from the office. Eye contact is perhaps a key indicator to the workings of a school. Do students, teachers, and office personnel look at you? Do they acknowledge your existence? The moment I walked into the HSPVA office unannounced, I was greeted and asked how I could be helped. I felt very much connected to the school within a few minutes. Students in the commons area, which is used as a cafeteria and rehearsal area, said hello as I walked in.

A Community of Learners.   I asked for a small space where I could talk with some students during their lunch time. Five students entered with their sack lunches, and we began our introductions. Shena, Mireille, Christina, Gumaro, and Russell are all seniors. They each specialize in one area of the arts in addition to working on their regular academic programs. The students reflect the diversity and richness of their city in terms of culture, ethnicity, and interests. Shena studies voice, and Mireille and Russell focus on theater. Christina studies instrumental music, and Gumaro studies dance. Yet in listening to them talk about themselves, their friends, and school, I was impressed with the great respect they have for each other and their teachers. This respect was a unifying theme that brought this diverse group together and made them collectively stronger than any one person alone.

Their school day is one hour longer than that of other high schools to enable each student to have three hours in an arts area and four hours in other academic subjects. Test scores are not used for entrance into HSPVA, yet the 1992 graduating class of 150 seniors received $2 million in college scholarships and countless awards. It is also a school without a football, baseball, or basketball team; cheerleaders; or prom king and queen. It is a school where everyone counts.

I asked a few questions of the six students, and they talked for nearly one and a half hours.

Question: You have talked about the freedom to do what's important. Would you describe this freedom for me?

Russell   It's controlled freedom, if that makes sense, it's freedom where you are safe. But day to day [you] allow yourself to grow, allow yourself to be an adult, you have the potential to be, so it's really just the freedom to become who you are.

Mireille   I think freedom gives you unknown boundaries that you're supposed to discover for yourself. Instead of someone saying, "Okay, this is how you are born and this is the way something is created," it allows you to realize it, which makes it a lot more satisfying. I think especially as teenagers we are all curious and that's why we do a lot of the things we do.

Russell If there are a lot of rules keeping you from discovering things, then you may be in your thirties before you actually get to discover something. It gives you so much more time to progress with it when you realize it in your youth.

Christina In another school if you don't want to play football, join the band, or be a cheerleader, you are nobody. Each of us here has some things that we are good at, and we can dedicate ourselves to it.

Question: Why is HSPVA special to you?

Shena I think a lot of it comes down to self-esteem. All of us are continually being built up and being told what potential we have.

Gumaro I can communicate with my teachers and my teachers can communicate with me.

Russell The major point is here, people want to learn, and teachers and students are on the same side.

Christina When I was in junior high school, my teacher spent thirty minutes disciplining the class and fifteen to twenty minutes teaching. You are here to learn, and you are here to grow, and discipline problems don't have any place here. And here we sort of wiped out the discipline factor. You don't have time to be bored, you have too much to do.

Russell We know the 623 people here, don't have to worry about someone going into school with a gun. We don't have to worry about gangs starting up during lunch or even during class or someone being thrown up against a locker; it's never a concern here.

Question: What can you tell me about your visiting teachers?

Shena They are great! They give us insights into the professional world.

Christina He [a visiting teacher] teaches us about life, and it's just great to talk.

Shena His name is Kirk Wayland, and he came last year. He's a jazz musician. After his master class, he told everyone who was thinking about a career in music to come up front and "we're gonna talk." He told us the three principles he follows in his life. They were, " . . . be true to your art, . . . never compare yourself, . . . and do what makes you happy."

Gumaro Well, they just lay it on the line. I mean, they come in and tell you exactly how it is, and they say if you can't do it, it's okay, you can get out.

They just really inspire faith in you, they really inspire you. I don't know, the whole key is just honesty and sharing, sharing what they have learned and fulfilling their dreams and carrying on the art.

Question: How do you receive feedback on your work?

Gumaro   We have a portfolio review. We sit down and show them our portfolio, and they look it over. I think it comes down to either you worked during the year or you didn't. They [the teachers] are really joking around with you. You're getting all this good time, and that's why I usually try and keep up with myself.

On Failure:

Russell   [Making mistakes now] is a lot easier, which is a nice feeling to know you can fail and it's not going to ruin your life or anyone else's.

Mireille   The teachers are really helpful because they let you know ahead of time if you are not doing well in an area. So, it's really helpful when the teachers sit with you and talk with you about how you are doing.

Question: Do you as seniors feel any particular responsibility for people coming in?

Mireille   I feel a lot of responsibility. I guess I have gained so much from being here, I just want everyone else to have the same kind of experience.

Christina   They [the freshmen] are coming from these middle schools. They are just so segregated from everybody. I mean last year, I remember, [at lunch] there was a Hispanic table, a Black table, a jazz table, and a dance table. I felt that was one of my responsibilities to teach them to go and meet with other people and get to know them so we can all be family. I want the freshmen to be themselves. They will come up to me and say, "Hey, Baby." Every time I see someone do that, I will go up to them and ask them how they are doing and teach them that they can be themselves, and they can talk to me. I try to let them know they don't have to do that to fit in; people will like you better if you be yourself.

Question: On a scale from "I hate school," "school is just so-so," "school is all right," "school is fine" to "I love school," where would you put yourself?

All students in unison   I love this school.

Russell   We all love the school. If you love something you are going to make it work.

Mireille   I love it; I couldn't, I wouldn't want to be anywhere else. I just want everyone else to feel the same way I do.

In 1987, the city leaders of Houston established, through private funds, the Houston Read Commission. The commission was charged with coordinating the literacy efforts of more than twenty different organizations in the city, organizations dedicated to helping the estimated five hundred thousand illiterate and semiliterate citizens in Houston. A staff of dedicated citizens, led by Barbara Kazden and Margaret Doughty, established the first Read Commission Literacy Center in a predominantly Latino area of Houston's inner city. Since its start, the Read Commission has expanded by opening additional centers throughout the city. It also has established sites within businesses so that employees have easy access to literacy services during the work day. Its most recent effort includes working with felons who have been recently released from prison and coordinating twenty-two other literacy providers throughout the city to help more than ten thousand adults advance their literacy.

The birth of the first center began with a staff composed of both volunteers and paid employees. They transformed a nondescript warehouse into a center for learning. They had three goals for each person who walked through the front doors: (a) Make the Read Commission Literacy Center a welcoming place for the student; (b) Provide curriculum and instruction different from what that student had in school; and (c) Give the student the freedom to come and go as needed, allowing learning to revolve around the student's schedule and not the center's.

The Read Center has been able to accomplish each of these goals. An extensive evaluation over a two-year period showed that students who spent 116 hours involved in learning at the center gained three years in reading and two years in mathematics skills (12). While the achievement gains were impressive, I was even more impressed with the interview responses of the young men and women who found new hope and meaning in their lives.

I asked the students if the center staff was assisting them in achieving their goals. One student responded, "I like that they go out of their way to help you one-to-one. That's what I like the most, everyone gets attention. Here, they come and ask you if you have any problems." Another student stated, "The people are friendly and take time out for me. They are caring. Sometimes I'm tired, and Bob takes the time to talk with me. That makes me keep coming." Yet they describe a relaxed, work-oriented environment. One student stated, "I just come for two hours. They get you started. They put attention to you." Another student also talked about the center: "[It's] excellent. They are right on the ball. There are some things that frustrate me, but they sit back and help me relax. In school, the class sizes were too big for that."

When asked if they would recommend the center to others, all the participants interviewed said they would. (Several students had already recruited others to the Learning Center.) According to one student, "We have one-to-one [teaching], no pressure, no stress, good environment, [and] good staff." Another responded, "Knowledge is power, and education will be more helpful in the long run." One student said, "The staff is open, kind, warm-hearted, and they treat you like family."

Comments.   Many students who come to this center are dropouts from public schools and other literacy programs established by school districts. It is clear from their comments that they need a different kind of learning environment than the kind presented in most schools today. When given a new approach and the opportunity to learn, they excel in reading and mathematics in a way that makes them feel great about themselves.

An Entire Province

During the late 1970s, when the United States was going back to the basics, the Toronto public schools in Ontario, Canada, took a road less traveled. They asked themselves what their students would need in order to enter the world in the future as educated citizens and how teachers and others could facilitate that need. They established, with students, parents, educators, and the general community in Toronto and the province of Ontario, a mission based on the kind of people they wanted to come out of their schools. What evolved was a mission statement focused on the needs of students. Local districts and their schools were the primary source for determining the best ways to achieve these goals.

The deputy minister of education explained on an ABC evening news report, *The American Agenda,* that there is no one best way to educate all children. Bill Blakemore, the interviewer from ABC, impressively listed the key ingredients in Toronto's mission for children preparing to leave school and enter an adult world (13):

Like to learn

Think clearly

Feel deeply

Act wisely

Work with others

Be problem solvers

Respect other cultures

Have basic skills

Teachers have become facilitators in the Toronto schools, using active learning and student involvement to engage the learner. Cooperative learning, in which students work in pairs or in teams of four, is an integral part of the learning day. It is used to expand educational opportunities and bring harmony to a racially and culturally diverse school system.

The ABC news report showed two boys of different races writing together in a book. When the interviewer asked them what they were doing, they explained, "We are writing a book." They planned to publish their book by placing it in the library where other students could read and learn from it. Rexford Brown of the Education Commission of the States, who visited the Toronto schools, explained in the ABC interview that the education system in the United States asked for low-level, threshold basic skills. "We have been asking for something less and we have been getting something less" (13).

CONCLUDING REMARKS

It is evident that our learning environments need to be changed. There are numerous examples and models of effective long-term, person-centered programs to provide a framework for this change, although some common goals are achieved by following different paths. The Toronto school system, HSPVA, the New Orleans Free School, and many others reflect the tip of the iceberg of opportunity for a revitalized and transformed learning community. The students we met in this chapter were given the opportunity both to learn and to facilitate the learnings of others. Being a facilitator of learning requires a special perspective on life. Facilitators are not performers or stars; they are people who place learners' needs and interests first. In the next few chapters we will begin to understand the dynamics of people who go beyond mere teaching to facilitate the learning of children and youth.

I often think the best facilitator was described by the Chinese philosopher Lao Tzu more than twenty-five hundred years ago. I want to end this chapter with his words:

A leader is best

When people barely know that he exists,

Not so good when people obey and acclaim him,

Worst when they despise him.

"Fail to honor people,

They fail to honor you;"

But of a good leader, who talks little,

When his work is done, his aim fulfilled,

They will all say, "We did this ourselves." (14)

REFERENCES

1. T. Peters and R. Waterman, *In Search of Excellence: Lessons from America's Best-run Companies* (New York: Harper and Row, 1982).

2. J. Hillkirk, "In Search of Excellence Ten Years Later" (interview with Tom Peters), *USA Today*, 11 November 1992, p. 7b.

3. K. Bachofer and W. Borton, *Restructuring: A View from the Trenches: The Continuing Evolution of O'Farrell Community School, Center for Advanced Academic Studies* (San Diego: San Diego Public Schools, 1992).

4. K. Bachofer, *Hidden Messages: Student Perceptions of Teacher Expectation Communication* (dissertation, Claremont Graduate School, 1993).

5. Y. Fournier, "Children Must Learn to Collaborate," *Houston Chronicle* (from Scripps-Howard News Service), 1 January 1993.

6. N. Flanders, *Analyzing Teacher Behavior* (Reading, Mass.: Addison-Wesley, 1970).

7. J. Goodlad, *A Place Called School: Prospects for the Future* (New York: McGraw-Hill, 1983).

8. H. J. Freiberg, *What to Do the First Days and Weeks of School* (Houston: Consistency Management Associates, 1992).

9. S. Conneley and B. Cooper, *The School As Work Environment: Implications for Reform* (Boston: Allyn and Bacon, 1991).

10. H. J. Freiberg, *High School for the Performing and Visual Arts* (Unpublished manuscript, University of Houston, 1980 interview).

11. D. Fadiman, *Why Do These Kids Love School?* (study guide) (Santa Monica, Calif.: Pyramid Film and Video, 1991).

12. H. J. Freiberg, L. Gauthier, and T. Stein, *Assessment of the Read Commission Learning Center* (Houston: University of Houston, 1992).

13. ABC World News Tonight, "Toronto Public Schools: Make the Difference," from the series *The American Agenda* (New York: ABC News, 1990). Video.

14. Lao Tzu, *The Way of Life according to Lao Tzu*, trans. Witter Bynner (New York: Capricorn Books, 1962).

CHAPTER 2

THE CHALLENGE OF PRESENT-DAY TEACHING

◆

Sometimes you want to go where everybody knows
your name and they're always glad you came.

What a splendid mission statement for our schools. But these words are from the theme song for *Cheers*, a long-running television series about a bar in Boston and relationships among its patrons. Unfortunately, instead of living up to the goals of the theme song, many schools have become places where there is little cheer or learning.

Chapter 1 illustrates the impact school can have on students when their needs *are* being met by caring and creative people: These students love school. Placing students at the center creates the conditions necessary for learning to occur. But perhaps we need to experience the worst to realize the best—to see the darkness to appreciate the light. Therefore, chapter 2 looks at the challenges we face in changing schools that function through mandates and bureaucracy rather than through the needs of the learner. Regrettably, too many of our public schools have become places that students and teachers try to avoid. The growth of home schooling—estimated by some to serve about 1.5 million students—and the movement toward private schools may leave our public school system, the foundation of any democracy, in shambles.

Increasingly, our schools are becoming isolated islands surrounded by indifference. Our classrooms have become rooms physically linked by hallways. Our future generations of children represent a dwindling population of healthy individuals. Now and in the future we are facing growing numbers of children with serious and severe problems. "Several years ago I would have one or two students in my class who were reluctant learners. Now I have an entire classroom of students with no motivation to learn," says a high school teacher from rural West Virginia. These thoughts are echoed by teachers from across the country. More often than not, children come to school devoid of the motivation to learn, and teachers lack the resources to meet the growing needs of students. Those children who *do* come to school with motivation to learn quickly lose it in the endless stream of imposed rules, tests, competition, and inflexibility.

Too many of our schools are silent. Dialogue and discourse are the exception, not the rule. Elementary students walk down halls with their fingers over their lips. Yet bullhorns blare in the cafeteria of a suburban middle school where five hundred students are expected to remain silent. Some teachers avoid group activities because "students need to talk, creating too much noise." The silence is broken, however, by the shrill of bells ringing to announce the change of classes. The squeal of the P. A. system breaks into the thoughts of students and teachers to make announcements to a few students: "Will Bill, José, Sarah, and Lantia come to the office? Remember, the band has practice at 4:00 P.M. today."

We have in our schools a curriculum of the absurd. Students can attend twelve years of school without ever seeing the integration of English, mathematics, social studies, literature, art, and history. Knowledge is taught in premeasured forty-two or fifty-minute cubes that are void of interrelationships. Students learn fragmented facts, are taught reading as if all students learn to read in the same way, are timed in mass drills, and do science without laboratory experience. Students are expected to be passive; and the lower the socioeconomic status, the more passive the child is expected to be. From the eye of the child sitting in the classroom each day, the school experience is at times bewildering, frustrating, and maddening. This bewilderment is compounded if the child's home and community are fragmented and provide limited support. A child leaves a place in the morning that lacks reading materials, arts, and other mental stimulation and enters a school equally limited. It is no wonder that millions of students leave school and that millions of other students attend school in body but not in spirit or mind.

HOW ARE THE REFORMS DOING?

In one word, abysmal. This assessment comes after nearly ten years of effort to improve and reform our schools. It is hard to find teachers, parents, legislators, or community members who will stand up and say that our children are better off today than they were ten or twenty years ago. The statistics paint a grim picture of youth in poverty and despair, isolated and frustrated. We live in a time when technology has provided the opportunity for the greatest comforts humans have known. From health care and communication, to computers and transportation, the world is a different place today than it was in 1969, when this book was first published. Despite all our technological advances, we seem to be crashing into an abyss of violence, crime, infant mortality, intolerance, isolation, apathy, and dissolving families. We must realize that a positive future is more than better technology; it is better relationships, which take time and a fertile climate of trust, caring, and positive self-regard. A cursory look at data from several sources shows that we face one of the greatest challenges our nation has experienced since the Civil War.

- The United States has the world's highest incarceration rate, with 426 prisoners for every hundred thousand people. This rate has increased threefold since 1970 (1).

- In Houston, a twelve-year-old boy was murdered for his Los Angeles Raiders jacket. In New York City, gangs within a space of a few months shot fifteen people and killed six in their quests for so-called status jackets (2).

- The New York City school system spends nearly $75 million on school security, while many school buildings are badly in need of repair and class size continues to increase.

- Nearly one child in four is poor, and children under five years of age represent the greatest level of poverty. Nearly 40 percent of the poor are children, and 10 percent are the elderly (3).

- 15.3 million children live with only one parent (90 percent with the mother) and 1.9 million children live with neither parent. They are raised by grandparents, by other relatives, or in foster homes (3).

- Inner-city teachers have the highest stress levels of any profession, including air traffic controllers and police officers (4).

- In a survey of 65,550 secondary students in Houston, 31,630 students (48 percent) disagree or strongly disagree with the statement "the school is a safe place." An additional 7,866 students (12 percent) indicated they did not know (5).

- Teenage suicide is the third leading cause of death. Among ten- to fourteen-year-olds, it has tripled from the mid-1960s to the mid-1980s and has doubled for fifteen- to nineteen-year-olds during the same time period. The greatest increase in suicides is among white teenagers.

Many blame drugs for our nation's and schools' problems, but drugs are a symptom of a more serious and deeper problem. The invisible bonds of connectedness that bring people together—family, community, neighborhoods, and schools—are being stretched to their limits. During the last three decades, the public, media, and educational community have focused primarily on the defects in our schools. The failure of our schools to prepare students for the workplace, the high financial expenditure for declining achievement gains (when compared with other economic peers in the international community), and the rising levels of social pathology (violence, suicide, teen pregnancy, gangs, and drugs) have taken center stage in our nation's assessment of the future.

When families, community, and values are strong, schools are strong, and the nation is strong. This is evident in the resources a nation spends for education. Of all industrialized countries, Japan spends the least for education of its youth. The United States is second highest in per-student expenditure (6). Japan spends far less because family, community, religious, and cultural groups expend something more valuable than money on the education of their youth: time and the social resources needed to support successful learning environments.

Forty years ago the education of students was sustained by five pillars of support: families, culture, religion, community, and the school. The high rate of divorce, combined with economic and personal needs for both parents to work outside the home, has shattered the ability of families to focus on and support the education of their children. Divorce, job changes, and housing mobility resulting from poverty also have destabilized the community. According to researchers, if current trends remain the same, by the year 2020 nearly 50 percent of all students will be educationally disadvantaged (6). This is due, in part, to a mismatch between the values, experiences, and resources of the home, community, and school.

When home and families, community, religion, and culture are not supporting the child, then the school is expected to increase its share, requiring money instead of more time from the other sectors. Money is an important resource, but alone it becomes a poor substitute for parental involvement, community support and awareness, and religious and cultural values. Countries that have a good balance between the five supporting pillars create an environment for strong leadership, quality of life, and economic success. The state of a nation's school and educational support system predicts the well-being of the country in the future and its ability to be resilient in challenging economic and political times.

It's not that teachers, principals, or parents are working less. In fact, everyone seems to be working more. In the 1970s studies predicted that the amount of adult leisure time would increase dramatically over a twenty-year period. The reality is that as adults we have less, not more, leisure time than in any period during the last fifteen years: seven hours less a week. Family members are working just to sustain a basic level of living, and there is evidence that the quality of life among the people of the next generation will be worse, not better, than their parents'.

While the statistics give a global picture of the problems, they also tend to dehumanize and minimize the fact that individuals are represented by the numbers. The problems of schools and society are complex, and the solutions need to be multidimensional (7). Schools alone cannot make lasting social changes without focused effort from all aspects of society. While much of the information is bleak, there is also hope. The hope comes not through technology or simple solutions but through the joining together of people with common concerns, beliefs, and interests, with people working together for the good of all children, a process in which the efforts of individuals are multiplied by cooperative efforts to achieve common good.

One Child's View

It is a warm August day. The air hangs heavy with humidity, and the sun shines brightly into Sarah's bedroom, which faces east. Sarah, who shares her room with three younger sisters, has been up for several hours. She is preparing for the first day of school, and she is very excited. Although Sarah didn't sleep much the night before, she isn't tired. She can't wait to get to her new school. Today she begins middle school.

I, too, remember the excitement of the first day of school. The thrill and anticipation of a new school are balanced by an uneasiness of the unknown. I used to wonder, "What will the new school, the other students, and—most important—my teachers be like?" Sarah's wonder and excitement are shared by millions of students on the first day of school. Some schools are warm and inviting places with bright colors, plants all around, students' work on the walls, and teachers and students who greet you with a smile as you enter. It doesn't matter how you're feeling as you walk in; you always walk out feeling good. There is an energy about the place that seems to give you a feeling of well-being.

In looking back at my own education, I can see that each school year brought different experiences. Some teachers demanded that I learn, others helped me want to learn; some laughed with me, others laughed at me; some made me want to cry, others made me want to cheer; some gave me hope, others gave me despair; some made me feel stupid, others made me feel smart. In other words, some felt they had to control my learning, while others gave me the *freedom to learn*.

Listen to the Students

Students tell us much about their conditions of learning. When we listen to students, we can gain an understanding about the reasons for both the successes and failures of our schools. For example, to some youth, school is an oasis, a safe haven from the crime, drugs, abuse, extremes of heat and cold, and dreariness of existence in decaying urban centers. To other students, school is a warm, dry place that is their only chance for a hot meal. I was visiting an inner-city elementary school early one morning and noticed a group of students huddled together against an outside wall. It was a cold morning, and the school was scheduled to open in fifteen minutes, at 7:00 A.M. I asked one of the students why they were here so early. The thin, somewhat shy boy said, "It's nice and warm inside and we get breakfast at 7:30." The principal told me later that she and some teachers planned to begin arriving earlier so the children wouldn't need to wait in the cold.

Other students, however, see school as a place that must be endured in order for them to participate in more interesting extracurricular activities like football and cheerleading. Still other students see school as a wonderful place, full of ideas, discussion, joy, friends, and excitement. I watched a middle school playground become a beehive of activity at 7:25 in the morning. Students were very animated as they shared their science projects with each other and discussed the details. I saw similar joy in a high school of two thousand students in North Kansas City where students worked until late in the evening preparing an art exhibition that included the works of all two thousand students and covered every square foot of wall space in the school. Students were guides for parents and visitors who came to see the exhibit, which lasted for three weeks.

Many adolescents see school as a place to socialize and meet others. Some even see school as a place to buy and sell drugs and share exploits of crimes committed against other students or people in the neighborhood. The media tend to sensationalize the latter problems, particularly those related to rising crime, drugs, and gangs. To many students, however, school is just boring.

Student Dissatisfaction

These problems of identity, isolation, and alienation are not unique to the United States. I have recently returned from trips to Italy, Spain, and Israel. During one visit, I spent time with Italian high school teachers and students in both urban and rural northern Italy, and I individually talked with several of the students, including the daughter of one of the teachers in the seminar. She described her experiences in school as one in which "we are treated as mindless beings with no respect, no ideas, and our opinions are judged as worthless, as if we don't exist."

Several dozen years ago, the level of student dissatisfaction in the United States was documented by an educational journal that requested student opinions for an issue called "Kids Talk about School." The journal was flooded with responses. The findings were summarized as follows: "3,157 students (U.S. and Canada, middle school, senior high, college and graduate school, male and female, black and white, public and private, rich and poor) wrote and told us that school is a BORE" (8, pp. 5–6). The situation has not changed since that time. In fact, it has grown worse.

It is clear from the national reports that this is an extremely difficult time in which to become a teacher. It is also a challenging time, and much of this book is devoted to ways of meeting that challenge. But I have no desire to overlook the very real negative elements affecting the education of our children today.

LEARNING CLIMATE

When he entered his job as head of the Houston Independent School District, which includes two hundred thousand students, Superintendent Frank Petruzielo asked the district's research and evaluation department to survey its educational *stakeholders:* students, parents, and community members throughout the district. The study was part of a shared decision-making program that the district was encouraging, and the superintendent involved members in the survey who are usually omitted from the decision-making process in large urban districts. While many of the survey's results (reported in 1992) were encouraging, several areas showed that a number of students may feel unwelcome and see school as a hostile rather than a supportive environment.

In the secondary schools, which included middle, junior, and senior high schools, 74 percent of the 64,550 students responding felt that their teachers encouraged them to do their best work, and 68 percent felt that their schools provided them with needed resources to learn. However, only 48 percent of the students felt that their teachers thought they were important, and only 47 percent agreed that their teachers respected them. Only 29 percent of the 63,997 students responding said that they enjoyed their classes. The school-district authors of the study concluded, "Thus, while most students responded that their schools are supportive of their efforts, many students believed that their teachers did not recognize them as individuals" (5). In the same survey, only 30 percent of the students said that their peers came to class on time, and only 27 percent felt that their peers were well-behaved. The report states, "These findings are areas of concern since they indicate a classroom atmosphere that would undermine instruction" (5).

Student unhappiness is not confined to elementary, secondary, and college levels. A high-ranking physician was able to make informal contact with students in a respected medical school. He met with nearly two hundred of them to learn their opinions of their professional education. The meeting started hesitantly as he endeavored to draw them out, but it soon changed:

❦ *The comments began—first slowly, then in a veritable avalanche—[and] an outpouring of frustration, disappointment, and real rage came crashing down about me. It soon became an enormous interactive song of anger. . . . The message . . . was simple and monotonous. They felt they were being lectured to death. . . . Every day they sat passively while faculty, whom they did not know and who did not know them, spewed enormous boluses of facts at them. There were blistering testimonials about the poor quality of the lectures, of insufficient time for study, of the absence of personal contact with the faculty, of school unresponsiveness to their needs or their complaints. Try as I might I was unable to coax out countervailing opinions.*

The students had developed an ingenious way of coping with this situation. They each contributed money to a fund. From this, selected students were paid to attend and record the lectures. These were transcribed, edited, and reorganized; references were added, and the material was distributed to classmates. Although the class numbered two hundred, an attendance of thirty-five at a lecture was not unusual, and sometimes as few as ten attended. "Even if there were only five students in the room, the lecturer would march to the podium and go through the whole incredible ritual of giving the lecture" (9, pp. 3–4).

Another reason for the boredom and unhappiness in our schools is the continual—and increasing—stress upon grades. One student wrote to me:

✺ *I seem to always feel anxious and pressured at school. I'm beginning to realize how painful the process of strict external evaluation of my work is to me. . . . I love to explore the new ideas or concepts that I come across when I'm reading, but my current environment hinders this almost completely for me. . . . Must I achieve the same as everyone else and live unhappy and dissatisfied along the way? These are very real questions for me right now. I know I have expressed the feelings of so many frustrated college students and teens. I'm beginning to sense in myself that frustration is turning into a type of hopelessness, and it is swallowing me up.*

A LOST GENERATION

Another reason for this feeling of hopelessness is the necessity of holding students against their will in schools that are little better than prisons. I remember vividly an experience that is as fresh to me today as it was when it occurred several years ago. I was visiting an inner-city school system that had worked wonders in many of its schools. Teachers and students were working together, learning together, and enjoying it. I was deeply impressed. I said to the administrator, "These schools are great, but there must be some schools you haven't been able to reach." He replied, "Yes, some of the junior high schools we haven't been able to touch." I said, "I'd like to see the worst." We visited it, a school in a severely impoverished inner-city area. The corridors were dark, with a few students furtively scurrying along. Every classroom door was locked, so that pupils could not get in or out. The doors originally had frosted glass windows, but most of these had been broken and replaced by plywood that had been nailed over the opening. We selected a door at random and knocked. The teacher unlocked it from the inside and peered out suspiciously. When he recognized the school official, he opened it wide. It was a strange scene. His face was red, and he was breathing hard, holding a large paddle in his hand. It was impossible to tell which student he had just paddled, because all the students, black and white, looked equally sullen and angry. Then began the farce. Laying down the paddle he said, "Now class, take your books and turn to page 73," and he started reading from his book. Very few students picked up their books. Their whole sullen stance was saying, "Just try to make me learn anything." We left, to spare him further embarrassment. I have often thought of that class and that teacher. Imagine the poor student having each morning to get up and go to a classroom he hates. And even worse for the poor teacher, no matter how many faults he may have. Think of earning a living by going to a classroom each day where he knew he was hated. It would be intolerable. It was not surprising that in this school there had been assaults on teachers and pupils and a great deal of vandalism.

It is clear the teacher saw only one choice, hitting a child to get him to do what he wanted. Not being aware of options, or not having the patience to seek out options, places extreme limits on interpersonal relations and learning. By nature, children are inquisitive and motivated, yet by the end of the second or third grade, many students lose both their inquisitiveness and motivation to learn. Punishment and bribes become the order of the day to catch their attention. I was reminded of that school, and others like it, when I read a portion of a commencement address by the president of Yale University in June 1981. He said, "America cannot allow itself to transform the public schools into warehouses for the angry" (10). What a description that is of so many of our schools: warehouses for the bored, the unhappy, the angry!

Most tragic of all are the desperately hopeless youngsters. A teacher in one of our cities has had the opportunity to work closely, over a period of time, with a small group of eight-year-olds from a deteriorating inner-city area. As she gained their confidence, their initial violence subsided, and the underlying despair came to light. One young girl, one of the brightest, confided that she didn't want to live. No one cared, she believed, and there was no point to living. She had already made one suicide attempt but was stopped in time. An African-American youngster, an active boy, said privately to this teacher, "I'm going to be the first one of this group to be dead." When she asked why, he said, "I don't want to live. I'm going to the top of a

FIGURE 2.1
Code Blue: A Medical Emergency

- One million teenage girls—nearly one in ten—get pregnant each year.
- Alcohol-related accidents are the leading cause of death among teenagers.
- The suicide rate for teens has doubled since 1968, making it the second leading cause of death among adolescents. The United States has surpassed Japan's suicide rate for teens.
- Teenage arrests among fourteen to seventeen year olds are up thirtyfold since 1950. Homicide is the leading cause of death among minority youth between the ages of fifteen and nineteen.

National Commission on the Role of the Schools and the Community in Improving Adolescent Health, *Code Blue: Uniting for Healthier Youth* (Atlanta: Centers for Disease Control, 1990).

building and jump off like Superman." The rest of the conversation gave evidence that he meant what he said. And these are eight-year-olds!

Frances Fuchs taught in a training program for adolescents who had been rejected by the regular schools. Early in the term she asked them to write a brief statement about what they envisioned for themselves five years from now. Here is one of the statements: "In five years I will either be dead or in the army or playing lead guitar in a band. I do think the war will come before five years and most of us will be dead" (11). More than half of this group believed they would be dead within five years or living desperate lives in polluted, overcrowded, crime- and drug-ridden towns and cities.

We have no way of knowing how many of our young people see death as being imminent, but a sobering report entitled "Code Blue: Uniting for a Healthier Youth" cosponsored by the National Association of State Boards of Education and the American Medical Association presents a bleak picture of our adolescents' well-being (Figure 2.1).

To know that in many classrooms today there are children and young people actively considering death, either by their own hand or in conflicts with street gangs or drug dealers, gives a new and somber dimension to the educational experience, one that challenges us to our very roots.

THE CHANGING SCHOOL

This is a period when education faces many disturbing circumstances originating outside itself. Budgets have been drastically cut throughout the country, affecting every type of education, limiting the resources needed to respond to changing needs in the school. Student demographics are changing. Since the 1980s, minority youth are the majority in one hundred of the largest city school districts in the nation. It is ironic that the term *minority* is being used to describe students of non-European ancestors when people of color are the majority in all major city school districts. However, teachers in these school districts usually come from European backgrounds, presenting a potentially serious gap in cultural understanding.

The Impact of Bureaucracy

The schools are, to a degree never seen before, regulated from the outside. State-designated curricula, federal and state laws, and bureaucratic regulations intrude on every classroom and every school activity. The teacher-student relationship is easily lost in a confusing web of rules, limits, and required objectives. One teacher gives her reactions to this situation. Here are excerpts from her journal:

> ❦ *Teaching frustrates me so much. There is always more to do, never enough time. There are stupid piles of paperwork or administrative duties which interfere with the real job in the classroom. . . .*
>
> *Teaching no longer offers the chance to be creative and stimulating. It's frustrating not to be able to try something different. How can you be a teacher without being creative? I feel angry when I feel stifled, not able to use everything that I've learned. . . . The students are not robots nor are the teachers, but with the demands of society for budget cuts and higher test scores, we are failing to realize that we are dealing with students who are feeling, total, human beings. . . .*
>
> *As a teacher, I feel I am expected to put in my time. Don't make waves, don't be creative or innovative. This causes too many problems for the administrators because the students begin to think and ask questions that the administration can't or won't answer. . . .*
>
> *People are so afraid of creativity because that might cause change and undermine their sense of security. I really want to help my students find a sense of security within themselves so that the inevitable change will not scare them. One thing that we had better learn to cope with is change!*

Anyone close to education knows that the feelings of this teacher are representative of the feelings of many others. I have talked with hundreds of teachers, and they echo the same message: "We are over-regulated, under-supported, buried with paperwork, watched like hawks, and treated as if all the school's problems are our fault."

In Texas, the state superintendent for education in 1992 told school leaders throughout the state that waivers of state regulations would be tried on an experimental basis. The Texas Education Agency was overwhelmed with two thousand school district requests for waivers from state regulation. Only one hundred waivers were approved!

WHAT DOES IT MEAN TO TEACH?

It seems that to most people, teaching involves keeping order in the class-room, pouring forth facts usually through lectures or textbooks, giving examinations, and setting grades. This stereotype is badly in need of over-hauling. I would like to quote a very sensitive, thought-provoking definition of teaching by the German philosopher Martin Heidegger:

> Teaching is even more difficult than learning . . . and why is teach-ing more difficult than learning? Not because the teacher must have a larger store of information, and have it always ready. Teaching is more difficult than learning because what teaching calls for is this: to let learn. The real teacher, in fact, lets nothing else be learned than—learning. His conduct, therefore, often produces the impres-sion that we properly learn nothing from him, if by 'learning' we now suddenly understand merely the procurement of useful information. The teacher is ahead of his students in this alone, that he still has far more to learn than they—he has to learn to let them learn. The teacher must be capable of being more teachable than the apprentices. The teacher is far less assured of his ground than those who learn are of theirs. If the relation between the teacher and the taught is genuine, therefore, there is never a place in it for the authority of the know-it-all or the authoritative sway of the official. It still is an exalted matter, then, to become a teacher— which is something else entirely than becoming a famous professor. (12, p. 75)

I would like to underscore some of Heidegger's thoughts because they express some of the central themes of this book. The primary task of the teacher is to permit the student to learn, to feed his or her own curiosity. Merely to absorb facts is of only slight value in the present, and usually of even less value in the future. Learning how to learn is the element that is always of value, now and in the future. Thus, the teacher's task is delicate and demanding—a truly exalted calling. In true teaching there is no place for the authoritarian nor for the person on an ego trip. I should mention that Heidegger first gave the previous statement as part of a lecture in 1951 or 1952. In other words, this kind of thinking about teaching is not new. It has very old roots. Yet in every era it is a radical way because it departs so far from the ordinary picture of the teacher. What this book endeavors to do is to portray fresh ways of implementing this central idea today in various sorts of school situations. It attempts to provide some practical answers to the question, "How can a teacher be creative in facilitating a student's learn-ing—and love of learning?"

WHAT IS LEARNING?

If the purpose of teaching is to promote learning, then we need to ask what we mean by learning. Here I become passionate. I want to talk about learning, but not the lifeless, sterile, futile, quickly forgotten stuff that is crammed into the mind of the helpless individual tied into this seat by iron-clad bonds of conformity! I am talking about *learning*—insatiable curiosity that drives the adolescent mind to absorb everything he can see or hear or read about a topic that has inner meaning. I am talking about the student who says, "I am discovering, drawing in from the outside, and making what I discover a real part of me." I am talking about any learning in which the experience of the learner progresses this way:

> ✺ *"No, no, that's not what I want."*
> *"Wait! This is closer to what I'm interested in, what I need."*
> *"Ah, here it is! Now I'm grasping and comprehending what I need and what I want to know!"*

This is the theme, the topic, of this book.

Two Kinds of Learning

Learning, I believe, can be divided into two general types along a continuum. At one end of the scale is the kind of task psychologists sometimes set for their subjects—the learning of nonsense syllables. To memorize *baz, ent, nep, arl, lud,* and the like is a difficult task. Because there is no meaning involved, these syllables are not easy to learn and are likely to be forgotten quickly. We frequently fail to recognize that much of the material presented to students in the classroom has, for the student, the same perplexing, meaningless quality that the list of nonsense syllables has for us. This is especially true for the underserved child whose background provides no context for the material with which he or she is confronted. But nearly every student finds that large portions of the curriculum are meaningless. Thus, education becomes the futile attempt to learn material that has no personal meaning. Such learning involves the mind only: It is learning that takes place "from the neck up." It does not involve feelings or personal meanings; it has no relevance for the whole person. In contrast, there is such a thing as significant, meaningful, experiential learning. When the toddler touches the warm radiator, she learns for herself the meaning of the word *hot*; she has learned a future caution in regard to all similar radiators, and she has absorbed these learnings in a significantly involved way that will not soon be forgotten. Likewise the child who has memorized "two plus two equals four" may one day in her play with blocks or marbles suddenly realize, "Two and two do make four!" She has discovered something significant for herself in a way that involves both her thoughts and feelings. Or the child who has laboriously acquired "reading skills" is caught up one day in a printed story, whether a comic book or an adventure tale, and realizes that words can have a magic power to lift her out of herself into another world. She has now *really* learned to read. Marshall McLuhan gives another example. He points out that if a five-year-old child is moved to a foreign country and allowed to play freely for hours with her new companions, with no language instruction at all, she will learn the new language in a few months and will acquire the proper accent too. She is learning in a way that has significance and meaning for her, and such learning proceeds at an exceedingly rapid rate. But let someone try to instruct her in the new language, basing the instruction on the elements that have meaning for the teacher, and learning is tremendously slowed or even stopped. This illustration, a common one, is worth pondering. Why, when left to her own devices, does the child learn rapidly in ways she will not soon forget and in a manner that has highly practical meaning for her? Why can all of this be spoiled if she is "taught" in a way that involves only her intellect? Perhaps a closer look will help us understand.

Let me define more precisely the elements involved in significant or experiential learning. One element is the quality of personal involvement: The whole person, both in feeling and in cognitive aspects, is part of the learning event. Self-initiated involvement is another element. Even when the impetus or stimulus comes from the outside, the sense of discovery, of reaching out, of grasping and comprehending comes from within. Another element is pervasiveness. It makes a difference in the behavior, the attitudes, perhaps even the personality of the learner. Yet another element relates to the learner's evaluation of the event. She knows whether it is meeting her need, whether it leads toward what she wants to know, whether it illuminates her dark area of ignorance. The locus of evaluation, we might say, resides definitely in the learner. Its essence is meaning. When such learning takes place, the element of meaning to the learner is built into the whole experience.

Whole-person Learning

Let me look at this from another angle. Educators have traditionally thought of learning as an orderly type of cognitive, left-brain activity. The left hemisphere of the brain tends to function in ways that are logical and linear. It goes step by step in a straight line, emphasizing the parts, the details that make up the whole. It accepts only what is sure and clear. It deals in ideas and concepts; it is associated with masculine aspects of life. This is the only kind of functioning that has been fully acceptable to our schools and colleges.

But to involve the whole person in learning means to set the right brain free, to use it as well. The right hemisphere functions in quite a different way. It is intuitive. It grasps the essence before it understands the details. It takes in a whole gestalt, the total configuration. It operates in metaphors. It is aesthetic rather than logical. It makes creative leaps. It is the way of the artist, of the creative scientist. It is associated with the feeling qualities of life. Frances Vaughn, in her classic work entitled *Awakening Intuition*, says,

> Intuition is known to everyone by experience, yet frequently remains repressed or underdeveloped. As a psychological function, like sensation, feeling, and thinking, intuition is a way of knowing. When you know something intuitively, it has the ring of truth; yet often we do not know *how* we know what we know. . . . Learning to use intuition is learning to be your own teacher. (13, intro.)

Significant learning combines the logical and the intuitive, the intellect and the feelings, the concept and the experience, the idea and the meaning. When we learn in that way, we are whole; we use all our masculine and feminine capacities.

The Dilemma

I believe that all teachers and educators prefer to facilitate this experiential, meaningful, whole-person type of learning rather than the nonsense syllable type. Yet in the vast majority of our schools, at all educational levels, we are locked into a traditional and conventional approach that makes significant learning improbable if not impossible. When we combine certain elements into one scheme—a prescribed curriculum, similar assignments for all students, lecturing as almost the only mode of instruction, standard tests that externally evaluate all students, instructor-chosen grades as the measure of learning—then we can almost guarantee that meaningful learning will be at an absolute minimum.

Do Alternatives Exist?

Educators don't follow such a self-defeating system because of any inner depravity. They are inhibited by bureaucratic rules; they fear making waves; they frequently do not know the steps they might take to implement a practical alternative. The fact that there are alternative ways to handle a classroom or a course—alternative assumptions and hypotheses upon which education can be built, alternative goals for which educators and students can strive—will, I believe, be amply illustrated in the chapters that follow.

The Balance

We can look squarely at all the elements that make teaching in the United States a difficult profession at this time, and I have endeavored to suggest some of these roadblocks and dangers. But we can never escape the exhilarating fact that when a student's eyes light up with a new discovery, a new learning that pervades and illuminates his or her life, all the hard work, the personal effort of teaching becomes completely worthwhile. How can that precious gleam occur more frequently? What can I, as an educator, do to kindle that spark?

The purpose of this book is to suggest some answers. It is not a handbook of methods or techniques. It is primarily an approach to the teaching-learning situation, a philosophy if you will, but a philosophy come to life in the experience of many teachers, and many students, who will be allowed to tell their own very diverse stories. Great changes in education and learning will not come from classroom activities; they evolve from values and beliefs that seek out ways to make changes. This book is about creating a vision for a better world where all people have a level playing field on which to live and learn.

I think I have said quite enough to indicate that our educational system is suffering from many elements of a crippling sort: decreased financial resources; dwindling enrollment; the tangled web of law and bureaucratic regulations that so often dehumanizes the classroom; political groups that aim to prevent freedom of thought and choice; and boredom, frustration, rage, and despair on the part of many students. Yet the other side of the coin needs to be equally stressed. This book is a celebration of students, teachers, parents, and other educators who have asked for more and are involved in exciting and creative learning experiences. There are school administrators with vision. There are teachers who inspire in their students a lifelong love of learning. There are students for whom school is the most exciting, most growing part of their lives—a place they *love* to go. I want now to introduce some of the fascinating challenges and opportunities that can make the teacher's task a most satisfying one.

References

1. "National Affairs: The Cities' Deadly Tally," *Newsweek*, 26 March 1991, p. 36.

2. "New York Teen Slain in Another Jacket Robbery," *Houston Chronicle* (from Reuters News Service), 12 January 1991, p. 12a.

3. H. L. Hodgkinson, *The Same Client: The Demographics of Education and Service Delivery Systems* (Washington, D.C.: Institute for Educational Leadership, Center for Demographic Policy, 1989).

4. "Most Stressful Jobs," *Men's Health*, cited by B. C. Oren, *Houston Chronicle*, 27 June 1991, p. 18a.

5. K. Sanchez, *Student/Parent/Community Surveys 1991–1992: Districtwide and Administrative Results* (Houston: Houston Independent School District, 1992).

6. A. Pallas, G. Natriella, and E. McDill, "The Changing Nature of the Disadvantaged Population: Current Dimensions and Future Trends," *Educational Researcher* 8, no. 5 (1989): 16–22.

7. H. J. Freiberg, "A Multi-dimensional View of School Improvement," *Educational Research Quarterly* 13, no. 2 (1989): 35–46.

8. "Kids Talk about School," *Media and Methods* 5 (April 1969).

9. D. E. Rogers, *Some Musings on Medical Education. Is It Going Astray?* (Unpublished paper, Robert Wood Johnson Foundation, 1981).

10. A. Bartlett Giamatti, quoted in *Time*, 11 June 1981.

11. Frances Fuchs, *The GUN on the Labor Market* (Unpublished manuscript, 1981).

12. Martin Heidegger, *What Is Called Thinking?* (originally published as *Was Heis Ist Denken?*) (New York: Hater Torchbooks, 1968). Book is based on lectures given in 1951–52.

13. F. E. Vaughn, *Awakening Intuition* (New York: Anchor Books, 1979).

CHAPTER 3

AS A TEACHER,
CAN I BE MYSELF?

◆

CAN WE BE HUMAN IN THE CLASSROOM?

A teacher friend of mine, knowing I was going to write this chapter, asked his class if teachers can be themselves in the classroom. One reply, typical of many, began, "Of course not!" and followed with some very eloquent reasons why both students and instructors believe that it is utterly impossible to be real, whole human beings in a classroom situation.

The Usual Class

In the first place, many an instructor, during all her* professional training and experience, has been conditioned to think of herself as the expert, the information giver, the keeper of order, the evaluator of products, the examination giver, the one who, at the end, formulates that goal of all "education," the grade. She firmly believes that she will be destroyed if she lets herself

---

* Throughout this chapter I use feminine pronouns for the teacher or instructor and masculine pronouns for the student.

emerge as a real human being. She knows that she is not as expert as she appears. She knows that, as a lecturer and information giver, she has her good days and her bad ones, that sometimes she should receive a failing grade on her own work. She knows, at some level, that if she lets her mask slip, if she shows herself as she is, she will answer some questions, "I don't know." She realizes that if she lets herself fully interact with her students, she will come to like some of them very much and feel real dislike for others. What then would happen to her "objectivity" in giving grades? Even worse, suppose some student she really liked did very poorly in his work. What a bind she would be in! Could she give a poor grade to someone she liked? In addition, if there were real interaction, some students would be bold enough to say that they found the class very uninteresting because it had little relationship to issues that really concerned them. In short, it would be very risky indeed to let students know her as a person. It would be risky within herself because she would be making herself vulnerable. It might well be risky in her profession because she would get the reputation of being a poor teacher and lecturer, of caring more about her students than about the content of the course, of having a noisy classroom where students talk a lot. Hence, she—and perhaps most instructors—prefers to play it safe. She firmly fastens her mask, maintains her role of expert, retains her "objectivity" at all costs, and keeps a proper distance between herself in her "higher"-level role in the room and the student in his "lower" role. She preserves her right to act as judge, evaluator, and sometimes executioner.

But many a student has his facade, too, and often his mask is even more impenetrable than the instructor's. If he wishes to be well thought of as a student, he attends class regularly, looks only at the instructor, or writes diligently in his notebook. Never mind that while looking so intently at the instructor, he is thinking of his weekend date, or while looking down, he is writing a letter in his notebook or wondering whether the family welfare check has arrived. He sometimes truly wants to learn what the instructor is offering, but even so his attention is contaminated by two questions: "What are this teacher's learnings and biases in this subject so that I can take the same view in my papers?" and "What is she saying that will likely appear on the exam?" If the student asks questions, the questions have the twofold purpose of showing his own informed knowledge and tapping a known reservoir of interest and information in the instructor. Therefore, he does not ask questions that might embarrass or expose himself. It makes no difference what he thinks of the course, his instructor, or his fellow students. He shuts such attitudes carefully within himself because he wants to pass the course, to acquire a good reputation with the faculty, and thus move one step further toward the coveted degree, the union card that will open so many doors for him once he has it. Then he can forget all this and enter real life.

For thousands upon thousands of students it is far too much of a risk to be a whole human being in the classroom. For the student it would mean letting his feelings show: feelings of indifference, resentment at the discrimination he feels is aimed toward him, occasional feelings of real excitement, feelings of envy toward classmates, feelings about the unpleasant family situation he has just left or the terrible disappointment or real joy he is experiencing with his girlfriend, his desire to learn important things, his sharp curiosity about sex or psychic phenomena or government policies—you name it. For him, as for the instructor, it is much safer to button his lip, preserve his cool, serve his term, cause no ripples, and get his paper credentials. He is not willing to take the risk of being human in class.

Perhaps I am too harsh, but I am sure you realize that this charade is played out every school term by thousands of instructors and hundreds of thousands of students. In this so-called educational atmosphere, students become passive, apathetic, bored—they become tourists in the classroom. Teachers, trying day after day to prevent their real selves from showing, become case-hardened stereotypes and eventually burn out. Here is some evidence from the student side—a panel of eight students in the Boston area from eighth grade through college and representing various economic levels:

> ❦ *School is just a place to meet your friends. Classes are something you have to live through. Lectures are so boring! I like some teachers as friends. But when they get into their teacher roles, they're boring, too. Students don't have the guts to confront the teachers and administrators and tell 'em what they feel. Before I went to school, I just dug books and encyclopedias. By the end of the first year, I wouldn't look at a book. I'd like to see a complete wipeout. Burn all the schools to the ground and start over.*

Now the question I want to raise is, Is this angry dissatisfaction necessary? Can a classroom be a place of exciting, meaningful learning related to live issues? Can it be a place of mutual learning where you learn from others and they from you, where the instructor learns from the class and the class from the instructor? I not only think it is possible; I have also seen it happen! If I didn't believe very deeply that this could come true in thousands of classrooms, I would not be writing this book. But how? Let's get down to the nitty-gritty.

My Own Learnings

I learned about the importance of being human in class in a kind of back-door way. As a psychological counselor dealing with students and others in personal distress, I found that talking to them, giving advice, explaining the facts, and telling them what their behavior meant did not help. But little by little I learned that if I trusted them to be essentially competent human beings, if I was truly myself with them, if I tried to understand them as they felt and perceived themselves from the inside, then a constructive process was initiated. They began to develop clearer and deeper self-insights, they began to see what they might do to resolve their distress, and they began to take actions that made them more independent and that solved some of their problems.

But this learning, which was important to me, made me question my role as a teacher. How could I trust my clients in counseling to move in constructive directions when I was not nearly so trusting of my students? Thus, I began a groping, uncertain change in my approach to my classes. To my surprise, I found that my classrooms became more exciting places of learning as I ceased to be a teacher. It wasn't easy, and it happened rather gradually. But as I began to trust students, I found they did incredible things in their communication with each other, in their learning of content material in the course, in blossoming out as growing human beings. Most of all they gave me courage to be myself more freely, and this led to profound interaction. They told me their feelings; they raised questions I had never thought about. I began to sparkle with emerging ideas that were new and exciting to me and also, I found, to them. I believe I passed some sort of crucial divide when I was able to begin a course with this kind of statement:

> ❦ *This course is called "Personality Theory" [or whatever]. But what we do with this course is up to us. We can build it around the goals we want to achieve within that very general area. We can conduct it the way we want to. We can decide mutually how we wish to handle those bugaboos called exams and grades. I have many resources that I have on tap to be available, and I can help you find others. I believe I am one of the resources, and I am available to you to the extent that you wish. But this is our class. So what do we want to make of it?*

This kind of statement said, in effect, "We are free to learn what we wish, as we wish." It made the whole climate of the classroom completely different. Though at the time I had never thought of phrasing it this way, I changed from being a teacher and evaluator to being a facilitator of learning—a very different occupation.

The reaction was not all positive by any means. While some students very quickly felt released and began to take initiative, others felt primarily suspicious. "This sounds good, but frankly we've taken so much guff from teachers that we don't believe you. How are you going to grade us?" Others were indignant. "I paid good money to come here and have you teach me, and now you're saying we'll have to learn the stuff ourselves! I feel cheated."

I understood very well how students could have these negative reactions; and when I tried to make my understanding clear, several things happened. The students discovered that they could challenge the instructor, even criticize him, and not be put down, rebuked, or humiliated. This in itself made the class totally different from any other class they were in. Little by little they experienced the concept of responsible freedom—not intellectualized it, not talked about it, but experienced it in their feelings and emotions and intellects. And then, in different ways and at different rates, they began to use that concept. A man named Samuel Tenenbaum, who was in a summer school graduate course with me, wrote about what it was like to be in that class—the surprise and the indignation of the students, the growing excitement, the closeness among class members, the incredible amount of learning, the self-insights that were a product. He wrote about a time when I had become quite fully what I wanted to be in relation to a class—namely, a resourceful, fallible, human facilitator. I used his account in one of my books (1, pp. 297–313), and you might find it of interest.

With more experience, I came to feel that the resentment and hostility I aroused at the outset of the class was not really necessary. Consequently, whether out of cowardice or wisdom, I have come to provide enough limits and requirements, which can be perceived as structure, so that students can comfortably start to work. Only as the course progresses do they realize that each "requirement" separately, and all of them together, is simply a different way of saying, "Do exactly what you wish to do in this course, and say and write exactly what you think and feel." But freedom seems less frustrating and anxiety-laden when it is presented as a series of requirements within a flexible framework using somewhat conventional-sounding terms. To make clear what I mean, I will give an example taken from one course.

Requirements

❦ *There are several aspects of the course that are required: I wish to have a list of the readings you have done for the course turned in before the end of the course, with an indication of the way you have read each book. For example, you might list a book and state, "Chapters 3 and 6 were read thoroughly." You might list another book and write, "Skimmed the book and found it was over my head." You might list yet another book and say, "I got so much out of this book that I read it twice and made careful notes on chapters 5 through 12." Or you might say, "I was repelled by the whole point of view and only read enough to become convinced that I was disgusted with the author." In other words, I want an honest account of what you have read and the depth to which you have read the material you covered. The books do not necessarily have to be on the course's reading list.*

The second requirement is that you write a paper, which may be as brief or as lengthy as you wish, about your own most significant personal values and the ways they have changed or not changed as a result of this course. A third requirement is that you turn in to me a statement of your own evaluation of your work and the grade that you think is appropriate. This statement should include (1) the criteria by which you are judging your work; (2) a description of the ways in which you have met or failed to meet those criteria; and (3) the grade that you think appropriate for the way you have met or failed to meet your own criteria. If I find that my own estimate of your work varies a great deal from yours, I will have a personal talk with you, and we will see if we can arrive at some mutually satisfactory grade that I can in good conscience sign and turn in.

The final requirement is your personal reaction to the course as a whole. I would like this turned in to me in a sealed envelope with your name on the outside. In this reaction I would like you to state very honestly what the course has meant to you, both positively and negatively. I would like your criticisms about the course and suggestions about ways in which it might be improved. This, in short, is your opportunity to evaluate the course, the instructor, and the manner in which the course has been carried out. It will in no case have any influence on your final grade; but if you are fearful that it might have such an influence, mark on the outside of your envelope, "Please do not open until the final grades have been turned in." If you mark the envelope in this fashion, I assure you that I will honor your request and not open your statement until all grades have been turned in.

I will not submit a final grade in the course until all of these requirements have been fulfilled.

Perhaps this example indicates how much freedom can be given within a framework that appears conventional. I believe it also suggests that instructions to students can be stated in a human way. I had to learn the hard way that I should never say I was granting some degree of freedom or some degree of trust if I was not willing to back up that statement with my whole being. When I granted some freedom and then felt I had to take it away, the resentment was incredible. It is better not to give it at all, I learned, than to extend it and then attempt to bring the authority back into my own hands. Where the freedom or trust is limited in certain ways, I have found that those limits had better be explicit: "I want this course to be as free as possible, but the department requires that we cover these two texts, and I will give an examination written and graded by the department on those texts." Or "I would like to say, 'Give yourselves the grade you think is fair,' but I realize that I must sign the grade sheet, giving it my approval, so I believe the grade must be mutually acceptable. If I find a discrepancy between my subjective evaluation of your work and your subjective evaluation, we will discuss it together and try to agree on a reasonable grade." (I found that I more frequently insisted on a higher grade than argued with a student about a high grade that was doubtfully deserved.)

All this had a great effect on the students and a great effect on me. I found myself so much freer to permit variety in student work; poems and artwork and experience in the community sometimes became student projects. More important to me was the fact that I felt far freer to express vague, ill-formed ideas (creative ideas are initially almost always half-baked) and to receive enormous stimulation from the discussion of them. Also, I felt more free—because I was no longer the power—to let a student know how I felt: "I don't know how others feel, but I resent the amount of class time you take with your talking," or "When you speak, it is always so much to the point, so incisive, that I wish you would speak up more often."

The effects of such human learning in a classroom persist. I received a letter from a young woman (now no longer so young) with whom I have had no contact for many years. In one paragraph, she says, "I have always meant to tell you that the two-course sequence with you twenty years ago (!!!) was the only genuine educational experience I found in about nine years of college and grad school at four different universities. I have never read so much psychology or with such pleasure as I did that year. The contrast between that and the rest was very painful." I can scarcely remember her, but she for twenty years has remembered a class where she was free to learn and to be.

A Facilitative Classroom

Why am I telling you about all these personal experiences? Because I think that from what I have said, you and your students might invent a way to develop a climate of free and creative learning in your class. You are not me, nor are your students the ones I have had, so laying down rules or telling you, "This is the way a class should be," is no answer. I am simply suggesting that if students and an instructor discuss the issue openly, they might find ways in which all of them could be whole human beings in the classroom. Occasionally, I have known miracles to follow from such discussions, but much more often it is painful, growthful struggles that ensue in the instructor, in each student, in the interactions of the whole group. It is only at the end of the course, or even afterward, that individuals may disclose how valuable it was to attempt to be whole human beings in a classroom interaction. Here are a few statements written, after the course was over, by students in a high school psychology course where discussion was free. Not even the most sensitive issues such as sex and drugs were barred; and movies, books, tape recordings, drawing materials, and many other resources were made available. The course was facilitated—certainly not taught—by Dr. Alice Elliott.

> ❦ *I think that there should be more classes where students would be able to speak out!!! In this class, people seemed to be more truthful than they are in other classes, and they seemed to be aware of other people's feelings.*

> ❦ *The class helped me to become more aware, a more interested person. I feel more independent and more like an explorer. I want to search, to know more.*

🦋 *This class has helped me realize more than before that I am an individual. I do not want to be measured with other people, but as myself.*

🦋 *This class or subject is about the greatest thing that ever happened to me in school, 'cause this subject makes you realize the object in your life. What are you doing in this world and what do you want to do in this world?*

🦋 *This class has made me realize that I am not the only person in the world, and everyone has just as many problems as I have. It also helped me to understand more fully why some people do the things that they do.*

🦋 *Ever since I started school and began to understand what I was doing I dreamed that one day it would be different. I never liked books and things that were written. I have learned more by being aware of what others liked and disliked.*

🦋 *For the last two years I have been a put-on. I've realized what I was, so I have changed. I try to be myself, do and say what I feel, no longer afraid of what people will think.*

These statements come from a classroom where the teacher is a real person who cares for adolescent young people and lets them know that she can understand their thoughts and feelings.

An Illustration of Classroom Changes

While working on this chapter, I received a surprising letter from a high school student describing a dramatic change in his math teacher. I was interested enough to write to the teacher asking to know more of her experience. It was indeed a dramatic story, almost melodramatic, and I thought that it could not be used because readers would be put off, feeling that it was too good to be true. On further thought, it seemed to me that the very sudden change in this teacher, which occurred within a few weeks, was much like the more gradual change I have observed in many teachers over a period of months or even years. So I decided to present the material from both the students and the teacher in this high school geometry class. Only the names have been changed. Here are some statements from the letter I received from Pete:

🦋 *It's been exactly two months and eleven days since a miracle took place at our public high school. A certain teacher came to school that Monday, March 9, as a completely different person. Yes, Mrs. Winnie Moore (an Algebra I and Plane Geometry teacher at our school) had changed. . . . We sit in a circle, kids teach kids.*

But in these classes we don't just learn math. We learn about life. . . . As I said earlier, Winnie changed my outlook on life. I now have a goal to work for—to become a teacher and to get this marvelous new way to work. I now can communicate with other people; I get along better with my parents; I care deeply about many things, and I notice things that I never noticed before. All this change in me came about because of this new method.

He also included statements from a number of other students who had been through the same experience. I will quote a few of them later. I must admit that my first reaction was, "What the hell do you suppose happened to that teacher?" Since Pete had given me her name, I wrote to her some weeks later to find out, asking, among other things, if she had been in an encounter group experience, which can sometimes produce a sharp change of this sort. She replied that she had not but wanted to tell me about "certain events that led up to my change in the classroom."

She had been taking an evening course in counseling during the winter in which she had come across some of my writings and the qualities that I have found to be productive of both learning and personal growth: genuineness (or realness), deep empathic understanding, and a warm, loving acceptance of the person as he or she is. She continued:

🦋 *These concepts intrigued me and, to my astonishment, I was able to use them in the next week. A student of mine who was deeply troubled came to visit me at my home. Paul is fifteen and well experienced with drugs. I sensed his desperate need to communicate to and with someone, and I felt God had designated me to be that someone. (I am sure the phenomenon could be thoroughly explained in psychological terms.) I tried to hear him at every level possible until I had internalized his difficulties almost to an intolerable extent. Suddenly, I realized how painful life seemed to him. More shocking still, I realized what he felt like as a student in my class. I was adding to his pain. I watched his agony at taking one of my quizzes. It became my pain, too.*

On Wednesday of that week I did some role playing in the evening counseling class. I had been chosen the week before to play the part of a client with a personal problem. I played a deeply troubled person who was thinking of suicide. In that role I believe that I played both Paul and me intertwined. The woman who played the counselor was astonished and told me, "If you can do this, you can do anything." She was, it seemed, almost on the verge of tears. I then went through an extraordinary experience on the following Friday—March 6—in which my husband, John, helped me to communicate with Paul. The three of us sat on the floor, and John started things off by saying that we all had to be very honest with each other even though that was difficult. I could not speak for a long time. Paul began to get tears in his eyes, so I moved toward him and whispered to him. I do not remember all that I said, but the words came very easily. I told him that I was sure that he had been trying to kill himself. (Later, he told me of four or five attempted suicides.) I also told him that I would see that he would not feel that lonely or despondent again. He told me that nobody had ever cared for him before. A bit later I was so released by this communication that I felt filled with power and strength. I really had reached somebody! The strength that I felt seemed to pour into Paul. I ran across this description in a personality text of Maslow's "oceanic feeling":

> *limitless horizons opening up to the vision, the feeling of being simultaneously more powerful and also more helpless than one ever was before, the feeling of great ecstasy and wonder and awe, the loss of placing in time and space with, finally, the conviction that something extremely important and valuable had happened, so that the subject is to some extent transformed and strengthened even in his daily life by such experiences.*

This was my experience! I had a fantastic feeling for four days. I could no longer tolerate the walled-in teacher that I had been. I had to change my teaching because I had to be true to myself. Teaching in the traditional way hurt me. I also had to show Paul that I could change, and then he could change. On the following Monday I changed all my classes as my students related to you. Paul was very dependent on me for several months, but our relationship now has eased into a friendship. He seems independent and more confident with his peers.

So that was what happened to her! Clearly, she had been through a conversion experience with profound effects. (I am always suspicious of conversions that take place because of external circumstance—an inspiring speaker or group pressure—but conversions that are brought on by internal experiences are quite different and tend to be lasting.) The work that she and her husband did with Paul may be questioned by many readers. Was she qualified to undertake the counseling of such a seriously disturbed boy? The alternative—to turn away a boy who had taken the great risk of coming to her for help—in my judgment would be a definitely hurtful thing, and I am glad she took the risk. There must have been a real psychic connectedness for her to know intuitively that he wished to commit suicide. I regard her initial whispered statement to him as very risky indeed, only justified by the fact that her intuition proved correct. I would have been more comfortable with a much more tentative communication on her part. But however we view her counseling sessions with Paul, the effect on her was profound. She had let herself move inside the world of one of her students, and not only experienced the pain he was in but the further pain she was causing him in her class. (Imagine the tremendous difference it would make if every teacher felt, even for a few moments, the way his or her class was being experienced by each and every student!) For Mrs. Moore, this profoundly empathic involvement with Paul caused her to change her whole way of being in her class. That this change was very observable is evidenced by the statements of other students, two of which are given here:

> 🦋 *A boy in her class*   *The things it's done for my geometry class cannot be put down in words on paper. But it all came about because Mrs. Moore was honest with us and with herself and took this small step. The things this small step did for me and the class and my education and my outlook on life just cannot be said adequately. I've gotten to learn so much about so many people in that class and I've gotten the will to work on geometry.*

> 🦋 *A girl writing to Mrs. Moore*   *I finally got myself believing that teachers were robots programmed to hurt people. I finally realized I had to shut them out and not listen to them for they scared me out of my mind. . . . My third-grade math teacher would call me stupid, lazy, and ungrateful when I messed up on a quiz or didn't understand my homework. She scared me so that when it was time to take a test, I was so scared of flunking that I flunked every one. My parents thought it was because I wasn't studying enough, so all my privileges were taken away and I was made to go to bed at 7:30 so that I would be rested for my next terrifying day at school. . . . It was like a dream—here a teacher was finally realizing that her students need her and want her to be their friend and to help them understand so many puzzling things! When I left your class, I felt like crying out to everyone that someone does care.*

I believe it is very rare and most unusual for a teacher and a classroom to change so suddenly. But whether slowly and gradually or within a short period, the response of students is overwhelming. To find a teacher who is human, to be treated as a human being in a class is not only a very precious experience but one that stimulates the learning of facts, as well as self-understanding and improved communication with one's fellows.

HOW CAN I BECOME REAL?

Thus far, I have frequently referred to "being real" and "being one's real self." What do these phrases mean fundamentally? I would like to approach them from several angles. To begin with, such queries are common. As I have come to know young men and women intimately in counseling relationships and encounter groups and less intimately in courses, seminars, and personal discussions, I have found one profound question underlying much of the surface talk. It appears that for almost all of them the vital questions are "Who am I, really? Can I ever discover or get in touch with my real self? Will I ever feel any assurance or stability in myself?" And these questions are not only those of the young, but of countless older men and women too.

The Search for Identity: A Modern Problem

We are, perhaps all of us, engaged in a struggle to discover our identity, the person we are and choose to be. This is a very pervasive search; it involves our clothes, our hair, our appearance. At a more significant level, it involves our choice of values, our stance in relation to parents and others, the relationship we choose to have to society, our whole philosophy of life. It is, in these days, a most perplexing search. As one college woman says:

> ❦ I'm confused. Just when I think I'm getting my head together, I talk with some fellow who's sure he knows what life is all about. And because I'm uncertain, I'm really impressed. And then when I get away I realize that's his answer. It can't be the answer for me. I've got to find my own. But it's hard when everything is so loose and unsure.

I see this search for one's real self, for identity, as much more of a problem today than it was in the historical past. During most of history, it made little difference whether the individual discovered himself. Perhaps he lived a more comfortable life if he did not because the identity he lived was defined for him. It is interesting to imagine ourselves back in feudal times. The serf was expected to be a serf throughout his life, as were his children after him. In return he was permitted to eke out a meager living, most of his work going to support the lord of the manor, who in turn protected him. The nobleman was, in a more luxurious way, also constricted. He was the lord, responsible for his followers, and his children would continue the role of the nobleman. In our own country, during one dark period of our history, the slave was always the slave and the master always the master. The difficulties of abandoning these role identities are still painfully with us. While the rigidity of the defined role seems incredibly restrictive to us now, it should not blind us to the fact that such rigidity made life simpler in many ways. The cobbler knew that he and his sons would always be cobblers; his wife knew that she and her daughters would always be primarily servants of their husbands. There were almost no options, and peculiarly enough this gave people a type of security that we have left behind. Perhaps one of the few analogies that are comprehensible to us is the peacetime army. Many men and women have come to accept army life with more satisfaction than they had supposed possible. There are almost no decisions: they are told what to wear, how to behave, where to live, and what to do. They can gripe as freely as they wish, without any responsibility for their lives. They are given an identity, told who they are; and the agonizing personal search that most of us must go through is at least temporarily abrogated.

It is for reasons of this sort that I say the search for one's real self is a peculiarly modern problem. The individual's life is no longer defined (though it may be influenced) by one's family, social class, color, church, or nation. We carry the burden ourselves of discovering our identity. I believe the only person today who does not suffer this painful search for self is the person who voluntarily surrenders his or her individual identity to some organization or institution that defines the purposes, the values, the philosophy to be followed. Examples include people who completely commit themselves to some strict religious sect that is sure of all the answers; those who commit themselves to a rigorous ideology (whether revolutionary or reactionary) that defines their philosophy, their life-style, and their actions; those who give themselves completely to science or industry or traditional education (though there are large cracks in the certainties of all these institutions); or, as I mentioned, those who give their lives to the military. I can thoroughly understand the satisfactions and securities that cause individuals to make such commitments, one of which is to gain a certain comfort. The transition from conformity to freedom creates a strong sense of disequilibrium and discomfort. Yet I suspect that the majority of young people prefer the more painful burden of choosing the uniqueness that is involved in discovering the real self. I know that is my choice. Still, one of the most common fears of people trying to discover who they really are inside is that this undiscovered "me" will turn out to be a worthless, bizarre, evil, or horrible creature. Something of this fear is expressed by a searching student:

> ❦ *I feel my mind is open, kind of like a funnel, and on top there are sparks and exciting things, but down deeper in the funnel it's dark, and I'm afraid to go down in there because I'm scared of what I might find. I'm not going to do it just now.*

This attitude is a very common one indeed.

Pathways to Self

There are a number of ways in which individuals pursue this goal of becoming themselves. Some lives have been badly distorted or warped by early childhood. For them, the search for solidity in themselves, for their own real self, may be a long or painful one. Others more fortunate are already in the process of discovery and have an easier time. Some are sufficiently frightened by the risks involved in the search that they endeavor to freeze themselves as they are, fearful of any road that would lead into unknown territory. I will briefly describe several of the ways in which people venture, as they search for the real self.

One Pathway: Counseling.   More and more people these days are seeking to find themselves through counseling and psychotherapy. The success of this venture depends heavily on the person and the attitude of the therapist. My colleagues and I have singled out three attitudes—three ways of being—that are especially important in a therapeutic relationship, and exhaustive research has confirmed this belief. The first is a *realness* or *genuineness* in the therapist. He is what he seems to be. His internal being is matched by his external expression. The second attitude is a *nonpossessive, nonjudgmental caring*—a type of love that creates a safe atmosphere for the person seeking help. The third is the therapist's *ability to listen* in a very special empathic way, leading to an acceptant understanding of the inner world of the client. This feeling of being fully understood without being judged is a very precious experience and one that enables the client to move forward. But this description is from the side of the counselor or therapist. I should point out that what I describe is a process that may take weeks, months, or even years to complete.

Here is a portion of a letter from Melanie. She is twenty-four years old, with experience as a teacher. She read one of my books and wrote me about her therapy:

> ❦ *I've found a new life, an aliveness and a sense of adventure. I found within me the strengths to give to others the love and understanding to help them grow in confidence and independence. I have returned to teaching where I have found joy in watching children who, in the right atmosphere, break through their defenses and reach out, who take the risk to bridge the gap from their separateness to mine.*

I think this illustrates the importance of finding in some other person trust, acceptance, and love if one is to become one's self, to become a separate person in one's own right. Clearly Melanie is now offering that kind of relationship in the atmosphere she creates for her pupils at school.

Another Pathway: The Learning Group.   It is increasingly common for people to have some sort of interpersonal experience in an intensive group. These groups exist under many different labels. The ones most pertinent to our present interest are those held in connection with university courses, often with a variety of purposes, including the opportunity for a student to grow in the understanding and acceptance of the self. A number of medical schools have organized such groups for students who are just entering medical school. Many businesses organize teams of people who participate in wilderness experiences together. At Prescott College in Prescott, Arizona, the entering class of students goes on a seventeen- to nineteen-day wilderness experience with the faculty. Public schools that also want to change have incorporated the intensive group as part of the transformation process.

Retreat groups usually include the students, the faculty members who will be teaching them, and members of the administrative staff. Students who are married are encouraged to invite their spouses. The sessions are held away from campus in some informal, camplike setting. When facilitated by an experienced person holding the sort of attitudes described previously for a psychotherapist, the outcomes are very meaningful for most participants. They build solid, personal, first-name relationships with faculty; develop friendships with other students; and make progress in discovering who they are underneath the usual facade. I, and many other instructors, have included such intensive group experiences as part of a course. My own preference is for two weekend groups, one early in the course and one toward the end. I would like to give some examples from a course of thirty students in which three former students assisted as facilitators. I have chosen reactions that bear on the issue of discovering one's true self:

> ❦ *I had always wanted to be loved, accepted, and esteemed and felt that this could only be brought about by certain values which came from others, that I could not rock the boat, and how I really felt didn't matter. In our first encounter group I felt mixed up but good when I related some of my deep personal problems, when the feedback was pleasant, when I tried to truly see myself. But I found that maybe that wasn't really me after all. Maybe there was another me who had something to say, but did he have the right to speak up? . . . [He tells how he began to express his feelings] here I was truly relating to others how I was really feeling, actually being aware of what I was experiencing. As I write this I am becoming emotional and have very wet eyes at this moment.*
>
> *I feel that I am definitely moving away from "oughts" and meeting expectations, that I don't always have to please others, that I can become myself, and actually become aware of what I am experiencing, and that this isn't any crime and I do have some rights. Truly a significant change in some of my personal values. I find that I am moving more toward trusting myself though this is going to take time.*

> ❦ *Since the last workshop encounter I have been turned on and have been experiencing myself, my wife and children, and my work, in a clearer, more involved, more meaningful way. Ideas, thoughts, emotional insights keep bubbling up and influencing me toward freer, more open behavior in these areas. I attribute these changes to my workshop experiences.*

> ❦ *As I reflect on the experiences afforded me in the small groups I realize that I had developed a kind of channeled perception; that is, I was filtering out those things that didn't fit my idea of the way the thing "ought to be."*

> *Small group members helped me to see my irrational behavior, not only by pointing it out to me, but by being open and interacting with each other. . . . As the group sessions drew to a close I began to experience a good feeling. I had developed a desire to face my problem in a positive way and in so doing I have since learned that what I had feared for five years really wasn't so important.*
>
> *Since the basic encounter group experiences I believe that I can learn to accept myself. I am well aware that this will take time, but I feel certain that as I learn to be less critical of myself, I will be happier. I am sure that this course has helped me in this regard.*

> ❦ *I became tellingly aware of the fact that I have been trying to prove myself. I don't have to prove myself. All I really have to do, that is, my only responsibility, is to be myself. I value myself more as a person—my dependency needs, my anxieties, my proving needs, my inadequacies, and limitations, as well as my warm feelings for others, my knowledge, my competencies, my worthiness, my potential.*

Not everyone profits from such group experience. In this class there was one negative reaction:

> ❦ *My negative reaction to the course is that for me personally it is a depressing experience to see how many truly deeply troubled people we have in our group, some with personal troubles so deep and complicated that I fear they will never overcome them. Of course, on the other hand, I can be thankful that I am not in their shoes, but somehow this feeling doesn't seem to overcome the concern that these weekends generated in me for the many troubled people we have drifting around as associates in this life. I myself personally received no help from these group encounters . . . but I accept the fact that they are of immense value to my troubled associates.*

Perhaps these student statements (with the exception of the last) are evidence of the progress an individual can make toward finding and being a deeper, more authentic self.

The Lifetime Journey of Self-discovery

This process of self-discovery, self-acceptance, and self-expression is not something that goes on only in therapy or in groups. Many people have neither of these experiences. For those who do, the therapy or the group exists for only a limited time. But for all of us, the search to become the person we most uniquely are is a lifetime process. I believe this is one reason why biography holds a fascination for so many readers. We like to follow the struggle of individuals to become what they are capable of becoming. For me, this is illustrated by the book I have just finished reading: the life story of artist Georgia O'Keeffe. There are many steps in her development. At fourteen, the inwardly independent but outwardly conforming girl won a gold medal for her ladylike deportment at a strict Catholic school. But by the age of sixteen, she was beginning to dress in a "tailored, midwestern corsetless style" (in 1903!), which was to be a characteristic throughout her many years. And at age twenty-nine she locked herself into her studio and analyzed all her work up to that point with "ruthless detachment." She could tell which paintings had been done to please one professor and which to please another. She could tell which had been influenced by well-known artists of the day.

> Then an idea dawned on her. There were abstract shapes in her mind integral to her imagination, unlike anything she had been taught. 'This thing that is your own is so close to you, often you never realize it's there,' she later explained. . . . 'I could think of a whole string of things I'd like to put down but I'd never thought of doing it because I'd never seen anything like it.' . . . She had made up her mind. This was what she would paint. (2, p. 81)

As you can imagine, this decision was the initial step toward becoming the great artist of her mature years. Even in her nineties, she relentlessly pursued that goal of painting her own unique perceptions of the desert, of bleached bones, of huge and gorgeous flowers—to the point that one has only to look at one of her paintings to realize "That's an O'Keeffe."

Like Georgia O'Keeffe, each of us is the artist or the architect of his or her own life. We can copy others, we can live to please others, or we can discover what is unique and precious to us and paint that, become that. It is a task that takes a lifetime.

The Invisible College

As professionals, many of us play roles that inhibit lifelong learning. The professional meetings where people stand at a podium and read their papers to a highly literate audience always seem to me to be a waste of precious resources. Clearly, I am not alone in this opinion. Starting in 1974, a group of university faculty who conduct research in schools began meeting to discuss important issues facing the teaching profession. No papers were presented. Researchers sat in a circle of chairs and discussed topics suggested by several members of the group. The group became known as *The Invisible College*. The term relates to the group's focus on dialogue and discussion without the need for a building or bureaucracy. Jere Brophy, distinguished University Professor at Michigan State University and one of the group's founders, is the keeper of the dream and organizer of its yearly meetings. Admission to the Invisible College is based on interest in the topics generated by the members. A nominal registration fee ($10–$15) is charged. The Invisible College's two hundred members meet two days prior to the national meeting of the American Educational Research Association. The sessions, which at times last into the night, are often filled with lively discussions, animated debates, and an occasional after-hours singalong. The yearly meetings, which are now into their twentieth year and have been expanded to include doctoral students, provide a real opportunity for university faculty to learn from each other in an informal setting. Finding opportunities to learn throughout one's life is more challenging than it first appears.

CELEBRATED LEARNING MOMENTS: LEARNING FROM OTHERS

The movement to improve the quality of learning begins with freeing teachers and others to become facilitators of learning. Beginning in the 1980s, more than twenty-five state departments of education established academies of learning for teachers, principals, and superintendents. The academies were one- or two-week resident retreats located away from the school building in a natural setting. The academies provided intensive interpersonal experiences for many teachers. The state of West Virginia initiated some of the first teachers' academies; teachers from around the state came to learn from each other and from educators across the nation. The concept was so successful that local school districts began their own academies. During an academy in the summer of 1992 in Charleston, West Virginia, teachers were asked to write about celebrated learning moments. These brief essays speak from the heart about the meaning of being a teacher today and the power of learning from others. The following selected essays reflect on some pathways to self-discovery.

Lessons a Student Taught Me

by Diana Ritenour, Cross Lanes Elementary School

❦ *Lesson One: First impressions are very important.   I do not believe in accidents, only opportunities. When I was hired as the only certified teacher for the Mulberry-Helm Center I received one of my greatest opportunities.*

Each and every child in my classroom served as my mentor. They filled in the gaping holes of my college education, providing insight and joy which continue to touch my life.

Every individual child has a story. I will share my lessons from Terry. They are numerous and humorous. Terry's clinical description was enough to raise the blood pressure of the most tenured special education teacher. It went like this: Terry was a twenty-one pound, five-year-old male, diagnosed as having cerebral palsy. His physical abnormalities included a hydrocephalic head, asymmetrical eye socket, recessed neck, barrel chest, large protruding bone mass in the middle of his back, lame left leg, and clubbed right foot.

He was able to hold his body in a sitting position and feed himself. All other body functions required assistance. He had a severe stuttering problem.

Whoa!! Nothing in my special education classes had, in any way, prepared me to work in this type of situation. To say I felt completely overwhelmed does not begin to express the depth of my level of concern. I was in way over my head.

Terry began instructing me the moment he entered my class. He flashed me his trademark dazzling smile and announced, "Hi, my name's Terry! Are you going to be my teacher?" All of Terry's abnormalities melted away, and there, in a fragile little body, was a child, eager to learn everything.

Lesson Two: People who are beautiful on the inside view other people's ugliness in a different light. *We were a federally funded program, and as such received many, many visitors. I imagined that we felt similar to the animals in the zoo when a parade of people would march through our room.*

Many times the visitors would interact with our kids in a kind, considerate way. Sometimes they would withdraw toward the door, with looks of disgust on their faces.

After one such visit, I was really angry! My body language, facial expression, and vocal tone made this quite apparent. Terry asked me what was wrong. I was trying to explain to him in a subtle way that those people didn't have the right to inflict their negative reaction to our class on us.

Terry, in his polite, kind, manner, simply said, "Maybe they aren't used to being around kids."

Lesson Three: Never let others impose their limits on you. *One of our daily activities was music class, instructed by Mrs. Rowe. The kids would get really excited and start making all kinds of noise. They really enjoyed the music! It was in one of these classes that Terry announced that he wanted to dance.*

As we looked back and forth, from one adult to the other, our first silent reaction was, "Oh no!" It struck us with great force. "Here was something else our kids couldn't do! How sad!" Not wanting the situation to end badly, Bonnie picked him up.

"N-n-no," he stuttered. "Put me on the floor, I want to da-da-dance like they do on TV."

Bonnie bent over to place Terry on the floor and looked at me, the certified, all-knowing teacher, to assure her that she had acted correctly. My heart beat wildly. I was in a state of utter panic! Terry, being the unique individual that he is, proceeded to demonstrate his ability to do the impossible. He danced! I mean he really danced. From his stomach, he raised his upper body up, at a right angle to the floor. He had rhythm! He was doing creative movements! He was accurately interpreting "the beat."

Lesson Four: You can tolerate anything to a point; beyond that point, you need to express yourself. One of our tasks was to teach Terry eating skills. He had developed the habit of storing food in his cheeks. His mother was concerned that when he was sleeping, he might aspirate it and die.

There were seven children in Terry's family and only enough food to go around. We learned, from Terry, that if you were slow in consuming your portion, you may leave the table hungry. Terry had learned to adapt to his environment.

After explaining the situation to the mother, it became our job to reteach Terry how to swallow what he put in his mouth. This was not a simple task. He had five years of practice in hoarding food. We began our task with soft, junior baby food kinds of things.

Every day, we would tell Terry what we planned to serve him for lunch. Every day, he would flash his smile and say, "Oh, boy!" We had a whole case of creamed corn, so he had that frequently.

One day, after about three weeks of this procedure, we announced what he would be having for lunch, just as we had always done. "Today you are having a sloppy joe, lime Jello, and creamed corn."

Terry took a deep breath, screwed up his face, and wailed! We were in shock! Terry, sweet little Terry, never whined, never pouted, never cried. He must be in severe physical pain! I dropped to my knees in front of him. I gently stroked his head and quietly asked, "Terry, what's wrong?"

He sobbed a few more times, took another deep breath, raised his head and looked painfully into my eyes. He softly sobbed, "T-t-teacher, I don't like creamed corn."

As a teacher, I continue to learn many invaluable lessons from my students and rediscover myself. (3)

A Quiet Celebration

by Tim Merrifield, Elkview Middle School

🦋 *Have you ever celebrated a moment in learning, and the student didn't know you were celebrating? My most celebrated moment was watching one student's biggest accomplishment by myself alone and crying with joy. The story unfolds as follows.*

My first year teaching I was an on-the-job trainer at Owens School. This job entailed my teaching mentally disabled students skills from the real world. I would go to employers and they would then tell me what skills the students needed [in order] to perform their particular jobs. I also had to teach the students how to get home from work. This meant riding a KRT bus from work to home. Have you ever tried to teach a mentally disabled student to pay a fare and ride the bus home?

Well, this one student (I'll call him Joey) had to go to a store that sells candy, where he worked. He lived in the city of Marmet. Every day we had to walk across a busy avenue in order to catch the bus.

From September to December we did the same thing. We went to work and then tried not to get hit by the vehicles flying down the street. Every day was an adventure just to get across the road, . . . [not to mention] trying to teach Joey how much to pay and where to get off the bus.

Finally the last day before Christmas break, the moment happened. I had told Joey he had to go from work to home by himself today. We had prepared for the day for months. All day Joey was nervous, anxious, excited, and apprehensive. He could hardly work because of his excitement and fear. Joey went on and on about how he had to have me on the bus with him. He said he couldn't do it, he wouldn't do it and he would go home with me. I told him he had to find his own way home because I had to go to the doctor right after work. When three o'clock came he was crying for me not to leave. I went around the corner crying myself. I don't know who was more nervous, he or I. Unknown to him I would follow the bus just to make sure that he did find his way home.

Joey left the candy store. I was around the corner watching. I was just hoping he didn't get killed or lose a leg or arm crossing the busy street. He went to the first corner, looked both ways and tried to cross. Just as he stepped into the road, a black Camaro came to a screeching halt. While this was happening I was running up the street trying to stop everything before I lost a student. Luckily, Joey didn't see me as he ran across the street. I was sweating, crying, and telling myself I didn't really want to teach anyway. The next big step was to cross McCorkle. Joey came to the stoplight, waited until it turned red so he could cross, and he did just that. There were no problems here except the teacher having major heart problems. I knew I wouldn't make it. When the bus came after what seemed like five days, Joey got on. When the bus started to pull out I ran to my car so I could follow. As I caught up to the bus, I became even more nervous. Joey had made it on the bus, but could he get off at the right stop? This drive to his home seemed to have taken days. Finally, when his stop came, I was praying he would stop the bus and get off. To my relief, he did just that. Joey got off the bus, crossed the road, and walked to his house. When he made it to his house, he started jumping up and down with joy. This is that moment. I stopped, got out of the car, and started jumping up and down. I was so excited. I wanted so much to share that joy with Joey, but I knew I couldn't. But I did stop at the first pay phone and call my principal and share the joy. To this day, that event brings back great memories. We each celebrated that moment, and I'm a better person because of it. (4)

Change Takes Time

by Janice Nease, Sissonville High School

❦ *When I arrived at Sissonville High School in the late sixties, at the height of the civil rights movement, I was astonished and appalled at the degree of intolerance and bigotry that existed among the majority of my students. Changing these attitudes became my goal. After a few years I did perceive minor changes which cheered me but were no cause to celebrate.*

Some years later, I was delighted by the arrival in my English class of a brilliant young man with all the attributes of the perfect student. Imagine my dismay to learn that he was an outspoken and extremely articulate bigot with a narrow, self-righteous view of religion.

Fortunately, by this time I realized direct confrontation was both inappropriate and unlikely to lead to any lasting change, so I developed a more indirect approach. I incorporated a number of contemporary black poets in our unit on poetry, and I chose as one of our novels one which I felt truly represented the black experience.

At first, David was a reluctant participant in this curriculum, but near the end of the year, he began carrying a volume of poetry by Langston Hughes to class. He never, however, articulated or overtly indicated that his views had changed. By the time David graduated, I was so impressed by his other attributes, I had long abandoned my crusade to directly open his view of the world.

No great reason to celebrate, you may say. In 1983, David, who had become chief psychologist of adolescent medicine at a major university, wrote a long letter nominating me for teacher of the year. More importantly, he described how our unit on Black literature had given him a new perspective on the Black experience and had proved invaluable in his understanding of and relationships with the Black adolescents with whom he had daily contact. Having become even more articulate, he affirmed the value of exposing oneself to new ideas and experiences and of striving for a better understanding of the world and people around us.

Ah! Now, we have genuine cause to celebrate, and I do. I celebrate the moment when, reading David's letter, I understood how truly and profoundly we touch our students and what power we have to effect lasting change. I celebrate, and I pray—I pray that the changes I effect in my students are always positive and that they affirm their worth as students and as individuals. (5)

The Beauty Is Here

by Betty W. Smith, St. Albans High School

❦ *The Shenandoah Valley is beautiful! Two weeks ago I was there—driving south on I-81—the weather was perfect. At my side sat my daughter, Jill. We were on our way home from NIH [National Institutes of Health]—a trip we make every eight weeks. Jill has a progressively fatal skin disease that necessitates these trips. Earlier in the day the doctors had told me that her condition was worsening. Reflecting as I was driving along, I recalled recent family events. My father had died earlier; my youngest son, an adopted biracial child, had married a lovely Caucasian young lady whose family has virtually disowned her; and my mother, a seventy-three-year-old victim of Alzheimer's dementia, requires complete care—diapers and feeding. This is coupled with a determination on my part not to put her in a nursing home but to keep her with me. Reality was very present! The Shenandoah Valley was beautiful, but my world somehow seemed grey.*

I looked at Jill doing a word find—thinking about her life—knowing how special she is. The world seemed very heavy at that moment—when suddenly Jill's voice interrupted my thoughts with a question, "Mom, why did you decide to be a teacher?" Startled, I responded to my weary traveler, "Why did you think to ask me that?" "Oh, I just can't see my mom doing anything else" was the reply. A tear in my eye, I looked at her and smiled,—"Yes, Jill, you're right!"

A teacher—all I ever wanted to be—a calling—a love—and suddenly I realized—the valley was ablaze with sun—the world was more beautiful. The reason I cope so well with my situation in life is because—I am a teacher! Through this medium, life has meaning. It brings happiness! A celebrated moment of learning brought about by a child's simplicity, a trip of anguish and the realization that I am what I want to be—a teacher!!!!!!!! (6)

It's Never Too Late

by Bernice Boggess, Sissonville High School

🦋 *Twenty years of teaching experience and a master's degree provided enough education. I wasn't interested in enrolling in graduate courses with the younger generation of teachers. My middle-aged mind could no longer compete with the intellect of youth. I already had adequate skills for performing my duties as a high school librarian. Since I was not a classroom teacher, I did not need to learn new teaching strategies. But one school day, my attitude changed.*

During lunchtime a colleague walked into the library and noticed the patrons. She asked why so many "misfits" spent lunch hour with me. Her question raised many questions of my own. Could I influence students? Could I make their school experience more rewarding? How could I encourage them to find acceptance and friendships among their peers? Did I have the enthusiasm to reach out to these teenagers? My self-questioning revealed that I had grown stagnant, but I had not outlived my usefulness as a teacher.

Learning began anew. I enrolled in graduate classes that taught effective communication skills and the building and maintaining of relationships. Courses in cooperative discipline and cooperative learning offered techniques for encouraging students' self-esteem. The Teacher's Academy has rejuvenated my mind and spirit.

Each new school year, some students enter the library and sit alone. Without intruding, I try to communicate with each by offering help with assignments, by complimenting an asset, or by offering a positive comment. Often after these students interact with me, they began interacting with other students. When the school year ends, most of these "misfits" are sharing a table with friends. Secretly, I am celebrating with them.

Since my moment of assessment, I have come to realize there are many stages of learning. Acquiring knowledge is only one element. Obtaining wisdom, compassion, and an appreciation for individual potential is a continuing process. My aging face may not reflect it, but inside my head is a young mind which says, "Teach me, so that I can touch the lives of others." (7)

Comments

Diana Ritenour and Betty Smith both learned a lifetime of understanding and hope from children who faced their own hardships in very special ways. Tim Merrifield, Janice Nease, and Bernice Boggess rediscovered a unique aspect of their lives from their students. Tim realized that independence for Joey meant that his role as a teacher must change. Janice discovered that opening a student's eyes to the world may not be very obvious until a child becomes an adult. And Bernice discovered that learning is truly a lifelong pursuit.

Each essay about a celebrated learning moment reflects on the opportunities around us to learn and discover ourselves. The five teachers learned from their students (and, in one story, from a daughter) because they were open enough to listen and see. To be facilitators of others' learning, people must first be facilitators of their own learning.

YOU CAN BE YOURSELF

Let me try to summarize what it means to me to find one's real self. In the first place it is a process, a direction, not some static achievement. In my estimation no one is ever completely successful in finding all her real (and ever-changing) self. But there are certain characteristics of this process. Persons move away from hiding behind facades and pretenses, whether these have been held consciously or unconsciously. They move toward a greater closeness to and awareness of their inward experiences. They find this development exceedingly complex and varied, ranging from wild and crazy feelings to solid, socially approved ones. They move toward accepting all of these experiences as their own; they discover that they are people with an enormous variety of reactions. The more they own and accept their inner reactions—and are unafraid of them—the more they can sense the meanings those reactions have. The more all this inner richness belongs to them, the more they can appropriately *be* their own experiences. An individual may become aware of a childish need to depend on someone, to be cared for and protected. In appropriate situations she can let herself be that childish, dependent self. She may discover that certain situations anger her. She can more easily express that anger as it arises in the situation that arouses it, rather than suppress it until it pours out explosively onto some innocent victim. A man can discover soft, tender, loving feelings (which are especially difficult for men to own) and can express them with satisfaction, not shame. These people are becoming involved in the wider range of their feelings, attitudes, and potential. They are building a good relationship with what is going on within themselves. They are beginning to appreciate and like, rather than hate and mistrust, all their experiences. Thus, they are coming closer to finding and being all of themselves in the moment. To me this is the way that the person moves toward answering the question, "Who am I?"

I should like to close this chapter with one more illustration from my course that included two weekend encounter groups. These words are not those of a young man, but of a man who has been a teacher and a high school principal, one who has carried heavy administrative responsibility. It is clear that he is just taking the first steps in finding and being himself. It seems tragic that he could have lived for more than thirty years without discovering himself, yet his pride in taking these steps and the excitement of getting acquainted with himself shine through his remarks.

> *As I sit at my desk to begin this paper I have a real feeling of inner excitement. This is an experience that I have never had. For as I write, I have no format to follow and I will put my thoughts down as they occur. It's almost a feeling of floating, for to me it doesn't seem to really matter how you, or anyone for that matter, will react to my thoughts. Nevertheless, at the same time, I feel that you will accept them as mine regardless of the lack of style, format, or academic expression. . . . My real concern is to try to communicate with myself so that I might better understand myself. I guess what I am really saying is that I am writing not for you, nor for a grade, nor for a class, but for me. And I feel especially good about that, for this is something that I wouldn't have dared to do or even consider in the past. You know I guess it bothers me if others don't think well of me. . . . But I now realize that I really want people to like me now for what I am, for what I really am, not just for what I pretend to be.*

THE CHALLENGE

I hope that this chapter has opened a door and given you a glimpse of what is beyond. It is a door that leads to being fully alive in the classroom; it is also a door to being more fully yourself. Some of you will want to close that door because what is on the other side seems too risky, too emotional, too frighteningly self-responsible, and the path it leads to seems too uncertain and unknown. Others may wish to peer cautiously inside and to take a few tentative steps. Others will feel, "This is for me," and realize from the examples they have read that it can truly open a pathway for them.

R*EFERENCES*

1. Carl R. Rogers, *On Becoming a Person* (Boston: Houghton Mifflin, 1961).
2. Laurie Lisle, *Portrait of an Artist: A Biography of Georgia O'Keeffe* (New York: Washington Square Press, 1980).

3. Diana Ritenour, *Lessons a Student Taught Me* (Unpublished manuscript, 1992).

4. Tim Merrifield, *A Quiet Celebration* (Unpublished manuscript, 1992).

5. Janice Nease, *Change Takes Time* (Unpublished manuscript, 1992).

6. Betty W. Smith, *The Beauty Is Here* (Unpublished manuscript, 1992).

7. Bernice Boggess, *It's Never Too Late* (Unpublished manuscript, 1992).

RESPONSIBLE FREEDOM
IN THE CLASSROOM

CHAPTER 4

A SIXTH-GRADE TEACHER EXPERIMENTS

◆

A diary constitutes the first section of this chapter (1). I feel that it speaks directly to the classroom teacher who is harassed by pupil apathy, discipline problems, complaining parents, a set curriculum, and the daily difficulties involved in being continuously in contact with a large and varied group of students. The diary is a deeply human document. I hope that it will have the meaning for teachers at all levels that it has had for me: a feeling that there is a basis for hope, even in so-called impossible classroom groups. I hope that it will release other teachers—helping them to be adventuresome and honest with themselves and their students and to risk themselves by taking steps, even if the consequences of those steps cannot be guaranteed but depend instead upon trust in human beings.

A Teacher's Diary

by Barbara J. Shiel

🦋 *This past year was my thirteenth year of teaching elementary school. I have taught all six elementary grades. The class mentioned in the document (originally intended only as a kind of personal diary) was one of the most difficult I had ever worked with in terms of discipline, lack of interest, and parental problems. There were thirty-six in the group, with an I.Q. range of 82 to 135. There were many who were "socially maladjusted," "underachievers," or "emotionally disturbed." I had exhausted my resources in an attempt to cope with the situation, but had made very little progress. The many discipline problems were notorious: they were constantly in the office or "on the bench" for varied offenses; their attitude and behavior kept them in constant trouble. Several were suspended for short periods. In addition, the parents were uncooperative and/or defensive. Most of them had a history of blaming the teachers or the school for the child's problems.*

March 5: We Begin

🦋 *A week ago, I decided to initiate a new program in my sixth-grade classroom, based on student-centered teaching—an unstructured or nondirective approach. I began by telling the class that we were going to try an "experiment." I explained that for one day I would let them do anything they wanted to do—they did not have to do anything if they did not want to.*

Many started with art projects. Some drew or painted most of the day. Others read or did work in math and other subjects. There was an air of excitement all day. Many were so interested in what they were doing that they did not want to go out at recess at noon!

At the end of the day, I asked the class to evaluate the experiment. The comments were most interesting. Some were "confused," distressed without the teacher telling them what to do, without specific assignments to complete.

The majority of the class thought the day was "great," but some expressed concern over the noise level and the fact that a few "goofed off" all day. Most felt that they had accomplished as much work as we usually do, and they enjoyed being able to work at a task until it was completed without the pressure of a time limit. They liked doing things without being "forced" to do them and liked deciding what to do. They begged to continue the experiment, so it was decided to do so, for two more days. We would then reevaluate the plan.

The next morning I implemented the idea of a "work contract." Each child was to write his contract for the day—choosing the areas in which he would work and planning specifically what he would do. Upon completion of any exercise, each student was to check and correct his own work, using the teacher's manual. The work was to be kept in a folder with the contract. Resource materials were provided, suggestions made, and drill materials made available to use when needed.

I met with each child to discuss plans. Some completed theirs in a very short time. We discussed as a group what this might mean, and what to do about it. It was suggested that the plan might not be challenging enough, that an adjustment should be made—perhaps going on or adding another area to the day's plan.

I found I had much more time, so I worked, talked, and spent the time with individuals and groups. At the end of the third day, I evaluated the work folder with each child. To solve the problem of grades, I had each child tell me what grade had been earned.

Also at this time, the group wrote a second evaluation of the experiment, adding comments their parents had made. All but four were excited and enthusiastic about the plan and thought school was much more fun. The four still felt insecure and wanted specific assignments. I talked with them about giving the experiment time—sometimes it took time to adjust to new situations. They agreed to try. The rest of the class was thrilled at the prospect of continuing for the rest of the year.

The greatest problem I've encountered is discipline. I have many problem individuals in my class, and there was a regression in terms of control when the teacher's external controls were lifted. Part of the difficulty stems from the fact that I let the children sit where and with whom they liked. The "problems" congregated together, spent much of their day fighting (verbally and physically), "bugging" each other, and generally accomplishing very little, which brings to mind another problem for me—internally I am having a difficult time watching them do nothing and am concerned at times about their progress, achievement, etc. I have to remind myself constantly that these pupils were "failing" under the old program and never turned in completed assignments under the old regime either. They only looked like they were doing something.

I've considered the possibility of moving some of the seats in the problem area, but I realize that I would be defeating an important aspect of the program if I reestablish my control. If we can survive this period, perhaps in time they will develop greater self-control.

It is interesting to me that it is upsetting to them, too. They all sit close to my desk and say it is too difficult this new way. The "temptation" is too great. This would indicate that they are not as recalcitrant as they seem.

The class has been delighted in general. They even carry their projects and work outside and have the whole school interested and talking about the idea. And I've heard the story that they think I've really changed (since I've stopped trying to make them conform to my standards and rules, trying to make them achieve my goals!!).

The atmosphere is a stimulating, relaxed, happy one (discounting the problem-area upheaval).

An interesting project has developed. I noticed that some of the boys were drawing and designing automobiles. I put up a big piece of paper for them to use as they wished. They discussed their plans and proceeded to do a mural on the history of cars, incorporating their designs of cars of the future. I was delighted. They used the encyclopedia as a reference, as well as books on cars they brought in. They worked together and some began models and scrapbooks, boys who had produced very little, if anything, so far this year.

Other ideas began to appear in other areas. The seed of initiative and creativity has germinated and begun to grow.

Many children are doing some interesting research in related (and unrelated) areas of interest. Some have completed the year's "required" work in a few areas, such as spelling.

Most important, to me, is the evidence of initiative and self-responsibility manifested.

March 12: Progress Report

🦋 *Our "experiment" has, in fact, become our program—with some adjustments.*

Some children continued to be frustrated and felt insecure without teacher direction. Discipline also continued to be a problem with some, and I began to realize that although the children involved may need the program more than the others, I was expecting too much from them, too soon—they were not ready to assume self-direction yet. Perhaps a gradual weaning from the spoon-fed procedures was necessary.

I regrouped the class—creating two groups. The largest group is the nondirected group. The smallest is teacher-directed, made up of children who wanted to return to the former teacher-directed method and those who, for varied reasons, were unable to function in the self-directed situation.

I would like to have waited longer to see what would have happened, but the situation for some disintegrated a little more each day—penalizing the whole class. The disrupting factor kept everyone upset and limited those who wanted to study and work. So it seemed to me best for the group as a whole as well as the program to modify the plan.

Those who continued the "experiment" have forged ahead. I showed them how to program their work, using their texts as a basic guide. They have learned that they can teach themselves (and each other) and that I am available when a step is not clear or advice is needed.

At the end of the week, they evaluate themselves in each area—in terms of work accomplished, accuracy, etc. We have learned that the number of errors is not a criterion of failure or success. Errors can and should be a part of the learning process. We learn through our mistakes. We also discussed the fact that consistently perfect scores may mean that the work is not challenging enough and perhaps means we should move on.

After self-evaluation, each child brings the evaluation sheet and work folder to discuss them with me.

Some of the members of the group working with me are most anxious to become "independent" students. Each week we evaluate their progress toward that goal.

I have only experienced one parental objection so far. A parent thought her child was not able to function without direction.

Some students (there were two or three) who originally wanted to return to the teacher-directed program are now anticipating going back into the self-directed program. (I sense that it has been as difficult for them to readjust to the old program as it would be for me to do so.)

March 19: Progress Report

❦ *Today, from my point of view as a teacher, has been the most satisfying since we began our new program.*

It began with an individual evaluation with each child in the teacher-directed program. (I had conferences with the nondirected group the preceding day.) Several of the children in the former group felt that they were ready to go back into the nondirected group. They decided they liked the freedom after all and thought they understood the responsibilities involved. It was decided that they would try it for one week to see if they really were ready. I would help them at any time they needed help with their work plan or actual work. At this point, I have only six in the teacher group. One wants to be in the other group, but since her mother was the one parent who complained, I told her she must discuss it at home first.

We had an oral evaluation; one of the topics discussed was parental reaction. One boy said his mother said it sounded as if I had given up teaching! Another boy said his father told him that he had tried self-responsibility with him before, and he thought I was nuts to try it with so many at once!

We discussed what we could do to help our parents understand the program. It was suggested (by the children) that we could take our weekly work folders home to show what we were actually accomplishing and that since the intangible work was on the work contract, it could be discussed as well.

The rest of the day was spent with as little interference as possible by me. Groups and individuals proceeded with their plans. It was a productive, rewarding day.

The days have fluctuated between optimism and concern, hope and fear. My emotional temperature rises and falls with each rung climbed on the ladder of our adventure.

Some days I feel confident, buoyant, sure that we are on the right track—on other days I am assailed by doubts. All the teacher training, authoritarian tradition, curriculum, and report cards threaten and intimidate me.

I must exercise great control when I see a child doing nothing (productive) for most of a day. Providing the opportunity to develop self-discipline is an even greater trial at times. I've come to realize that one must be secure in one's own self-concept to undertake such a program. In order to relinquish the accepted role of the teacher in a teacher-directed program, one must understand and accept oneself first. It is important as well to have a clear under-standing of the goals one is endeavoring to work toward.

In another statement written later, Shiel describes the elements of a school day during the experiment. I insert it here in order to give readers more of a picture of the way that students, as well as Shiel, operated.

A Sample Day in the Class

🦋 *Each day began informally; the first task of each individual was to design his or her work plan, or "contract." Sometimes children planned with one or two others. There was constant self-grouping and regrouping, or withdrawal from a group for inde-pendent work.*

As soon as the contract was made, the child began to study or work on his plan. He could work as long as he needed or wanted to. Because I was not free to discard the state-devised curriculum time schedule, I explained the weekly time-subject blocks to the children. This was to be a consideration in their planning. We also discussed sequential learning, especially in math, mastering a skill before proceeding to the next level of learning. They discov-ered that the text provided an introduction to a skill, demon-strated the skill, and provided exercises to master it and tests to check achievement. When they felt they were ready to go on, they were free to do so. They set their own pace, began at their own level, and went as far as they were able or self-motivated to go.

I have been constantly challenged, "But how did you teach the facts and new concepts?" The individuals inquiring apparently assume that unless the teacher is dictating, directing, or explain-ing, there can be no learning. My answer is that I did not "teach." The children taught themselves and each other.

When individuals or groups wished to share their projects, learnings, or research with the class, or when there were audiovisual materials of general interest to the class, they were announced on the board and incorporated into the individual planning. For example, if we had a film on South America, the entire class viewed it; but what they did with the film was up to the individual. They could outline it, summarize it, draw pictures of it—or ignore it if they chose.

Whenever the children felt the need to discuss individual, group, or class "problems," we arranged our desks in a seminar circle and had a "general semantics" session. We also functioned as one group in music (singing) and in physical education.

Since evaluation was self-initiated and respected by the teacher, there was no need for cheating to achieve success. We discovered that "failure" is only a word, that there is a difference between failure and making a mistake, and that mistakes are a part of the learning process.

In art, the children were free to explore with materials: paper paints, crayons, chalk, clay, etc., as well as with books and ideas. They discovered for themselves, through manipulation and experimentation, new techniques and new uses of media. No two products were alike—although there was considerable dependency on the discoveries of others in the beginning. In time, individuals developed confidence and openness to experimentation. The results were far more exciting than those achieved in teacher-directed lessons in spite of the fact that I consider art my greatest strength, or talent!

The children developed a working discipline that respected the individual need for isolation or quiet study, yet allowed pupil interaction. There was no need for passing notes or subversive interaction. There was respect for meditation and contemplation as well as for overt productivity. There were opportunities to get to know one another. The children learned to communicate by communicating.

Final Entry

April 9: Progress Report

🦋 I prefer the term self-directed to nondirectional in describing our program. I believe it better describes the goals, as well as the actual implementation, of the program. It is directed, in the sense that we must work within the structure of the curriculum, the specific units of study. It is self-directed in that each child is responsible for his own planning within this basic structure.

At this point, I have only four pupils who are not in the program. I try to provide a period each day for them when they are able to assume some responsibility, make some decisions. They are children who need much additional help and are insecure and frustrated without my guidance.

As I went through the process of putting grades on report cards, I began to realize that the most valuable aspects of the children's growth could not be evaluated in terms of letter grades. For some, there is no observable change, or it is intangible—yet one senses growth, a metamorphosis taking place.

Day to day one can sense the growth in communication, in social development. One cannot measure the difference in attitude, the increased interest, the growing pride in self-improvement; but one is aware that they exist. And how does a teacher evaluate self-discipline? What is easy for me may not be easy for someone else.

The report cards are only an indication, but I know the children will be as pleased as I am at the improvement in their grades and the great decrease in citizenship checks.

In evaluating their work, I find them to be fairly perceptive, aware of their capacity and how it relates to their accomplishment. I rarely need to change grades. When I do, sometimes I must upgrade!

I mentioned earlier how many "problems" there have been in this class both disciplinary and emotional. This program in fact developed out of an attempt to meet the challenge that the "problems" presented. At times, I felt whipped, defeated, and frustrated. I felt I was making no headway and resented my policing role.

Since our program has been in full swing, I've found that I've undergone change, too. Early in the year I could but bide my time until I could send the "gang" onward and upward—at least see them off to the seventh grade.

I find now that I see these children with different eyes, and as I've watched them, I've begun to realize that there is hope. I have asked to take this class on, in a self-contained situation, to seventh grade. Scheduling may prevent this from becoming an actuality but I feel these children would continue to progress toward self-actualization within the framework and freedom of the self-directed program.

I feel that now that the mechanics of the program are worked out, now that there is greater understanding and rapport between the children and myself (since I have discarded the authoritarian role), there is greater opportunity for self-growth, not only creativity, initiative, imagination, but self-discipline, self-acceptance, and understanding.

At times when I see children who are not doing what I think they ought to be doing, I must remind myself again of the ultimate goals and the fact that they did not produce "required" work when it was assigned previously. They may be drawing something that is not aesthetically pleasing to me, but they are drawing, and it is imaginative! They may not be "busy," but they may be thinking. They may be talking, but they are cooperating and learning to communicate. They may fight and respond with signal reactions—abuse one another verbally—but it may be the only way they know. They may not do as much math, but they understand and remember what they do do.

Best of all, they are more interested in school, in their progress. I would venture [to say] that this program might result in fewer dropouts and "failures" in school.

It is not the panacea, but it is a step forward. Each day is a new adventure; there are moments of stress, concern, pleasure— they are all stepping stones toward our goal of self-actualization.

I continued the program until the end of the term, two months past the last report. In that time, there was a continuing change in these children. They still argued and fought among themselves but seemed to develop some regard for our social structure: school, adults, teachers, property, etc. And as they began to better understand themselves, their own reactions, the outbursts and quarrels diminished.

. . . They developed values, attitudes, standards of behavior on their own and lived up to those standards. They did not become "angels" by any means, but there was a definite change. Other teachers and playground supervisors seldom had to discipline them and commented on the change in behavior and attitude. They were rarely in the office for infractions, and there was not one parental complaint the balance of the year! There was a tremendous change in parental attitude as the children evidenced success and growth, both academic and social. I have neglected to mention the students who were not problems and those who are above average academically. I firmly believe that the gifted children were the ones who benefited most from this program. They developed a keen sense of cooperation among themselves, interest in mutual projects, and they sailed ahead, not being restricted by the slow learners. Their achievement was amazing to me.

I found that the children who had the most difficulty learning also made great progress. Some who had been unable to retain the multiplication tables (which should have been learned in fourth grade) were able to multiply and divide fractions (!) with a minimum number of errors by June.

I cannot explain exactly what happened, but it seems to me that when their self-concept changed, when they discovered they could, they did! These slow learners became fast learners. Success built upon success.

. . .I am well aware of the fact that in many schools or districts I would have not been allowed the freedom I was permitted to have.

Both my principal and superintendent were interested in, and gave support to, my effort. The schedule was structured to enable me to continue on to a self-contained seventh grade. Then it was learned that the people who had been hired for the intermediate positions did not have elementary credentials and therefore could not take my place. I had to be put back into a sixth-grade position. The children, the parents, and I were very disappointed.

Partly as a result of this disappointment, Shiel accepted another position. She did not, however, lose all contact with her class. The following autumn a report came to her.

🦋 *I received a letter from my principal this week in which he states: "I must relate to you . . . that your former students are dedicating themselves to building rather than destroying. . . . really, you can take honest breaths about your contribution . . . as I have not had any negative dealings with any of your former pupils, even those who unfortunately find themselves in poor environments. . . . Your "impress" method, or whatever, seems to have done the job, and their commitment (to you really) is something to behold."*

Shiel concludes:

🦋 *If three months of "self-direction" produced such tangible results at this age level, imagine the potential inherent in a program of greater length! It is an exciting thing to contemplate.*

COMMENTS ABOUT THE EXPERIMENT

Although Shiel's account speaks for itself, I should like to point out some salient features of the way in which she dealt with this experiment and some of the learnings that I see as transferable to other educational situations.

Commitment

Shiel was clearly and deeply committed to a philosophy that relied upon self-direction and freedom to lead to the most significant learning. This

face the struggle and pain of trying to change perceptions and behaviors. Shiel reports her experience:

> ❦ *The participating teachers spent the morning working with the children, then met in the afternoon with a psychologist in an encounter group to explore together the morning experiences and their feelings and attitudes. The purpose of the workshop was not to show "one way," but to illustrate that possibly "other ways" exist. We wanted the teachers to experience self-direction in the same milieu that was provided for the children. Almost every teacher experienced great anxiety and apprehension in working with these problem children in an atmosphere of freedom. For all concerned, it was an emotionally trying time, painful—as growth can sometimes be. However, various forms of evaluation indicated [that] the workshop was successful in helping teachers change their perceptions and attitudes.*

One teacher was unable to cope with the situation and eventually resigned. The general reaction from teachers, students, and parents ranged from favorable to enthusiastic, and more than thirty additional teachers signed up for a new workshop.

We will talk more about this workshop approach in later chapters. Suffice it to say that it is, in part, an opportunity for exploration of self and one's relationship with others.

Shiel concluded her report with the following words:

> ❦ *Writing in retrospect, one can never capture the actual tears, pain, and guts that go into such exploration. Many of us went deep into our inner selves and discovered that our anxieties, hostilities, and needs profoundly affect us as teachers. The structure of the system can be a refuge of sorts, and to deliberately "rock the boat" can be terribly threatening.*
>
> *For me, the experience of finding myself an "instant administrator" (lacking preparation or courses), was a new challenge—at first frightening. "Could I do it? What if I 'failed'? Had I gotten in over my head?" I found it difficult to wear so many hats, and I learned that my patience with the "child" in big people is more limited than it is with little people. I learned that to be truly facilitating is quite different from articulating about facilitating.*

Certainly this whole program is evidence that the approach Shiel used with her own sixth-grade class can, in its essential attitudes, be conveyed to others. But it is clear that this new learning on the part of teachers can only be effective when they *experience* greater self-direction, greater freedom to communicate. It is *not* conveyed on an intellectual level.

SUMMARY

I am deeply indebted to Barbara J. Shiel for her willingness to have this material used. It is of special practical help because it portrays her own uncertainties and confusions, as well as those of her students, as she launched into this new approach. Clearly it takes courage to attempt the new, and many teachers at every level lack this courage. Shiel's experience is most certainly not a model for another teacher to follow. Indeed, one of the most meaningful elements in this account is that she risked giving freedom to her pupils only so far as she dared, only so far as she felt reasonably comfortable. Thus, it is an account of a changing, risky approach to a classroom situation by a changing, risk-taking human being who felt at times defeated and at times very moved and stimulated by the consequences of what she was attempting.

POSTSCRIPT

Barbara Shiel's story has been told many times over as teachers have moved from controlling managers to liberating facilitators of learning. The stages of introspection, questioning, and change—while unique for each teacher—seem to form an evolutionary pattern, a process that has few shortcuts. The teachers, administrators, and others who seek to facilitate learning, those described throughout this book, all have their own pathways to freedom.

REFERENCES

1. Barbara J. Shiel, *Evaluation: A Self-directed Curriculum, 1965* (Unpublished manuscript, 1966).

CHAPTER 5

A FRENCH TEACHER GROWS WITH HER STUDENTS

◆

What about high school students? Is it possible to trust them to want to learn? Can they make appropriate choices about what to learn?

Talking with Gay Swenson (now Dr. Swenson, a psychologist), I learned of her experiences in teaching French a number of years ago. Because she had ample notes and material on which to base an account, I encouraged her to write about her experience. This helped her decide that her experiences were still relevant today and might well be helpful to teachers of, and those preparing to teach, any subject.

Here she shares her very personal development as a French teacher, in addition to the exciting growth of her students (1, pp. 115–27). I feel indebted to Gay Swenson and her students for permitting us to see this extremely pervasive, ever-changing learning process.

Grammar and Growth

The Beginning

🦋 *When I began substitute teaching in 1966–67, many factors were in my favor. I was young, enthusiastic, and very committed to French and social studies, my two major fields, so my experi-*

ences were quite rewarding. At the end of that year I was accepted for a teaching position at a high school well known and respected for its innovative atmosphere. I spent the summer preparing materials, audiovisual aids, and sample lessons for French.

That fall semester I applied the best principles gleaned from my recent graduate education courses and entertained the students with humor and personality. I sometimes felt as though I were tricking them into learning something through cleverness and catchy techniques. Apparently they were enjoying it for the most part, so in the name of good pedagogy to "keep them motivated" I continued. At the end of the year I felt rather satisfied that we had enjoyed ourselves together; they liked the new teacher, and they had learned a considerable amount of French as well. My department head, principal, and fellow teachers gave me encouraging feedback about my potential as an exceptional teacher, and I was given an intern to supervise the following year, a rare assignment for an untenured teacher.

Yet I felt something was missing. My "great" lesson plans sometimes mysteriously fell through unpredictably, and my modest ones would succeed as well as if I had spent hours preparing them. I would reason that the success or failure was probably related to the time of day, the heat of the season, their or my personal lives, or any other possible chance variable. At the worst, I would take out my frustration about crisis-filled days by angrily saying they could just "go home and turn on their darn TVs if what they expected was entertainment from me all the time. . . . "They were here to learn, and it wasn't all fun, etc., etc.

Among these highs and lows, a pattern clearly emerged that later developed into an incipient principle. I noticed that whenever learning involved either (a) creativity from the individual, (b) personal choice by the student in determining a project, or (c) controversy around an issue applicable to their personal world, learning invariably occurred [and] lasted, and something intangible flourished for us all. Following is an example that illustrates these observations.

Two students chose to teach the entire class for a week in French 1. The students were to select the concepts they wanted to teach, design appropriate approaches and audiovisual aids, teach the unit, develop and administer tests for it, and then grade the students. They were then to evaluate their own and the class response to their efforts. The entire class was electric with various reactions during and after the unit—amusement, enthusiasm, anger, frustration, but always aliveness. They readily criticized clarity or lack of it in the lessons, the tests, grading, etc. The results for both the learners and teachers, including myself, were significant: (a) generally high grades overall, (b) clear evidence of skill acquisition, (c) a voiced insight into the difficulties inherent in developing a coherent lesson comprehensible to everyone, and, therefore, (d) empathy for teachers. The key principles which appeared most clearly here were that involvement and excitement occurred when learning was self-directed and initiated by personal choice of the student. This early experience of freeing students to learn was to be the foundation for further changes in me as a teacher [during] the following years.

The importance of controversy as a catalyst for learning in class appeared frequently as we began to discuss current issues relating to their private lives and the larger world. Although we may not have all felt similarly, we discussed delicate issues openly in French whenever we could at whatever level of competency, from beginning French on. I shared my personal values and views with them as they did with me. It seemed to be unique for them, and us, to do this, and they would strain to speak in French to get their ideas across. Finally, significantly, they seemed to find it supportive that I respected them and valued their worth as persons enough to engage in controversial dialogues. They often expressed this to me in the anonymous class evaluations which I requested regularly.

With this and similar experiences behind me I was beginning to develop some clearer sense of direction. During the summer I did intensive reading on innovative education and attended conferences given by people concerned with educational and social change.

School in Transition

🦋 Our school itself had long been planning and preparing for a major structural and social change, which occurred during my second year of teaching. Later this innovation was to involve the community at large in several ways. The change was marked most overtly by our school beginning "modular or flexible scheduling," an event exciting and challenging to us all. Modular scheduling is a pattern of class attendance similar to that at universities. Classes meet at stated times throughout the day and week rather than following a lock-step order hour after hour. Classes vary in length from twenty minutes to two hours, depending on the course; they vary in size from eight students to nearly two hundred, and in numbers of teachers involved, from one to teams of five. Students are scheduled into classes from 60 percent to 90 percent of the day, and therefore have varying amounts of "open" or "free" time. The problems and advantages of flexible scheduling are numerous, and vary depending on the individual perspective. I personally found it a long overdue approach to dealing with several aspects of compulsory education.

One significant change built into the new schedule, and a precursor to the total change I attempted later, was the small-group seminar. As applied in the Foreign Language Department, this was designed to provide more time for listening and speaking. The third-year language students met in seminar once a week for forty-five minutes in groups of not more than twelve. The material and content used for these conversation seminars was based on vocabulary lists topically organized around the house, body, clothes, idioms, and specific situational dialogues such as movies and restaurants. If done with some imagination by the teacher, the students took to it and used the time well. But again, it was when the content involved an issue which concerned them that they really tried to get their ideas across to one another. The effectiveness of such an approach remained vividly with me as we continued. So I began to make lists of issues which the students had suggested, and appropriate vocabulary upon which to build oral skills. Some of the topics which students suggested and we discussed were sex, drugs, ecology communes, school curriculum, grading, drinking, dating, driving, prejudice, politics, parents, peace, and . . . teachers. The changes in student participation were amazing. Their fluency developed, their interest and involvement increased, and ideas buzzed through the small room as opinions differed [and] emotions flared and [as] they struggled to communicate all this "en français." Student evaluations indicated that it was generally fun to be learning.

Early Contracting

❦ Despite innovations in schedule and curriculum, emphasis on small-group discussions and student-led lessons, I felt that there was still no fundamental change in the class structure and hierarchy system. It was still the teacher who held the power and control in matters of attendance, curriculum, and grading. There were still students who were unchallenged [or] bored or [who] felt held back. I wanted to find alternatives for these people. I tried several alternatives, each very different. They gave me incentive to later apply such principles to an entire class.

One such alternative approach was that selected by two very capable young women in third-year French. We worked out an interdepartmental approach for English and French. One young woman studied children's literature in her English classes and created her own book—a fairy tale written in French and illustrated by her as well. Additionally, in cooperation with her friend, the two of them analyzed and compared American and French romantic poetry. Each wrote serious papers on poetry styles and translated a series of very difficult poems by Victor Hugo, attempting to retain the flavor, sound, and imagery of the originals. This they did well. To this day, both young women retain an active interest in French, corresponding or visiting with me once or twice a year.

Emerging Values

❦ With such small successes after two years of teaching, several values were solidified for me. Yet I still had many concerns about the learning process. There were pitfalls and potentials in freeing students to learn; therefore, how to best maximize the potentials became the issue.

I asked myself, "How does one meet all the different needs of all these different students so that they are using both their scheduled in-class time and free time creatively and uniquely?" Related to this concern was how to keep the students in class and involved while they were there, for with the new flexible schedule there was an initial heavy pattern of cutting, or selective class-cutting and nonproductive use of open time. I did not personally have heavy cutting. I assumed it had something to do with the kinds of students I was lucky enough to have and perhaps more importantly with something different we were doing together in class.

Operating primarily on this latter assumption, I began my third teaching year with the belief that all the best features of the partially individualized approach which I had experimented with so far could be and should be made a permanent part of the structure of the class. Having that summer just finished reading Freedom to Learn, the book by Carl Rogers, I felt even more strongly . . . [the importance of] making a commitment to individualized learning.

But where to begin? I certainly couldn't radically individualize all my classes at once since this year I was to teach all five levels of French. What would be my criteria for selecting a class? After taking some time to come to know the various groups, I selected one which had the widest cross-section of potential.

The Free Learners

❦ The "free learners," then, in 1969–70 were to be my third-year French class. In makeup, it was a class of twenty-eight students, mostly sophomores, a few juniors, and a couple of seniors. They ranged from very motivated, sophisticated, and good-willed people, to [those who were] not so, . . . who in the past had been more than willing to let me know when they were bored or uninvolved. The class met three times a week for about an hour, then, in addition, once a week in a conversation seminar, and again once a week in a large group with the other two French teachers' third-year classes for a film or lecture.

I did not begin the "project approach," as we came to call it, in the fall. Still afraid of the risk, hesitant, procrastinating, I stopped myself by my own fear that they would not "get in" the necessary grammar if given too much freedom of choice. Instead I reached into my bag of tricks and tried to make palatable the usual short stories, grammar, dictations, essays, and listening comprehension.

At the same time I was coordinating the development of a tutorial program whereby some three hundred French students would be tutored by volunteer fellow students in addition to their regular assigned class time. This monumental logistical effort took much energy, many hours, and some guts and nerve, which I consequently did not put into the project approach. While a rational "stopper," it also gave me incentive, for this experience did teach me much about self-motivated teaching/learning which later became applicable to our project.

Hesitant Steps

✸ My first hesitant attempt to destructure the class involved my planning a unit, rather highly structured at that, based on the words and music of Jacques Brel: a unit which I developed in advance for the students. In retrospect I see my hesitancy apparent in the very pronouns used above. Even at the end of the unit I felt that were I to do it again I would leave the course principally in the hands of the students to develop and coordinate. Although the unit was highly enjoyable according to the students, I believe that it would have been much more imaginative and, importantly, more meaningful had they initiated it themselves.

After Christmas vacation we began to use another textbook. The students did not want to return to the traditional approach, so they suggested forming groups again to work on different chapters, present them to the class, build their own vocabulary lists and tests as they had in the Brel unit. But this time it was old hat. They were quickly bored with the pattern as well as with the light nature of the book itself; the semester was nearly over and we were going nowhere. They were annoyed and I began my old line of "You just want to be entertained." We had several frank and painful sessions on what was wrong with the class. They were just not interested anymore. Some even wanted to drop French. We were all discouraged and I became even more resistant to *freeing them to learn their own way. Yet this very crisis acted as the final push that helped me to plunge . . . with them into a turbulent and buoyant sea of change.*

Researching and Self-searching

❧ *First, if they weren't interested anymore, what would renew their interest? I asked and they told me in a series of preference sheets—poetry, music, art, history, fashion, drama, cartooning, cooking, literature of every sort, philosophy, and even grammar. For weeks, the students and I dug out every bit of written or audiovisual material we had on hand in the language department, researched additional school library resources, and added from our own personal home libraries and record stocks. The pile of literature alone included works from* Peanuts, Winnie-the-Pooh, *and* The Red Balloon *to [those written or composed by]* Brel, Piaf, Baudelaire, Verlaine, La Fontaine, Molière, Sartre, Camus, Villon, *Prevert, and others. It took the form of short stories, poetry, music, magazines, anthologies, college texts, and references on every aspect of literary analysis, history, or grammar.*

From these materials I made up what came to be known familiarly as "the cart"—a moveable book cart and overhead projector overflowing with records, tapes, and books from which groups or individuals were to select their initial project when the spring semester began.

The Project

❧ *As we began this totally individualized approach, there were organizational and personal issues to be dealt with carefully and constantly. How we dealt with them varied from day to day as we moved along, but the general themes occurred fairly consistently as follows:*

To deal with the personal aspects of the change we had informal groups or class meetings. Some of the issues dealt with at length were (a) the problems and opportunities involved in this approach, (b) the responsibilities to oneself and others, (c) confronting the frustrations as they appeared and not allowing feelings to build up, (d) handling feelings of great expectations about an individualized program and the possible disappointments and sense of failure when goals changed or did not materialize. In time we were to express precisely this wide emotional spectrum and more—anxiety, acting out, anger, false starts and frustrations, sadness in facing one's lack of self-directive abilities, need to blame, problems with working in groups or alone—all had their day in each of us. Every feeling and issue demanded attention, caring, understanding, and encouragement. We gave it to each other as individuals or as a class. Later I will give examples from specific incidents which will vividly demonstrate this aspect of the change.

A second factor requiring creative solutions was the ongoing logistics problems, such as (a) the mechanics of developing a personal contract, (b) choice in selecting a project, (c) use of time, (d) keeping accurate records of one's work progress and a record of newly learned materials, (e) being responsible to turn in materials when completed and deciding when one was ready to take tests on work done; perhaps developing these tests from one's unit for oneself or other group members, (f) selecting new goals as one project was completed, (g) altering goals and/or demanding more work from the "cart" or elsewhere. The underlying theme in all the above was personal and shared responsibility for constant movement and change.

A third and crucial learning—or, more accurately, unlearning—process occurred as the students became more involved in their projects and completed them: that of evaluation. Here the adjustment involved learning to look inward for signs of progress and growth and not through peer comparison or teacher evaluation alone. At first we experienced a high level of resistance to self-evaluation. This was not surprising, for the evaluating responsibility is a difficult one for teachers to abdicate and for students to assume after years of conditioning. During this project I found it a vital shift to make, if the students were to learn to become self-evaluators rather than persons waiting for the traditional authority to say, "Yes, that is good; you are right; go on." As with the logistics issue, students learned to assume this responsibility, or rather to share it with me, with varying degrees of efficiency and comfort. This again required guidance and encouragement which hopefully led to personal satisfaction at the growth experienced.

As the projects got further underway, the realities of the physical situation itself were both frustrating and humorous. It was not unusual to see me and several students lugging tape recorders, record players, and slide projectors across campus to class, then later, running off to the next class with materials scattering windward en route. Sudden room changes, assembly day schedules, or switches in the time a student was to present a project to the class added to the flurry of activity and the need for constant flexibility. [After we had] . . . taken a deep breath and settled down in one location for the day, the creative chaos began. Since each student had selected an individual or group activity, an unprepared visitor might walk into a room where he would find one group acting out a scene from a play, another reading a story aloud or translating, a single student silently spread out on the floor over an art project or engrossed in a poem, [while] nearby a friend [was] leaning over the record player, struggling to hear it over a neighboring tape recorder in the corner; others would be trying to grasp the emotionality of the use of the subjunctive, calling for help from me while the usual conversation "nuts" would be talking away in French about men, sex, life, or the current ecological crisis, and, of course, someone would be goofing off altogether in English until I came close by, while others coolly handled it all. Over the din and to the astonishment of our visitor some anxious soul might yell, "I don't know what the hell I'm doing and this chaos is driving me crazy."

Admittedly, there was all that seeming chaos. The physical, philosophical, logistical, and emotional factors were ever-present. It was not an easy change for the students or for me. It was an exciting one, for there was a vitality and aliveness present through it all. We never knew if that vitality would take the form of guilt, anger, and blame, or jubilance and joy at the discovery or accomplishment of the moment. It was an electric time.

Doubts in the Community

🦋 *In the language of the graduate education school, what has been discussed up to this point has remained primarily in the "affective domain"; . . . what actually happened to the "cognitive progress" of the student? In other words, "what did they really learn that we can measure?"*

Correlated closely to the question of "measurable results" are two events which had an impact on the effectiveness of the project approach. One event affected us particularly as a class and the second involved the entire school.

First, during the spring our school came under heavy criticism from a vocal minority in the community as to the merit of this new flexible schedule in which students were given so much freedom to determine how they used or abused their time. In this regard the group was strongly supported by a local newspaper. As the conflict intensified there were days and nights of meetings. Student, parent, and faculty committees were formed pro and con and conciliatory. There were long weeks of anxiety and pressure on everyone with hope for resolution of the impasse.

Many of my students and I were deeply involved in the issues during the entire spring semester both in and out of class. Our minds were often not involved with the "cart." Putting the cart before the horse in this case would have been not only a cliché and bad pun but a catastrophe as well. However, in class our small-group discussion seminars were like local town meetings where the conflict was played out in miniature—in French.

During this dialoguing an esprit de corps *developed and intensified among us in support of the school and its innovations while students also offered fine suggestions for modifying the system to improve it. School ended with the issues still smoldering, to burn again the following year.*

A second event which affected us personally as a class was my health. During this period I became quite ill. Only five weeks after having begun the project approach, I was in the hospital for ten days and home for a month following. The adjustments to this event were hardest on the teachers replacing me. For [them] . . . the project was at the least a surprise and, at the most, a shock. Often appalled at what was going on—or not going on—in class, one substitute would rapidly retreat to be replaced by another and another. For students it was easier in some respects since they were in charge as they had been all along. Since it was their individual responsibility to help the substitute, my files and desk were opened to them and they knew where the "cart" was and the materials and equipment to be checked out. They would tell a substitute not to worry; they knew what they were doing; [and] then [they would] phone me at the hospital to ask where something was or tell me which student was teaching with the sub for that week. Often they would visit the hospital or my home during their open time, bringing with them delightful presents, jokes, good wishes, and, significantly, serious questions and concerns about their work in French. During this period I believe they felt a responsibility and freedom rarely experienced in the normal classroom situations: [the] choice to goof off and/or grow, as they felt inclined, and to reap the appropriate harvest.

Fruits off the Cart

❦ *Four weeks later when I returned with barely a month left of school and not much spark or gumption, fears bubbled up in my stomach. I feared that the fruits of their individual efforts would be stunted or blemished due to the halting, hit-or-miss nourishment. I wondered if my faith and values built up over the last years would have some foundation in fact. Answers to these inner questions would be the crucial telling point as to the merit of the project we had ventured into together. When it came time to present the results or "harvest," the creative individual and group efforts which had emerged out of the not-so-well-nurtured soil of confusion and first attempts were astonishing. The fruits were so much more abundant than I had ever expected that I could hardly believe it. Following are the collected examples of such growth— work and play and learning.*

1. *One girl wrote some fifteen papers and personal essays in French on poetry, music, and literature.*

2. *One student read twelve short stories and condensed them into an imaginative single French composite, developing tests, vocabulary, and grammar units on each of the readings.*

3. *Several students translated and drew popular or original cartoons in French.*

4. *One student made a pictorial adaptation of a poem from newspaper clippings and explained the story line in French orally.*

5. *Many students adapted stories and poems, which they had first translated, into art forms—collages, pictures, and photos.*

6. *Several students read, listened to tapes, analyzed, and wrote essays based on the fables of La Fontaine and the underlying themes.*

7. *Students studied grammar and applied the points learned in various story forms or essays or personal journals.*

8. *Several students read and learned vocabulary from dozens of poems by various French poets and discussed in French the significance to them personally.*

9. *Singers Piaf and Brel continued to be popular sources for looking at personal values and life meanings.*

10. *Tales such as* The Red Balloon *and* Babar the Elephant *were approached from direct translation to acting out, writing about, or developing increasing grammar competency and vocabulary.*

11. *Many students wrote their own poetry or journals expressing intimate feelings from their inner lives.*

12. *Grammar study was continued in differing formats. Those students continuing a traditional intensive approach covered much more material than I would normally have assigned during the same time period.*

Comparative Facts

🦋 *During such a similar period of seven weeks' time, we would normally have read some short stories or* The Little Prince *together as a class and done grammar, dictations, and listening comprehension as we had in the past. Indeed, 80 percent of the students did at least three different projects each, and everyone did at least one project which included translation, a paper, testing, and vocabulary and grammatical growth. Only one person turned in no work at all. She read poetry in class when she was there. When she was not [present], we took time together to discuss the effect of her choice for the following school year and in her personal life at home and elsewhere.*

Evaluations

✺ *Obviously there were drawbacks and advantages to the approach as seen by the students and myself. As abstracted from their written evaluations at the end of the school year, the following points were mentioned either repeatedly or with decided emphasis in individual cases.*

1. *My absence was mentioned most frequently. Many felt it had led to less productivity, particularly for those students who were experiencing a need for more direction. This need was not expressed by just one type of student or learner but came from an A-plus student, a timid student fearing self-direction, another student needing to be "pushed," she said, in order not to flunk, and one who "would have done better if you had told me what to do more."*

2. *Mistranslations occurred. When work was done alone or in a group, since they could not or would not always check with me or a dictionary for every idiom or grammatical subtlety, some inaccurate learning took place.*

3. *Several students expressed a desire for a more rigid system of deadlines to be set by me. This was to include expectations for each week, a demand to turn in or achieve so much during a specific time slot. Old conditioning feels safe and operates well.*

4. *Some students admittedly did not do work commensurate with their ability. They did not set or achieve goals well or clearly, and one did not even come to class very often. These same students did learn something valuable about themselves in the process according to their reports.*

5. *Many wished [for] more oral work in French such as that provided . . . in the small conversation seminars held once a week.*

6. *Some students feared they may not have learned traditionally enough to prepare them for demanding college work.*

On the more positive side the gains were clearly stated. In terms of the subject matter students frequently expressed a sense of excitement, involvement, renewed interest, or intensified interest in French. Many said they read more in French and enjoyed it more for themselves, often voluntarily not even submitting it for a project but just doing it from getting "turned on." In personal terms they expressed good feelings about group cooperativeness in becoming noncompetitive learners, helpers to learn together, thus minimizing competition; they valued highly the removal of fear about tests; they praised the warm, relaxed feelings in class.

The fairly neutral students expressed increased interest because the goals did not seem so unattainable since they could choose a project more appropriate to their level of competency or commitment. All types of learners appreciated the freedom to create, the feeling of self-direction and responsibility, the elimination of pressure to cheat, the facing of their own potentials and limitations, and [the] ability to direct and pace their learning process. Lastly, and frequently mentioned, was the feeling that they will remember what they did much longer and with greater joy. Only one student in the project approach suggested returning to the traditional classroom method.

My personal point of view as a participant in this project naturally reflects my own bias and valuing process. Additionally, my views express as well my sensibility to young people and a respect for my own intuitive and intellectual strengths; therefore, I would like to share some conclusions with you.

1. *A new and significant element to me was that student learning was not spatially one-dimensional: i.e., occurring only in class. Outside of class, in the offices, under the trees, in the halls, students would be found discussing "their" poet or writer with someone else with a real notable concern and excitement. Nor was learning limited to "the assignment." They would sit together with friends and become interested in some other person's project. Often they exchanged books, bought or "borrowed" copies of their own, or kept books long after projects were over. It was common practice to stop in the office for additional references or help from me or just to talk in French and/or English. We went places together and spoke French in the car and at the park or museum or restaurant until it was "too much, let's stop." Perhaps some changes were merely because they now had time outside of class to do this. Perhaps not merely that.*

2. *Very significant to me was the fact that we became learners together. Since I obviously was not an expert in every one of the areas in which they often became immersed, I was discovering and researching along with them. I did not know all the grammar nor the entire French literary vocabulary, and we all accepted this perfectly comfortably. I was never afraid to say, "I don't know," and they became more and more comfortable and pleased with this reality.*

3. *The changes in personal growth and in interpersonal relationships among students and between student and teacher were highly visible and moving to me. We were very open about our moods, and let each other know clearly where we were when we sensed some changed feelings. Anger, joy, grief, belly*

laughs, and tears were freely shown by me and them. It was not unusual to hear from them or from me, "You may notice I talk too much, so stop me when you've had enough," "I am really depressed today; can you handle this for me for a while until I get out of it?", "I just had this huge fight and my head's in a mess," "The most fabulous thing happened to me this weekend!" "I'm sorry, I really wasn't listening to you at all," "You've given me so much," "I really love you," "I'm really getting angry," "You don't give a damn about me!" We discussed our problems about sex, drugs, abortion, etc., at length very openly, both in the small-seminar hour or outside of class as a group. When I was in the hospital a miniature rose tree was sent with a note from The Little Prince *saying, "Tu es unique au monde," among dozens of individual presents, visits, etc. I know that every teacher has experienced such caring and concern which in no way relates to the approach or the curriculum; however, I do feel that the context in which we operated during the year made such ways of relating easier. The growing trust that each of us felt was of very special value and worth to the other in some way and, most importantly, of increasing value to ourselves as we emerged intellectually and emotionally, facilitated the possibility of the following occurrences.*

When I had been particularly upset about a possible personal change in my life, my emotions were rather transparent. So there would be flowers on my desk, notes, and special caring contacts with many sensitive students. One day a student came to me in my office and sat down and from a real sense of her own worth as a supportive human being, regardless of our differences in age, "roles," etc., said, "Mrs. Swenson, you don't seem to be your usual self these days. A lot of us are really concerned. I know we're only students, but you are so often there when we're upset, we want you to know that if you want to talk about it, we'd like to listen." I am still deeply touched recalling this incident, both for the caring for my well-being and for the self-respect that this young woman's statement exemplified. Movement toward maturity is more than mastery of subject matter alone, and together that past year we had been enabling such mutual growth.

Old Fears

❧ *However, as the year came to an end the old feelings held fast, the old fears reappeared in students and in me. In gestalt terms, what had been "ground" for some time was emerging as "figure" in the form of doubts. Have they learned as much as they would have with a traditional method? Will they do well on those ever-present, and important, achievement tests? Questions such* as "Will they learn values and ideals needed for their own worth? Will they become free learners? Will they concern themselves with humanity's needs?" fell back in timid retreat.

We were all faced with those fears, students and I both, this first time around, so before final exam week I told them we had better review fast in grammar areas we might not have "covered" well enough individually. I suggested they go through the grammar workbook we had used in the earlier part of the year and intermittently since, and we would take an eighty-point multiple-choice test, all verbs and grammar, with one change. [The change involved how the final exam was taken.] During the three-hour final they would bring up each page as they finished it, I would mark the incorrect answers with a dot, and they would be given a second chance to determine the right answer. Only this time, they had to justify and explain their answer, indicating in writing or orally that they understood the rule behind its selection; in that way the factor of guessing or chance selection was to be eliminated. We did this. The test was very difficult and [the] results excellent, frequently without the added second chance for many students. Some, of course, had still "never understood" grammar and several of these had been the most creative students in the class. When I asked the class how it was that they had done so well, the answer was a comment, both humorous and sad, on our usual approach to learning. "What difference does it make? You always study for the final the week before—then forget everything the next day. So we did the same thing this time. The only difference was we did a lot more interesting things all year long too."

All but three of the twenty-eight students who were not graduating continued on into fourth-year French the following year, expressing hope that the class would be organized—or rather not organized—as it had been this year.

Some Conclusions

🦋 Having outlined the major drawbacks and personal and academic potentials of our project, I would like to summarize the major beliefs which I hold some years after initiating the program. These values and premises had been long incubating in me as "inner promptings." When I listened to them and acted upon them, these beliefs became tangible evidence that learning can be self-directed, as postulated in Freedom to Learn. In fact, many of the values listed below closely resemble those stated by Rogers.

I strongly feel that:

1. The curriculum can be self-selected by the student, based on his or her own current interests and abilities.

2. *There can be self-testing, self-evaluation, self-set goals, which are valid.*

3. *Frequent evaluation of the effectiveness of a program can occur [through] . . . a combination of input from the individual learner, the teacher, the entire class.*

4. *Such an approach requires miniature "encounter groups" or "keeping-current sessions" which might be highly charged with complaints, positive feelings, mixed feelings and creative problem solving.*

5. *When interests alter, change need not be considered failure or something about which to feel guilty; . . . rather [it is] a self-selected rerouting of direction and growth.*

6. *Cooperation rather than competition can accrue and be encouraged.*

7. *Grades can be based on individual expectations and will differ greatly; this will mean that one student's "A" will be very different from another student's "A."*

8. *Varying amounts of time will be put in by different students at different time periods, some coming in for additional work because they are shy in class [or] less confident in one area, or because they want more in-depth intense work in addition to that in class and others may invest very little time or effort.*

9. *Students can be involved at every level possible in designing curriculum or selecting materials and approaches to achieve their goals.*

10. *Language learning is fundamentally a cultural and oral communicative tool which can increase insights and understanding among diverse people and can aid in decreasing disharmony and stereotypic reactions to differences.*

11. *Therefore, the most appropriate and satisfying content for conversation seminars are student-selected controversial topics which they might discuss with a young French person of their own age.*

12. *Values and beliefs regarding the human condition can be integral to the study of literature and grammar.*

Doing It Your Way

🦋 *Implementing such a belief system can be risky, frightening, and open to challenge. It will take considerable preparation on the part of the teacher, both psychologically and in the way of research. However, as the project continues, even more potential will emerge or be suggested by fellow students and teachers. It can be an electrifying and varied experience when team-taught by excited cooperative colleagues; it can be made more conve-*

nient by a language center where materials and equipment and "ambiance" are available in one location; students can help develop a core cultural approach (such as that used by the Spanish team in our school); mini-courses can evolve based on student interests such as crafts, drama, politics, or social action, and can be led by the students themselves.

None of the above is necessary to begin. All that is needed is one's courage, one's students, and one's commitment to trust the human ability to discover oneself. It is then we begin to become more of what we really are—free, excited learners and growers.

Postscript

❦ *Years later, letters and visits continue to come from students who shared the experience described above. The contents reassure me that the problems encountered and the opportunities offered during that time helped these young people to become more competent decision makers and, very importantly, open, risking adults, affirming their personhood.*

In closing I think of a student from whom I heard only this week. The woman writes, "I think a lot about my experiences there, especially the cooperative group of friends (teachers and students) and the stimulating environment and intellectual excitement which I have rarely experienced anywhere else, even at the university, which I thought would be better. The environment there [in our French class] was so rich for me and I could explore so many directions. . . . I remember being awakened to something new every day. . . . The places I've lived and studied have not been nearly so supportive or rather have not encouraged the kind of growth I experienced in our class."

So I am touched and encouraged to know that our ways of coming together academically and personally have lasted through the years beyond the classroom time and space, that it did indeed offer as an alternative more humanistic classes where people were persons together as well as learners.

COMMENTS

I would like to underscore some elements I see as important in Dr. Swenson's account, most of them already stated by her.

It is a splendid example of the way in which a teacher may start taking small risks, small enough that he or she can afford to fail. As each risky step provides new learnings and new confidence, the teacher can go on to greater and more pervasive innovation in permitting students to take responsibility. To put it another way, providing responsible freedom in the classroom is not an all-or-none thing. It is a gradual growth process, involving both the teacher and the students.

It is clear that the underlying philosophy, the fundamental belief in the potential of each student, can then be flexibly implemented. Techniques, or special teaching methods, are secondary.

From the outset Gay Swenson was committed to students and her subject. She was eager to learn from each experience. Being open to learning from her experience led to developing a new personal educational philosophy. This increased her capacity for permitting students to grow.

Following Swenson's experiences allows us to see her change from being originally an accusative and evaluative teacher to one who listened and learned from her students. She began with "You just want to be entertained" and "Don't think school is all fun." But later she asked her students, "What would renew your interest?"—and they told her! It is clear that this kind of learning process demands a teacher who is continually growing.

Her increasing openness in expressing her feelings—whether joy, anger, or conviction—while leaving room for others to have different feelings—is striking.

Her caring for her students came through in many ways, and it was fully reciprocated: when she was ill and, most movingly, by the young woman who offered her help in a psychological crisis.

Involving parents and community was a most valuable step in a crisis situation. Dr. Swenson says, "It was a reminder of how important it is that we listen to each other and to the multiplicity of voices and views before, during, and after an innovation."

Swenson's report gives evidence that with freedom and responsibility, the students became cooperative learners, competent decision makers, and responsible leaders (especially when she was ill).

In the climate Dr. Swenson initiated and that students and teacher created, they learned far more French than they would have in a traditional class. In addition they learned to live responsibly and creatively with themselves and with others.

One last point. The students are quite right that learning in order to pass an exam need take only a relatively small amount of time, and that when this fact is faced, there is ample time for creative personal and group learning.

It is exciting to see how both teacher and students, even as they focus on learning a particular subject, can also learn and grow in personal responsibility, openness of communication, an increased sense of self-worth, creativity, and warm interpersonal relationships. That these learnings can last for years afterward adds to the significance of the whole experience.

REFERENCES

1. Gay Swenson, "Grammar and Growth: A French Connection," *Education* 95, no. 19 (1974): 115–27. Used by permission and revised for this chapter.

CHAPTER 6

ADMINISTRATORS AS FACILITATORS

◆

A leader is best

When people barely know that he exists,

Not so good when people obey and acclaim him,

Worst when they despise him.

"Fail to honor people,

They fail to honor you;"

But of a good leader, who talks little,

When his work is done, his aim fulfilled,

They will all say, "We did this ourselves." (1)

The quote by Lao Tzu concluded chapter 1 and begins this chapter. It reminds me that being a facilitator is much more difficult than being a leader. Leadership requires followers, but facilitating requires standing among others rather than standing apart. The best facilitator blends in with the group.

OXYMORON OR CONGRUENCE?

The concept of administrators as facilitators is not an oxymoron; the terms are not incongruous. Administrators can and do facilitate learning. This chapter highlights examples of facilitators of learning who created schools that kids and teachers love. It also gives examples of the way one of the most difficult areas of interaction between teachers and principals—supervision and evaluation—can become a facilitative and building process. The students mentioned in chapter 1, who discussed their reasons for loving school, had administrators, teachers, and other concerned and caring people whose goal and mission in life was the well-being of young people. What these facilitators did and said were in congruence with each other and their students' comments in the previous interviews in chapter 1. Schools and communities have many types of leaders. We are going to visit with a few who see their role in life as facilitating the development of others.

CALL ME BOB

"Twenty years ago the Free School strongly proclaimed local control for schools at the school-site. Today, I can proudly state that on the front burner of educational reform is moving power from the statehouse and the [school] boardroom to the schoolhouse" (2). This statement is by Robert Ferris, a facilitator of learning at the New Orleans Free School at its twentieth-anniversary celebration.

The students at the New Orleans Free School call their facilitator "Bob." Other people know him as the school's founder. The kindergarten through eighth grade public school in New Orleans consists of an old building constructed at the turn of the century. It has wooden floors, high ceilings, and no air conditioning for the steamy New Orleans days. At the central district office, Dr. Robert Ferris (aka Bob) is known as the principal.

I visited the school during its twentieth-anniversary celebration. Bob Ferris met me at his office, which is furnished with used office furniture. His work area, an old student desk saved from the trash heap, measures no more than two-by-three feet. The school serves low-income students in New Orleans, with about 90 percent of the students participating in the free-lunch program. For the school's twentieth anniversary, the parents and students sponsored a dinner and dance. The anniversary celebration was also a part of the never-ending fund-raising activities to which schools, by necessity, must devote time and energy if they are to have resources for change. Rather than giving a speech, Bob wrote out his thoughts, which he titled "From Gadfly to Mainstream: The New Orleans Free School Twenty Years Later." The following excerpts are from his twentieth-anniversary letter to students, parents, teachers, and community members.

✤ *We are sharing our twenty years of operation. As I reflect upon our journey over these years, I realize that the process has been long and difficult, though often rewarding. We started out with just an idea that became a reality. We now celebrate the adulthood of that idea.*

Twenty years ago we were strong-willed, full of energy, sure we were right, and hell-bent on changing the course of history. The only difference now is that we are older and no longer wild and crazy; we have become pensive and reflective. The innovator is no longer viewed as a lawbreaker and a rule bender, a rebel and a gadfly; rather, the innovator is now considered a lawmaker and a visionary, a thinker and a pathfinder.

When we started the Free School back in 1971 the key concept was that education must be relevant to the life of the child, that learning best occurs from the life involvement of the unique individual. I am proud today to be able to say that our program still offers an inquiry-based, experimental, and creative program. Instead of an emphasis on right answers, rigidity, routine, and reproducing the known, the thrust of our program is to actively engage the students in the learning process, to get them personally involved in their development of knowledge.

Twenty years ago we argued that if America was to truly revitalize our public schools, we must seek and establish small schools. No student must be allowed to go through our schools anonymously—unnoticed. In this great industrialized nation of ours, we must guarantee that education will be an intensely personal experience for every student.

Twenty years ago we took a strong position for offering a nongraded program. We argued then as now that grades do little for the bright students while all too often crush and obliterate the struggling student.

. . .We are offering children from New Orleans an environment which achieves academic progress without the fear of traditional, harmful social comparisons which all too often lead to low self-esteem and self-image.

Grades are not as much of an issue today as they were back in 1971. The battle today is over standardized testing. Standardized tests are now so pervasive and powerful in our public schools that they have greatly diminished the quality of our schools.

. . .The emphasis all too often is not on the joy, excitement, and/or challenge of learning; rather, it is on the skill development, mastery of isolated skills, sequence of skills, test-taking skills, etc. Curricula are no longer based on interests, needs, or curiosity, but are dominated by what is on the tests. While we as educators are told not to cheat on these tests, we are instructed to teach what is

on the tests. The result of this overemphasis on achievement tests is that it narrowly defines curricula content in an age when we must be concentrating on the expansion of knowledge through individuals who have a love for learning, who know how to learn, and who have thought processes intricate enough to deal with the complexities of the modern world. Testing has now reversed the process of learning. Instead of using testing to facilitate and evaluate learning, we are now using testing to test our ability to teach the test. Instead of learning dictating testing, testing is determining learning. Instead of [our] utilizing testing for human development, [testing] . . . has become the yardstick of human . . . worth.

Our large bureaucratic public school structure forces compliance and convergency on us all. This political and bureaucratic structure forces schools to be "compromised organizations," to use the words of the recent Rand study titled "High School with Character." The isolated few schools which work because of wealth and/or practices notwithstanding, the public school political structure's message is "This is the way you do it." School-site personnel are reduced to mental dwarfs, forcing the best and brightest to crawl into a hole and sacrifice principles and thoughts, leave the system, or spend a life in the lonely position of being an adversary.

. . . Twenty years ago we were on the outside looking in. We were strongly attacking bureaucratic control of schools and we were critical of corporate America. . . . Now instead of a concentration on attacking bureaucracy, our efforts remain on the cutting edge of education but with an emphasis on serving as a model of responsive, humanistic education for mostly low-income students. We have even joined corporate America. We now have two business partners. . . . We have come to the realization that with society's complex and entrenched problems, only together can we make a difference.

. . .We must change our schools from convergent compliancy to divergent creative living organizations. [We] are not talking about the rhetoric of change. School-based management, shared decision making, empowerment are all buzz words of the bureaucracy. . . . Do we have to sink the boat in order to rock it? I do not know. I do know that we must pop the cork to drink the champagne. I also know that twenty years is a long time. Let's drink the champagne. (2)

Comments

I am struck by the strong sense that Bob Ferris has given a lifetime to the facilitation of learning. The students come *first*, the bureaucracy *last*. It appears that during the last twenty years Ferris has grown as a facilitator.

The bringing together of resources, including local businesses, to help children requires a fine balance between staying outside the system to maintain independence and being connected enough to marshal resources to support the learning community. Bob is a person who lives education on a daily basis, and we can see through his words the effects of testing, grading, competition, and, at times, indifference on the lives of children. It is also clear that after twenty years, he does not have all the answers. Bob is still searching for ways to improve the lives of children in New Orleans. In his search for answers, he may improve the lives of children in many other places as well.

INTERVIEW WITH BOB FERRIS

Bob's unusual record and national reputation as a principal/facilitator resulted in my visit and interview in 1991 and a follow-up conversation in 1993. The issues of order, trust, and barriers to communication were discussed. Bob also revealed some ways in which administrators facilitate learning. The following are excerpts primarily from the 1991 interview, with additional information provided in 1993.

On Barriers to Communication

Question: I would describe your office here as having an eclectic furniture style, with the desk about the size of a student desk. Do you think it makes it more comfortable for parents to come in?

BF I . . . think if I had a really formal type of office it would be intimidating. . . . Really the office is used for everything. It's been used for a costume room, it's used as a dance studio, sometimes when I teach the kids the folk dances, I get two or three kids in here and we go over the steps, and I try not to be in here very much.

On Quiet and Order

BF I think we basically model schools after the industrial age and they really are factories and run that way. The order is more important in these places than the life of the learning. Unfortunately most people want really quiet, orderly schools. Kids are not always quiet and orderly and it makes it more of a challenge when you loosen the reins . . . and you try to make learning more relevant, more active, and more fun. The noise we have here is a noise of interaction and learning. You lose some of the control, and most people don't want to lose that control. . . . They don't realize that shared control is better for both student and teacher.

On Trust

Question: I could not help overhearing your conversation with a parent. The child had lied to you and the issue you raised was a breach of trust.

BF   She [the middle school student] had brought a student into the building telling me that it was her brother. . . . But it's a big problem; she'd lied to me saying that it was her brother, a kid that none of us knew. . . . I just talked to the child and her mother in trying to express the seriousness of it and that it was a breach of trust, because I want to be able to trust kids.

On Student Choices

Question: How do the kids interact across grade levels?

BF   Well, they interact a lot because we have a program called "Sign-up Time" which is our enrichment program. Every Monday morning a list [of classes] floats through the school. In fact, it's going through the school now, and they get choices of different kinds of classes. They pick the classes and then go to that class during the last period of the day, Monday through Thursday. Each week the classes change. First grade though fourth grade can sign up together, and then fifth graders through eighth graders sign up together. So a fourth grader can be working right alongside . . . a first grader, and a fifth grader can work alongside an eighth grader. This is done on purpose, and it causes . . . a lot of the mixing of students. Students can take, for example, sign language, band, folk dancing, tap dancing, choir, photography, chess, and arts and crafts.

In addition to . . . "Sign-up Time," students beginning in the seventh grade complete "internships" at the children's museum, city hall, nursing homes, and other civic places. They write a résumé, go for an interview, and we give them one afternoon or morning a week to complete their internship. In 1993, students were asked to select an issue facing New Orleans and direct their service toward that issue. The students elected to provide services to the homeless.

On Hitting Kids

BF   We don't hit a child in any way, shape, or form. To its credit, Orleans Parish has a rule against corporal punishment. And we are up front [to the students]: "We are not going to hit you."

On State Mandates

BF   We make it [the curriculum] comply with state mandates, which bothers me. Again, basically, schools are organizations of compliance, not vital living organizations and that's one of the major flaws, that we are spending too much time attending to other people's agendas instead of . . . [doing] it according to our agenda. We are told to be creative, but teacher evaluations determine how we teach, textbooks determine what we teach, and standardized tests determine the value of what we teach.

On Successes and Failures

BF   Not every student succeeds at the Free School. The earlier they start school here, the more success we and they have. Students who start in the elementary grades and progress until eighth grade are very successful. We have had a few students who come in the seventh or eighth grade and can't adjust to the freedom. They are so programmed to being told what to do, how to do it, and when to do it that they don't know how to handle the choices and options we provide. It's a sad commentary on our schools and society when kids would rather do worksheets than a project or see our freedom to choose as a license to disrupt the choices of others. Fortunately, there are very few students . . . [to whom] we failed to give the opportunity to succeed.

On Projects

BF   We belong to the Arts Connection and we have two artists come in and teach two and one half days and work in our classrooms with our students and teachers.

In all the subject areas we asked students and teachers to develop projects that have a creative arts component and incorporate the arts in their classroom presentations. For example, we don't use textbooks for science. Students conduct research projects and experiments and present their findings to the class. The students are asked to include the arts in their classroom presentations of their science projects.

On Being without a Principal

BF   Well, for many years, fourteen to be exact, we didn't have a principal. The school started out in the private domain. We became part of the public school system in 1973, as one of the free schools that started out in the late 60s, early 70s, and we moved to this building in 1980 and started growing. When we started growing, they [the district administrators] said, "You have to have a principal." In other words, they wanted to put us into their bureaucratic line of functioning. . . . Honestly, it was too hard to try to run a school and run a fund-raising organization. It was too much. We really didn't want to, but it was . . . [get a principal] or die. We wanted to demonstrate that this philosophy [of freedom] could work in an urban situation with urban children. This is the only magnet school in New Orleans dedicated to low-income children.

Comments

Bob Ferris, after more than twenty years as a facilitator, sees his role as inviting others to learn and share in the learning. From his basic office to a truly open-door policy about his office—it may be used by all who have a need for space—Bob is the embodiment of the ideals he presents. In a world of territoriality, his office has a welcome mat. He also facilitates in other ways: by his walkabouts in the school. He has little need to be in his office. The action, it seems, is going on throughout the school. He spends a majority of his time in classrooms and in the building. He has a willingness to be a facilitator at all levels—from the student selection of classes during the last period of each day, to giving folk dancing lessons himself. He has been able to provide students with real-life experiences through internships in the community and choices of classes through "Sign-up Time," giving students opportunities to meet, interact, and learn from each other across grades. Projects are designed to afford students an opportunity to see the whole picture of learning, not to be lost in isolated facts or disconnected concepts.

The Arts Connection is another example of using all the resources of the community to facilitate learning. We saw how Houston's High School for the Performing and Visual Arts, also founded in the early 70s, draws from the community to support a holistic approach to learning. Whether in New Orleans, Houston, Chicago, Preston County, or anywhere else in our nation, community interaction is an important ingredient in providing the best education for all students, regardless of who they are or where they come from. I have noticed that schools that children love have two or three times the number of community partnerships than other schools.

PRINCIPAL TEACHER

It is interesting to note that the New Orleans Free School functioned very well without a principal for fourteen years. There was a time before bureaucracy when most schools were organized around teachers and students, not administrators. The faculty selected one of its own to be the principal teacher. From this basic concept came the modern-day principal, who usually has little contact with students' learning and is primarily a manager.

Many principals I have met, who are facilitators of learning, find the time to be in the classroom each day. They teach regularly scheduled classes—not because they have so much extra time, but because they realize the importance of being in contact with students and experiencing what the other teachers are experiencing. Dr. John McClellan, who until recently was principal of Milby High School, a 3,600-student, predominantly Latino high school in Houston's inner city, taught a class each day. The principal and the assistant principals, whose first language was English, all learned to speak Spanish. The assistant principals also taught regularly scheduled classes. I asked McClellan about the reaction of teachers and students to his teaching a class. He described that reaction in the following way.

> ❦ *Well, I'll tell you what a teacher said: "He is going to handpick the kids." We told the counselor, "You assign us anybody," [and] I had ninth grade through twelfth. I had outlaws and good guys. Then the teacher said, "Oh well, he's the principal and they're gonna. . . ." You know, after the first week kids don't care who you are. They don't know you're a doctor or anything; that don't mean zip to them. They just want to know, "You care about me," and we did. . . . I'm not going to negate the fact that I'm the principal but as the course goes on, they forget that and you're just another teacher, and they'll talk back if they have something to say. . . . I had one teacher who came up to me and said, "I've been here twenty years, [and] I've never seen an administrator go into the classroom; I really appreciate that you guys do that." Right now we are team-teaching a course on leadership for kids.*

When people share both problems and solutions, the collective results are often far more creative than one person's ideas alone.

FACILITATING GREAT IDEAS

When principals facilitate their teachers and students and allow people to learn from failure, success may be around the corner. There are many examples I could recount, but one stands out among the others.

In many of our schools, teachers leave their teaching positions in the middle, some even at the beginning, of the school year. They become quickly frustrated, the social fabric in the classroom breaks down or is never created, and teachers walk away from their students. Teachers who leave may be unable to establish a climate for learning or a learning community; discipline is often cited as a reason for leaving.

While leaving may help the teacher and in some cases the students, many students I talked with felt angry, hurt, and abandoned by their teacher. Once the teacher leaves, the usual procedure is to hire a short-term substitute until a long-term substitute can be found. In many classes, students may see five or six substitute teachers before a permanent substitute is hired. Students vent their anger and feelings of abandonment on each new teacher. In many classrooms, chaos reigns as teacher after teacher is driven away. It is understandable that students ask why they should trust or listen to the adult in front of them. "She will only leave us in a few weeks" was the response of one fourth grader.

This situation is repeated thousands of times a year with the same disastrous outcomes. Teachers become interchangeable parts, warm bodies to baby-sit the kids, as several teachers have described it to me.

Collective Solution Finding

This same scenario occurred in one inner-city elementary school, but with a different ending. A fourth-grade teacher resigned before Thanksgiving from a class of students known as the outlaws of the school. This time the principal met with the other four fourth-grade teachers and asked for their suggestions for a replacement. The teachers asked for time to think about a possible solution. Their solution focused on the needs of the students in the abandoned classroom. They suggested that the students be divided equally into each of their fourth-grade classrooms. Each teacher would personally invite seven students to come to his or her class for at least a six-week period. A substitute teacher would work with small groups of students in each of the four classrooms every day for an hour and half. Once a permanent teacher was hired, the teacher would have at least a week to work with small groups of students, learn their names and interests, review the readings and other materials, and then bring all the students back together to form a new class. The principal agreed to their plan; the class, which had been a serious discipline problem, became a working team with a teacher who wanted to be with the students.

The students went from being abandoned to being invited to learn. The principal and the teachers sought solutions that benefited the students and ultimately the entire school. It was more work for the other four teachers, but they realized that the children in the school were everyone's responsibility, not one teacher's. The principal became a facilitator rather than an administrator (who would have followed the book on teacher replacement), a problem solver rather than a problem ignorer. The principal bent some rules in the process to meet the children's needs, but facilitative principals always look out for the best interests of their students and teachers.

CAN VISION CARRY FORWARD?

The best leaders allow others to lead. In schools that have facilitated learning in students for decades, how does the leader continue the vision of being person-centered? What happens when the leader leaves? Too often the school or program collapses.

I studied a school that brought in a dynamic leader to an inner-city elementary school. Just a year earlier the school had been identified by the state education agency as among the 5 percent of the lowest performing schools in the state. The new principal brought great energy to the school. New teachers were hired; some older teachers retired, and others left within the first two years to find work in a less demanding profession. The principal built around her a revitalized team from new and veteran teachers to better meet the children's needs.

The principal worked with an impoverished community to marshal meager resources in order to build community ownership in the school. A minister was encouraged to move his children from a private religious school to the public school. Gradually, the minister became a strong advocate for the school, encouraging others in the community to bring their children back to this public school. Soon other resources began to flow to the school. Business and community sponsors joined with the school to provide programs of pride and academic excellence throughout the year, including Saturday and summer-enrichment programs. Thousands of dollars were raised to build a needed community park and playground on the school's campus. The climate and learning environment at the school, as measured by student perceptions, was very high. Within five years, the same state agency that had placed the school on a watch list honored the principal, teachers, community, and students for their exceptional academic achievement. But shortly after receiving the state award, the principal and several teachers left to open another school in a different school district. The programs and community support at the once revitalized school began to fade. Achievement and school climate also began to change. Soon the school was drifting back to its former self.

This process of improvement and decline is becoming a common pattern for schools, particularly those in urban areas. Dynamic leadership leaves, revealing that the interpersonal endowment that had been created was tied to one leader, not the school, its students, or its mission. The next leader, who can never be as dynamic, enters an environment that is loyal and affiliated to the previous administrator. It's little wonder that after the arrival of a new principal or a new superintendent all ties with previous programs and practices are cut. The new leaders perceive a need to build their own constituency of teachers and parents. Programs that worked for the benefit of the students are suddenly dropped, and new programs are added—in many cases with little input from teachers, students, parents, or the community. It seems that education is constantly reinventing the wheel. This scenario may explain one of the contributing factors to the lack of movement toward open and healthy schools.

Another reason may be related to the leader's inability to entrust others with the vision and opportunity to become builders of the future. If there is not a sense, as Lao Tzu phrased it long ago, that "we did this ourselves," then the vision goes when the leader leaves. When a school has clearly identified a vision and taken ownership of it, then leaders can come and go; the vision grows because there is a foundation upon which to build new ideas. The current shareholders—parents, students, and the community—become participants in an evolving process that facilitates the needs of children and youth. Are there examples of schools that sustain a vision over time? Clearly there are. The following example shows that leadership can become a shared vision.

More than twenty years after its founding, and after much growth and evolution, Houston's High School for the Performing and Visual Arts (HSPVA) still clearly recognizes its original mission. The high school (also discussed in chapter 1) has had three principals in twenty-three years. The current principal, Annette Watson, was an art teacher in 1970 and became part of the first planning group with Ruth Denney, the founder and first principal of HSPVA. Watson, who taught at the school for seven years, left for twelve years and then returned recently as principal. She reflects about the start of the school, both from the perspective of a teacher and from her current position as principal.

> ❧ *Well, it was an experience; actually I don't know if we knew what it was going to be like. Ruth Denney called me and said she had this wild idea. She had been asked by the superintendent of schools and the school board to investigate setting up a high school for the performing and visual arts as a way to naturally [racially] integrate the school district, through a magnet concept. But in addition, Ruth knew [that] the arts cut across all socioeconomic and ethnic barriers.*
>
> *She [Denney] knew from her own experiences as a drama teacher that you can take a lot of kids who would not have been productive citizens in school without the arts, . . . and . . . a total arts setting . . . may turn them around in a lot of ways. So she called me and asked if I would be on the planning committee [for the school]. I was, and she hired me to teach art here.*
>
> *. . . Nobody had ever done anything like this. Who would want their kids to get on a bus and go across town to a performing arts high school that didn't have football, basketball teams, didn't have clubs or organizations?*
>
> *The vision of the school came from Ruth and the faculty. She visualized the high school made up not only of arts educators and content teachers, but professionals in the community who could come in and support the educational program.*
>
> *. . . We found that experience in the arts prepares you best for helping others. A dancer who is dancing with the Houston Ballet, a musician who plays for the symphony can bring something to the students. Now you also need people who like kids, who work well with people, who have human skills. So you have to find that special artist, that special musician, that special dancer, who communicates with people and really wants to do something. They supplement, they do not supplant the certified teacher; they*

enrich. It gives both students and teachers a constant influx of new ideas and experiences from the professional world. You can become very ivory towerish and cut off from the real world of the arts, . . . [and then] the dynamics would be lost.

But from the very beginning her [Ruth's] motto was . . . "Education Is an Adventure in Trust." She trusted us to do the very best job possible and in turn we trusted the students who came to us to do the very best job possible.

. . .We found that if you give kids freedom to succeed, you also have to give them choices, and those choices may put them in a situation where they are failing. So you have the freedom to fail. . . . It's not a matter of not succeeding so much as determining this is not the way I want to spend the rest of my life.

Ruth Denney said, "What you're teaching in that math class ought to make sense to those kids in the arts." That's why she hired math teachers who had music backgrounds and experiences, and language teachers who had opera experiences, and English teachers who had piano and acting experiences, and so forth. I will never forget a group of students who did a dance demonstrating the whole process of cell mutation. It was in a science class and it was these cells dividing again and again; it was beautiful. I remember going into a social studies classroom and they were studying Indian cultures and a student, who was a flutist, had an original composition that dealt with the music concepts he connected with the American Indian. I mean he did a lot of research on this. There was an art student who had done a sculpture about women emerging from servitude and bondage. The beautiful sculpture of these arms and bodies rising from out of itself—it was splendid.

We came from this concept and it's still here. I just hired a young woman to teach English. In addition to being a wonderful English teacher, she does the yearbook and newspaper, and she takes classes at the Houston Ballet Academy, so she has an understanding of dance.

I asked Annette, "How do you maintain the vitality?" Her response focused on the link between the school and the arts community.

❦ *First of all, you have new people continuously coming in to add vitality and that's what happens with our guest artists. You can't be static when you have twenty to thirty people coming every day from another context; it brings vitality to it, an energy that could be missing if the same people, year after year, are doing the same thing, year after year. You can really get into a rut. That has to do both with the teachers and the administration. It has to do with every level, so something has to happen to shake you up, shake you loose from your everyday habits.*

One of the things that I think is essential as an administrator is [that] you stay in contact with the professional world. You don't isolate yourself and you need to look at yourself as an administrator. You look at yourself as a liaison to bring all the resources to bear, to help students and teachers. Administrators need to be open-minded, and not close off options before they are even explored. I believe good administrators say, "Anything is possible and let's find out how we can do it." A good administrator finds the very best people possible, the most intelligent, caring, and dedicated, and you give them the freedom to do what they need to do. I think a quality administrator has to protect the students. You have to keep students' best interests in mind at all times. But you're not ruthless with your faculty to that end. I try to treat faculty the way I want to be treated as a person. If you find that there are problems that they're encountering as teachers, you sit down with them and you are very honest; you discuss those problems in a caring way. You want . . . teacher[s] to succeed and . . . [they need] to feel that you want them to succeed and you will find ways to support . . . [them] and give them time.

As an administrator you have to have courage; if you don't have courage to do the things that in your heart of hearts, you know . . . [are] right, then you don't belong in the job. . . . If they would take time to sit down and get very quiet and look inward and say, "What is the right thing to do?" There's an inner voice that tells me if it's really right or if it's really wrong, and if you go against your inner voice, you pay the price every time, because sometimes you let your mentality override your intuition. You have to trust yourself. One of the things I think the arts does, is it helps you become a risk taker. If you do everything the safe way, you turn into a real bureaucrat, you become a bean counter, a rule follower to the detriment of the kids.

When we started school the first seven years I was here, nobody looked at kids' grades or test scores as part of the criteria for entering. While I was gone, and I don't know where the pressure came from or how it originated, there was an emphasis on being sure that the student who auditioned not only pass a rigorous audition, but meet certain test and grade requirements. I knew about it before I returned here, and it disturbed me for several years because I knew that was not the reason we set up the school.

The only things we are looking for are kids who say they want to spend three hours a day in the arts and they want to do a rigorous academic program [for the other four hours]. If they say they want to do it, schedule them for an audition and the audition will determine who gets in.

What has happened is [that] the scores haven't gone down. We have all these students coming in with varying degrees of academic preparedness. The teachers are working to be sure that the kids continue to do well, not so we look good on test scores, but so the kids are prepared to do what they want to do.

Comments

The sense of vision and continuance is a thread that runs through the interview with Annette Watson. The mission of using talent in the arts as the criterion for entrance into HSPVA is one easily lost by many people who are charged with the operations of schools. HSPVA continues to provide an environment in which students love learning, and the comments from students in chapter 1, both from 1980 and 1992, reflect the power of providing the freedom to learn.

Watson's role of liaison to the world allows her to bring learning into the school through the medium of the guest artists and to bring the school into the community through performances by HSPVA students. The HSPVA motto, "Education Is an Adventure in Trust," which originated with Ruth Denney, is still in evidence more than twenty years later. The legacy that continues at the school reflects its ability to select administrators who feel an affinity with the mission of the school. Change has occurred over time; but rather than having resources revolve around one person, they are there to support a pathway for students to shape their own learning. People need to experience the freedom to learn themselves, which in turn enables them to facilitate others. Ruth Denney provided that experience to the teachers, and Watson was able to take that experience and continue to facilitate the learnings of others.

OPEN SCHOOLS/HEALTHY SCHOOLS

The examples provided in this chapter are supported by a wide range of research that studied whether principals are either supportive or directive. Research about school health and climate, which was conducted by Wayne Hoy, John Tarter, and Robert Kottkamp, is reported in a text entitled *Open Schools/Healthy Schools*. It describes the attributes of administrators in seventy-two high schools in New Jersey. The researchers found that "when teachers are not given the freedom to make professional judgments and are watched closely [by the principal], they tend to be distrustful of the principal." The more supportive and open the principal, the more trust the teachers had in their principal. Teachers who are involved in their schools through "shared sentiments of pride in their school, commitment to students, . . . concern for colleagues, and . . . trust [are] likely to promote engaged teacher behavior" (3, p. 121). While principals in this study have a direct role in developing trust between themselves and teachers, they have a more indirect role in developing colleaguality and trust among teachers. According to Hoy and his associates, "The primary role of the principal, however, is to improve instruction indirectly through the development of an open, healthy, and trustful climate" (3, p. 121).

It seems that a principal's directive and controlling behavior can make for unhealthy schools. Although the researchers never use the term *facilitative*, the principals discussed in their study are facilitative by creating a learning environment for students and teachers that is supportive, finding resources to assist the learning community, and encouraging an open and healthy environment for learning. The need for principals to minimize their constant monitoring of teachers may run counter to state mandates for principals to evaluate and rate teachers according to predetermined teaching categories. Bob Ferris at the Free School said, "It [evaluation] is not a way of enhancing education; it is a way of controlling it. It's a control mechanism to get teachers to be very traditional along with tests and textbooks." There are other more indirect ways to encourage teachers to improve their work with students, which I would like to explore further.

SELF-ASSESSMENT: CREATING FULLY FUNCTIONING PROFESSIONALS

How does a principal facilitate teachers who want to move from being givers of information to being facilitators of learning? Compare the following event with what typically goes on between teachers and principals during an evaluation in which teachers are assessed on their teaching. Imagine an instructional conference between the principal and a teacher where the teacher, rather than the administrator, initiates discussion about the way her instruction has been developing. The science teacher confidently explains the areas of strengths and weaknesses of a particular lesson.

> 🦋 *I talked 40 percent of the time during a lesson in which students were discovering chemical elements during the time of Mendeleyev. They each had the elements of his time and I gave them cards to write [down] the elements. They worked in groups and brainstormed possible new elements based on the information they had. The students began to place their cards on the wall and soon our modern-day periodic table took shape. I am really pleased that the students were able to talk without my dominating the discussion. The last time I taught a similar lesson, I talked over 80 percent of the time. The only person to discover anything in that class was me. I was also able to use student ideas and we set the stage for the next class. The students talked*

about creativity and what Mendeleyev must have experienced in discovering new elements in his day. I also reduced the number of recall questions from the last time we met. I am able to realize that asking students to think means I need to stop asking so many lower-level questions. I waited for their answers and did not make a comment after each student statement, which has been my usual pattern. My nonintervention resulted in students asking more questions of each other and allowing student-to-student interactions.

The conference continues for another fifteen minutes with the teacher and principal reading from the data sheet the teacher had prepared.

The teacher was able to create this self-assessment by listening to an audiotape of her class and analyzing the results using a format described in the last chapter of *Universal Teaching Strategies:* "Self-improvement through Self-assessment" (4, pp. 413–453). The teacher cued the tape, and she and the principal listened to samples of classroom discussions. In addition to the audiotape analysis, the teacher used a student survey instrument to measure the health and climate of the classroom, also found in the book chapter. The two sources of data provided authentic feedback about what she and the students were doing in the classroom. She played the tape so the students could listen to their own discussion. Student feedback indicated that they were seeing her as inflexible and not willing to listen to them. She shared this information with her principal, and they spent the remainder of their meeting talking about ways in which she could listen more to student views. She decided to devote some time to a class meeting to raise issues about the way the class was functioning. She and the principal would talk about this more during their next meeting.

Internal Locus of Assessment

Knowledge is power, but knowledge about self is the greatest power. The teacher and principal in the previous example have changed their roles. Usually, it is the principal who sits in the classroom, writes notes or codes on an observation sheet about what the teacher is doing, and gives feedback to the teacher at some later date. From the time a young adult enters teaching to the time that person retires, she is dependent on others to answer the question, "How am I doing?" The locus of control is always external rather than internal. Fully functioning professionals need a degree of independence to grow. Being constantly dependent on others to tell you how you're doing inhibits individual growth and creates a dependency that stifles an entire profession. Meaningful and lasting change occurs when we look inside ourselves for answers.

The audiotape process is one tool for allowing teachers to examine their interactions with students. If your goal is to be person-centered, then a pattern that shows that 70 or 80 percent of class time is spent in teacher talk will identify a need to change the way you and your students interact in the classroom. The principal in the previous example was facilitating the process of change. In the past, this principal had been part of a charade in which one or two observations a year were expected to improve the quality of instruction, interaction, and learning in the classroom.

In other schools, facilitative administrators support the development of teacher dialogue groups. Small groups of teachers complete their audiotape analyses and share their self-assessments with each other. I have seen this process work in schools across the nation. The open sharing of ideas and discussion of teaching philosophies build a remarkable degree of colleagual openness. A middle school English teacher made the following assessment of her lesson: "My most glaring weakness, in my opinion, is my tendency to *tell* instead of *ask,* and I frequently restated or answered my own questions without having allowed sufficient time for student thought" (5, p. 91). Teachers are able to build an internal locus of assessment when the principal and school environment support self-learning. Learning from one's successes and mistakes can be the best teacher of all.

Administrators can facilitate a climate in which teachers learn and have the opportunity to share successes and failures. Principals can also become partners with teachers, students, parents, and community members in developing open and healthy schools. We have seen in this chapter the importance of the vision of facilitation in schools that focus on students and not on any one person. Schools that have stars rather than facilitators as their leaders leave a hollow legacy. But those that sustain their mission do so with people who share in that vision and are willing and able to facilitate others. Annette Watson experienced what it meant to be trusted and facilitated by her principal, Ruth Denney. Now a principal herself, Annette is able to carry forward that vision of trusting others to be co-learners.

Is seems reasonable that for change to occur, more people need to experience the benefits of working with facilitative people. As the number of people who facilitate others grows, so will the opportunities for the next generation of leaders to free others to learn. Administrators *can* be facilitators, but they must see "education as an adventure in trust" and feel pride when others say, "We did this ourselves."

REFERENCES

1. Lao Tzu, *The Way of Life according to Lao Tzu*, trans. Witter Bynner (New York: Capricorn Books, 1962).

2. Robert Ferris, "From Gadfly to Mainstream: The New Orleans Free School Twenty Years Later" (Unpublished letter to the community, presented at the twentieth anniversary of the founding of the New Orleans Free School, 1991).

3. Wayne K. Hoy, John C. Tarter, and Robert B. Kottkamp, *Open Schools/Healthy Schools* (London: Sage, 1991).

4. H. Jerome Freiberg and Amy Driscoll, *Universal Teaching Strategies* (Boston: Allyn and Bacon, 1992).

5. H. Jerome Freiberg, "Teacher Self-assessment and Principal Supervision," *NASSP Bulletin* 71, no. 498 (1987): 85–92.

CHAPTER 7

OTHER FACILITATORS OF FREEDOM

◆

One of the most prevalent misunderstandings about a person-centered approach to education is that it is applicable only in certain kinds of subjects or in certain special situations. We have, in previous chapters, observed the use of a person-centered approach in secondary schools across the nation as well as in an elementary grade and in a foreign-language class. In this chapter I wish to show how it can be implemented in a wide variety of other situations.

By presenting the experiences of very diverse individuals, I hope to make clear that we are not talking about a method or a technique. A person-centered way of being in an educational situation is something into which one grows. It is a set of values, not easy to achieve, that places emphasis on the dignity of the individual, the importance of personal choice, the significance of responsibility, the joy of creativity. It is a philosophy, built on a foundation of the democratic way, that empowers each individual. So in this chapter you will find the following:

◆ A science teacher whose bold effort at creating freedom in his classroom is marred by one mistake

◆ A department chairman who believes in the democratic process and goes the limit in empowering both students and faculty

◆ A mathematician who learns what constitutes a nurturing environment for creative thinking

◆ A teacher of teachers who uses childhood memories as a way of changing teacher attitudes

◆ A counselor in a conventional school who cultivates a limited garden plot of freedom, the fruits of which are highly nutritious and long-lasting

COURAGE, INTEGRITY, AND ONE MISTAKE

I am quite aware that up to this point I have presented examples in which both the process and the outcome of the learning were positive for the instructor as well as for the student. However, I don't want to leave you with the impression that the change to a person-centered approach occurs without some problems and adjustments. I should like now to present an innovative course in which, in my judgment, a real error was made with some unfortunate consequences.

Dr. John Barkham teaches environmental science in an English university. He sent me a long, very thoughtful analysis of a course that he taught in a most innovative manner (1). The course was a valuable learning experience for the instructor as well as the students. I cannot in a short space do credit to the dedicated way in which Dr. Barkham prepared for the course and evaluated it using ingenious research methods. I wish to focus only on some of its salient features, which I quote from his report. Though it is unfair to the course as a whole, I wish to emphasize some of the things he did and did not do, which in my judgment constituted serious mistakes and kept the experience from becoming all that it might have been.

Dr. Barkham had been moving toward an innovative style for some time.

> ❦ *Over a number of years I have been developing and changing my approach to teaching Ecosystem Management. . . . In 1978 I began to realize the potential power of participatory learning in groups. [He tells of developing discussion groups during 1970–80.] At this point I read two books for the first time which have influenced me enormously. Adam Curle's* Education for Liberation *[2] got to my guts and gave me a little revolutionary zeal, Carl Rogers'* Freedom to Learn *[3] confirmed those feelings but actually helped me find the tools I was at that precise moment looking for to facilitate my students more effectively. If you want to be stuck where you are in your thinking about teaching, don't read either of these books.*

He was very honest about his internal struggle, stating it in a way that rings true to many teachers.

🦋 *I realized for the first time that many students' difficulties in "EcoMan" in 1970–80 actually mirrored my own confusion of role. They could hear me saying, "I want to give you freedom to explore . . ." but what they felt was that I was simply controlling and, at worst, manipulating them in another way. And indeed I was. Giving freedom and responsibility to students for their own learning is a very scary business. I was scared of the possible consequences, of losing control. After all, if I know so much more than the students surely I have a duty to put it all there before them? And anyway they wouldn't respect me if I allowed them to think that their ideas are as important and as valid as my own. . . . I know what is important; what is important is the syllabus and all students must accept that I know best, etc., etc. These were some of the fears in me which in general I failed to articulate to myself. So, I realized that if the students were to feel genuinely free, I would genuinely have to leave go of the reins. Having read Rogers' book, I immediately wrote the handout for the course 1980–81 in the space of a day.*

This handout, which several months before the course began was given to the thirty-seven students who had signed up, is exceedingly thorough and detailed: an eleven-page, single-spaced document. A brief segment gives its tone and purpose.

🦋 *Can you and I together run a really worthwhile third-year course with so many people involved? . . . My own personal goal for this course is to give you all possible freedom to pursue the study of ecosystem management and nature conservation. You are not the empty vessels into which I will pour some of the contents of my own vessel. I must remember all the time that this is your course, not mine. You have expressed an interest by signing up, and my role must be as facilitator: to enable you as far as my own skills allow to pursue your interest. I want to set up an environment in which freely self-directed and creative learning can take place.*

An initial trace is already evident of the inner conflict that definitely affected the course. Note the discrepancy between "you and I together" and "this is *your* course, not mine." Which statement will he stand by?

The handout goes on to discuss various topics. Dr. Barkham suggests the questions that the student may use to define his or her own goals. He outlines the many resources: books, field trips, outside experts. He suggests the kind of projects on which students might embark. He deals at length with the problem of assessment of student work, stating that his aim is "to work out together a solution to this problem which satisfies the University while at the same time not destroying our freedom to learn, the ethos of the course. I think this will be the main item on the agenda for our first meeting." He also lets them know that he will ask for a report at the end of the course, signed or anonymous, evaluating the instructor and the experience of the course, which may be negative or positive.

In describing the resources available, he states that one of the resources is "me."

> ✷ *My perception is that, at least initially and for some of you, how to use me most effectively will be a tricky problem. You're used to a lecturer making all or most of the running. Now you've got to run yourselves. I'm sure you can overcome this problem. What do I think I have to offer which may facilitate your learning? What I think I have may be different from what* you *think I have! Here are some things I think I can offer and which you may wish to use at some point. [He then lists his experience and his interests.]*
>
> *There may be other ways in which you expect me to help. To facilitate your use of me I must be available to you in a predictable way. Here are the times I will nearly always be so, at least during the Autumn Term. [He gives a list of his office hours.] Almost certainly you will need to book my time in advance. Please do it wisely, out of perceived need, because almost certainly there will be many calls upon my time. You must make it clear precisely what you want of me and how you are going to use me so that I can prepare accordingly. If I don't understand or cannot meet your demands or [if I] take exception to them I will say so. Otherwise I will do my best to oblige.*

In this offering of himself there appears to be a certain formality and distance that is out of line with the rest of the handout.

He concludes the handout by giving the date, hour, and place of the first meeting and ends with this rather abrupt statement:

> ✷ *I will start the meeting at 3:30 and, within five minutes, hand it over to you to manage as you think fit. I suggest at least the following items for the agenda. [He lists questions about how groups might form, the use of outside experts, the problems of examinations and assessment, etc.]*

It appears clear from this final statement that he was distancing himself still more from the course. The first meeting had some of the chaos that any such learning experience involves, but he was not a significant part of it.

🦋 *The initial class meeting was tense and anxious. I introduced it and then relinquished control and direction. Obviously most students found it very difficult to handle themselves in such a large group. There were many bids and counter-bids for leadership and many silent members. Much of the time was spent thrashing [out] the issue of assessment, and worries about such a course with an exam at the end of it were freely expressed.*

That he had indeed left himself out of the course is told in two uneasy but revealingly honest excerpts.

🦋 *By and large the early weeks were very anxious ones for me. After the first meeting, a few of the students I never saw again for the entire course. I found this difficult to handle. I could only make one response: I had given them freedom and if they wished to use it to work entirely on their own then it was their decision for which they were responsible. The fear in me that in some cases no work was being done at all could neither be substantiated nor denied.*

My activities. *Apart from sitting worrying, I eventually freed myself to take my own independent action. I had intended, apart from responding to student requests, to use any available time for my own new learning in nature conservation, thereby making myself a more effective resource person for the students.*

The gap in group leadership was not left empty. One student by this time had taken a leadership role in organizing events. He was determined to get things moving and took all manner of initiatives, carrying others along with him—arranging seminars, etc., etc. Professor Barkham did take two initiatives: he invited a number of professional nature conservationists to meet informally with the class, and these meetings were well attended and appreciated. Significantly, he did not lead one of these sessions. He also gave a few lectures. The first was at the request of the students, in which he stated his personal values in the area of nature conservation. The students enjoyed this particularly.

The outcomes of the course, as shown by student productivity and their reactions and evaluations, were generally satisfactory or better. It was, for most of the class, a period of independent study. One rather typical reaction follows:

🦋 *I think that the structure of the course is good in enabling you to develop your own lines of thought. From the outset it is made clear that you are on your own. This encouraged me to look at the course as more of a voyage of self-discovery than just another course. Also because there are no "set" things to do, I found myself able to develop more freely than if lectures were set. It is impossible to become indoctrinated doing this course. . . . I think that the course actually teaches you how to be interested.*

However, the students wished he had taken a more active role.

> ❦ *Your contribution was inadequate to my mind. I would have preferred more talks . . . or even real seminars . . . where you actually have to prepare something.*

> ❦ *I personally feel you should play a larger part—not in the sense of lecturing, but in guiding the discussions.*

Comments

I should like to comment on Dr. Barkham's experience. He was clearly ambivalent about whether it was to be "our" course or "your" course, but his actions made it definitely the latter. He effectively left himself out of the group experience, and once out he had no way back except to intrude. This he did apologetically. He says in his report that when he decided to give some lectures, his decision was "not simply a response to their anxieties . . . or mine about my lack of usefulness." When he arranged for the informal sessions with visitors, he speaks of "my justification for taking this initiative." Clearly he felt he had no real right to take action in the course.

Although I believe Professor Barkham made a real error in shutting himself out of his own course, I feel very sympathetic. I recall vividly a weekend session with an important high-level faculty group that had the purpose of helping them rethink their educational goals. Like Professor Barkham, I made it clear that it was *their* group, and they could use the time as they wished. To my dismay, they chose to spend it mostly in small talk, and I had no effective way of changing the situation. If it had been *our* group, my anger at the waste of precious time could have been voiced as a participant member and would have been heard. As it was, I chalked up the weekend as a real disaster.

In my case, and I suspect in Professor Barkham's, the error was made out of an excess of zeal in trusting others. What I failed to do was to trust *myself* to be a useful member of the group. Thus, I cheated them of what I might have contributed. I feel the same thing can be said of Dr. Barkham. He lost the opportunity to be a coparticipant and, even more important, he missed out on the chance to be a *co-learner.*

The second consequence of shutting himself out of the course was that the stimulation and creativity that comes from full and open interaction among the members was lost. Because he kept himself and his feelings to himself—sitting uneasily in his office—the group tended to react in the same way. They held some discussion groups, but for the most part they went their own ways in independent study. This is one excellent way to learn, but it would have been greatly enriched if there had been regular sessions facilitated by the instructor. In the climate of freedom thus created, one mind strikes sparks in another, one person's fresh insight stirs many creative reactions in others, and the dynamics of the group process enhance the process of learning in all.

As I see it, the instructor's isolation from the group robbed both him and the members of important co-learnings. Then the failure to develop a facilitative *group* experience robbed them all of many creative insights that would almost certainly have occurred. This was a bold experiment carried out with great attention to detail, and its outcomes were largely good. But it could have been a great deal more valuable for instructor and students had it not been for one error in implementation: the instructor's failure to regard himself as a significant learning member of the group.

GEOLOGY GOES RADICALLY DEMOCRATIC

Bill Romey had a dream of how learning might take place in the fields of geology and the earth sciences. He finally found a home for his ideas at St. Lawrence University. I will let him tell about his plan in his own words (4, pp. 680–96).*

🦋 *In discussions at St. Lawrence the dream of an academic department focusing on its people rather than any narrow construct called a discipline was set forth. The university bought the dream, and initial conversations suggested an open willingness to support implementation. The plan involved the following elements:*

1. *Independent project work at all levels, for all students and faculty, would replace all standard courses.*
2. *Students would evaluate their own work.*
3. *Students would keep portfolios of their own work as an alternative means of showing what they had accomplished. There would be no more examinations of conventional types.*
4. *Students and faculty would participate fully and equally in the governance of the department.*
5. *Students would define for themselves what they wanted to study in the department, when, for how long, and with whom.*

---

* Reprinted by permission from Bill Romey, "Radical Innovation in a Conventional Framework: Problems and Prospects," *Journal of Higher Education* 48 (November/December 1977): 680–96.© 1977 by the Ohio State University Press. All rights reserved.

"Geology" and "geography" would be given the widest possible interpretations.

6. *The faculty would accept responsibility, in cooperation with the students, to create and maintain a rich and stimulating learning environment for the benefit of all.*

7. *The department was to run as an open organism with free access for everyone in the university, whether or not they were formally enrolled for credit.*

8. *Everything was to be negotiable and faculty members and students would agree not to try to use power on, to manipulate, or to try to control anyone else.*

9. *The community would strive to create and maintain open communication leading to respect for each other and for the physical facilities. Friendship, mutual support, and closest possible interpersonal relationships would be sought.*

10. *Each person would function both as a teacher and as a learner.*

11. *A horizontal administrative structure would give all participants equal power, authority, and access. The chairmanship was to be a coordinating position for at least minimal integration of a horizontally organized group like ours into a larger university context organized in a strictly vertical hierarchy. The chairmanship would rotate.*

12. *The department would evolve from its primarily preprofessional orientation toward a more liberal department where general learning about the earth would be at least as important as the preparation of narrowly defined geological and geographic specialists. Thus, people in business, politicians, musicians, historians, linguists, and people going out into almost any career would have a chance to become more aware and knowledgeable about the earth.*

Comments

As one might imagine, problems quickly arose. One big problem concerned grading. Romey and his group finally gained acceptance for a system in which there were only two evaluations recorded with the registrar: either *credit* or *continuing* (in progress). In other words, there were no grades at all in the usual sense of comparative evaluations. The other major issue revolved around the faculty of the five areas involved in this experiment. Some of the instructors became very uncomfortable with the lack of scheduled courses. So gradually such courses were reintroduced. After five and a half years, the program had become a dual system, with more than 60 percent of the students in project-oriented groups and the remainder in labeled courses of a more traditional sort.

It is difficult to evaluate such a far-reaching experiment. One outside observer noted:

> ✹ *By a narrow measure, the experiment could be said to have failed, since some faculty have returned to older ways of teaching. But to talk of this return as a simple reversion would be a mistake. The atmosphere has been wholly transformed and this has affected even the conservative teachers more profoundly than they themselves may realize. Moreover if the objective was to set up an environment offering the maximum range of choices for the learner, the experiment has been a great success. . . . The diversity of teaching styles and assumptions is obvious to everyone in the department, so that there is a heightened consciousness about education among the students. (5, pp. 16–17)*

What Romey and a few colleagues did was to establish, in essence, an alternative college within a fairly conventional liberal arts university. Furthermore, this alternative college was highly democratic.

Why do we so much prefer to teach democracy rather than to practice it? Now the students and faculty at this alternative college at St. Lawrence University participate in all important decisions. It is even democratic enough to permit divergence from innovation. Neither faculty nor students are *forced* to be free. They can choose the mode of learning and teaching with which they are most comfortable. The extent to which they have departed from a hierarchical system is astonishing. This is a small revolution growing in a healthy fashion inside of a larger conventional university envelope. It could be a model for others.

It is significant that during the five years the experiment has been underway, the number of students majoring in this field has nearly tripled. The number of seniors completing honors theses, mostly of publishable quality, has increased. The number of students going on to graduate school has shown a slow but steady increase. Clearly students are learning, and enjoying learning, in this program.

CREATIVE KNOWLEDGE: BORN OF LOVE AND TRUST

Alvin White of Harvey Mudd College in Claremont, California, is an unusual teacher of mathematics. Years ago he described his experiment in making a course called "Calculus of Variations," (I don't know what that means, either!) a human, person-centered learning experience (6, pp. 128–33). It was such a growing learning process for all concerned that he has continued in ever bolder ventures—for example, educating faculty members and trying out even more unique ideas in the classroom. In a report, he tells of a remarkably varied seminar whose primary purpose was to enable students to learn how we gain knowledge and how we create. His account has some fascinating aspects (7).

🦋 *An experience sometimes has such a profound effect that it leads one to infer general principles of which the particular is an instance. If the insights are true, then the general illuminates the particular which evoked it.*

I shared such a fortunate experience with students at MIT [Massachusetts Institute of Technology] several years ago. The quiet glow of remembrance still inspires me. The Division for Study and Research in Education offered me a visiting professorship and an invitation to lead a seminar of my choice for the spring term. The invitation was an opportunity to consider questions which are common to all disciplines, and therefore are studied by very few if at all. I proposed a series of questions:

> *How do people obtain knowledge? What are the limits of certainty? What is the relation between general and scientific knowledge? What is the role of beauty, simplicity, or intuition in creative discovery? Our present knowledge in the arts, humanities, and sciences is the legacy of creative imagination. How can this legacy influence education at all levels?*

Appropriate readings were suggested. The scope was at once frightening and exhilarating to me. Being a visitor encourages audaciousness.

There were twelve students. Artificial intelligence, biology, computer science, electrical engineering, environmental studies, linguistics, mathematics, physics and visual arts were represented. The group was interdisciplinary or multidisciplinary. Our experience was transdisciplinary or transcendent! We reported on, considered and discussed the writings of various authors in search of answers. The answer, however, as to how we were obtaining knowledge was, for us, embedded in the process and its context.

We were scheduled to meet twice a week from 9:00 to 10:30 A.M. We quickly found ourselves continuing the discussions until noon. Everyone cancelled other morning appointments. Students invited their professors to participate. Visitors would ask permission to observe quietly, although their reticence was usually soon overcome. One student remarked that the popularity of our seminar among visitors was probably because openness, honest listening, and caring for each other were evident. Every contribution was accepted in a nonjudgmental way. No one was forced to speak, and everyone had a chance to speak. We examined writings by Dewey, Kant, Polanyi, Popper, Russell, and others.

The last week of the term was a time to discuss and evaluate the seminar. Why was it so successful? What had happened to us? How had we been transformed from strangers to a group of friends and colleagues? It was as if we had chanced upon a semester-long celebration, and like Alain-Fournier's Wanderer, we had been caught up in the spirit of the place. A student observed that this was the first course where her presence in the room had "made a difference."

Why had the seminar been so remarkably satisfying? What had we learned and what should we do if we wanted to find that spirit of celebration again? An unexpected answer emerged, one that answered some of the questions of the seminar as well as the questions about the seminar. The answer which came from one of the students in a moment of insight was "Love and Trust."

What did that phrase mean? The concept came from the process of our exploration, not from any of the disciplines represented. Love and trust contributed to the spirit of celebration and were essential ingredients in the process of obtaining knowledge. Some instances were remembered where those ingredients were absent, and then only minimal learning had occurred. Should love and trust have been such a surprising answer? Was my surprise a legacy of my formal education? In the past was I too unseeing to have noticed those qualities, or is my memory influenced by the cruelties and meanness often found in the academic scene? The students and I recognized our experience as real and exceptional. The rarity of such an experience for us made us treasure it. And yet, would such an answer be considered sentimental or worse?

Love and trust seem far removed from mathematical logic or electrical engineering as they are encountered in the classroom. Yet if we are engaged in learning and teaching, then all of the disciplines share the process involved in intellectual imagination and creation. Love and trust were natural parts of our learning in the group setting. We came together, attracted by the description of the seminar. Some progress toward understanding was made. Our understanding, however, went beyond the seminar.

Perhaps my surprise came from the absence of love and trust as explicit items in the syllabus or objectives of any course or table of contents of a text. The syllabus is focused on the discipline. How we obtain knowledge is considered outside of the discipline and is therefore usually not discussed.

Traveling on the road, however, is as important as finding the road of knowledge. Obtaining knowledge is presumably an objective of a course. Why not assume that our seminar was the natural mode and that teaching and learning without love and trust are unnatural? Reflection on that seminar has been an impetus to seek confirmation that the student's insight about our success was an instance of a general principle; that those who adopt this mode are not sentimental, but are natural.

Mathematics is considered by some of the uninitiated to be devoid of any emotional content. By extension, perhaps, the teaching and learning of mathematics may be thought to be independent of emotional content. Recently, however, the concept of Mathematical Anxiety has been recognized (8). In describing programs to overcome Math Anxiety at Wesleyan, Stanford and Mills College, the consensus was that notwithstanding any superficial differences in the various approaches, there was a common element that was probably essential to their successes. That element was that the anxious student knew that there was someone who could help him or her and who had faith in the student's ability to succeed. Whatever the cause of anxiety, the cure was love and trust between two people.

In addition to reading what others had said about knowledge, [we discovered that] the seminar itself was an example of how one obtains knowledge. The supportive, anxiety-free environment of our seminar is a simple idea, although it may be difficult to achieve. And the idea is not unanimously endorsed by teachers or students. We, however, found it liberating. The students studied with joy and a sense of ownership and personal meaning. Our discussions were not only an aid to memory and an occasion for sharing ideas and insights; they were for the creation of ideas and insights. Knowledge was created by the process of our discussions.

Comments

A mathematician's striving toward the establishment of love and trust as the basic elements in his classroom is so different as to be almost unbelievable. Yet a human climate fosters learning in mathematics, in philosophical issues such as those that concerned his seminar, in "hard" sciences, and in psychology and the humanities. White's work has been of special interest to me because it is often assumed that a humanistic approach to learning applies only to the "soft" subjects. He has demonstrated that it not only applies to the learning of such subjects as calculus, but that it induces creative new learnings in mathematics or, as in his seminar on epistemology, in the investigation of human knowing.

In the manuscript from which the previous excerpt came, Alvin White shows that various philosophies and a national committee have come to much the same conclusions as his seminar did, although they couch their views in slightly more academic language. He says, "Now my surprise is not about a student's insightful answer; it is that whereas I thought a new frontier had been discovered, I now see that it is a well marked path!" It is indeed a well-marked path, trodden over many years by many people. Yet it has always remained the path of the minority. Society as a whole, education as a whole, has not dared to trust, and certainly not dared to love. But the teacher who is bold enough to include these ingredients is opening a gate to creative learning for both student and instructor.

FANTASY IN TEACHER TRAINING

Dr. Julie Ann Allender uses a special method to help teachers become aware of experiences that inhibit or promote real learning (9). Her way would, I believe, be especially appropriate to the in-service training of teachers.

> For the past eight years I have been training teachers—part-time at Temple University—[in] the methods of teaching affectively and effectively, i.e., differences between traditional and open education. Basically, the major variables are the instructor, the style of teaching, group dynamic techniques, a grading system based on a contract system, and open education techniques based on people such as Rogers, Maslow, Dewey.
>
> At the beginning of each course I begin on a negative note looking at the problems of education. I call it "mis-education." We look at how learning has been prevented. We look at how teachers create an unpleasant atmosphere for themselves and for their students. We look at how students' motivation and curiosity are stifled. We look at students' and teachers' fears and resentments. We begin by looking at what doesn't work and then for the next two-thirds of the course we look at what does work. What does enhance learning? What promotes curiosity? What creates a pleasant positive atmosphere conducive to learning? What does motivate students and increases curiosity? We look at students' and teachers' appreciations and their resentments. We learn how to give constructive feedback.
>
> One of the first things I do in order to orient the class into thinking about what the problems are or what doesn't work is to form a circle on the floor and pass out a multitude of stories that I label as "mis-education stories," and I have the students read them aloud to the group. Many of the stories are well known, others are less well known, ones that I have collected over the years.
>
> This activity always stimulates feelings of shock and horror at the realization that many of these stories are true and as the students begin talking about them among themselves they begin to tell each other their own horror stories about their schooling experiences, and the reality of these "mis-education stories" begins to set the stage for many of the following experiences and learnings that we will share together during the semester.

It is at this point that I introduce the Fourth Grade Fantasy Activity. I tell [people] . . . to find a comfortable spot, to close their eyes and I then turn off the lights. (This always produces a lot of stirrings and giggling. Remember that most of these students are used to a traditional lecture series.) I then proceed to have them quietly breathe deeply for two to three minutes, listening to the air flowing in and out of their bodies, and then two to three minutes tensing and untensing each part of their bodies beginning from the feet up to the head. When I feel they are relaxed I begin the activity.

I take them (in fantasy) out of the room and back to their elementary school building. I have them slowly walk up and look all around them as they approach the building, trying to take in all that they can. I then inform them that they are fourth graders and that it is time for their classes to begin so they should hurry along to their classrooms. (I also offer fifth grade for those who have trouble remembering fourth grade.) I have them spend about ten minutes in their fourth grade fantasy classrooms with me guiding them. We look at the students' desk arrangements, where the teachers' desks are, what was on the walls, the atmosphere of the classroom, their feelings of being there, etc. I give them plenty of time to really concentrate on what it was like for them in that classroom and then . . . it is the end of the school day. Everybody gets ready to leave. I then instruct my students that when they are ready to return to our classroom here they should slowly open their eyes. When all eyes are open I then turn on the lights.

The next step is for them to quietly draw a diagram or picture, not too elaborate, of their classroom and when that is finished I have them find three other people, getting into groups of four, and sharing with that group of four what each person's fourth grade classroom was like. As one final piece, when this process is finished I have the whole class come together and share with each other the things that the small groups had discussed.

I have used this fantasy activity in recent years with a total of about 195 students, mostly educated in Philadelphia. Of these students I never had more than one student per class who had had anything but a traditional row by row structured classroom. Some of the teachers' desks were in differing spots of the room (to the side, back or front) but otherwise the classrooms were all the same. The desks were all in single or double rows and the furniture never moved. Some of the more rigid school rooms even had the desks nailed to the floor. It was not unusual to have at least two students in each classroom who came from Catholic parochial schools in which they had had fifty to ninety pupils per classroom per teacher. To my class this information was shocking. To me it is becoming common knowledge. After three or four years, I was no longer surprised. Saddened, yes, at how the size and rigid class structure affected their learning, but not surprised.

How does this affect learning? Well, the next step in my process was to have the students brainstorm or throw out words that came to mind. Words that could be placed on the board under one category; words that describe learning. The left half of the board being positive and right side of the board being negative. Each time the board filled up very quickly . . . well, at least half of the board did . . . words that described learning to them through their eyes. . . .

The right side would always be overflowing. Students could not wait to put up their words concerning what was negative. However, with the left side, the positive side, I would have to prod and pull to get even half as many positive words up there. The negative words were mainly concerned with discipline, behavior, punishment, hidden agenda items, grades, tests, etc. Nothing to do with learning. Words such as embarrassment, fearful, failure, sit up straight, don't talk, no noise, *etc. The positive side had to do with escaping school: recess, lunch, vacation, meeting friends, and again nothing to do with learning. Once in a while a teacher's name would get in under the positive side as a friend, caring and considerate, but that was rare.*

I guess what I did not realize was how much information I as an instructor have and might be sitting on. This is just one example, but it is true. It is very powerful. These 195 students represent a great many schools and if their education is thought to be so negative by them, then something is wrong with education and we need to get more of these true stories published. We need to encourage more schools to use affective/effective means of educating. This is not to say positive learnings and positive recollection do not exist concerning education. The three or four students that I have had (out of the total 195) that have experienced open *education felt very different. Their descriptions of the classrooms all varied. I could never put them in a box and describe their learning situations as easily as I did the other 190! These students tended to begin my class on a more positive note.*

Their words of recalling their fourth grade classrooms were positive. In fact, most of the positive words on the board would come from these few students. It did not take me the fourteen weeks to get them to trust education. They began excited and remained so throughout the course. It is the other 97–98 percent who have only experienced the traditional and have had limited other experience that have very few positive memories of their educational process. Encouragingly enough by the end of the course I can get most of these students to really become active and interested learners. However, then the inevitable happens. The ultimate question is asked . . . "What now? Do we have to go back to the other teachers and their traditional style of teaching which we do not like?" And sadly I must reply, "Yes. However, there is a light at the end of that tunnel." I tell them, "Now at least you know the difference and you do have the power to change things."

Comments

When we contemplate the full meaning of this experience, the shock is great. Here are classes of teachers or teachers-in-training. Presumably they would not have chosen that profession if they had not found some value in their education. Yet when they think back on their schooling, the feelings are almost all negative, and even the positive feelings have to do with escaping from school. Their experience has been composed of fear, failure, humiliation, resentment, constriction. These are the important learnings—the personal ones. The *content* of their courses—what they were *supposed* to have learned—doesn't even come to mind! What an incredible fact! We have paid our taxes in order to have our children scarred, damaged, hurt, and stultified—changed from eager learners into active rebels against education.

The stupidity and tragedy of it all is that this outcome is completely unnecessary. That this is so is shown by the reaction of the very few students who have experienced an open, varied, individualized education. We have seen in the first chapter that kids can love school and that positive learning experiences are real and obtainable. These students have not been scarred. Why do we, as a community, continue to insist on a school experience that damages when a proven alternative exists? The question is a most troubling one.

FREEDOM PART TIME AND ITS CONSEQUENCES

The basic ideas and philosophy of this book are not new. They have many roots in the past, which I should like to illustrate with an account of an innovative project in one school that started with the dissatisfaction felt by one person in the early 1960s. The story is completed by a participant who tells of the project's impact then and fifteen years later. The project was a most unusual one. It involved both students and teachers on a part-time basis only. The pupils ranged from slow learners in seventh grade to gifted eleventh graders. Out of thirty to thirty-five periods in a week, the students spent from six to ten in EXP, as the program was called, and the teachers and the coordinating counselor spent approximately the same amount of time. The enormous flexibility of scheduling was made possible only because the project had the full support of the principal.

Here is an account of the eight-year program, as told by the person most responsible: Ruth Sanford (10).

🦋 *This experiment in learning began with an almost desperate need to save myself. As a counselor with administrative responsibilities in a public school district, I had felt for some time that I was dying a little every day. I had begun to feel like a shock absorber, taking in the pressures, the anxieties and frustrations of students, parents, administrators, teachers, the board of education and the community, trying to be at the same time an advocate for student growth and learning. It seemed to me that everyone was losing, especially me. There had to be a better way! Unless I could find one, my energies and enthusiasms would ebb away and I would become another drop-out from the educational system.*

One of my strong points is, I believe, that once I have gained an insight, I do something about it.

My first step was to apply for a sabbatical leave, which I used for research into "Creativity, Intelligence and Achievement in a Public Secondary School: Implications for the Classroom." It grew the following year into an experiment in education in which I, a counselor, worked first with a group of teachers, and later with those teachers in their classrooms. Our purpose was to create a climate in which the creative urge to grow and the excitement of learning would be nurtured. Much to our surprise we found that in the nurturing climate which we were striving to create, we ourselves were nourished, and found within ourselves a renewal of excitement in learning.

The next eight years were the most vital and adventurous of my professional life—up to that time.

The program kept the title chosen by the students, "EXP," although its form and the students involved varied from year to year depending upon the grade level and the school schedule for that grade. Perhaps like many living creatures, plant and animal, characteristics most essential to its survival were its adaptability and its will to live. It provided a place and a time for students to learn what they wanted to learn—in their own way—an opportunity to supplement and synthesize their regular schedule of required subjects.

The principal of the building, having shared in the enthusiasm of the preliminary workshop groups, was cooperative in setting up his master schedule. Some groups met two double periods each week plus time usually allotted to art, music and reading; others met one or two periods daily with adjacent free periods used, with student consent, to make larger blocks of time available for films, discussions and art work. The "prep" and free periods of teachers were also so placed in the schedule that they could meet once each week for workshop and processing sessions with the counselor or counselors.

We centered the subject content around a loose-leaf "Living Textbook"* divided for convenience into what we called "The Four Worlds": the natural world, the esthetic world, the technological world and the human or social world.

The introduction was a personal message to the learner, assuring her/him that "worlds" could be combined or separated into others or ignored, saying to the learner, "This is the beginning of your book. The moment you make a change, add, delete or rewrite, illustrate an article, make something and include a photograph of it, or do a page of your own, it becomes uniquely yours, living as you are living and changing. Even if today you only write a note in the margin it becomes yours."

We also used as a focus the "Being and Becoming" film series, developed by Dr. Drews under a federal grant. These films presented self-actualizing men and women, at work, at play, with their families and in their communities—as whole persons. The films, by selection, challenged the men/women career stereotypes, presenting, for example, a woman judge, a man artist, a woman doctor. The "Living Textbook" together with the films, stimulated heated discussions on ideas and values, prejudices and ambitions. They encouraged original work, wide reading; some students were stimulated to become authorities on topics of special interest to them, often newly found interests. We discovered later that some of this adventuring spilled over to after school hours and family dinner tables—even to social gatherings of their parents.

Some students worked almost exclusively in their "Living Textbooks" and "hated" the films; some "loved" the films and did very little in their "LTBs"; some were highly verbal in class and others rarely spoke; some withdrew and worked on sculpture or mobiles while others wrote poetry or stories—or gazed at the sky: A few who had never written an acceptable "composition" talked with a student friend or with one of the adults in the group, into a recorder, then edited a transcription and were amazed at the result—"Did I write that?"

---

* The book was patterned after *Living Textbook*, developed by Dr. Elizabeth Drews, who was then at Michigan State University.

For purposes of measurement and "feedback" most of the sessions were taped, in whole or in part, ready to be played back on request. Playback of tapes, along with the group process of establishing confidentiality and trust, became important parts of the learning process. After years of feeling manipulated by adults, trust came slowly, but by the second semester it became, for many, permission to be a whole, real person in the classroom.

Students, teachers and counselors involved directly in the program, teachers who knew students only in "outside" classes, and parents, all had a part in the evaluation process, and a brief composite of the evaluations was placed in the student's folder along with the transcript of academic record. There were no grades.

Students, adult members of the groups and parents also evaluated the program. One boy wrote, "This is the first time in nine years of school that I felt I had a place." Another said, "This course did nothing for me," then added, "except to give me a few new ideas on education." A tenth grade girl asked, "Why is it that in this class with no teacher I have learned more than in my other classes with regular teachers?" An eleventh grade student wrote, "This EXP has brought me nothing but trouble. When I have an idea now or disagree with someone, I speak up. Usually the teacher doesn't like it, especially if I disagree with the teacher." We learned that we could not measure a student's participation or learning by what was apparent in class: One young woman, whom the teachers and counselor had felt "probably gained the least" from the program, came back four years after she graduated from high school to tell us with great excitement about what her EXP experience was meaning to her in her practice teaching. She was full of questions about the planning—"Or," she asked, "did it just happen that way?"

Teachers learned that students, on the whole, accomplished more without the goad of grades, and that discipline problems diminished, much to their surprise.

In general, students in these groups showed an improvement in their English and social studies grades following their experience; most were more selective in the subjects in which they did well, most were observed by other-subject teachers to be more self-directed in their work and more able to weigh values in class discussions rather than "to see issues in terms of black or white"; most took a more active part in diversified activities associated with special interests after a year or more in the program.

Eight years after EXP ended as a formal program, there is a lasting effect on the teachers who were closely involved. I was in personal touch with four of the five who constituted a core of the experiment. Two of them use almost the same words: "After those

*years in EXP, I could never be the same again." One is in adminis-
tration, one teaching music, another English, the fourth works
with disadvantaged children and adults in an impoverished farm-
ing community. In every case they continue to see learning as a
partnership, to trust others to choose, to participate, to learn. EXP
is still having its effect.*

*We are also seeing the impact on education of some of the par-
ticipating students, who are now themselves teachers or counselors. The long-lasting impact of the EXP experience is best
exemplified by the story that follows. It is written by one of the
young women who was for two years a participant and another
year a student assistant. Her account has special meaning for me
because my notes at the time describe her as a quiet, shy girl who
didn't open her mouth in the group until almost the end of the first
semester, and then with tentative uncertainty. This memory is
supported by her own comments at the end of her first year in
EXP.*

Jeanne Ginsberg writes of what it was like for a student (11).

Looking Back

Shock and Confusion

🦋 *EXP—my first impression was that I had stepped into a carni-
val funhouse; nothing was as it should have been. There were no
grades; teachers offered minimal direction, students were
addressed with the same respect given adults.*

*There seemed to me to be little point in working or in partici-
pating since there were no external standards to meet. Even in
our discussions there seemed to be no right or wrong answer.
Most students seemed to feel the way I did and our beginning discussions were somewhat dull, guarded comments punctuated by
long silences.*

*Even then, teachers did not interfere. I began to feel that
something was not right and that no one was doing anything
about it. I began to feel anxious as the realization hit me that
since there was no external approval or punishment—no adult
with a special knowledge and power telling me what was
"right"—I was going to have to figure out for myself what was
"right," what I wanted to get from this experience. If someone was
going to make this interesting or meaningful or fun, it would have
to be me.*

*It was this realization which helped me to open and fill with
light and air and movement a door which until that moment had
been tightly closed. The first component of the program which*

caught my attention was the film series. I come from a home in which the roles and options for men and women are clearly defined. There are correct and incorrect ways to behave in each situation and there was a tremendous amount of fear associated with any move away from the standard ways of acting.

The film series "Being and Becoming" (I remember an interesting discussion about what these words mean and how they fit together) represented unconventional professions and did not always present the "proper" (that word again) gender for that role. Suddenly the options, which had previously been so constricted, widened for me. I began to gain a sense of independence and enthusiasm and self-respect.

Learning and Self-discovery

❦ *Soon after this, I read one line in an article from the "Living Textbook" which suggested the possibility that dolphins had a language of their own and [said] that a man named John Lilly was studying this language. The idea that people could actually learn to decipher dolphin language, in a sense to realize what it felt like to be a mammal living in the sea and to share their history, caught hold of me and I began to explore this tidbit of information for no end other than my own interest. I wrote to John Lilly, found articles and books in the library, talked to people about my findings, and felt enthused about something I had discovered at school for the first time. Eventually I turned my exploration into a paper for a biology class and received an A+. The difference, however, was that I did this paper for myself. The grade was incidental.*

I gradually stopped doing things for a teacher's approval and started doing things because I wanted to do them. How did this happen? I think one of the main factors was that the teachers seemed to accept everything I said. They didn't approve or disapprove; there didn't seem to be any judgment attached. They simply seemed interested. So, there was no point doing something for someone else's reaction.

As I stopped doing things for someone else I began to realize what I was interested in; what I wanted to learn; what was important to me; essentially, who I was. I began emerging from the shell of my parents' and teachers' expectations and into my own self.

Freedom vs. Rigidity

❦ *Perhaps the image which is most vivid to me now, years later, is that of the difficult trip down one hallway, through a crosswalk, and down another hallway to the left from EXP to Latin class. The entire trip took no more than two minutes but within that time I had to adjust myself from what seemed to me at fourteen years old the difference between life and death.*

Life: I think of change, action, conflict, colors, feelings, risk-taking, growth, choices. Death: I think of stagnation, sluggishness, no conflict, grays, controlled emotion, certainty, and no choice— the belief that there is only one way to do or think or feel. I remember reading a statement of Maya Angelou's: "Children's talent to endure stems from their ignorance of alternatives." In EXP I was asked to think about things, to delve more deeply, to explore, to feel, to develop and to be myself. Our textbook was the Living Textbook. *The class provided a place to "jump off" into material, into discussions, into interaction, and into the world outside of the classroom. It was an introduction into a way of relating to the world and to other people.*

In Latin class, I was told to sit in a row in alphabetical order by my last name; the notes to be copied from the board made up our notebooks. Our text was a translation of Julius Caesar. *The teacher moved up and down the rows to see that we were copying the notes neatly and exactly. A test was given daily on the material we were instructed to memorize the evening before. Homework: work in the most dead sense of the word. I remember practically nothing of my two years of Latin study. No wonder I was often late for this class, had nightmares about it, and dreaded eighth period.*

The Present Impact

🦋 *Now I am a teacher of emotionally disturbed and neurologically damaged children. In developing my own style of teaching I thought back to the walk between Experimental and Latin class and the feeling of darkness I experienced on that walk. These particular children need a tremendous amount of order and structure in their routine and work since their inner worlds and perceptions are often fraught with disorder and confusion. Yet, I have learned that while modes of learning can be classified into certain groups (visual learner, auditory learner, kinesthetic learner) there are as many learning styles as there are children. One child needs to learn math through understanding and experimenting with the concept. Another needs to learn the rote operation, practice it fifty times, and only then begin to understand the concept. A child who throws his reading book on the floor every day may be doing so because he perceives the symbols on the page to be jumping up and down. Another child who is presently enamored with dinosaurs (I remember my dolphins) has become an expert on the subject and learned division only when I superimposed the prob-*

lems on the back of a dinosaur. Each child is unique to me and I find one of the most exciting aspects of teaching is discovering and working with these differences.

It is most important to me to make the learning experience meaningful and personal by encouraging the children to use their minds rather than simply accept information. I want to challenge the one dimensional viewpoint and offer alternate ways of experiencing the world. In this way, I hope each child can feel in part responsible for his or her own learning experience.

This sometimes gives the class the appearance of being slightly more noisy or disorganized or less disciplined than a traditionally run classroom. Actually, tremendous planning and a very carefully organized program must be developed in order to enable disturbed (or for that matter, any child) to make discoveries and come up with ideas and conclusions based upon their own experience.

I think one of the most difficult insights for the children in my class to gain is that there may be more answers or viewpoints than their own. As one child screamed when I was helping to process a fight between him and another child: "Case is closed! He did it on purpose. Why won't you believe me? I'm right and he's wrong!!" Actually, the other child had hit this child with a ball accidentally because he has severe problems with eye-hand coordination. The first child only perceived the hurt as purposeful.

When I heard this, I felt frightened. It brought back old memories of Nazi Germany where Jews, gay women and men, really anyone who expressed a differing viewpoint to the government was deemed not deserving to be free or even to survive. It brought up new fears of a "Moral Majority" who know they are right; of a proposed Family Protection Bill which forbids the federal government from interfering with issues of child or wife abuse, forbids Legal Services Corp. from using money for cases involving abortion, divorce, homosexual rights or busing to achieve racial desegregation, and over thirty more subsections which would destroy the work and progress American people have made over the years. It brought up fears of the rising power of the Ku Klux Klan and the killer of Black children in Atlanta. If I react to this child's statement or run my classroom with the same closed and stuck finality of his thought pattern, I believe I am helping to feed this child's pathology and helping to create an individual who is incapable of empathy or reason or the possibility of change.

Very simplistically, in order to form valid opinions, I feel a child must learn how to listen, to consider what he's heard, to form an opinion based on his new information as well as his past experience, culture, and individual personality, and to express this opinion. I usually devote a large part of my curriculum to

*developing these skills with lessons as structured as copying let-
ters or words exactly from a model, to sharing a personal experience in three full sentences, to writing creative stories on a specific topic, to discussing feelings and thoughts, and value systems.*

*I can trace a great deal of my excitement with the learning
and growth process to the Experimental class. "Experimental"—
even the name suggests that anything can happen if only you
open your eyes and mind and ears and feelings. I hope that I
carry this excitement with me into my classroom in a way that
the children can feel its energy and power.*

To insert a radically free learning environment into a conventional
school, on a part-time basis, required a very strong sense of the importance
of the person, both teacher and student. Why did it work? It had the back-
ing of the principal. It involved many of the regular teachers and the regular
counselor, thus defusing much of the criticism that would have arisen if the
program had been brought in by outsiders. It did not force anyone—teacher
or student—to do anything. It simply provided an opportunity. Students
used this opportunity in such constructive ways that the program sold itself
to parents and to those who at the outset were skeptical.

As I read the two accounts, I am struck by the many valuable learnings
that occurred. There was clearly an increase in ability to take initiative,
excitement about learning, independence of thought, ability to make
choices, ability to organize a project and persist in it, creativity, openness,
and honesty, the appreciation of self. All this came about in a climate of
nonjudgmental caring, stimulating resources, and a trust in the student.

There are three elements in Jeanne Ginsberg's statement that stand out
vividly. One is the contrast between the living joy of self-directed learning
and the deadening nightmare of a highly traditional class. Another is the
evidence that the impact of EXP was lasting. Clearly it has affected her
teaching. She does not try to duplicate EXP in her class because her students have special problems and structure is required; but her attitudes are
those fostered by EXP. Finally, the program played a part in helping her to
become a thoughtfully independent citizen, willing to make and voice her
own considered judgments on personal, moral, and political issues. And
she is helping all her students to become similarly thoughtful citizens. I can
only conclude that an experience of freedom to learn, even if it is only for a
few hours a week, can have a positive influence that lasts for many years.

CONCLUDING REMARK

I am indebted to the six people who have permitted us to enter their diverse
worlds through what they have written about their experiences. I am also
indebted to the students who come so expressively into the stories. I trust

that the point has been made that any facet of education is drastically altered when the person responsible for it holds a humanistic, person-centered view. Revolutions—major or minor—occur.

REFERENCES

1. John P. Barkham, "Environmental Sciences 365: Ecosystem Management" (Unpublished evaluation of the course, 1980–81).

2. Adam Curle, *Education for Liberation* (London: Tavistock Publications, 1979).

3. Carl R. Rogers, *Freedom to Learn*, 1st ed. (New York: Macmillan/Merrill, 1969).

4. William Romey, "Radical Innovation in a Conventional Framework: Problems and Prospects," *Journal of Higher Education* 48 (November/December 1977): 680–96.

5. C. J. Sugnet, "Metamorphosis of a Geology Department," *Change* (July 1977).

6. Alvin M. White, "Humanistic Mathematics: An Experiment," *Education* (Winter 1974).

7. Alvin M. White, "Process and Environment in Teaching and Learning," in *New Directions for Teaching and Learning: Interdisciplinary Teaching,* No. 8, ed. Alvin M. White (San Francisco: Jossey-Bass, 1981).

8. S. Tobias, *Overcoming Math Anxiety* (New York: Norton, 1978).

9. Julie Ann Allender, "Fourth Grade Fantasy," *Journal of Humanistic Education* 6 (1982): 37–38.

10. Ruth Sanford, *Eight Years of an Experimental Program* (Unpublished personal document, 1981).

11. Jeanne Ginsberg, *Looking Back* (Unpublished personal document, 1981).

FOR THE TEACHER

CHAPTER 8

THE INTERPERSONAL RELATIONSHIP IN THE FACILITATION OF LEARNING

◆

This chapter is passionate and personal because it endeavors to probe my relationship to the learning process and the attitudinal climate that promotes this process. It has been presented in different forms at different times, the first at Harvard University (1, pp. 1–18). It has, however, been changed and revised for this volume. I believe that it expresses some of my deepest convictions in regard to the process we call *education*.

I wish to begin this chapter with a statement that may seem surprising to some and perhaps offensive to others. It is simply this: Teaching, in my estimation, is a vastly overrated function. Having made such a statement, I scurry to the dictionary to see if I really mean what I say. *Teaching* means "to instruct." Personally, I am not much interested in instructing another in what she should know or think, though others seem to love to do this. It also means "to impart knowledge or skill." My reaction is, why not be more efficient and use a book or programmed learning? Another meaning: "to make to know." Here my hackles rise. I have no wish to make anyone know something. "To show, guide, direct." As I see it, too many people have been shown, guided, directed. So I come to the conclusion that I *do* mean what I said. Teaching is, for me, a relatively unimportant and vastly overvalued activity.

But there is more in my attitude than this. I have a negative reaction to teaching. Why? I think it is because it raises all the wrong questions. As soon as we focus on teaching, the question arises, What shall we teach? What, from our superior vantage point, does the other person need to know? I wonder if, in this modern world, we are justified in the presumption that we are wise about the future and the young are foolish. Are we *really* sure as to what they should know? Then there is the ridiculous question of coverage. What shall the course cover? This notion of coverage is based on the assumption that what is taught is what is learned; what is presented is what is assimilated. I know of no assumption so obviously untrue. One does not need extensive study to provide evidence that this is false. One needs only to talk with a few students.

But I ask myself, "Am I so prejudiced against teaching that I find no situation in which it is worthwhile?" I immediately think of my experiences in Australia long ago. I became much interested in the Australian aborigine, a group that for more than twenty thousand years has managed to live and exist in a desolate environment in which modern humans would perish within a few days. The secret of the aborigines' survival has been teaching. They have passed on to the young every shred of knowledge about how to find water, about how to track game, about how to kill the kangaroo, about how to find their way through the trackless desert. Such knowledge is conveyed to the young as being *the* way to behave, and any innovation is frowned upon. It is clear that teaching has provided aborigines with a way to survive in a hostile and relatively *unchanging* environment.

Now I am closer to the nub of the question that excites me. Teaching or the imparting of knowledge makes sense in an unchanging environment. This is why it has been an unquestioned function for centuries. But if there is one truth about us, it is that we live in an environment that is continually changing. It seems, as we approach the start of a new century, that rapid change is our only constant. The one thing I can be sure of is that the physics taught to the present-day student will be outdated in five years or less. The teaching in psychology will certainly be out of date in ten years. The so-called facts of history depend very largely upon the current mood and temper of the culture. Chemistry, biology, genetics, and sociology are in such flux that a firm statement made today will almost certainly be modified by the time the student gets around to using the knowledge.

We are faced with an entirely new situation in which the goal of education, if we are to survive, is the *facilitation of change and learning*. The only person who is educated is the person who has learned how to learn; the person who has learned how to adapt and change; the person who has realized that no knowledge is secure, that only the process of seeking knowledge gives a basis for security. Changingness, a reliance on process rather than on static knowledge, is the only thing that makes any sense as a goal for education in the modern world.

So now with some relief I turn to an activity, a purpose, that really warms me—the facilitation of learning. When I have been able to transform a group—and here I mean all the members of a group, myself included—

into a community of learners, then the excitement has been almost beyond belief. To free curiosity, to permit individuals to go charging off in new directions dictated by their own interests, to unleash the sense of inquiry, to open everything to questioning and exploration, to recognize that everything is in process of change—here is an experience I can never forget. I cannot always achieve it in groups with which I am associated, but when it is partially or largely achieved, then it becomes a never-to-be forgotten group experience. Out of such a context arise true students, real learners, creative scientists, scholars, and practitioners. From this flexible environment, then, comes the kind of individuals who can live in a delicate but ever-changing balance between what is presently known and the flowing, moving, altering problems and facts of the future.

Here, then, is a goal to which I can give myself wholeheartedly. I see the *facilitation of learning* and the *aim* of education as one process, the way in which we might develop the learner and the way in which we can learn to live as individuals. I see the facilitation of learning as the function that may hold constructive, tentative, changing *process* answers to some of the deepest perplexities that beset humankind today. But do we know how to achieve this new goal in education or is it a will-o'-the-wisp that sometimes occurs, sometimes fails to occur, and thus offers little real hope? My answer is that we possess a very considerable knowledge of the conditions that encourage a whole person's self-initiated, significant, experiential, gut-level learning. We do not frequently see these conditions put into effect because they mean a real revolution in our approach to education and revolutions are not for the timid. But we do, as we have seen in the preceding chapters, find examples of this revolution in action. We know—and I will briefly mention some of the evidence—that the initiation of such learning rests not upon the teaching skills of the leader, not upon scholarly knowledge of the field, not upon curricular planning, not upon use of audiovisual aids, not upon the programmed learning used, not upon lectures and presentations, not upon an abundance of books, though each of these might at one time or another be utilized as an important resource. No, the facilitation of significant learning rests upon certain attitudinal qualities that exist in the personal relationship between the facilitator and the learner. We came upon such findings first in the field of psychotherapy, but now there is strong evidence showing that these findings apply in the classroom as well. We find it easier to think that the intensive relationship between therapist and client might possess these qualities, but we are also finding that they may exist in the countless interpersonal interactions between teacher and pupils.

QUALITIES THAT FACILITATE LEARNING

What are these qualities, these attitudes, that facilitate learning? Let me describe them very briefly, drawing illustrations from the teaching field.

Realness in the Facilitator of Learning

Perhaps the most basic of these essential attitudes is *realness* or *genuine-ness*. When the facilitator is a real person, being what she is, entering into a relationship with the learner without presenting a front or a facade, she is much more likely to be effective. This means that the feelings that she is experiencing are available to her, available to her awareness, that she is able to live these feelings, be them, and be able to communicate them if appro-priate. It means that she comes into a direct personal encounter with the learner, meeting her on a person-to-person basis. It means that the facilita-tor is being herself, not denying herself.

From this point of view, we see that the teacher can be a real person in her relationship with her students. She can be enthusiastic, bored, inter-ested in students, angry, sensitive, and sympathetic. Because she accepts these feelings as her own, she has no need to impose them on her students. She can like or dislike a student product without implying that it is objec-tively good or bad or that the student is good or bad. She is simply express-ing a feeling for the product, a feeling that exists within herself. Thus, she is a person to her students, not a faceless embodiment of a curricular require-ment or a sterile tube through which knowledge is passed from one genera-tion to the next. It is obvious that this attitudinal set, found to be effective in psychotherapy, is sharply in contrast with the tendency of most teachers to show themselves to their pupils simply in *roles*. It is quite customary for teachers rather consciously to put on the mask, the role, the facade of being a teacher and to wear this facade all day, removing it only when they have left the school at night.

But not all teachers are like this. Take Sylvia Ashton-Warner, who took resistant, supposedly slow-learning primary school Maori children in New Zealand and let them develop their own reading vocabulary. Each child could request one word each day—whatever word he wished—and she would print it on a card and give it to him. *Kiss, ghost, bomb, tiger, fight, love, daddy*—these are samples. Soon they were building sentences, which they could also keep. "He'll get a licking." "Pussy's frightened." The children simply never forgot these self-initiated learnings. But it is not my purpose to tell you of her methods. I want instead to give you a glimpse of her attitude, of the passionate realness that must have been as evident to her tiny pupils as to her readers. An editor asked her some questions, and she responded: "A few cool facts you asked me for. . . . I don't know that there's a cool fact in me, or anything else cool for that matter, on this particular subject. I've got only hot long facts on the matter of Creative Teaching, scorching both the page and me" (2, p. 26).

Here is no sterile facade. Here is a vital person, with convictions, with feelings. It is her transparent realness that was, I am sure, one of the ele-ments that made her an exciting facilitator of learning. She doesn't fit into some neat educational formula. She *is*, and students grow by being in con-tact with someone who really and openly *is*.

Take another very different person, Barbara Shiel, whose exciting work in facilitating learning in sixth graders has been described earlier. She gave her pupils a great deal of responsible freedom, and I will mention some of her students' reactions later. But here is an example of the way she shared herself with her pupils—not just sharing feelings of sweetness and light, but anger and frustration. She had made art materials freely available, and students often used these in creative ways, but the room frequently looked like a picture of chaos. Here is her report of her feelings and what she did with them.

> ✹ *I find it maddening to live with the mess—with a capital M! No one seems to care except me. Finally, one day I told the children . . . that I am a neat, orderly person by nature and that the mess was driving me to distraction. Did they have a solution? It was suggested [that] there were some volunteers who could clean up. . . . I said it didn't seem fair to me to have the same people clean up all the time for others—but it would solve it for me. "Well, some people like to clean," they replied. So that's the way it is. (3)*

I hope this example puts some lively meaning into the phrases I used earlier, that the facilitator "is able to live these feelings, be them, and be able to communicate them if appropriate." I have chosen an example of negative feelings because I think it is more difficult for most of us to visualize what this would mean. In the previous instance, Barbara Shiel is taking the risk of being transparent in her angry frustrations about the mess. And what happens? The same thing that, in my experience, nearly always happens. These young people accept and respect her feelings, take them into account, and work out a novel solution that none of us, I believe, would have suggested. Ms. Shiel wisely comments, "I used to get upset and feel guilty when I became angry. I finally realized the children could accept my feelings too. And it is important for them to know when they've pushed me. I have my limits, too" (3).

Just to show that positive feelings, when they are real, are equally effective, let me quote briefly a college student's reaction, in a different course:

> ✹ *Your sense of humor in the class was cheering; we all felt relaxed because you showed us your human self, not a mechanical teacher image. I feel as if I have more understanding and faith in my teachers now. I feel closer to the students too.*

Another said:

> ✹ *You conducted the class on a personal level and therefore in my mind I was able to formulate a picture of you as a person and not as merely a walking textbook.*

Another student in the same course said:

> ❧ *It wasn't as if there was a teacher in the class, but rather someone whom we could trust and identify as a "sharer." You were so perceptive and sensitive to our thoughts, and this made it all the more "authentic" for me. It was an "authentic" experience, not just a class. (4)*

I trust I am making it clear that to be real is not always easy, nor is it achieved all at once, but it is basic to the person who wants to become that revolutionary individual—a facilitator of learning.

Prizing, Acceptance, Trust

There is another attitude that stands out in those who are successful at facilitating learning. I have observed this attitude; I have experienced it. Yet it is hard to know what term to put to it, so I shall use several. I think of it as *prizing* the learner—prizing her feelings, her opinions, her person. It is caring for the learner, but nonpossessive caring. It is an acceptance of this other individual as a separate person who has worth in her own right. It is a basic trust—a belief that this other person is somehow fundamentally trustworthy. Whether we call it prizing, acceptance, trust, or some other term, it shows up in a variety of observable ways. The facilitator who has a considerable degree of this attitude can be fully acceptant of the fear and hesitation of the student as she approaches a new problem as well as acceptant of the pupil's satisfaction in achievement. Such a teacher can accept the student's occasional apathy, her erratic desires to explore byroads of knowledge, as well as her disciplined efforts to achieve major goals. The teacher can accept personal feelings that both disturb and promote learning: rivalry with a sibling, hatred of authority, concern about personal adequacy. What we are describing is a prizing of the learner as an imperfect human being with many feelings, many potentialities. The facilitator's prizing or acceptance of the learner is an operational expression of her essential confidence and trust in the capacity of the human organism.

I would like to give some examples of this attitude from the classroom situation. Here, in this context, any teacher statements would be properly suspect since many of us would like to feel we hold such attitudes and might have a biased perception of our qualities. But let me indicate how this attitude of prizing, of accepting, of trusting appears to the student who is fortunate enough to experience it. Here is a statement from a college student in a class with Dr. Morey Appell:

> ❧ *Your way of being with us is a revelation to me. In your class I feel important, mature, and capable of doing things on my own. I want to think for myself and this need cannot be accomplished through textbooks and lectures alone, but through living. I think*

you see me as a person with real feelings and needs, an individual. What I say and do are significant expressions from me, and you recognize this. (5)

College students in a class with Dr. Patricia Bull describe not only these prizing, trusting attitudes, but the effect these attitudes have had on their other interactions.

❦ *I still feel close to you, as though there were some tacit understanding between us, almost a conspiracy. This adds to the in-class participation on my part because I feel that at least one person in the group will react, even when I am not sure of the others. It does not matter really whether your reaction is positive or negative, it just IS. Thank you.*

❦ *I appreciate the respect and concern you have for others, including myself. . . . As a result of my experience in class, plus the influence of my readings, I sincerely believe that the student-centered teaching method does provide an ideal framework for learning; not just for the accumulation of facts, but more important, for learning about ourselves in relation to others. . . . When I think back to my shallow awareness in September compared to the depth of my insights now, I know that this course has offered me a learning experience of great value which I couldn't have acquired in any other way.*

❦ *Very few teachers would attempt this method because they would feel that they would lose the students' respect. On the contrary. You gained our respect, through your ability to speak to us on our level, instead of ten miles above us. With the complete lack of communication we see in this school, it was a wonderful experience to see people listening to each other and really communicating on an adult, intelligent level. More classes should afford us this experience. (4)*

These examples show the facilitator who cares, who prizes, who trusts the learner to create a climate for learning so different from the ordinary classroom that any resemblance is purely coincidental.

Empathic Understanding

A further element that establishes a climate for self-initiated, experiential learning is *empathic understanding*. When the teacher has the ability to understand the student's reactions from the inside, has a sensitive awareness of the way the process of education and learning seems to the student, then again the likelihood of significant learning is increased. This kind of understanding is sharply different from the usual evaluative understanding, which follows the pattern "I understand what is wrong with you." When there is a sensitive empathy, however, the reaction in the learner follows something of this pattern: "At last someone understands how it feels and seems to be *me* without wanting to analyze me or judge me. Now I can blossom and grow and learn." This attitude of standing in the other's shoes, of viewing the world through the student's eyes, is almost unheard of in the classroom. One could listen to thousands of ordinary classroom interactions without coming across one instance of clearly communicated, sensitively accurate, empathic understanding. But it has a tremendously releasing effect when it occurs.

Let me take an illustration from Virginia Axline as she talks with a second-grade boy. Jay, age seven, had been aggressive, a troublemaker, slow of speech and learning. Because of his cussing, he was taken to the principal, who paddled him, unknown to Ms. Axline. During a free work period, Jay fashioned very carefully a man of clay, down to a hat and a handkerchief in his pocket. "Who is that?" asked Ms. Axline. "Dunno," replied Jay. "Maybe it is the principal. He has a handkerchief in his pocket like that." Jay glared at the clay figure. "Yes," he said. Then he began to tear the head off and looked up and smiled. Ms. Axline said, "You sometimes feel like twisting his head off, don't you? You get so mad at him." Jay tore off one arm, another, then beat the figure to a pulp with his fists. Another boy, with the perception of the young, explained, "Jay is mad at Mr. X because he licked him this noon." "Then you must feel lots better now," Ms. Axline commented. Jay grinned and began to rebuild Mr. X (6, pp. 521–33).

The other examples I have cited also indicate how deeply appreciative students feel when they are simply *understood*—not evaluated, not judged, but simply understood from their own point of view, not the teacher's. If any teacher set herself the task of endeavoring to make one nonevaluative, acceptant, empathic response per day to a student's demonstrated or verbalized feeling, I believe she would discover the potency of this currently almost nonexistent kind of understanding.

WHAT ARE THE BASES OF FACILITATIVE ATTITUDES?

A Puzzlement

It is natural that we do not always have the attitudes I have been describing. Some teachers raise the question, "But what if I am *not* feeling empathic, do not, at this moment, prize or accept or like my students. What then?" My response is that realness is the most important of the attitudes mentioned, and it is not accidental that this attitude was described first. So if one has little understanding of the students' inner world and a dislike for the students or their behavior, it is almost certainly more constructive to be real than to be pseudoempathic or to put on a facade of caring. But this is not nearly as simple as it sounds. To be genuine or honest or congruent or real means to be this way about *oneself*. I cannot be real about another because I do not *know* what is real for him. I can only tell, if I wish to be truly honest, what is going on in me.

Let me take an example. Earlier in this chapter I reported Ms. Shiel's feelings about the mess created by the artwork. Essentially she said, "I find it maddening to live with the mess! I'm neat and orderly and it is driving me to distraction." But suppose her feelings had come out somewhat differently, perhaps in the disguised way that is much more common in classrooms at all levels. She might have said, "You are the messiest children I've ever seen! You don't take care about tidiness or cleanliness. You are just terrible!" This is most definitely not an example of genuineness or realness, in the sense in which I am using these terms. There is a profound distinction between the two statements, which I should like to spell out.

In the second statement the teacher tells nothing of herself, shares none of her feelings. Doubtless the children will sense that she is angry; but because children are perceptively shrewd, they may be uncertain about whether she is angry at them or has just come from an argument with the principal. It has none of the honesty of the first statement in which she tells of her own upsetness, of her own feeling of being driven to distraction.

Another aspect of the second statement is that it is made up of judgments or evaluations; and like most judgments, they are all arguable. Are these children messy, or are they simply excited and involved in what they are doing? Are they *all* messy, or are some as disturbed by the chaos as she? Do they care nothing about tidiness, or is it simply that they don't care about it every day? If a group of visitors was coming, would the children's attitude be different? Are the students terrible, or simply children? I trust it is evident that when we make judgments, they are almost never fully accurate and hence cause resentment and anger as well as guilt and apprehension. Had she used the second statement, the response of the class would have been entirely different.

I am going to some lengths to clarify this point because I have found from experience that to stress the value of being real, of being one's feelings, is taken by some as a license to pass judgments on others, to project on others all the feelings that one should be *owning*. Nothing could be further from my meaning. Actually the achievement of realness is most difficult; and even when one wishes to be truly genuine, it occurs but rarely. Certainly it is not simply a matter of the words used. If one is feeling judgmental, the use of a verbal formula that sounds like the sharing of feelings will not help. It is just another instance of a facade, of a lack of genuineness. Only slowly can we learn to be truly real. For first of all, one must be close to one's feelings, capable of being aware of them. Then one must be willing to take the risk of sharing them as they are, inside, not disguising them as judgments or attributing them to other people. This is why I so admire Ms. Shiel's sharing of her anger and frustration without in any way disguising it.

A Trust in the Human Organism

It is most unlikely that one could hold the three attitudes I have described, or could commit herself to being a facilitator of learning, unless she has come to have a profound trust in the human organism and its potentialities. If I distrust the human being, then I must cram her with information of my own choosing lest she go her own mistaken way. But if I trust the capacity of the human individual for developing her own potentiality, then I can provide her with many opportunities and permit her to choose her own way and her own direction in her learning.

It is clear, I believe, that the teachers and principals whose works are described in the preceding chapters rely basically upon the tendency toward fulfillment, toward actualization, in their students. They are basing their work on the hypothesis that students who are in real contact with problems that are relevant to them wish to learn, want to grow, seek to discover, endeavor to master, desire to create, move toward self-discipline. The teacher is attempting to develop a quality of climate in the classroom and a quality of personal relationship with students that will permit these natural tendencies to come to their fruition.

Living the Uncertainty of Discovery

I believe it should be said that this basically confident view of the human being and the attitudes toward students that I have described do not appear suddenly, in some miraculous manner, in the facilitator of learning. Instead, they come about through taking risks, through acting on tentative hypotheses. This is most obvious in the chapter describing Ms. Shiel's work where, acting on hypotheses of which she is unsure, risking herself uncertainly in new ways of relating to her students, she finds these new views confirmed by what happens in her class. The same is definitely true of Ms. Swenson in her foreign-language class. I am sure the other teachers we have discussed went through the same type of uncertainty. As for me, I can only state that I started my career with the firm view that individuals must be manipulated for their own good; I only came to the attitudes I have described and the trust in the individual that is implicit in them because I found that these attitudes were so much more potent in producing learning and constructive change. Hence, I believe that it is only by risking herself in these new ways that the teacher can discover, for herself, whether or not these attitudes of implicit trust in students are effective, whether or not they are for her.

I will, then, draw a conclusion, based on the experiences of the several facilitators and their students who have been included in this book so far: when a facilitator creates, even to a modest degree, a classroom climate characterized by all that she can achieve of realness, prizing, and empathy; when she trusts the constructive tendency of the individual and the group; then she discovers that she has inaugurated an educational revolution. Learning of a different quality occurs, proceeding at a different pace with a greater degree of pervasiveness. Feelings—positive, negative, confused—become a part of the classroom experience. Learning becomes life and a very vital life at that. Students are on the way, sometimes excitedly, sometimes reluctantly, to becoming learning, changing people.

The Research Evidence

The research evidence for the statements in the previous paragraph is now very convincing indeed. It has been most interesting to watch that evidence accumulate to a point where it seems irrefutable.

In the 1960s several studies in psychotherapy and education led to some tentative conclusions. Let me summarize them briefly, without presenting the methods used. (To learn more, consult the references at the end of the chapter.) When clients in therapy rated their therapists as high in genuineness, prizing, and empathic understanding, self-learning and therapeutic change were facilitated. The significance of these therapist attitudes was supported in classic research by G. T. Barrett-Lennard (7).

Another study focused on teachers. Some teachers saw their urgent problems as "helping children think for themselves and be independent," "getting students to participate," etc. These teachers were regarded as the "positively oriented" group. Other teachers saw their urgent problems as "getting students to listen," "trying to teach children who don't even have the ability to learn," etc. These teachers were termed the negatively oriented group. Research found that students perceived the first group as exhibiting far more empathy, prizing, and realness than shown by the second group. The first group showed a high degree of facilitative attitudes; the second did not (8).

A study by R. Schmuck showed that when teachers are empathically understanding, their students tend to like each other better (9). In an understanding classroom climate, every student tends to feel liked by all the others and has a more positive attitude toward self and school. This ripple aspect of the teacher's attitude is provocative and significant. To extend an empathic understanding to students has effects that go on and on.

The foregoing are samples of studies that are beginning to provide clear directions for healthy learning environments. But we may still ask, Does the student actually *learn* more when these attitudes are present? Back in 1965 David Aspy did a careful study of six classes of third graders (10). He found that in the three classes where the teachers' facilitative attitudes were highest, the pupils showed a significantly greater gain in their reading achievement than those in classes with a lesser degree of these qualities. Aspy and a colleague, Flora Roebuck, later enlarged this research into a program that extended for more than a decade. The overwhelming evidence that they accumulated is presented in a later section of this book, "What Are the Facts?" Their study makes it very clear that the attitudinal climate of the classroom, as created by the teacher, is a major factor in promoting or inhibiting learning.

In the 1990s, Wayne Hoy, John Tarter, and Robert Kottkamp synthesized a thirty-year period of research on school health and climate in their book *Open Schools/Healthy Schools* (11). They conclude, in part, that 59 percent of the reason for student learning can be attributed to the health of the school. Healthy schools have a very strong sense of partnership and community among all their members. "Teacher affiliation, a key mechanism for integrating school life, is the friendliness and commitment of the teachers to the school, colleagues, and students that make a school a community. . . . The healthy school has no need to coerce cooperation; it is given freely by professionals" (11, p. 194).

Evidence from Students

Certainly before the research evidence was in, students were making it clear by their reactions to student-centered or person-centered classrooms that an educational revolution was underway. This kind of evidence persists to the present day. The most striking learnings of students exposed to such a climate are by no means restricted to greater achievement in the three R's. The significant learnings are the more personal ones: independence, self-initiated and responsible learning, release of creativity, a tendency to become more of a person. I can only illustrate this by choosing, almost at random, statements from students whose teachers have endeavored to create a climate of trust, of prizing, of realness, of understanding, and, above all, of freedom.

Again I quote from Sylvia Ashton-Warner about one of the central effects of such a climate: "The drive is no longer the teacher's, but the children's own. . . . the teacher is at last with the stream and not against it, the stream of children's inexorable creativeness" (2, p. 93). If you need verification of this, here is one of a number of statements made by students in a course on poetry led (not taught) by Dr. Samuel Moon:

> ❦ *In retrospect, I find that I have actually enjoyed this course, both as a class and as an experiment, although it had me quite unsettled at times. This, in itself, made the course worthwhile since the majority of my courses this semester merely had me bored with them and the whole process of "higher education." Quite aside from anything else, due mostly to this course, I found myself devoting more time to writing poetry than to writing short stories, which temporarily interfered with my writing class.*

> ❦ *I should like to point out one very definite thing which I have gained from the course; this is an increased readiness on my part to listen to and to seriously consider the opinions of my fellow students. In view of my past attitude, this alone makes the course valuable. I suppose the real result of any course can be expressed in answer to the question, "Would you take it over again?" My answer would be an unqualified "Yes." (12, p. 227)*

I should like to add several comments from Dr. Patricia Bull's sophomore students in a class in adolescent psychology. The first two are midsemester comments (4):

> ❦ *This course is proving to be a vital and profound experience for me. This unique learning situation is giving me a whole new conception of just what learning is. . . . I am experiencing a real growth in this atmosphere of constructive freedom. . . . the whole experience is challenging.*

> ❦ *I feel that the course had been of great value to me. . . . I'm glad to have had this experience because it has made me think. . . . I've never been so personally involved with a course before, especially outside the classroom. It has been frustrating, rewarding, enjoyable, and tiring!*

The other comments are from the end of the course:

> ❦ *This course is not ending with the close of the semester for me, but continuing. . . . I don't know of any greater benefit which can be gained from a course than this desire for further knowledge.*

> ❦ *I feel as though this type of class situation has stimulated me more in making me realize where my responsibilities lie, especially as far as doing required work on my own. I no longer feel as though a test date is the criterion for reading a book. I feel as though my future work will be done for what I will get out of it, not just for a test mark.*

> ❦ *I think that now I am acutely aware of the breakdown in communications that does exist in our society from seeing what happened in our class. . . . I've grown immensely. I know that I am a different person than I was when I came into that class. . . . It has done a great deal in helping me understand myself better. . . . thank you for contributing to my growth.*

> ❦ *My idea of education has been to gain information from the teacher by attending lectures. The emphasis and focus were on the teacher. . . . One of the biggest changes that I experienced in this class was my outlook on education. Learning is something more than a grade on a report card. No one can measure what you have learned because it's a personal thing. I was very confused between learning and memorization. I could memorize very well, but I doubt if I ever learned as much as I could have. I believe my attitude toward learning has changed from a grade-centered outlook to a more personal one.*

If you wish to know what this type of course seems like to a sixth grader, let me give you a sampling of the reactions of Ms. Shiel's youngsters—misspellings and all.

> ❦ *I feel that I am learning self abilty [sic]. I am learning not only school work but I am learning that you can learn on your own as well as someone can teach you.*

> ❦ *I like this plan because there is a lot of freedom. I also learn more this way than the other way you don't have to wate [sic] for others you can go at your own speed rate it also takes a lot of responsibility. (3)*

Or let me take two more, from Dr. Appell's graduate class:

> ❦ *I have been thinking about what happened through this experience. The only conclusion I come to is that if I try to measure what is going on, or what I was at the beginning, I have got to know what I was when I started—and I don't . . . so many things I did and feel are just lost . . . scrambled up inside. . . . They don't seem to come out in a nice little pattern or organization I can say or write. . . . There are so many things left unsaid. I know I have only scratched the surface, I guess. I can feel so many things almost ready to come out. . . . maybe that's enough. It seems all kinds of things have so much more meaning now than ever before. . . . This experience has had meaning, has done things to me and I am not sure how much or how far just yet. I think I am going to be a better me in the fall. That's one thing I think I am sure of. (13, pp. 143—48)*

> ❦ *You follow no plan, yet I'm learning. Since the term began I seem to feel more alive, more real to myself. I enjoy being alone as well as with other people. My relationships with children and other adults are becoming more emotional and involved. Eating an orange last week, I peeled the skin off each separate orange section and liked it better with the transparent shell off. It was juicier and fresher tasting that way. I began to think, that's how I feel sometimes, without a transparent wall around me, really communicating my feelings. I feel that I'm growing, how much, I don't know. I'm thinking, considering, pondering and learning. (5)*

I can't read these student statements—sixth grade, college, graduate level—without being deeply moved. Here are teachers, *changing* themselves, *being* themselves, *trusting* their students, adventuring into the existential unknown, taking the subjective leap. And what happens? Exciting, incredible *human* events. You can sense persons being created, learnings being initiated, future citizens rising to meet the challenge of unknown worlds. If only one teacher out of one hundred dared to risk, dared to be, dared to trust, dared to understand, we would have an infusion of a living spirit into education that would, in my estimation, be priceless.

The Effect on the Instructor

Let me turn to another dimension that excites me. I have spoken of the effect upon the student of a climate that encourages significant, self-reliant, personal learning. But I have said nothing about the reciprocal effect upon the instructor. When she has been the agent for the release of such self-initiated learning, the faculty member finds herself changed as well as her students. One teacher says:

> ✺ *To say that I am overwhelmed by what happened only faintly reflects my feelings. I have taught for many years but I have never experienced anything remotely resembling what occurred. I, for my part, never found in a classroom so much of the whole person coming forth, so deeply involved, so deeply stirred. Further, I question if in the traditional setup, with its emphasis on subject matter, examinations, grades, there is, or there can be, a place for the "becoming" person with his deep and manifold needs as he struggles to fulfill himself. But this is going far afield. I can only report to you what happened and to say that I am grateful and that I am also humbled by the experience. I would like you to know this for it has enriched my life and being. (14, p. 313)*

Another faculty member reports:

> ✺ *Rogers has said that relationships conducted on these assumptions mean "turning present day education upside down." I have found this to be true as I have tried to implement this way of living with students. The experiences I have had have plunged me into relationships which have been significant and challenging and beyond compare for me. They have inspired me and stimulated me and left me at times shaken and awed with their consequences for both me and the students. They have led me to the fact of what I can only call . . . the tragedy of education in our time—student after student who reports this to be his first experience with total trust, with freedom to be and to move in ways most consistent for the enhancement and maintenance of the core of dignity which somehow has survived humiliation, distortion, and corrosive cynicism. (5)*

TOO IDEALISTIC?

Some readers may feel that the whole approach of this chapter—the belief that teachers can relate as persons to their students—is hopelessly unrealistic and idealistic. They may see that in essence it is encouraging both teachers and students to be creative in their relationship to each other and in their relationship to subject matter, and feel that such a goal is quite impossible. They are not alone in this. I have heard scientists at leading schools of science and scholars in leading universities argue that it is absurd to try to encourage all students to be creative—we need hosts of mediocre technicians and workers, and if a few creative scientists and artists and leaders emerge, that will be enough.

That may be enough for them. It may be enough to suit you. I want to go on record as saying it is not enough to suit me. When I realize the incredible potential in every student, I want to try to release it. We are working hard to release the incredible energy in the atom and the nucleus of the atom. If we do not devote equal energy—yes, and equal money—to the release of the potential of the individual person, then the enormous discrepancy between our level of physical energy resources and human energy resources will doom us to a deserved and universal destruction.

I'm sorry I can't be coolly detached about this. The issue is too urgent. I can only be passionate in my statement that people count, that interpersonal relationships *are* important, that we know something about releasing human potential, that we could learn much more, and that unless we give strong positive attention to the human interpersonal side of our educational dilemma, our civilization is on its way down the drain. Better courses, better curricula, better coverage, better teaching machines will never resolve our dilemma in a basic way. Only persons acting like persons in their relationships with their students can even begin to make a dent on this most urgent problem of modern education.

SUMMARY

Let me try to restate, somewhat more calmly and soberly, what I have said with such feeling and passion. I have said that it is most unfortunate that educators and the public think about, and focus on, *teaching.* It leads them into a host of questions that are either irrelevant or absurd so far as real education is concerned. I have said that if we focus on the facilitation of *learning*—how, why, and when the student learns and how learning seems and feels from the inside—we might be on a much more profitable track. I have said that we have some knowledge, and could gain more, about the conditions that facilitate learning, and that one of the most important of these conditions is the attitudinal quality of the interpersonal relationship between facilitator and learner.

Those attitudes that appear effective in promoting learning can be described. First of all, is a transparent realness in the facilitator, a willingness to be a person, to be and live the feelings and thoughts of the moment. When this realness includes a prizing, a caring, a trust, and a respect for the learner, the climate for learning is enhanced. When it includes a sensitive and accurate empathic listening, then indeed a freeing climate, stimulative of self-initiated learning and growth, exists. The student is *trusted* to develop. I have tried to make plain that individuals who hold such attitudes, and are bold enough to act on them, do not simply modify classroom methods; they revolutionize them. These bold individuals perform almost none of the functions of teachers. It is no longer accurate to call them teachers. They are catalyzers, facilitators, energizers; they give students freedom and life and the opportunity to learn. Most important, they are co-learners with students.

I have brought in the cumulative research evidence that suggests that individuals who hold such attitudes are regarded as effective in the classroom; that the problems that concern them have to do with the release of potential, not the deficiencies of their students; that they seem to create classroom situations in which children are disliked and not admired, but in which affection and liking are a part of the life of every child; that in classrooms approaching such a psychological climate, children learn more of the conventional subjects. But I have intentionally gone beyond the empirical findings to try to take you into the inner life of the student—elementary, college, and graduate—who is fortunate enough to live and learn in such an interpersonal relationship with a facilitator, in order to let you see what learning feels like when it is free, self-initiated, and spontaneous. I have tried to indicate how it even changes the student-student relationship, making it more aware, more caring, more sensitive, as well as increasing the self-related learning of significant material. I have spoken of the change it brings about in the faculty member.

Throughout, I have tried to indicate that if we are to have citizens who can live constructively in this kaleidoscopically changing world, we must free our children to become self-starting, self-initiating learners. Finally, it has been my purpose to show that this kind of learner develops best, so far as we now know, in a growth-promoting, facilitative relationship with a *person*.

REFERENCES

1. Carl R. Rogers, "The Interpersonal Relationship in the Facilitation of Learning," in *Humanizing Education*, ed. R. Leeper (Washington, D.C.: National Education Association, 1967), pp. 1–18. © Association for Supervision and Curriculum Development.
2. Sylvia Ashton-Warner, *Teacher* (New York: Simon and Schuster, 1963).

3. Barbara J. Shiel, *Evaluation: A Self-directed Curriculum, 1965* (Unpublished manuscript, 1966).

4. Patricia Bull, *Student Reactions, Fall, 1965* (Unpublished manuscript, New York State University College, 1966).

5. Morey L. Appell, *Selected Student Reactions to Student-centered Courses* (Unpublished manuscript, Indiana State University, 1959).

6. Virginia M. Axline, "Morale on the School Front," *Journal of Educational Research* (1944): 521–33.

7. G. T. Barrett-Lennard, "Dimensions of Therapist Response as Causal Factors in Therapeutic Change," *Psychological Monographs* 76, no. 562 (1962).

8. F. C. Emmerling, "A Study of the Relationships Between Personality Characteristics of Classroom Teachers and Pupil Perceptions" (Ph.D. diss., Auburn University, 1961).

9. R. Schmuck, "Some Aspects of Classroom Social Climate," *Psychology in the Schools* 3 (1966): 5–5; "Some Relationships of Peer Liking Patterns in the Classroom to Pupil Attitudes and Achievements," *The School Review* 71 (1963): 337–59.

10. David N. Aspy, *A Study of Three Facilitative Conditions and Their Relationship to the Achievement of Third Grade Students* (Ph.D. diss., University of Kentucky, 1965).

11. K. W. Hoy, J. C. Tarter, and R. B. Kottkamp, *Open Schools/Healthy Schools* (London: Sage, 1991).

12. Samuel F. Moon, "Teaching the Self," *Improving College and University Teaching* 14 (Autumn 1966): 213–29.

13. Morey L. Appell, "Self-understanding for the Guidance Counselor," *Personnel and Guidance Journal* (October 1963): 143–48.

14. Carl R. Rogers, *On Becoming a Person* (Boston: Houghton Mifflin, 1961).

CHAPTER 9

BECOMING A FACILITATOR

◆

*As a teacher, I must first slow down in order to acknowledge
the voices of my students—to take these moments to give
value to what is being said no matter how loud or soft, gentle
or angry, relevant or irrelevant it may seem.*
Elementary school teacher *(1, p. 30)*

A MAGIC WAND

Not long ago, a teacher asked me, "What changes would you like to see in
education?" I answered the question as best I could at the time, but it
stayed with me. Suppose I had a magic wand that could produce only one
change in our educational systems. What would that change be?

I finally decided that my imaginary wand, with one sweep, would cause
you and every other teacher at every level to forget that you are a teacher.
You would develop complete amnesia about the teaching skills you have
painstakingly acquired over the years. You would find that you are abso-

lutely unable to teach. Instead, you would find yourself holding the attitudes and possessing the skills of a facilitator of learning: genuineness, prizing, and empathy. Why would I be so cruel as to rob teachers of their precious skills? Because I feel that our educational institutions are in a desperate state; and that unless our schools can become exciting, fun-filled centers of learning, they are quite possibly doomed.

You may be thinking that *facilitator of learning* is just a fancy name for a teacher and that nothing at all would really change. If so, you are mistaken. There is no resemblance between the traditional function of teaching and the function of the facilitator of learning. On the one hand, as a traditional teacher—a *good* traditional teacher—you ask yourself questions like these:

> What do I think would be good for a student to learn at this particular age and level of competence? How can I plan a proper curriculum for this student? How can I inculcate motivation to learn this curriculum? How can I instruct in such a way that he or she will gain the knowledge that should be gained? How can I best set an examination to see whether this knowledge has actually been taken in?

On the other hand, as a facilitator of learning, you ask *these* questions, not of yourself but of the students:

> What do you want to learn? What things puzzle you? What are you curious about? What issues concern you? What problems do you wish you could solve? [When you have the answers, further questions follow.]
>
> Now how can I help my students find the resources—the people, the experiences, the learning facilities, the books, the knowledge in myself—that will help them learn in ways that will provide answers to the things that concern them, the things they are eager to learn? [And then later,] How can I help them evaluate their own progress and set future learning goals based on this self-evaluation?

The attitudes of the teacher and the facilitator are also at opposite poles. Traditional teaching, no matter how disguised, is based essentially on the *mug-and-jug* theory. Traditional teachers might ask, "How can I make the mug hold still while I fill it from the jug with these facts that the curriculum planners and I regard as valuable?" But your attitude as a facilitator has almost entirely to do with climate:

> How can I create a psychological climate in which the child will feel free to be curious, will feel free to make mistakes, will feel free to learn from the environment, from fellow students, from me, from experience? How can I help him or her recapture the excitement of learning that was natural in infancy?

Once this process of facilitating wanted learning is underway, a school will become, for the child, "my school." In previous chapters we discovered that students who love school see the classroom as "our classroom" and the learning as "my learning." Each student feels like a living, vital part of a very satisfying process. Astonished adults begin to hear children say, "I can't wait to get to school today," "For the first time in my life I'm finding out about the things I want to know," "Hey, drop that brick! Don't you break a window in *my school!*"

Beautifully, the same phrases can be used by the child who is mentally impaired, the gifted child, the urban child, the underserved child. This is because students can work on problems of real concern and interest at levels where they can grasp a problem and find a useful solution. Each can have a continuing experience of success. When Christina, a senior at Houston's High School for the Performing and Visual Arts (HSPVA), talked in chapter 1 about the "Black table, the Hispanic table, the jazz table" at lunch and that it was "one of my responsibilities to teach them to go and meet with other people so we all can be family," she communicated the essence of what can be reality.

Some educators believe that such individualized learning is completely impractical because they think it will involve an enormous increase in the number of teachers. Nothing could be further from the truth. For one thing, when children are eager to learn, they follow up their own leads and engage in a great deal of independent study. The teacher also saves time because problems of discipline or control drop tremendously. Finally, the freedom of interaction that grows out of the climate I have so briefly described makes it possible to use a great untapped resource—the ability of one child to help another in learning. For John and Roberto to hear, "You gentlemen have worked together beautifully in carrying out the long division to solve this problem," is a marvelous experience for both students. It is even more marvelous for the two of them to work together, helping each other learn, *without being asked!* John really learns long division when he helps another learner understand. Roberto can accept the help and learn because he is not shown as being stupid, either in public or on a report card.

It is a risky thing for a person to become a facilitator of learning rather than a teacher. It means uncertainties, difficulties, setbacks—and also exciting human adventures as students begin to blossom. One teacher who took this risk told me that one of her greatest surprises was that she had more time to spend with each child, not less, when she set each child free to learn.

I cannot stress too strongly how much I wish that someone could wave that magic wand and change teaching to facilitation. I deeply believe that traditional teaching is an almost completely futile, wasteful, overrated function in today's changing world. It is successful mostly in giving children a sense of failure when they can't grasp the material. Traditional teaching also succeeds in persuading students to drop out when they realize that the material taught is almost completely irrelevant to their lives. No one should ever be asked to learn something in which the person sees no relevance. No child should ever experience the sense of failure imposed by our grading system, by criticism and ridicule from teachers and others, by rejection when he or she is slow to comprehend. But it is healthy for children to feel a sense of failure when they try to achieve something that is actually too difficult, for that feeling drives them to further learning. It is a very different thing to experience this sense of failure from a person—imposed failure, which must ultimately devalue the learner as a person.

WHAT IS THE WAY?

If you as a teacher desire to give students the freedom to learn—in other words, if you want to become a facilitator—how can you achieve this goal?

I cannot answer for anyone else, as there are many ways by which one may change. So I am simply going to speak personally and raise the questions that I would ask myself or the students if I were given responsibility for the learnings of a group of children. How would I meet the challenge posed by such a group?

What Is It Like to Learn?

I think this is the first question I would raise: What is it like to be a child who is learning something significant?

I believe the most meaningful answer I can give is to speak from my own experience. I was a very good boy in elementary and high school. I got good grades. Frequently I annoyed my teachers by being clever enough to get around the rules they had set up, but I was not openly defiant. I was a very solitary boy with few friends, isolated from others by a strictly religious home.

My family moved from a suburban setting to a large farm with acres of woodland when I was thirteen. At that time Gene Stratton Porter's books were popular, books that involved a wilderness setting and made much of the great night-flying moths. Shortly after we moved to the farm, I found a pair of luna moths—great pale green wings with purple trimmings—on the trunk of an oak tree. I can still see the six-inch spread of shimmering green with its iridescent lavender spots, bright against the shaggy black bark. I was enthralled. I captured them, kept them, and the female laid hundreds of eggs. I got a book about moths. I fed the baby caterpillars. Though I had many failures with this first brood, I captured other moths and gradually learned to keep and sustain the caterpillars through their whole series of life changes: the frequent molting of their skins, the final spinning of their cocoons, the long wait until the next spring when the moths emerged. To see a moth come out of its cocoon with wings no bigger than a thumbnail and within an hour or two to develop a five- to seven-inch wingspread was fantastic. But most of the time it was hard work: finding fresh leaves every day selected from the right varieties of trees, emptying the boxes, sprinkling the cocoons during the winter to keep them from drying out. It was, in short, a large project. But by age fifteen or sixteen, I was an authority on such moths. I knew probably twenty or more different varieties, their habits, and their food, as well about those moths that ate no food during their life span but only during their period as caterpillars. I could identity the larvae by species. I could spot the big three- to four-inch caterpillars easily. I never took a long walk without finding at least one caterpillar or cocoon.

But it interests me as I look back that to the best of my recollection I never told any teacher and only a few fellow students of my interest in moths. This consuming project wasn't in any way a part of my education. Education was what went on in school; a teacher wouldn't be interested. Besides, I would have so much to explain to that teacher when, after all, he or she was supposed to be teaching me. I had one or two good teachers whom I liked during this period, but my project was personal, not the thing one could share with a teacher. So here was an enterprise at least two years in length—scholarly, well researched, requiring painstaking work and much self-discipline, wide knowledge, and practical skills. But to my mind it was, of course, not a part of my education. So that is what real learning was like for one boy.

I am sure that significant learning is often very different for children whose life experiences contrast with my own. If I see education only through my own eyes, I will miss many opportunities to grow with my students. As a boy growing up in a rural setting and in a religious home, as one who also lived in China, I developed a view about the world that may not have been experienced by girls, urban children, or physically disabled children. But as a facilitator, keeping my own childhood learning in mind, I want to try very hard to find out what it is like to be a child who is learning. I want to get inside the child's world to see what has significance for him or her. I want to make school at least a friendly home for such meaningful learning, no matter where it might be occurring in the child's life.

My experiences in school settings have also shaped my view of the world and learning. Too often I am tempted to *teach* in the way I have been taught. Breaking this mold requires reflection about what is best for the learner, not about what is familiar to me.

Can I Risk Myself in a Relationship?

A second cluster of questions runs along these lines: Do I dare to let myself deal with this boy or girl as a person, as someone I respect? Do I dare reveal myself to him and let him reveal himself to me? Do I dare to recognize that he may know more than I do in certain areas—or may in general be more gifted than I?

Answering these questions involves considering two aspects. One is the question of risk: Do I dare to take the risk of giving affirmative answers to the queries I have raised? The second aspect is the question, How can this kind of relationship come about between the student and myself? I believe that the answers may lie in some kind of intensive group experience—sometimes called a communications group, human relations group, cooperative group, or whatever. In this kind of personal group it is easier to take the risk because the group provides the sort of psychological climate in which relationships build.

I am reminded of a very moving film, *Because That's My Way* (2), in which a teacher, a narcotics agent, and a convicted drug addict were participants in a group experience. At the conclusion of this filmed group, the high school drug addict said with wonderment in his voice, "I've found that a teacher, a cop, and a drug addict are all human beings. I wouldn't have believed it!" He had never found such relationships with teachers in school. Another film, *Stand and Deliver*, describes the real-life efforts of math teacher Jaime Escalante at Garfield High School in inner-city East Los Angeles. Before Escalante began teaching, no student at Garfield had passed the national Advanced Placement calculus examination. He believed that his eighteen students could learn calculus and take the advanced placement tests for college (3). Escalante began with his students' interests and showed them that mathematics could be a building block for their lives. All eighteen students passed the Advanced Placement calculus examination, twice. They had to retake the exam because the testing agency didn't believe that all the students had passed the first test honestly. Ironically, the students had made similar mistakes on the examination because they had learned from the same teacher. His limitations became their limitations. From 1982 until 1987, 354 students at Garfield High School passed the AP calculus examination. In 1992 Jaime Escalante resigned from Garfield, citing problems with the bureaucracy and the lack of colleagual support. He is now teaching at a high school in northern California.

The level of expectations and the opportunity and desire to learn represents a fork in the road for many students. When students don't have caring persons as teachers, they may take a path that leads to destruction for themselves and others. A colleague once shared with me his experiences of teaching in a maximum security prison at night after teaching sixth grade in an inner-city middle school during the day. He found three barriers to breaking the cycle of crime and imprisonment: All the inmates had a reading problem that placed them outside societal success; they could not identify a teacher in high school that related to them as a person; and the only time someone did pay any attention to them was when they were causing trouble (4). Humanizing our schools may be a better solution to the crime wave sweeping our country than building more prisons.

In conferences about humanizing medical education, we have found the need for relationships in learning to be much the same. Here is one of the outstanding learnings that evolved in those intensive groups: The physicians-in-training discovered that their department chairpersons, medical school deans, and faculty members were human beings—people like themselves. They regarded this discovery as incredible. We had the same experience in dealing with the Immaculate Heart school system at both the high school and college levels: Students and teachers were able to relate as persons, not as roles. It was a totally new experience on both sides.

Although I have seen the highly positive results of an open and personal relationship between learner and facilitator, I don't mean that it would be easy for me to achieve it in every class or with every student. I know from experience that to show myself as I am—imperfect and at times admittedly defensive—seems to be a personal risk. And yet I know that if the relationship between myself and my students were truly a relationship among people, much would be gained. If I were willing to admit that some students surpass me in knowledge, some in insight, some in perceptiveness in human relationships, then I could step off the teacher pedestal and become a facilitative learner among learners.

What Are the Students' Interests?

Here is another question I would ask myself: What are the interests, goals, aims, purposes, passions of these students? I would want to ask the question not only collectively, but individually. What are the things that excite them, and how can I find out?

I may be overconfident, but I think the answer to this question is an easy one. If I genuinely wish to discover a student's interest, I can do so. It might be by creating a climate in which it is natural for interests to emerge. Although young people have been greatly deadened by their school experience, most do come to life in a healthy psychological atmosphere and are more than willing to share their desires.

It impresses me as I think back that I can recall no teacher who ever asked me what my interests were. That seems an amazing statement, but I believe it is a true one. Had a teacher asked, I would have told her about wildflowers and woodland animals and the night-flying moths. I might even have mentioned the poetry I was trying to write or my interest in religion, but no one asked.

Although more than sixty years have gone by, I remember one question a teacher penciled in the margin of a freshman theme. I had written, I believe, about something I had done with my dog. Alongside the description of some action I had taken, the teacher wrote, "Why, Carl?" I have always remembered this marginal note, but it is only in recent years that I realize the reason for the memory. It stands out because here was a teacher who seemed to have a real personal interest in knowing why I, Carl, had done something. I have forgotten all the other wise comments written on my themes, but this one I remember. To me it shows how rarely a student realizes that a teacher really wants to know some of the motives and interests that make the student tick. So if I were a teacher, I would like very much to make it possible for students to tell me just these things.

How Can I Unleash Curiosity?

This is the fourth question I would ask myself: How can I preserve and unleash curiosity?

There is evidence to show that as children go through our public school system they become less inquiring, less curious. It is one of the worst indictments I know. The provost of the California Institute of Technology has told me that if he could have only one criterion for selecting students it would be the degree to which they show curiosity. Yet it seems that we do everything possible to kill, in our students, this inquisitiveness, this wide-ranging, searching wonder about the world and its inhabitants.

A California university professor whom I know is finding his own way of preserving the zest of inquiry. He wrote a letter to me in which he said, "I want to tell you about some of the outcomes your *Freedom to Learn* has had for me and my students" (5). He told me that he had decided to adapt each of his psychology courses to make them freer:

> ❦ *I was careful to explain to the students the assumptions underlying the approach we were going to try. I further asked them to consider seriously whether or not they wanted to take part in such an "experiment." (My courses are elective. . . .) No one decided to drop out. We—the class and I—created the course as we went along. (There were sixty in the class.) It was the most exciting classroom experience I have ever had, Carl! And, as it turned out, the students were equally excited. They turned in some of the best work . . . that I have ever seen from undergraduates. Their excitement was contagious. I found out later, from several different sources, that students in this course were constantly being asked by roommates, by peers in the cafeteria, etc., "What did you do in class today?" "How is the course going?" I had a constant stream of students requesting to visit the class.*
>
> *Perhaps the most meaningful evaluations for me came from those students who said that they had not learned as much as they could have, but that this was their own fault: they took the responsibility for it. There is so much more to tell, Carl, but I don't want to belabor the point. What I did want is that you know how enthusiastically these students responded to the opportunity to learn—in ways that were important for them. And how freeing it was for me as a fellow-learner.*

How Can I Provide Resources?

Another question I would ask myself is, How can I imaginatively provide resources for learning—resources that are both physically and psychologically available?

I believe that a good facilitator of learning should spend the majority of preparation time in making resources available to the young people with whom he or she works. To a large extent with all children, but particularly with bright children, it is not necessary to *teach* them, but they do need resources to feed their interests. It takes a great deal of imagination, thought, and work to provide such opportunities.

My son is a physician. Why? Because in a forward-looking school in the junior year of high school, each student was given a number of weeks and considerable help in trying to arrange a two-week apprenticeship. My son was able to obtain the consent of a physician who found himself challenged by the naive but often fundamental questions of a high school boy. He took Dave on hospital rounds and home visits, into the delivery room and the operating room. Dave was immersed in the practice of medicine. It enlarged his very tentative interest into a consuming one. Someone had been creative in thinking about resources for his learning. I wish I could be that ingenious.

How Can I Nurture Creativity?

If I were a teacher, I hope that I would be asking myself questions like this: Do I have the courage and the humility to nurture creative ideas in my students? Do I have the tolerance and humanity to accept the annoying, occasionally defiant, occasionally oddball questions of some of those who have creative ideas? Can I make a place for the creative person?

I believe that in every teacher education program there should be a course on "The Care and Feeding of Infant Ideas." Creative thoughts and actions are just like infants: unprepossessing, weak, easily knocked down. A new idea is always very inadequate compared with an established idea. Children are full of such wild, unusual thoughts and perceptions, but a great many of them are trampled in the routine of school life.

Then, too, as the work of Getzels and Jackson has shown, there is a difference between those students who are bright and those who are both bright and creative (6). The latter tend to be more angular in their personalities, less predictable, more troublesome. Can I permit such students to live and find nourishment in my classroom? Certainly education—whether elementary, college, or professional training—does not have a good record in this respect. So Thomas Edison was regarded as dull and stupid. Aviation only came about because two bicycle mechanics were so ignorant of expert knowledge that they tried out the wild and foolish idea of making a heavier-than-air machine fly. Educated professionals would not have wasted their time on such nonsense.

I hope that perhaps in my classroom I could create an atmosphere of a kind often greatly feared by too many educators—an atmosphere of mutual respect and mutual freedom of expression. That, I think, might permit the creative individual to write poetry, paint pictures, produce inventions, or try out new ventures without fear of being squashed. I would like to be able to do that.

Chase McMichael, a senior majoring in physics at the University of Houston, received two patents in 1993 as the co-developer of a levitation bearing that nearly eliminates mechanical friction. Perhaps what is most interesting about this inventor are his memories about school and the route he took to making a milestone invention that could save the world billions in electrical costs by cutting down on friction in motors.

He was labeled in high school as having attention-deficit problems and dyslexia. His high school guidance counselor indicated that he was "not college material" (7, p. 1e). According to a lengthy interview in a Houston paper, he was mostly a *B* and *C* student in high school. "He wasn't much interested in classes. He always wanted to know the point of the knowledge" (7, p. 10e). The lack of support from his school did not stop him from dreaming about coming to a major university and working with the leader in the field of superconductivity, Professor Paul Chu. After doing some reading on his own, he became intrigued with the idea of creating a flywheel that would spin forever. "I'm going to have to build the best bearing in the world" (7, p. 10e). From the beginning, the university has adjusted to his needs. Because of his dyslexia, he is allowed extra time on his tests and is making *A*'s and *B*'s in college. I wonder how many potential Chase McMichaels have succumbed to negative school feedback, resulting in a tremendous loss for the individual and the world.

Is There Room for the Soma?

Perhaps a final question would be, Can I help the student develop a feeling life as well as a cognitive life? Can I help him or her become what Thomas Hanna calls a *soma*—body and mind, feelings and intellect?

I think we are well aware of the fact that one of the tragedies of modern education is that only cognitive learning is regarded as important. I see David Halberstam's book *The Best and the Brightest* as the epitome of that tragedy. Those men who surrounded presidents Kennedy and Johnson were all gifted, talented people. As Halberstam says, "If those years had any central theme, if there was anything that bound these people, it was the belief that sheer intelligence and rationality could answer and solve anything." Certainly they learned that viewpoint in school. So a complete reliance on the cognitive and the intellectual caused this brilliant group to lead us little by little into the incredible quagmire of the Vietnam War. The computers omitted from their calculations the feelings, the emotional commitment, of people who had little equipment and no air force but who were fighting for something in which they believed. This omission proved fatal.

The human factor was not put into the computers because "the best and the brightest" had no place in their computations for the feeling life, the emotional life of individuals. I hope very much that the learning that takes place in my classroom might be a learning by the whole person—something difficult to achieve but highly rewarding in its end product.

AN EXAMPLE

You may well ask if there are schools in which the teachers can give generally positive answers to the questions I have raised. There are many such schools, and one is carefully described by Karen Volz Bachofer, who followed the development of O'Farrell Community School in San Diego for four years (8). We can visit O'Farrell Community School through Bachofer's words:

> ✹ *Only in schools do we expect the new to occur while everyone is still working on the old. It's like trying to rebuild an airplane while it's in the air. At some point, one must either land the plane to make repairs or take the time to design an aircraft which meets the increasingly rigorous specifications and customer demands. If real change is to occur in schools, we need to start thinking differently about the ways in which we approach school reform. We must begin to realize that we can no longer afford to patch the plane while it is in flight. Instead, we must take the time to thoughtfully and purposefully redesign our schools so that they meet both the needs of all students and world-class standards.*
>
> *O'Farrell Community School, which opened on September 4, 1990, is a middle-level school in San Diego, California, that evolved as a result of such thoughtful and purposeful planning. It represented one of the most extensive restructuring efforts in San Diego city schools. In January 1988, following the decision to move San Diego's School of Creative and Performing Arts (SCPA) to a new facility, district planners began discussing the possibility of opening a new neighborhood school concept in the old SCPA buildings. That school would become O'Farrell, the future home for 450 students during its first year and over thirteen hundred students in subsequent years.*
>
> *In October of 1989, O'Farrell's principal and the first seven teachers began to meet weekly to plan a school that would meet the educational needs of young adolescents. District personnel, university professors, social service agency representatives, parents, community members, and colleagues were invited to join the team at their planning meetings. In addition to on-going planning meetings, team members visited a number of schools involved in*

similar restructuring efforts nationwide, and participated in a number of faculty development activities throughout the summer. These planning efforts, supported by both the district and private foundations, were essential to the development of O'Farrell's vision, program and structure.

Visitors to O'Farrell Community School almost always get their first look at the campus by participating in a student-led school tour. Tour guides lead visitors through classrooms, where students are working with base-ten blocks to solve algebraic equations, discussing a piece of literature in a Socratic seminar, working in pairs to identify the parts of a cow's eye, or creating a Civil War adventure game in one of the school's Macintosh computer labs. Student tour guides also demonstrate the use of the computerized reference systems in the library, explain the services offered in the school's Family Support Services Wing (which brings social and health services . . . directly into the school), and provide an overview of O'Farrell's philosophy, history, and structure. And, as one might imagine, they answer question after question after question. The fact that O'Farrell students take responsibility for welcoming almost one thousand visitors to the school each year is noteworthy. What is remarkable is the fact that every O'Farrell student serves as a tour guide at least once while a student is at O'Farrell.

Currently, O'Farrell Community School is a restructuring inner-city magnet school serving an ethnically and linguistically diverse group of approximately 1,350 sixth, seventh, and eighth grade students in southeast San Diego, California. The school is divided into nine educational families, and all but the most severely emotionally and physically handicapped students receive the same high-level, enriched curriculum within the educational family structure. Daily instructional blocks link the subject areas of Humanities (language arts and social studies), Technics (mathematics, science, and computers) and physical education into an interdisciplinary core curriculum. Fine arts, music, and foreign language share a Discovery block each day. These interdisciplinary programs are tied together through schoolwide nine-week thematic units.

The O'Farrell program, developed by different thinkers including teachers, administrators, parents, and community members, blends student-centered, activity-oriented learning experiences with state-of-the-art technology and community service in an effort to meet the social, intellectual, psychological, and physical needs of middle-level youth. Every decision made at the school reflects a commitment to provide the best education possible for all students. At O'Farrell, the students come first.

All students at O'Farrell have teacher-advocates and meet in homebase advisory groups on a daily basis, and all-school-wide town meetings are held regularly to share information, have discussions on issues important to the school community, and strengthen their identity with each other. Innovative scheduling allows teachers in every educational family to have daily common preparation time, to develop interdisciplinary curricula, make educational family decisions, and meet with students and parents. The professionalization of teachers and environments which support high-quality teaching and learning are central to O'Farrell's approach, and echo the philosophy described in Caught in the Middle, the 1987 California Middle Grades Task Force Report. "When teachers and students are grouped together into interdisciplinary teams it creates an educational glue that holds together almost every other aspect of the school program."

In order to achieve a reduced class size, approximately 23:1, O'Farrell elected not to fill the traditional vice-principal and counselor positions at the school. Instead, they used funds which would have gone to these positions to supplement the school's staffing budget, reducing the student-teacher ratio during the core instructional time. As a result, the leadership and administrative duties that would have been handled by a vice-principal and head counselor are shared by the teaching staff. The position that normally would be described as the principal is held by the Chief Educational Officer (CEO), who provides leadership for all of the educational families, is another advocate for students, and fulfills schoolwide organizational duties.

At first glance, O'Farrell's innovative structure, interdisciplinary curriculum, and staffing patterns might seem to be the most important features of the school's program. The O'Farrell staff is quick to point out, however, that the single most significant element of the program is the school's shared vision statement, which clearly articulates the staff's commitment to ensuring that all students have the same access to and success in an academically enriched curriculum. The development of the O'Farrell vision was the staff's first priority during the planning process, and that vision continues to focus all decision making at the school on what is best for students—not what is most convenient for teachers, what is easiest to schedule, or what is aligned most closely with district procedure.

A commitment to academic excellence and equity, a structure which ensures strong relationships among teachers, students, and parents, and a school culture which communicates high expectations to all students contribute to the success of the O'Farrell program. Students at O'Farrell know that their teachers expect that *they will do well, and rely on their teachers' encouragement, assistance, and unwavering belief in their abilities as they move toward becoming independent learners.*

In February 1993, we asked a group of O'Farrell students what they thought about their school. One student noted, in typical seventh-grade fashion, that the "food at O'Farrell can blast your taste buds—Cajun fries, ice cream bars, and other excellent foods at a low price!" Most of the other students, however, said that their teachers were what they liked best about O'Farrell.

Amy   The best thing I like about O'Farrell is the teachers, because they try really hard to help us learn and be respectful. They also try really hard to understand our feelings and our modern ways of life.

Raquel   Another great thing about O'Farrell is that the teachers care about the students very much. They try to make changes that involve helping the students. Sometimes the teachers will go out of their way to help the students and make sure that students understand the assignments either for class or homework. Some teachers will stay after school to make sure that the students can finish their assignments.

Ikeo   The teachers are not just teachers, they are also friends.

Laurie   The teachers here are always there for you and you can count on them to teach interesting things that get you really into it.

Johnetta   I really admire the teachers because it seems like they really care about our grades and about our futures. If you want to come to this school you'll probably think the same.

Glen   One of the things about O'Farrell that I like is the teachers. They stretch their neck for us to get an education, but some of us still lay around and do nothing.

Shonna   I think the best thing about O'Farrell is the teachers because they help you learn. Even though they can sometimes be strict, they always know how to respect the students' ideas and not make unremarkable [*sic*] statements about them. When my little sister comes to O'Farrell next year, I hope the teachers treat her with the same respect they treated me with.

Antoinette   There is a lot I like about O'Farrell, but the main thing is the teachers because they never stop believing in you. No matter what, they always go out of their way just so that they can help you to do better. The people here care.

These responses illustrate students' strong identification with, and appreciation for, their teachers' efforts, as well as an awareness of their own responsibilities in the teaching-learning process. Clearly, the O'Farrell vision has become an integral part of the school's culture, and is valued by students and teachers, alike. Each O'Farrell teacher wears a name tag identifying him or her as a member of the "O'Farrell Dream Team," and the CEO's name tag identifies him as the "Keeper of the Dream." The O'Farrell Dream is exemplified by a sign that hangs on one teacher's wall— "Smart is not something that you just are. Smart is something you can get."

Comments

It is remarkable that when a student's well-being and discovery of the world become the focus of our efforts and we work as a team toward this end, no one person becomes the star. All the students who shared their thoughts at O'Farrell talked about the *teachers*, not a specific teacher. As we also discovered from the responses of students at HSPVA in Houston, the learning environment and all the facilitators of that learning environment become the key.

The schools served as a place where teams of people from throughout the community could build, not with bricks but with ideas, an environment that had the learner as the center of attention. The team concept also became the foundation for the school's structure, which was built around well-defined families of learners. While the size of the school presented many potential problems, the use of *families* as a unit of learning and caring and as student advocates enabled the teachers and others to break down the barriers to success. These barriers have too long been a detour or, even worse, a dead end for meaningful learning for many students. As the quote from the elementary teacher at the beginning of the chapter indicates, becoming a facilitator requires first listening to the voices of your students.

References

1. The Institute for Education in Transformation at the Claremont Graduate School, *Voices from the Inside: A Report on Schooling from inside the Classroom* (Claremont, Calif.: Claremont Graduate School, 1993).

2. W. H. McGaw, C. R. Rogers, and A. Rose, *Because That's My Way* (Lincoln, Neb.: Great Plains TV, 1971). Film.

3. R. Mendez and T. Musca, *Stand and Deliver* (Burbank, Calif.: Warner Brothers, 1988). Film.

4. H. Jerome Freiberg, *A Conversation with Carl Rogers on Educational Change* (Unpublished manuscript, University of Houston, 1984).

5. L. Rock, Personal correspondence, 1972.

6. J. Getzels and Jackson, *Creativity and Intelligence* (New York: Wiley, 1962).

7. Cheryl Laird, "Big Dreams: Physics Student Is Patented Success," *Houston Chronicle*, 1993, pp. 1e, 10e.

8. K. V. Bachofer, *O'Farrell Community School* (Unpublished manuscript, San Diego City Schools, Planning Research and Evaluation Division, 1993).

CHAPTER 10

WAYS OF BUILDING FREEDOM

◆

"Could I do this in my classroom?" This question, it seems to me, might be raised by the teacher or educator who has been favorably impressed by the preceding chapters. In this chapter, I point to some of the specific ways in which teachers have been able to provide opportunities for more self-reliant learning. I hope these ideas will give both reassurance and stimulation to teachers and others who wish to step into the chilly waters of classroom innovation.

If you want to give your students freedom to learn, how can you do it? We've reviewed some personal and subjective attitudes that are basic to the creation of such a climate. And there is no doubt that the teacher who is in the process of achieving these attitudes will develop modes of building freedom suited to his or her own style, one that grows out of free and direct interaction with students. Yes, you will undoubtedly develop a growing methodology of your own—always the best procedure. Yet it is quite natural for those who are taking the risk of being creative to want to know what others have tried and what ways they have found to implement these personal attitudes in the classroom in such a way that students can perceive and use the freedom offered to them. It is the purpose of this chapter to set forth briefly a few of the approaches, methods, and techniques that have been successfully used by teachers endeavoring to give students and themselves the freedom to learn.

BUILDING ON PROBLEMS PERCEIVED AS REAL

It seems reasonably clear that for learning of the sort that we are discussing, students must be confronted by issues that have meaning and relevance for them. In our culture, we try to insulate our students from any and all of the real problems of life, and this insulation constitutes a difficulty. It appears that if we desire to have students learn to be free and responsible individuals, then we must be willing for them to confront, to face problems.

It seems wise for any teacher to try to draw out from students those problems or issues that are real to them and also relevant to the course at hand. Because students in school are so insulated from dilemmas, it may be necessary to confront them with situations that will later become real problems to them. It is possible to set up circumstances that can involve students and confront each one with a problem that becomes very real.

Young human beings are intrinsically motivated to a high degree. Many elements of the environment constitute challenges for them. They are curious, eager to discover, eager to know, eager to solve problems. A sad part of most education is that by the time our children have spent a number of years in school, this intrinsic motivation is pretty well dampened. Yet the motivation is there, and it is our task as facilitators of learning to tap that motivation, to discover what challenges are real for young people, and to improve the opportunity for them to meet those challenges.

PROVIDING RESOURCES

Teachers concerned with the facilitation of learning rather than with the function of teaching organize their time and efforts very differently than do conventional teachers. Instead of spending great blocks of time organizing lesson plans and lectures, facilitative teachers concentrate on providing all kinds of resources that can give students experiential learning relevant to the students' needs. These teachers also concentrate on making such resources clearly available by thinking through and simplifying the practical and psychological steps the student must go through in order to use the resources. For example, it is one thing to say that a given book is available in the library. This means that the student may look it up in the catalog only to find that it is already on loan. Not every student will have the patience or interest to wait for the book to return. I have found that if I can make a shelf of books and reprints available for loan in the classroom, the amount of reading done and the resulting stimulation to use the library in pursuing individual needs grow by leaps and bounds.

In speaking of resources, I am thinking not only of the usual academic resources—books, articles, work space, laboratory room and equipment, tools, maps, films, recordings, and the like. I am also thinking of human resources—people who might contribute and interest students. Frequently, there are people in the community who might be brought in to illuminate certain problems with which the students are concerned. But clearly, the teacher is the most important resource. By allowing students to know themselves as people, by making knowledge and experience clearly available to the students, a teacher can give help without imposing. The facilitator can outline the particular competencies he or she possesses, and the students can call for help in those areas.

We have examined some of the ways in which a teacher may thus make himself or herself available. Barbara Shiel made herself available for individual consultation to students who were having difficulty with the tasks on which they were working. Gay Swenson made herself available in ways too numerous to list. Bill Romey arranged it so that students could sit in on any course in the department. Ruth Sanford took the students on field trips. Without exception, all of the teachers made themselves personally available in the class sessions.

Richard Dean of the California Institute of Technology taught a course in higher mathematics in a very free fashion. He provided feedback sheets in which he tried to summarize the major problems discussed or resolved in each session (as well as the problems opened up and not resolved) for the use of the class. A student coming into any class meeting was supplied with a feedback sheet from the previous session; the information helped students refresh their minds on what the class had done. Later Dean stated that any student could also volunteer to provide a feedback sheet; in this way, both he and some of the students shared in summarizing the discussions. In addition, Dean or the students frequently would add their own analysis of what had gone on or their own solution to issues and problems that had been raised.

If, instead of spending our time on planning for prescribed curricula, lectures, and examinations, we spent it on the imaginative provision of a multitude of resources for learning, we could come up with many new ways of surrounding students with a learning environment from which they could choose those elements that best meet their needs.

LEARNING OBJECTIVES

Since the 1950s, much of what teachers have been taught about learning has revolved around behavioral objectives. A product of World War II and a hand-me-down from the industrial age, behavioral objectives were designed to segment what students will learn into *observable actions*. Three types of objectives were identified: behavioral, affective, and psychomotor. While the developers encouraged the use of all levels of objectives, in practice most objectives settled at the behavioral and factual recall levels. Few higher-level, affective, or psychomotor objectives were written or included in the teacher's classroom.

Experiential Learning vs. Behavioral Objectives

What was an experiment in the 1950s became the order of the day, as textbook publishers and test developers geared their efforts to low-level thinking, relying on behavioral objectives to improve the quality of teaching. As we saw in chapter 1, this path led many of our nations' schools on journeys of lowered expectations and low-level threshold skills. While many schools continue today to require lesson plans and objectives from their teachers, there are alternatives. If behavioral objectives state what the student will learn, *Experiential Learnings* talk not about an end product but about the conditions of learning. Facilitative classrooms focus on creating the climate for learning and the experiences that support student understanding of the whole rather than its modularized parts.

The following written examples show the differences between behavioral objectives and experiential learnings as reflected in two teachers' classrooms:

> 🦋 *The students will list five contributions of ancient Egypt to modern world societies with 100 percent accuracy.*

> 🦋 *Class members will design, plan, and go on a field trip to visit the ancient Egyptian collection at the fine arts museum.*

In the first statement—the behavioral objective—what the students will learn is predetermined. In the second statement, which encourages experiential learning, the experience is described but the learnings are not predetermined. The teacher's role in the first classroom was to determine that the students could tell the five contributions. In the second classroom the teacher's role was to facilitate learning by supporting her students in their planning and design of a field trip to the Egyptian collection at the fine arts museum. The inclusion of the entire class in designing their learning experience through a field trip provided a broader experience for the students.

These types of experiences are not limited to elementary and secondary schools. At Prescott College in Prescott, Arizona, experiential learnings began in 1966 with a three-week wilderness experience for all incoming freshmen. Twenty-eight years later, the three-week experience continues. It is designed to give new students meaning to the environment that will be their classroom and home for four years. At Prescott College, students learn through field components, independent studies, group independent studies, internships and practica, learning journals, and learning contracts. Each student also designs a graduation proposal with a team of faculty, which sets a path for completing one part of a lifetime journey of learning. Jim Stuckey, the president of Prescott College, wrote in 1990 about the school's philosophy, one that he believes creates a climate for individual learning:

> ✸ *The liberal arts indicate a way of being as much as a body of knowledge. Go beyond gathering information and gaining technical skill. . . . Think about work and procedures and products, about their ultimate costs and values not only to a particular consumer but to society, humankind, and to the earth. Question your own value assumptions, recognize how tentative all our knowledge and understanding are, and yet remain willing to take a reasoned and moral stand. (1, p. 12)*

Prescott College uses many tools for learning. It gives each student and faculty member a repertoire of options and opportunities to learn.

INSTRUCTIONAL CONTINUUM

We learn in many different ways: by listening, watching, questioning, doing, and helping others learn. In most middle and high school classrooms, teaching is framed within a very narrow range of options—usually lecture, questioning, drill, and practice. Studies conducted during the 1980s by Larry Cuban (2), John Goodlad (3), and Jere Brophy and Tom Good (4) support the fact that most classrooms reflect a limited number of approaches to teaching and learning. The strategies followed in too many classrooms conform to a teacher-centered rather than a student-centered approach. The issue is not either one or the other, but a classroom where all participants are co-learners in the educational journey.

   A person-centered classroom can include a variety and range of opportunities for the teacher and students to learn. A continuum of options (Figure 10.1) for teaching and learning should be part of each person's repertoire. In order for teachers and students to become co-learners, teachers need to incorporate the student-focused strategies on the continuum into a person-centered classroom. This chapter highlights a few strategies and identifies resources for many others.

USE OF CONTRACTS

One open-ended device that helps to give both security and responsibility within an atmosphere of freedom is the use of student contracts. There is no doubt that this also helps to assuage the uncertainties and insecurities the facilitator may be experiencing, and we have seen how Barbara Shiel

FIGURE 10.1
Instructional Continuum

Teacher-focused

- Lecture
- Questioning
- Drill and practice
- Demonstration
- Discussion
- Cooperative groups
- Guided discovery
- Contracts
- Role-play
- Projects
- Inquiry
- Self-assessment

Student-focused

Adapted from H. J. Freiberg and A. Driscoll, "Instructional Continuum" in *Instructor's Manual: Universal Teaching Strategies* prepared by H. J. Freiberg, A. Driscoll, and R. H. Stetson. Boston: Allyn & Bacon, 1992, p. 46.

quickly made use of daily contracts with her students. Contracts allow students to set goals and to plan what they wish to do. They provide a sort of transitional experience between the complete freedom to learn whatever is interesting and a learning process that is relatively free but that stays within the limits of some institutional demand or course requirement.

Arthur Combs has used a type of contract for college and graduate students that has some interesting features. He explains at the beginning of the course that each student may obtain any grade she or he chooses. Students who desire a passing grade in the course and want to receive credits for it may certify that they have read a certain amount of assigned textbook material and then pass examinations covering the material. No stigma is attached to this decision. Students who want higher grades must plan for themselves, individually, work that would justify a *B* or an *A* grade. Once the work is completed, the student will receive the contracted grade. This removes any fear and apprehension from class sessions and makes genuinely free discussion possible. Students can differ with the professor without feeling that they may be endangering their grade. They can express what they really feel and think.

Contracts are also helpful in resolving doubts that may exist in the mind of the instructor or the student. If the teacher is dubious that students will be responsible learners and if some students have difficulty believing they can learn without being pushed, then time spent developing contracts will be very helpful to both. Indeed, a number of initial hours in the course may be given over to this process. Using student contracts is one way to evaluate students based on a shared view of both quantity and quality. Traditionally, teachers have decided upon criteria for an *A* grade without including any input from the students. With the use of contracts, the student has an opportunity to share in decisions about evaluation. Contracts can provide activities, motivation, and reinforcement to help students achieve cognitive objectives. They can be used in any subject matter or at any grade level. But like many classroom techniques, contracts should be recognized as an aid to learning and not the only method of teaching.

An Example of a Contract

Because contracts are such a helpful bridge between conventional approaches and a classroom of greater freedom, I present here a very specific description of how a contract may be used (5). An independent study contract was developed with a sixth-grade middle school student in a social studies class. The particular course of study was African history, and this contract was related to the study of Africa (Figure 10.2).

One day in class Cynthia (who is African-American) asked, "How can people survive if Africa is hot and there's not enough food?" We sat down and discussed the assumptions made by her question: (a) that Africa is hot, and (b) that there is no food. The assumptions that she developed were very similar to hypotheses, and they became the basis for our contract. (There should only be a few assumptions because too many may signal the need for a more specific question.)

The first step in using the contract was to explain its function and how it operates in general terms. As I went through the process of explaining the use of contracts, Cynthia was allowed to decide on her level of participation. (Developing a contract with one student was a good way to ease into the use of student contracts. It allowed the teacher to see the problems associated with individualizing instruction, the difficulties of evaluation, and the use of resources.)

Once the contract was written, both parties agreed to try to abide by it. In this particular case (this was Cynthia's third contract), the length of the project was two or three weeks. But in other cases it may be desirable to begin with contracts of a much shorter duration and then gradually increase their scope. During the allotted time period, it is important to interact with the student to find out how things are going. Then you can see if the contract is too difficult, or if it is not challenging enough for the student.

We scheduled a student-teacher conference for every Tuesday and added others as needed during the time of the contract. We also scheduled regular independent working time for Cynthia so that she could use resources in the library or work independently in the classroom. The decision to work in the library or in the classroom was Cynthia's.

FIGURE 10.2
Independent Study Contract

Independent Study Contract

Cynthia S.
Mr. Freiberg

Question: How can people survive if Africa is hot and there is not enough food?

Assumptions:

1. Africa is hot.
2. There is no food.

Independent study time:	Every Tuesday if needed Cynthia will go to the library.
Length of project:	Two to three weeks
Scheduled meetings with Mr. Freiberg and Cynthia S.:	Every Tuesday, plus meetings as needed.
Activities:	Cynthia will find out the answers to the above questions by presenting her findings in the following form:

1. Weather and rainfall maps
2. Interview of Mr. Awad and Mr. Schikongo with a list of ten questions and answers.
3. Diary of films and slides about Africa.
4. Present the findings of her questions to the class.
5. Answer questions about the topic from the class and Mr. Freiberg.

Evaluation:	Cynthia will receive an *A* if all the above (1–5) are answered.
Possible resources:	Almanac Atlas Films and slides in library Mr. Schikongo and Mr. Awad interview Books in the library

Signed:_____

Cynthia S.

_____

Mr. Freiberg

The questions posed at the beginning of the contract—Cynthia's original assumptions—were answered by the activities developed by both the student and the teacher. A rainfall map helped her see that it does snow in parts of Africa and that there is a great deal of rain and vegetation. An interview with two people from different parts of Africa allowed her to learn more about the continent. By keeping a log of films and slides, Cynthia could describe the kinds of things she had seen in them.

She agreed to present her findings to the class, at which point both the class and the teacher were able to question her. During this period of time, the class as a whole had also been discussing Africa, and Cynthia had been in class except on Tuesdays when she went to the library. As a result, she completed much of the regular classwork while she also worked on her independent study project (the two overlapped).

To review: Contracts can be written for any length of time. First contracts usually have a short duration; later they can be expanded according to the student's own abilities. It is important to vary the activities—combining reading, writing, artwork, interviews, oral presentation, and reports in the activity section of the contract. If films are not available, use books. Allow the student to progress to the point of going to the library rather than use library work as an initial activity. It is important, initially, for you and the student to sit down and go over the possible resources. It is also important that the contract be signed and dated.

Now that you have completed a review of the contract, it might help to list the specific elements involved.

Elements of a Contract

1. Decide if the contract will be short term or long term.
2. Develop a general format for a contract.
3. Gather resource material and information.
4. Have a few feedback sessions with the student about progress.
5. State in the contract how the student will be evaluated.
6. Begin with one student; and if the operation is successful, begin the process with another student.

Questions You Should Ask Yourself

1. What is to be done in the contract?
2. Who will do it? (Students may work in groups after their first attempt with a contract has been successful.)
3. What will the student have at the end of the contract?
4. What is the expected outcome for the student? (What will the student take away from the learning experience?)

5. How will you evaluate questions 3 and 4?

6. What resources will be needed?

7. Where will the student find resources independently?

To help yourself write contracts more effectively, you might sit down, perhaps during one of your in-service programs, and simply write a contract with another teacher. For example, you could role-play a student, and the other person could role-play a teacher. You could negotiate a contract, switch the roles, and then negotiate another contract. In that way you could see how close your contract comes to some of the criteria in this particular activity.

At first the learning contracts and other tools for student learning may be primarily teacher-directed; but as students acquire greater understanding of their own power to learn, the contracts will become more student-focused. Jim Stuckey describes the process of developing learning contracts at Prescott College, a process that has been in operation for more than thirty years:

> ✹ *Early in her [the student's] Prescott College career she [may] feel too naive to do a good job of it [developing a learning contract], so her professor will suggest more of the curriculum design for the course or study. As the student becomes more skilled with the processes of the College and more knowledgeable about the world of knowledge and how to access it, she will contribute an ever greater portion to her learning contracts. (1, p. 17)*

Learning that is person-centered provides many options, and the development of contracts is just one of many tools to build freedom.

ENGAGING THE COMMUNITY

Another avenue of approach is to use the learning resources of the community. For example, students at the New Orleans Free School, an inner-city public school in Louisiana, provided community support to the homeless. The students began with background work and study on the homeless. They had to learn how to approach people and how to listen, to analyze their notes to discover the salient points that emphasized the need for this project in their community. As a result, this activity was a far more valuable learning experience than any classroom course I can imagine. There are many other types of community projects. A group of students at the California Institute of Technology (Caltech) in Pasadena decided to study the smog problem in Los Angeles and finally developed such an impressive plan that they were financed by a federal grant.

I should mention one other type of possibility. If a student is particularly interested in working with people, she or he might, with the instructor's help, become an apprentice to a working psychologist, psychiatrist, or social worker in the community. She or he might enroll in a peer group for individuals with similar interests. The student might, in other words, wish to learn psychology experientially.

These very tentative suggestions add up to one major view that I hold—that students, if given real freedom, frequently come up with very exciting learning experiences that they have developed on their own and from which they profit deeply. They can become searchers after knowledge, not passive and temporary recipients of it. They can enter into the process of learning and discover what an adventure it is.

LEARNING THROUGH PROJECTS

Contracts have been used by student-centered teachers to bring life to a lifeless curriculum and meaning to a seemingly unrelated barrage of information. We have read about the need to prepare our youth for a future where information and change become one, where yesterday's knowledge becomes today's history and is outdated in a year or two. Many teachers have made their classrooms person-centered by encouraging students to help build the curriculum through projects. Projects allow both teacher and students to bring together disparate ideas, concepts, and facts into a level of meaning that can last a lifetime. Projects like those at the New Orleans Free School (discussed earlier) allow students to select from areas of interest that also meet a social need in the city of New Orleans. Other projects may reflect the needs of students to find out about issues that concern their age group. Projects may begin with a brainstorming discussion in which ideas are listed on the board and topics are discussed by the class. The teacher's role in designing and implementing projects is to guide, provide resources, and generally facilitate opportunities to learn from the experience.

Projects allow students to find out about something interesting and meaningful. Some projects start with the teacher but quickly become a shared learning experience. There are too few opportunities for teachers and students to be co-learners, and projects provide this chance. Those that present learning opportunities usually are designed to afford a holistic picture to a problem or question posed by students. Some of the best projects are those that lead to more questions. Much like student contracts, projects can begin with a question or a situation that arises in class or in the lives of the students. Projects stimulate all the senses and bring a student in touch with everyday issues from which other learnings can be connected, and they may be completed by students working on their own or in cooperation with others.

The use of projects is perhaps more prevalent in the elementary grades than in middle or high schools, due in part to the way time is structured in our secondary schools. Given the forty-two minute time period in secondary schools, thinking and planning for projects may take several days. However, even this limitation can be surpassed with some collaborative planning with students. As we will see in future chapters, many secondary schools are changing the way in which time is allocated to provide greater learning opportunities.

How often do teachers build bridges between students' daily realities and the classroom? The following example shows how Diane Rabinowitz, a middle school teacher in an ethnically and linguistically diverse middle school with more than 1,100 students in San Francisco, developed a project with her students (6). Using computers, she journeyed with her students as they built bridges between the world of school and other parts of their lives. The class developed a project that looked at the television viewing habits of more than four hundred students at their school. Diane describes this journey with thirty eighth-graders in a computer classroom, providing a picture of how this project began and asking her students to talk about their views of the project (6, p. 1–5):

> ❦ *A familiar scene—I look out across a chasm of yawning students as I present my most well-planned, interesting lesson. I can't seem to catch these students, yet I know there's nothing wrong with their attention span—they spend many hours concentrating in front of the TV set, as recent research tells us. They seem to have more sophisticated awareness of the world than I did at their age. And I think that one major contributing factor is the amount of hours they spend in front of the television set. Young people are assaulted by a barrage of images, characters and situations, which are perhaps their most influential teachers as they construct their own reality; yet little or no effort is made to help them critically examine this experience. These images affect how young people feel about themselves, how they behave with the people in their lives, and any "universal laws" they can glean about how life works. How can we as teachers allow this valuable viewing time to go unexamined? At one time, it was enough to reflect on one's self to heed the warning: "The unexamined life is not worth living." But today, with television media so integral to our lives, we have to say, "The unexamined life in relationship to the media is not worth living." How can this media viewing experience become a bridge between student experience and classroom learning?*
>
> *Many young students also spend over fifty hours a week in front of the television screen absorbing images, fictional and actual, about our world. And nobody fully understands the hold*

that television has had over us, either. For example, has television affected our family structure? In the film "Avalon," one subtheme was that as television viewing increased, family members became increasingly isolated from one another. The large multi-generational family that had gathered together to share Thanksgiving at the beginning of the film was reduced to a lone nuclear family in the blue light of the television by the end of the film. Secondly, has television viewing affected our verbal and written expression? During the Civil War series, aired on Public Television, many people remarked at the eloquence with which the soldiers expressed themselves in letters written home from the front. People wondered what has happened to that eloquence of written expression today. Has it in some way been eradicated by television viewing?

So popular media is not going away; in fact, it is becoming more integrated into our lives and a more accepted way to learn about the world. If I don't watch much television I may not worry about its hold over me, but I do have to be concerned about the youngsters for whom TV watching is a primary activity. To what degree do they believe that this narrow band of experience represented on television is representative of reality? Especially when the producers are primarily interested in ratings, not for the quality of the production, but for the amount of advertising they are able to sell. Can young people's curiosity be aroused about this phenomenon, and will they be interested in studying it?

My interest in this project began with an article by Harlem educator John Taylor Gatto, who, as teacher of the year in New York, called for "Ferocious Debate on Education Aims and Methods" [7]. He cited statistics about how young peoples' hours are so scheduled that they have only minutes per day for self-reflection in which to carve out an identity. Among these statistics was the fact that the average child watches fifty-five hours of TV per week. This figure astounded me, so I gave a simple assignment—a journal entry in which my students were to answer the question: "Name your three favorite TV shows, and tell what you like about one of them." My curiosity was further piqued by their answers. Almost without a plan, our discussion evolved into a mini-survey. We began to ask each other, "How many hours of TV do you watch per night?" (Many students responded seven hours—from 4:00 to 11:00.) We all participated in a lively discussion from which many questions were generated. The next class we wrote and discussed five questions they'd like to ask fellow students about their TV watching habits.

They were very curious about what their peers in the school thought about television. At our next class meeting we developed the beginning of our survey. Their questions were written on the board and the answers were tallied as we went through each question. We decided to take these questions to other seventh period classes to find out if their responses were similar to our class's. Questions focused on student TV watching habits and motivations for watching television.

At first, the students were a bit shy to go to other classes, introduce the survey, and answer any questions fellow students might have. But after their first time out, their spirits were boosted by their success. There is great ethnic and cultural diversity in our student body—a very high percentage of Chinese, Russian, and Latino ESL students who were just learning English, mainstreamed students who had been in special education classes, and students the school has identified as at-risk students. This wide range of students was fully represented in all aspects of creating and administering the survey, as well as responding to it.

We decided to poll all the eighth graders which included about four hundred students. The thirty students created a database and entered the results into their computers. Students worked in pairs to type in the responses. They had to learn how to pose questions to the database, and techniques of rearranging the layout and sorting by category to obtain data for analysis. Suddenly, students were eager to learn computer and statistical techniques because they had both a need and interest.

The following excerpts are from interviews with the students at the completion of the project:

Fan Wa I've never done this kind of work before. It was different from the other projects. The feeling of independence that you don't have to do what the teacher assigned you, instead now you're on your own like a child in a complicated society without any help from parents. It changed my view toward what is called the old method of studying—that is, the students are always . . . passive.

Melissa I [have] never done this process, but I was really excited. When we went interviewing, it really trained us to talk in public. I felt independence and this [will prepare me] for future work. Using a computer to do this survey [is] giving me idea[s] that we shouldn't learn only from remembering. At the last day, when we hand[ed] in the bundle of papers, it really felt great.

Meagan I like mostly going to different classrooms and interviewing other people. I didn't like typing it into the computers because it was kind of boring and I like talking better than typing. . . . I liked the project. It was fun because we got to interview people our own age and see what TV shows [that our] friends liked.

Selby   Our group never had a project like this. Jessica felt excited and interested in the project. Scott thought it sounded dumb and stupid, but later on he liked it. . . . [He] liked going around to different classes and answering their questions. . . . I thought it sounded strange because I never had anything like it before. . . . I liked going around to different classes and passing out the surveys. . . . It made me ask more questions in other classes.

Angie   The . . . thing that made me scared was going to other classes and talking to them. . . . I have never spoken to a lot of people. . . . The . . . thing I mostly liked was finding out information about other students. I think doing a project like this could let me find out information I didn't know, such as finding out how TV affects others, and that would make me sit far back from the TV so it wouldn't affect me. . . . I was shock[ed] to know that a lot of Asian people watched "Fresh Prince of Bel Air" because usually I thought Chinese people watch Chinese channels. And that made me feel better that I could relate to a lot of Chinese people. . . . I felt the project was fun, and hope to do more projects like it.

Dimple   We have never done a project like this before. . . . I liked programming the information into the computer the best. I was really scared when I had to go to other classes to interview the people because I am really shy, but this project helped me get over my fear of being in front of a group of people.

❦ *Students were encouraged to predict how the majority of their peers responded to the survey questions, then used the database to find the statistics to answer their questions. Working in groups, they checked each other's work, making sure the categories searched were relevant to their questions and the statistics backed up the conclusions reached.*
  Here are some of the results they found:

♦ *Most students agree that they learn about current events from watching TV.*

♦ *The majority of students agree that they enjoy reading, and also watch less TV than the fifty-five hours quoted by J. Gatto—between 0–20 hours per week.*

♦ *Among those students who report that they don't like reading, the majority watch over fifty hours of TV per week.*

♦ *The majority of students agree that they learn more from reading than from watching TV, but most also report that TV helps them with their schoolwork and their problems.*

♦ *Although the greater majority of students agree that TV is educational, a majority also agree that they watch it because they have nothing else to do.*

- *Most students reported not knowing if they were physically fit, but among those who say they are not physically fit, the majority watch more than fifty hours of TV per week.*

- *Students were evenly divided over the question of TV helping them with their grammar.*

- *The four favorite shows, in order, were, "In Living Color," "Fresh Prince of Bel Air," "Family Matters," and "The Simpsons." There was very little difference in favorite TV shows between males and females.*

One of the most interesting findings was the following, by a Chinese ESL student: A much greater percentage of males than females reported that watching TV helped them with their moral development. The females were unsure of the moral merit of watching TV. Given that television is still male-dominated, his finding makes sense. Also, given that females are still frequently used as sexual lures to sell products, it is not surprising that the majority of females were doubtful of the moral value of watching TV. . . .

The most challenging part of the project was that students were overwhelmed by the amount of information the survey yielded, possibly because they've never been asked to discuss this topic in school before. And by discussing it, they began the first stages of self-awareness. Yet the investigation has barely begun, and there are many more questions that can be raised about television's influence on perception, thinking, learning, and reality construction. Teachers and their students can compare the mythical heroes and archetypal situations in literature and history with characters in the media. This student-centered study can transform television watching from a passive to an active activity. It is an opportunity for young people to reflect on their generation and the times they live in, as well as how the times are reflected back to them in the media. And it is one bridge between their daily reality and the classroom, which engages them in meaningful learning.

Comments

Reflecting on her role as teacher-facilitator, Diane Rabinowitz concludes with the following observation: "This project represents the beginning of a teacher's journey—the journey of relating authentically with students, of being a facilitator, and of a relationship of trust with students." The students were also touched by the experience of creating new knowledge and the interpersonal experiences of conducting the study with their peers.

Melissa's and Fan Wa's comments reflect a strong sense of independence. Angie, too, realized that there are students different from herself who have similar viewing habits, which presents the opportunity for a common point for discussion. The students learned many lessons, including the use of computers to help gather data. Although the analysis and synthesis of the data led to the students' conclusions, they emphasized the affective experiences in their comments.

It is also noteworthy that both teacher and students learned from the project's experience. Because she was new to the idea of projects for her class, Diane guided the process. As she and the class become more experienced in the use of projects as a learning tool, she will be less a teacher and more a facilitator of learning.

PEER TEACHING

The tutor-tutee relationship is one mode of promoting learning that has many advantages both for the student who is being helped and for the older or more advanced student who is doing the teaching. A noteworthy project of this sort was carried out by two faculty members at the University of Cincinnati (8). They carefully selected seventy-six sixth-grade children to be tutors for an equal number of second and third graders. The children were from inner-city, suburban, and rural schools; and the subject was mathematics. The researchers selected sixth-grade students on the basis of personality, achievement, sense of responsibility, and enthusiasm. They found that these students already had a very good idea of what it took to facilitate learning. There were three training sessions of thirty minutes each. Letters were sent to parents of both tutors and tutees, explaining the project and enlisting their support. On the basis of observation and teacher suggestions, tutors were matched with tutees. There were six thirty-minute tutoring sessions during a two week period.

An evaluation of this very brief experiment showed that many of the tutees increased their mathematical skills; only 12 percent showed little or no progress. Perhaps a more important observation indicated that the tutees "showed greater confidence, more motivation to work, and an improved attitude toward mathematics." The main complaint of the tutors was that there were not enough tutoring sessions. "Tutors gained in their own self-assurance and their willingness to assume responsibility. Several of them worked hard to extend and improve their own knowledge of mathematics" (2, p. 431). Recent synthesis of research supports positive earlier work on peer teaching for student learning (9). Especially in a time of reduced budgets and large classes, tutoring is a resource that might be much more heavily used with gains for all concerned.

CHOICE OF A GROUP

It does not seem reasonable to impose freedom on anyone who does not desire it. When students are offered the freedom to learn on their own responsibility, teachers should also provide for those who do not want this freedom and prefer to be instructed and guided. Shiel recognized this problem and divided her sixth graders into two groups, one self-directed and one conventional. The fact that the children had freedom to move back and forth between these two approaches made this a very happy solution. Richard Dean, in teaching higher mathematics, made it possible for students who did not like the freedom to transfer into conventional sections of the same course.

Such easy solutions may not always be possible, but the facilitator of learning will always wish to consider the problem. If students are free, they should be free to learn passively as well as to initiate their own learning. Those who prefer to follow their own directions and initiate their own learning can meet as a group or can follow any of the various patterns that have thus far been described.

Organization of Facilitator Learning Groups

Is it possible to provide any freedom of learning within large classes? This question is often and deservedly raised. Weldon Shofstall, when teaching prospective high school teachers, came up with an interesting way of handling this problem (10). He set the climate for the class with some general comments:

> ✺ *I am a facilitator of learning, and you are the learner. There is no teacher in the traditional sense. Whether you learn or not is entirely your own personal responsibility. My sole job is to allow you to take this responsibility by using your own initiative. . . . I am always available for personal conferences. You are urged and advised to start these personal conferences during the first week. . . .*
>
> *In addition, personal conferences are very helpful to me as your facilitator because I wish also to be a learner. I can learn only if you raise questions, objections, and make suggestions to me personally.*

He then provides for the formation of relatively autonomous facilitator learning groups:

> ✺ *You will be assigned to an FL group . . . [composed of] seven to ten students. Within this group you can either waste your time and the time of others, or you can find this one of the most stimu-*

lating and worthwhile learning experiences you have ever had. For most of you there will be no middle ground. . . . I will attend your FL group upon the invitation of the group only. Please let me know the day before if you want me to attend your group meeting.

The FL group should select a chairman. It is suggested that the chairman serve for not more than one week at a time. The chairman is the group moderator and must report to me before every FL group meeting. In addition to selecting a chairman, one member of the group should be designated as the group reporter. This person will report to me after each group meeting. It is suggested that the group plan the FL group work and make assignments for not more than two meetings in advance. . . . Failure on the part of individual members to prepare for the group meetings is a serious handicap to the effective functioning of the group.

At the end of each course, Shofstall asked the students to write letters to new students who planned to take the course the following year. Here is an excerpt from one of those letters:

🦋 *To begin with, friend, if you have gone through all of your college career sitting in lectures, taking notes on what the teacher wanted you to get, reading what the teacher wanted you to read, writing or reporting what the teacher wanted you to write or report on, and taking tests over what the teacher wanted you to know at the end of his course—and you like this method of education—then drop this course. . . . But if you are willing to try honestly and sincerely to become involved with assuming responsibility for your own learning, then welcome!*

There are many other ways of dividing up large classes into small, functional, self-motivated groups. Members can be clustered in terms of special interests, in terms of particular topics, or in other ways. The description of Shofstall's method is simply intended to indicate that if we are willing to give as much attention to planning for the facilitation of learning as we ordinarily do for the preparation of lectures, many of the seemingly insuperable problems can be resolved.

The Cooperative Group

A very important example of a development that fosters a climate for significant learning is the cooperative learning group. This approach helps in educating not only students but teachers and administrators about the newer goals in education. There have been volumes written during the past twenty years on cooperative learning groups. Some of the volumes are included at the end of this chapter or at the end of the book.

Cooperative groups are usually created in a class by forming several groups of four students who have different rather than similar abilities. Cooperative learning begins with students learning how to work together. Many teachers begin with simple tasks and graduate to having the groups of four solve problems provided by the teacher and, ultimately, solve problems developed by the group. In general, cooperative groups help with racial and interpersonal relations among group members, help special education students mainstream into regular education classrooms, improve learning as measured by achievement tests, and allow students to develop cooperative strategies for solving problems (11).

The teacher's role in cooperative learning groups is that of a consultant-facilitator and resource to the groups. Changing roles from givers of information to facilitators and resource providers is a difficult transition for many teachers, so begin where you feel most comfortable. It is better to give a little freedom that students can call their own than to give more than you feel comfortable with and then have to take it away. A study conducted by J. M. Moskowitz and associates and reported in a research summary indicates that some teachers use a modified jigsaw approach to cooperative learning, which requires each student to be responsible for one element of the project (12). Each student's work then becomes a piece of the puzzle. For example, a group of four students selected Algeria for their cooperative project. Each student in the group was independently responsible for a piece of important information about the country (such as products, culture, language, or geography). Teachers in this study, however, modified the cooperative approach to the point that it became more like traditional teaching, with which they felt more comfortable. This highlights the importance, for teachers and other educators, of understanding a person-centered philosophy of learning and having the commitment to follow through with giving freedom to students. Activities like cooperative grouping provide opportunities for greater learning only if teachers and students are able to break with tradition and explore other ways of learning.

THE CONDUCT OF INQUIRY

A specialized type of participative and experiential learning, which has been receiving increasing emphasis in recent years, has been developing in the field of the sciences. Various individuals and national groups have been working toward a goal of helping students to become inquirers by working in a fluid way toward discovery in the scientific realm. The impetus for this movement grew out of an urgent need to have science experienced as a changing field, as it is in the modern world, rather than as a closed book of already discovered facts. The possession of a body of knowledge about science is not an adequate achievement for the student today. Today's aim is to get the student away from the misleading image of science as absolute, complete, and permanent.

In order to achieve this aim, the teacher sets the stage for a mind-set of inquiry by posing the problems, creating a responsive environment, and giving assistance to the students in the investigative operations. This environment makes it possible for pupils to achieve autonomous discoveries and to engage in self-directed learning. As described previously in this chapter, Diane Rabinowitz's class became scientists themselves on a simple level, seeking answers to real questions, discovering for themselves the pitfalls and the joys of the scientist's search. They may not learn as many scientific facts, but they develop a real appreciation of science as a never-ending search, a recognition that there is no closure in any real science. It is obvious that if prospective teachers are to facilitate this kind of stimulation of inquiry among their pupils, they must first experience it themselves. It follows that courses in teacher training must be taught in the same fashion as those we have just read about if teachers themselves are to experience the satisfaction of self-initiated discovery in the scientific realm.

This new development in the area of science constitutes a deep challenge to present concepts of teaching. Current educational practice tends to make children less autonomous and less empirical in their search for knowledge and understanding as they move through the elementary grades. This trend is strictly at variance with the aim of those who focus on inquiry. When children are permitted to think their way through to new understandings, the concepts they derive in the process have greater depth, understanding, and durability. They have become more autonomous and more solidly based in an empirical approach.

There is a need to offer teachers a variety of learning experiences. Today, more than ever, the educational system and teachers in particular are faced with a continuing barrage of seemingly insoluble problems. However, we continue to give teachers fifteenth-century tools to deal with twenty-first-century education. The gap between the verbalization of problems and the solutions to those same problems becomes wider. As educators we need to offer those tools that are closest to being practical. We do not expect a carpenter to build a house with only a hammer. Why do we expect teachers to build the educational foundations of children with only one approach?

Like any of the methods described in this chapter, the procedures involved in developing an inquiring state of mind can themselves simply become more ways of imposing a teacher-directed curriculum on the students. I have known this to happen. None of the methods mentioned in this chapter will be effective unless the teacher genuinely desires to create a climate in which there is freedom to learn.

SELF-ASSESSMENT

The evaluation of one's own learning is one of the major means by which self-initiated learning also becomes responsible learning. When the individual has to take the responsibility for deciding what criteria are important to him, what goals must be achieved, and the extent to which he has achieved those goals, then he truly learns to take responsibility for himself and his directions. For this reason, it seems important that some degree of self-assessment be built into any attempt to promote an experiential type of learning.

We have already seen a number of ways of implementing self-assessment. Barbara Shiel settled the problem of grades by mutual discussion with her pupils. Gay Swenson worked cooperatively with her students to establish highly individualized grades. In a class of mine, the students were primarily responsible both for the criteria and for the grade assigned. In other classes, fulfillment of the contract is itself a completion of the self-assessment. Weldon Shofstall gives his students summaries of learnings and self-evaluations made by previous students so that they have some notion of the task. During the whole course, students analyze their personal strengths and weaknesses and confer with other members of the group for feedback. Class grades are decided upon by representatives selected by each group, who meet with the instructor to make their recommendations. In chapter 6 we saw how teachers and administrators could work together in building a foundation of supervision through self-assessment.

It is obvious that there are many patterns to follow in making an appraisal of personal efforts and learning. The particular pattern is far less important than the feeling of responsibility for intelligent pursuit of specific learning goals. One student may choose a very rigid goal such as simply amassing a certain amount of testable information in the field of study. Another may use a course to become more spontaneous in learning, more open to a wide range of stimuli, or more free to be himself in reacting to the available resources. Obviously the criteria are very different for these two individuals. Yet each has functioned as a responsible, professional person functions in society.

OTHER SOURCES

I have purposely limited this chapter to a few general areas and methods that the teacher may wish to consider. There is a wealth of other ideas and ingenious procedures described by those who are directly involved in classroom teaching. The following volumes (although there are many more) may prove helpful to teachers eager to humanize their classrooms:

E. Cohen, *Designing Groupwork: Strategies for the Heterogeneous Classroom* (New York: Teachers College Press, 1986). This book contains strategies for developing practical and humane cooperative learning activities for classroom groups.

H. J. Freiberg and A. Driscoll, *Universal Teaching Strategies* (Boston: Allyn and Bacon, 1992). Written by authors with classroom experience, the book blends research with practical examples of how to implement a range of teaching and learning strategies in elementary and secondary classrooms. In the book teachers talk about the way they implement strategies in their own classrooms.

Gerald I. Pine and Angelo V. Boy, *Learner-centered Teaching: A Humanistic View* (Denver: Love Publishing, 1977). The book was developed from the rich experiences of two teachers. It contains helpful lists of books, films, and organizations that are devoted to a humanistic approach to education.

Shlomo Sharon, ed., *Handbook of Cooperative Learning Methods* (Westport, Conn.: Greenwood, 1993). The *Handbook* provides a comprehensive and practical view of methods for developing cooperative learning in the classroom. The text includes strategies for implementing cooperative learning across content disciplines and examples of implementation in specific subject-matter areas. The book also provides examples of how cooperative learning could be developed throughout a school to the benefit of both students and teachers.

Additional reference sources appear in the section "Resources for Change" at the conclusion of this book.

CONCLUDING REMARKS

I trust that this chapter has made it clear that if you wish to create the conditions for responsible self-directed learning, there are a number of methods already at hand that are congenial to this approach. A few have been discussed and reference made to other sources. These will, I hope, serve as a stimuli for you to develop an expanded repertoire of facilitative approaches that span the instructional continuum. Teaching the way we have been taught is not an option if that way has been dominated by an active teacher and a passive learner. It is reassuring to know, as you work toward creating a classroom climate of responsible freedom, that the relevant research studies and practice in schools show that your students will profit in ways highly important for their future living in a changing world.

REFERENCES

1. J. Stuckey, *Prescott College: A Case Study in Intuitive Quality Management* (Paper presented at Conference on Quality, sponsored by the Sacramento Area Council for Total Quality, Sacramento, August 1990), pp. 12–17.

2. L. Cuban, *How Teachers Taught: Constancy and Change in American Classrooms, 1890–1990* (New York: Teachers College Press, 1993).

3. J. Goodlad, *A Place Called School: Prospects for the Future* (New York: McGraw-Hill, 1984).

4. J. E. Brophy and T. L. Good, "Teacher Behavior and Student Achievement," in *Third Handbook of Research on Teaching,* ed. M. L. Wittrock (New York: Macmillan, 1986), pp. 328–75.

5. H. Jerome Freiberg, "Recipe of Classroom Ideas," in *Professional Development Modules,* ed. W. R. Houston and S. White (Houston: University of Houston, College of Education, Professional Development Center, 1973).

6. D. Rabinowitz, *Bridging the Student Interest Gap Through Media Study* (Unpublished document, San Francisco, 1993).

7. J. T. Gatto, "Teacher of the Year Calls for Ferocious Debate on Education Aims and Methods" (Reprint of keynote address, Santa Cruz, Calif.: New Society Publishers, 1990).

8. I. C. Hill and Tanveer, "Kids Teaching Kids: It Works," *Educational Forum* 45 (1981): 425–532.

9. D. Berliner and U. Casanova, "Peer Tutoring: A New Look at a Popular Practice," *Instructor* 97, no. 5 (1988): 14–15.

10. W. Shofstall, *Training High School Facilitators of Learning* (Unpublished manuscript, Arizona State University, 1966).

11. T. Graves and Nancy Graves, "Recent Research in Cooperative Learning," *International Association for the Study of Cooperation in Education* 9 (1988): 2–23.

12. J. M. Moskowitz et al., "Evaluation of a Cooperative Learning Strategy," *American Educational Research Journal* 20 (1983): 687–96.

CHAPTER 11

THE POLITICS OF EDUCATION

◆

A humanistically oriented teacher often finds that she simply does not fit into a conventional school. The humanistic teacher may feel that she is an alien being in a conventional system. This is not surprising because there are two sharply different approaches to the learning process. I would like to consider these in more detail.

Traditional education and person-centered education may be thought of as the two poles of a continuum. I think that every educational effort, every teacher, every institution of learning could locate itself at some appropriate point on this scale. You may wish to consider your own placement on this continuum as well as your school or educational enterprise's placement.

THE TRADITIONAL MODE

I believe that the following are the major characteristics of conventional education as we have known it for a long time in this country and as it is experienced by students and faculty:

♦   *The teacher is the possessor of knowledge, the student the expected recipient.*   The teacher is the expert who knows the field. The student sits with poised pencil and notebook, waiting for the words of wisdom. There is a great difference in the status level between the instructor and student.

♦   *The lecture, the textbook, or some other means of verbal intellectual instruction are the major method of getting knowledge into the recipient. The examination measures the extent to which the student has received it. These criteria are the central elements of this kind of education.*   Why the lecture is regarded as a major means of instruction is a mystery. It made sense before books were published, but its current rationale is almost never explained. The increasing stress on the examination is also mysterious. Certainly its importance in this country has increased enormously in the last couple of decades. It has come to be regarded as the most important aspect of education, the goal toward which all else is directed.

♦   *The teacher is the possessor of power, the student the one who obeys.*   The administrator is also the possessor of power, and both the teacher and the student are the ones who obey. Control is always exercised downward.

♦   *Rule by authority is the accepted policy in the classroom.*   New elementary school teachers are often advised, "Make sure you get control of your students from the very first day." Another common maxim, expressing the grimness of this control, is "Don't smile at your kids before Christmas." The authority figure—the instructor—is very central in this education. Whether greatly admired as a fountain of knowledge or despised as a dictator, the teacher is always the center.

♦   *Trust is at a minimum.*   Most notable is the teacher's distrust of the student. The student cannot be expected to work satisfactorily without the teacher's constant supervision. The student's distrust of the teacher is more diffuse—a lack of trust in the teacher's motives, honesty, fairness, competence. There may be a real rapport between an entertaining lecturer and those who are being entertained. There may be admiration for the instructor, but mutual trust is not a noticeable ingredient.

♦   *The subjects (students) are best governed by being kept in an intermittent or constant state of fear.*   Today there is not as much physical punishment in schools, but public criticism and ridicule and a constant fear of failure are even more potent. In my experience, this state of fear appears to increase as we go up the educational ladder because the student has more to lose. The individual in elementary school may be an object of scorn or regarded as stupid. In high school there is the added fear of failure to graduate, with its vocational, economic, and educational disadvantages. In college all these consequences are magnified and intensified. In graduate school, sponsorship by one professor offers even greater opportunities for extreme punishment due to autocratic whim. Many graduate students have failed to receive their degrees because they have refused to conform to every wish of their major professor. Their position is often analogous to that of a slave, subject to the life-and-death power of a despot.

♦ *Democracy and its values are ignored and scorned in practice.* Students do not participate in choosing the goals, the curriculum, or the manner of working. These things are chosen for the students. Students have no part in the choice of teaching personnel or any voice in educational policy. Likewise, the teachers often have no part in choosing their administrative officers. In addition, they often have no part in forming educational policy. This is in striking contrast to all teaching about the virtues of democracy, the importance of the free world, and the like. The political practices of the school stand in direct opposition to what is taught. While students learn that freedom and responsibility are the glorious features of our democracy, they see themselves as powerless, with little freedom and almost no opportunity to exercise choice or carry responsibility.

♦ *There is no place for the whole person in the educational system, only a place for her intellect.* In elementary school the bursting curiosity of the normal child and the youngster's excess physical energy are curbed and, if possible, stifled. In secondary school the one overriding interest of all students is sex and the emotional and physical relationships between the sexes. Teachers almost totally ignore these issues and certainly do not regard them as major areas for learning. There is very little place for emotions in the secondary school. In college the situation is even more extreme—only the rational mind is welcomed.

THE POLITICS OF CONVENTIONAL EDUCATION

In discussing the politics of this traditional mode, I use the term *politics* in its sociological sense, as in "the politics of the family," "the politics of psychotherapy," or "sexual politics." In this sense, politics has to do with control and with the making of choices. It has to do with the strategies and maneuvers by which one carries on these functions. Briefly, it is the process of gaining, using, sharing, or relinquishing power and decision making. It is also the process of the complex interactions and effects of these elements as they exist in relationships between people, between a person and a group, or between groups.

Looked at from this perspective, the politics of traditional education is exceedingly clear. Decisions are made at the top. "Power over" is the important concept. The strategies for holding and exercising this power are (a) the awarding of grades and vocational opportunities; and (b) the use of aversive, punitive, and fear-creating methods such as failure on exams, failure to graduate, and public scorn. It is the politics of a "jug and mug" theory of education: The faculty (the jug) possesses the intellectual and factual knowledge and causes the student to be the passive recipient (the mug) so that the knowledge can be poured in.

We see this concept of conventional education practiced all around us. It is not often openly defended as the *best* system. It is simply accepted as the inevitable system. Occasionally, however, it acquires a spokesperson, as in the case of Dr. Jay Michael, who was the vice president of the University of California. Michael strongly opposed two recommendations that had been made to the legislature. One recommendation was that a small percentage of the budget be set aside for innovation in education. This suggestion was completely unacceptable to him. The other recommendation was that education should include both affective and cognitive learning. Of this Michael said, "There is knowledge that exists separate and apart from how a person feels . . . and that accumulation of knowledge is *cognitive*. It can be transmitted, it can be taught and learned." To include affective learning would, he feared, reduce the importance of cognitive learning "to a level unacceptable to scholars" (1). Here is explicit support for the politics of the jug and mug theory. Teachers know best what should be transmitted to the student.

THE PERSON-CENTERED MODE

The person-centered approach is at the opposite end of the scale. It is sharply different in its philosophy, its methods, and its politics. In our present educational culture, it cannot exist unless there is one precondition. If this precondition exists, then the other features listed may be experienced or observed at any educational level, from kindergarten through graduate school.

This is the precondition:

> A leader or a person who is perceived as an authority figure in the situation is sufficiently secure within herself and in relationships with others to experience an essential trust in the capacity of others to think for themselves, to learn for themselves. She regards human beings as trustworthy organisms. If this precondition exists, then the following aspects become possible, and tend to be implemented.

◆ *Facilitative leadership has a ripple effect.*   Leaders who facilitate others are themselves facilitated. Shared decision making gives a new voice and weight to decisions, allowing all those affected to support and be supported. Many administrators feel isolated and exposed in the decision-making process. Being inclusive allows a sharing of the responsibility for the learning process. It is difficult to imagine a positive learning environment in which all adults in the school are not supporting each other in the pursuit of the best learning climate for each student.

◆   *The facilitative teacher shares with others—the students and possibly parents or community members—the responsibility for the learning process.*   Curricular planning, the mode of administration and operation, the funding, the policy-making are all the responsibility of the particular group involved. Thus, a class may be responsible for its own curriculum, but the total group may be responsible for overall policy. In any case, responsibility is shared.

◆   *The facilitator provides learning resources from within herself and her own experience and from books, materials, or community experiences.*   She encourages the learners to add their own resources based on their knowledge and experience. She opens doors to resources outside the experience of the group.

◆   *The student develops his or her own program of learning, alone or in cooperation with others.*   Exploring their own interests, facing their personal wealth of resources, students make choices about their individual learning directions and carry the responsibility for the consequences of those choices. They work within a facilitative learning climate. In meetings of the class or of the school as a whole, an atmosphere of realness, of caring, and of understanding listening is evident. This climate may spring initially from the person who is the perceived leader. As the learning process continues, it is more and more often provided by the learners for each other. Learning from each other becomes as important as learning from books or films or work experiences.

◆   *The facilitator focuses on fostering the continuing process of learning.*   The focus is primarily on fostering the continuing process of learning. The content of the learning, while significant, falls into a secondary place. Thus, a course is successfully ended not when the student has learned all she needs to know, but when she has made significant progress in learning *how to learn* what she wants to know.

◆   *A student reaches personal goals through self-discipline.*   The learner recognizes and accepts that discipline is her own responsibility. Self-discipline replaces external discipline. (See chapter 12, which focuses on the question, "Is there discipline in person-centered classrooms?")

◆   *A student evaluates her own learning.*   The learner is the primary evaluator of the extent and significance of student learning, although this self-evaluation may be influenced and enriched by caring feedback from other members of the group and from the facilitator.

◆   *In this growth-promoting climate, the learning tends to be deeper, proceeds at a more rapid rate, and is more pervasive in the life and behavior of the student than is learning acquired in the traditional classroom.*   The direction is self-chosen, the learning self-initiated; and the whole person (with feelings and passions as well as intellect) is invested in the process.

THE POLITICS OF PERSON-CENTERED EDUCATION

Consider the political implications of person-centered education. Who has the essential power and control? Clearly, the learner does—or the learners as a group, including the facilitator-learner. Who is attempting to gain control over whom? The student is in the process of gaining control over the course of her own learning and life. The facilitator relinquishes control over others, retaining only control over herself.

I see two strategies used in relation to power. The facilitator provides a psychological climate in which the learner is able to take responsible control. The facilitator also helps to de-emphasize static or content goals and thus encourages a focus on the process, on experiencing the way in which learning takes place. The decision-making power is in the hands of the individual or individuals who will be affected by the decision. Depending on the issue, the choice may be up to the individual student or the students and facilitators as a group. It may also include administrators, parents, members of the local government, or community members. Deciding what to learn in a particular course may be entirely in the hands of each student and the facilitator. The decision to build a new building affects a much larger group and therefore must be dealt with by that group.

Each person regulates modes of feeling, thought, behavior, and values through her own self-discipline. So it is obvious that the growing, learning person is the politically powerful force in such education. The learner is the center. This process of learning represents a revolutionary about-face from the politics of traditional education.

THE THREAT OF THE PERSON-CENTERED APPROACH

I have slowly come to realize that it is in its *politics* that a person-centered approach to learning is most threatening. The teacher or administrator who considers using such an approach must face up to the fearful aspects of sharing power and control. Who knows whether students or teachers can be trusted, whether a process can be trusted? One can only take the risk, and risk is frightening.

Person-centered education is threatening to the student. It is much easier to conform and complain than to take responsibility, make mistakes, and live with the consequences. In addition, students have been directed for so many years that they long for the continuance of the security of being told what to do. Just this week, a faculty member told me of sharing with students the responsibility for learning in a course on marriage and the family. Even in a course with such an enormous potential for significant personal development, the initial student reactions were largely ones of alarm: "How will we be graded?" "How many exams?" "How much of the text are we supposed to study?" Clearly, responsible choice is frightening, a fact we do not always recognize. Another colleague who teaches high school geometry shared her gradual movement away from worksheets to projects. The students complained that worksheets would better prepare them for the college tests. The teacher responded that the projects they selected may better prepare them for life.

I hardly need to mention the threat to the administrator. Time and again I have observed that if one teacher in a traditional system, without talk or fanfare, institutes a person-centered process of learning in one classroom, that teacher becomes a threat to the whole system. The ferment of responsible freedom and shared power is recognized for what it is—a revolutionary force—and it may be suppressed. Naturally, the conventional members of the system do not say that they are opposed to a democratic process or to responsible freedom. The most frequent reaction to the threat is "This idealistic notion is very commendable as a dream, but it just wouldn't and couldn't work in practice."

This statement implies that person-centered education is neither practical nor effective. But the facts and examples presented throughout this book stand in complete contradiction to the statement. The comments of students from public schools like Houston's High School for the Performing and Visual Arts, the New Orleans Free School, O'Farrell Community School, Amy 6, Milby High School, and others are also supported by research studies conducted during the past twenty years and presented in chapter 13, "Researching Person-centered Issues in Education." The day is now past when teachers or administrators can dismiss the person-centered approach as an impossible mode of conducting education or as ineffective in promoting learning. The facts support a person-centered approach to facilitating learning.

THE POLITICAL IMPLICATIONS OF THE EVIDENCE

Facilitative conditions make a profound change in the power relationships in the educational setting. To respect and prize the student, to understand what the student's school experience means to her, and to be real as a human being in relation to the pupil is to move the school a long way from its traditional authoritarian stance. These conditions make the classroom a human, interactive environment, with much more emphasis upon the student as the important figure who is responsible for the evaluation of her own experience. Research demonstrates that politics of this humane sort foster all kinds of constructive learning, both personal and intellectual. Furthermore, a lack of such a humane environment works against such learning and is associated with less than normal progress. Under sharply and measurably defined humane politics, students improve in their way of perceiving themselves and in their social behavior. The students who spoke their thoughts about school in the previous chapters reflect a growing sense of what could be: Many, if not all, students, teachers, and administrators could thrive in a person-centered environment. All this is a striking affirmation of the value of a person-centered approach in education.

CAN WE INFLUENCE A PROFESSION?

Would it be possible to move a whole profession toward a more humanistic, person-centered approach? Obviously if we were to attempt this, the strategic approach would provide person-centered experiences for those who were involved in the preparation of the professionals. For instance, there is a bias that the "hard" sciences are more difficult to change than the social or "soft" sciences. To many people, the field of medicine represents a profession that is resistant to interpersonal change. But there does exist an interesting example of an effort to involve a whole profession—the medical field—in a person-centered approach to learning. The story is one from which we may learn.

More than twenty years ago Orienne Strode-Maloney, a member of our Center, whose former husband had been a physician until his death, initiated a plan for helping physicians to be more human in their relationships. She elicited support and encouragement from the dean of Johns Hopkins University Medical School and from others, including me. A program was developed; it was aimed at medical educators, the people most responsible for the attitudes of young physicians.

The first four-day workshop on Human Dimensions in Medical Education was held in June 1972. We had been worried that high-status medical personnel would not respond to a program carried on by a nonmedical staff. Consequently, we were surprised and pleased that more than fifty chose to come, a large proportion of them deans of medical schools or chairpersons of departments. We found the attendees to be generally dubious about whether or not the experience would be worthwhile. For a few, the program was not very profitable, but the great majority left the workshop with many new personal and professional learnings. We also included some medical students and interns, so that the viewpoint of the physician-in-training would be represented. This proved to be a very wise move. Our staff was surprised to find that those attending this conference and the succeeding ones felt that they gained more of what they wanted from the small, often highly personal intensive groups than from the sessions on how institutions might be changed. Consequently, the small groups were made more of a central focus for future conferences.

What did the participants gain? I think it might be best to let a few of them speak for themselves through their letters and questionnaire responses:

Faculty member   Enjoy "teaching" more—don't feel the fantastically unreal drive to "keep up" or "get ahead" or get "one-up" as much—don't feel guilty when you haven't read the latest. Relate on a much more human level to students, faculty, and personnel.

Medical school dean   In these weeks since our experience, I'm still gaining drive, understanding, warmer relations at home, an urge to know colleagues better, an ability to relate to others. . . . It works! I sense a closeness to my group members that has rarely happened before.

Professor   It gave me a far greater awareness of students as persons.

Third-year medical student   My experience there was the most meaningful and valuable part of my medical education to this date. The exposure to genuine, dynamic interactions between people from the medical community has sustained me throughout the process of becoming a physician.

Chairman, Department of Surgery   To say it in a few words, I learned a lot. Medicine and medical education desperately need what sessions like this have to offer. On the plane coming back I decided to build a requirement for training in human relations into our surgical internship and residency program as we develop it.

Notice that many of these responses indicate a freer communication and a greater sharing of power.

Since that beginning, the program has grown very rapidly. There have now been many of these four-day conferences with more than one thousand participants. Nearly every medical school in the United States has been represented, and members of foreign schools are beginning to attend. A number of those attending wished they might have more extensive training in group facilitation so that they could be more effective back home. As a consequence, a number of ten-day conferences have been held. Somewhat more cognitive material has been presented in them, although the best training for a facilitator is still the experience of learning to be more of oneself with a group. A frequent reaction was the wish that others in one's department or medical school attend. Consequently, team attendance was encouraged. A number of medical schools have had five to fifteen educators attend, and they constitute a support group for each other when they return to their school.

Most important of all have been the many requests to hold similar conferences in the medical school itself. Here is one example from the chairman of a Department of Surgery:

❦ *I would be interested in pursuing the idea of a cooperative venture between your group and perhaps four medical schools to set up a specific program aimed toward the development of the whole physician and a more humanistic approach to the teaching and practice of medicine.*

A number of medical schools have now initiated such humanistic programs, adopting different forms suitable to the situation but having a common goal of turning out doctors with experience and training in effective interpersonal relationships.

In one of these medical schools, a unique and pioneering program was strongly supported by the dean who had himself attended one of the early workshops. This school held a four-day conference involving intensive group experience for all of their incoming students, the thirty faculty members who would be facilitating those students, and the school staff (registrar, secretaries, librarians). The facilitators of the intensive groups were physicians from other medical schools in the region who had attended our ten-day programs. Deep levels of communication were achieved among faculty, students, and staff. Can you imagine a situation in which ninety incoming students and spouses were on a first-name basis with all of their teaching faculty—sharing as equals their hopes, dreams, anxieties, concerns, fears; interacting as persons in their classes, not as roles? The situation constituted a revolution in professional education! Feedback from all levels has been enthusiastic. This same group of students and their teaching faculty continued to meet in a two-day, off-campus conference every six months throughout their medical school career. Another revolution!

This whole program for humanizing medical education has led to dramatic changes in curricular thinking in a number of schools. It is bringing about in faculty and students the very attitudes we have described as being effective in promoting a humanized process of learning. It is creating a person-centered context for turning out physicians who are both competent and human.

CONCLUSION

I ask myself why such a program is growing so rapidly in medical education while there are few comparable programs—and, so far as I know, no real sustaining desire for such programs—in most of our schools of education and other teacher-training institutions. I believe there are several answers. In the first place, physicians are accustomed to changing their practice as new knowledge and new ways of treatment develop. A doctor eagerly seizes upon the newest, most effective way of dealing with an old disease and is rewarded for so doing. I believe there are very few rewards in the teacher-training field for educators who are trying out new ways. Another element is that the physician is continually exposed to feedback and is accustomed to learning from mistakes. The death of a patient, the autopsy, and a review by a board of peers may tell the physician that either a serious mistake was made in diagnosing a disease or selecting a treatment or that death was unavoidable. A patient who develops a serious side effect from some new drug confronts the physician with the necessity of fresh learning. It is to physicians' political and financial advantage to be open minded and changing. But long-term feedback is very rare in education. A teacher educator almost never learns about the curiosity killed, about the people damaged or the potential lost as part of a misguided pathway to the classroom. In the same light, teacher educators rarely see their successes. Feedback that could give vitality to teacher education is too politically threatening.

My conclusion is that we may see a person-centered approach to education developing strong roots in alternative schools, in universities-without-walls, and in specialized situations such as medical education before it has a major impact on our larger teacher-training institutions. A rigid power structure recently imposed by state mandates results in a greater barrier to the person-centered change.

But colleges of education do not have a monopoly on resistance to change. Recently at a conference on Effective Practices in Urban Schools, a high school teacher stood up during a small group meeting and announced: "I went through an alternative certification program in which we were told to sit on the kids, not let them get to us. You were the only person to say treat the students like people, don't wait until Christmas to smile and it's OK to be real in the classroom." A second teacher at the same high school came up after the session and explained that she (the first teacher) was a great teacher and the kids were always the center of her attention.

Yet the challenge and the possibility remain. Clearly, steps could be taken in teacher education not unlike those beginning to have a real influence on physician education, with the purpose of bringing about a more human and effective learning climate in our classrooms. Becoming a facilitator is more rewarding and energizing if you share your experiences with others—you don't need to be alone on this journey. The politics of person-centered education lends itself to creating friends and allies who will facilitate your own process of becoming a facilitator, as you in turn facilitate theirs. The section called "Resources for Change: A Learning Community" at the end of this book provides a wealth of resources including people who could become part of your learning network. Do we, as educators, wish to take those steps or will the politics of traditional education continue to stand in the way?

REFERENCES

1. As reported in the *Los Angeles Times*, 3 December 1974.

CHAPTER 12

IS THERE DISCIPLINE IN PERSON-CENTERED CLASSROOMS?

◆

Good question. And one usually asked by teachers, parents, and administrators who have not experienced person-centered learning. Yes, there is discipline in a person-centered learning environment: *self-discipline.*

In the broader context of life, self-discipline is knowledge about oneself and the actions needed to grow and develop as a person. The goal of most teachers is to encourage self-discipline, but the path many take to this goal is misdirected. Too often the cooperation teachers seek from students in order to teach does not allow for real engagement in the learning process. Teachers find themselves imposing their requirements for order without relating them to student requirements for learning. Discipline becomes mandated rather than developed. The differences between building self-discipline and imposing discipline is the balance point between the traditional classroom and a person-centered learning environment.

Self-discipline is built over time and encompasses multiple sources of experiences. There is no one path, model, or program that leads to self-discipline in all students. Self-discipline requires a learning environment that nurtures opportunities to learn from one's experiences—including mistakes—and to reflect on these experiences. But what does self-discipline look like and how is it achieved? Perhaps the best way to describe it is through a series of brief vignettes based on school and classroom examples.

EXAMPLES FROM THE CLASSROOM

Self-directed Active Learning

❧ *The students in this active second-grade classroom are working at four learning centers scattered around the room. At the writing center, four students are writing about butterflies they saw earlier in the day. There is only room at the writing center for four students at one time, and two additional students want to enter the center. The two students look at a board near the writing center and see that all the "tickets" have been taken. They also look at the timer and see that two students have another ten minutes left at the center. The two waiting students write their names on a small notebook-sized chalkboard, which will hold a place at the writing center for them. Then they go to the reading bookshelf and continue reading books they started the previous day.*

Choice, managing one's time, setting goals and priorities, and maintaining a sense of order are part of self-discipline. Very young children can flourish in environments that have freedom of choice and yet have structure. The limitations of space, materials, and time require some form of organization. Too often the organization benefits a few students or the teacher, but rarely both. In the previous example the organization avoided unnecessary conflict between the students at the writing center and allowed them to make good choices. Students in this class had freedom to move about, make decisions regarding what they would learn for parts of the day, and interact with each other. The teacher provided the structure, but students had freedom of choice within that structure.

The Helping Tree

❧ *In a preschool for four and five year olds, children are walking to a board that has a paper tree attached to it. On the tree are leaves that show the names of every student in the classroom. Why are students placing their names on the tree? They're not. They are placing the names of students who have helped them in some way that week. The names on the tree are put there by students, the teacher, or other teachers and people in the school. Parents and siblings may also add leaves in recognition of help and support provided at home. The child's help is described on the back of the leaf in a drawing or in simple words. The leaves are not counted, but each month the leaves are removed and placed in a box by the teacher, and the helping tree is ready for new leaves. The teacher and children are all smiles when the tree is full and leaves are ready to be stored. At the end of the month all the leaves are piled on the table so that everyone can see how many times children in the class have been helpful to others.*

Helping and caring for each other is part of self-discipline. In a considerate and cooperative environment, the *Helping Tree* can be an important lesson about caring for each other. In a competitive environment, however, the *Helping Tree* can result in a competition for who gets the most leaves. The teacher in the previous example tried to avoid this pitfall by emphasizing the combined efforts of the class.

In building self-discipline, the importance here is not the *Helping Tree* activity but the philosophy behind it. Person-centered activities without a person-centered philosophy can be harmful to building authentic self-discipline. This is an important point, and one that is misunderstood by many people. The attainment of leaves, rather than caring for and helping one another, is a misdirected goal that needs to be avoided.

Classroom Constitution

🦋 *It is the first day of school, and an eighth-grade class is gathered around in a circle talking about class rules that need to be included this year to allow everyone to learn. The class decides to develop a classroom constitution that everyone will sign. The teacher sets the tone by suggesting that the rules need to be stated in the positive and that everyone, including herself, will sign the constitution. The students start with a preamble: "We the people of Room 213, to have a more perfect learning environment, agree to the following rights and responsibilities."*

The teacher follows this same process in each of her six classes. Because of limited wall space, all six constitutions are on a wall chart. A student from each class volunteers to flip the chart to his class's constitution each day.

By the middle of the year, the students in the fourth-period class decide to revise the constitution to delete an area that is no longer needed (tardies) and add one that is becoming a problem (listening to each other). The teacher notices that students take more responsibility for their actions when they have a part in developing a framework for those actions.

A social fabric is created in the classroom not unlike the social compact that is part of our democratic foundation. Behaviorist-oriented approaches to discipline ignore the potential growth experienced by students who use democratic principles in the classroom. Instead, hierarchical and at times authoritarian models require that all things flow from the top—which is exhibited, for example, when rules are posted in the class-room prior to the beginning of school. However, many teachers have found that students become reluctant participants in this process. When a school system operates from the top down, each person on the hierarchy passes on the orders to the next level. The ripple effect ends in classrooms where teachers and students have minimal input into decisions that directly affect them. If the school does not operate in a caring way for teachers, they have more difficulty finding the physical and emotional energy to be more caring for their students.

Trying to create a cooperative social fabric in the classroom that excludes 99 percent of its participants is counter to what we know about building human interpersonal relations. Students begin seeing the rules as *your* rules not *our* rules. As the previous classroom example indicates, there are reasonable ways to create a compact of understanding for the type of classroom each person needs.

Classroom Opportunities for Dialogue

🦋 *Each morning the sixth-grade students in Ms. Gomez's class write in their journals, read while they are propped up on pillows, or talk into a tape recorder about their thoughts. The teacher may read the journal if the page is left open, but a folded page signals that the student's writing is confidential. The same is true for the tape recording. In addition to this morning activity, the students have a regular class meeting to talk about what's going well and what's an issue for group concern and problem solving. As the students gather around in a circle, anyone, including the teacher, may bring a topic to the group for discussion. Ms. Gomez finds that the journal time and the class meetings help connect the students with each other and with her. Many of the problems she had last year with students, such as not respecting each other, fighting, and name calling, have nearly disappeared.*

Listening to others and to one's self is part of the building blocks to self-discipline.   Children bring to school more than their pencils and books. With increasing frequency, they also bring trauma, abuse, conflict, and anger from a world that is anything but child-centered. Before children can learn about the rain forests, they must often learn about themselves. Time spent in talking, listening, and providing productive outlets for children and youth is time well spent.

Students As Peacemakers

🦋 *Two students from an inner-city middle school square off to fight in the school yard. A crowd of students gathers around. There is high excitement and tension in the air. The usual situation is for the crowd to shout encouragement for the fight to begin. But this time two students in the crowd, who are known as medi-*

ators, begin talking to the two combative students: "Come on, a fight's not going to solve anything," says one. "You're smarter than this," says the other. After listening for a few minutes to words of peacemaking from the mediators, the combative students drop their hands and a discussion begins among the four students. The crowd thins, but the two students trying to defuse the situation still remain. After a short while the conflict is resolved, and the four students head off to their classes.

The two middle school students from the crowd had mediator training, learning how to defuse conflict and potentially violent situations without placing their own safety in jeopardy. They talk about mediating.

"No one loses face," explains one. The other says, "We try to help you solve your problems if you have difficulties with another person. We get together and mediate. It's like a council." The council is a schoolwide meeting held each week to discuss issues and solve problems. "Another kid can relate to you closer than maybe the teacher can."

"Does it work all the time?" I ask.

They say, "It doesn't always help, but sometimes it does."

Peacemaking is an important part of self-discipline. With the level of day-to-day media-generated violence in our society, the need for peacemakers is of prime importance. Students need to see specific role models of peacemaking and experience the benefits of seeking alternatives to violence. There will always be some level of conflict when people come together with different attitudes, values, and beliefs. However, conflict can lead to greater understanding rather than greater hostility.

Student mediators learn several important lessons. First, that they can have a positive influence on their learning environment. Second, as students they have additional tools for mediating their own conflicts with others. Third, they begin to understand that self-discipline is an outgrowth of helping others work out their conflicts.

Students As Facilitators

Substitute Teacher Managers

🦋 *Ms. Johnson, a second-grade teacher, is home with the flu and a substitute teacher will have her class today. The following is a sequence from the first five minutes of class.*

"Good morning, class. My name is Mr. Davis and I will be your teacher for the next few days." He acknowledges a student's raised hand: "Yes?"

"Mr. Davis, I am the Substitute Teacher Manager, *and Ms. Johnson gave me a picture seating chart for you and a brief description of how our class works. I am also your assistant today, along with Sarah, Lanita, Sedrick, and José who will take*

care of getting the forms to the office and passing out and collecting papers. There are other students listed on the pocket chart on the wall who have responsibilities in class if you need them to help." Unlike the select few who become teachers' helpers in many other classrooms, the management positions in Ms. Johnson's classroom are open to all students (1).

After school Mr. Davis writes a long letter to Ms. Johnson about how great her class behaved. He explains that he had not realized that students so young could take such responsibility. He would welcome teaching in her class again.

Teaching Ourselves

❧ *At 5:00 A.M. the telephone rings at the assistant principal's home. His wife answers the phone and takes the message that Ms. Wilcox is sick and cannot be in school today. The assistant principal's wife hangs up the phone and goes back to sleep.*

Ms. Wilcox has taught world, American, and state history for nearly twenty years at a rural high school that serves students from a nearby town and several counties. After attending a summer university course that emphasized the human side of learning and the need to involve students in the day-to-day operations of the classroom (1), she implements a program entitled Consistency Management in her own classroom.

Initially she meets with each of her seven classes and encourages them to talk about the conditions necessary for the classroom to work for all of them; she explains that she has needs for herself just as the students have needs for themselves. Together they list the jobs that will allow the classroom to operate as a place in which everyone has an opportunity to be a citizen rather than a tourist. A list of twenty jobs is posted (for each class), and students volunteer to secure a job by writing a job résumé that explains why the position is important and how they can do the job. Once the students select their jobs, Ms. Wilcox has a short job training orientation for all students. Because there are more students than jobs, she sets a time period of three weeks for each job. All students taking a new job work with the previous job holder to learn the specifics of the job. The jobs are posted on the wall with the job descriptions developed by the classes. No student is ever fired from a job. The teacher just spends a little extra time with any student who is having difficulty. If a student is absent, another student who has held the job previously takes responsibility for the day.

What happens next becomes the talk of the community. The message about Ms. Wilcox's absence does not make it to the assistant principal, and a substitute teacher is not notified. All seven of Ms. Wilcox's classes meet without her. In every period, student facilitators teach the day's lessons, present projects, have discussion groups, and send the attendance slips and other paperwork to the office on time for each period. Neither the teachers in the rooms around her class nor the administration know that Ms. Wilcox is not at school. Not until seventh period, when the office needs her for an unrelated matter, does anyone realize that her classes have taught themselves all day. While the administration is quiet about the "day the students taught themselves," word quickly spreads throughout the school and into the community. Ms. Wilcox later praises the students in each of her classes for taking the responsibility and having the self-discipline to learn and cooperate without her being there. She describes as both satisfying and rewarding the degree of responsibility students can take when given the opportunity.

Trust is part of building self-discipline.   Ms. Johnson and Ms. Wilcox trusted their students. The students, in turn, took the responsibility to conduct class and respond to the usual administrative demands because they had participated in all the responsibilities of the classroom throughout the year. I have been told by substitute teachers that in classes in which teachers rule with an iron hand, students explode into a frenzy of misbehavior when a substitute is their teacher. Ms. Johnson and Ms. Wilcox both had an implicit relationship with their students, one that had been built over time and resulted in each student in their classes taking responsibility without being told by an adult what was necessary to learn. These students didn't need a baby-sitter for the day; they could work and learn on their own. One striking point in the Wilcox vignette is the lack of interaction teachers have with other adults. A teacher was missing for seven hours and no one knew but her students. The example highlights the isolation many teachers experience during a typical day.

A Circle of Friends in a 1st Grade Classroom

❦ *Susan Sherwood, a first-grade teacher of eighteen years, describes one of her classes, which included a student with severe multiple disabilities (2, p. 41). Her reference sources are noted at the end of this chapter.*

> *Ann. Age 6. Severe multiple disabilities. Birth trauma. Head injured. Moderate to severe mental disabilities. Hemiplegia to right side of body but ambulatory. No right field vision. Small amount of left peripheral and central vision. Color-blind. Verbal.*

Pacing back and forth in the entryway, I pondered the details in my mind. As I anticipated Ann's arrival on the area agency education bus, I vacillated between calm conviction and near panic. Three days before, the special education teacher had greeted me with a request for a full-time integration placement. In light of my conviction to meet the needs of all students, my answer was instantaneous. Now I wasn't quite so sure.

As a teacher of young children for 18 years, I know that every class has a wide range of abilities and problems. This particular group of 21 students was no different. Their intelligence range, as measured by the Cognitive Abilities Test was 68–137 (excluding Ann's evaluation). She was reading at the 8th grade level; Sarah had been diagnosed as learning disabled, James as hyperactive; Mike was adept at mathematics problem solving; Erica was a 6 year old in puberty; and so on. Indeed, Ann was not so different. All needed to belong to our classroom community and to accept their own strengths and limitations before they could freely accept others. To develop confidence, instill love of learning, and enhance self-concept, the teacher builds on each child's uniqueness—creating a motivating and challenging atmosphere where all children are free to work cooperatively. Learn from mistakes, take risks, and rejoice in accomplishments. Such a classroom community is a support system for each of its members.

Special educators coined the term "a circle of friends" to describe the framework of peers, friends, and adults in the natural environment that surrounds a child with severe multiple disabilities and offers mainstream support [a, b]. Only the term itself, however, is new to the classroom teacher who has worked to build these relationships in his or her classroom all along.

Just as circles of friends draw the lives of children together, networking within the classroom links special educators and regular educators together in common goals. . . .

In social interactions, nonhandicapped children are good role models. By observing what they see, the handicapped imitate appropriate social behaviors and engage in fewer inappropriate ones [c, d]. I was amazed at the ability of my students to provide structure for Ann's activities in the absence of an adult aide. For example, when Mike noticed that Ann needed assistance, he would gather the necessary materials, quietly approach her, and firmly direct her task. On one occasion, when she flatly refused to participate, he unemotionally prodded her, "You have to because you're a 1st grader, and these are the things first graders do." Then, without a pause, with the same sense of purpose as an adult, he directed her to trace the letters.

Of course, to promote Ann's independence, we had to adapt basic 1st grade materials to enable her to follow directions and participate routinely. For example, to allow her easy access to her supplies, we affixed a wooden block to the top of her desk to hold pencils, crayons, and her name stamp in an upright position.

On some academic tasks, such as rote counting by one's and five's to one hundred, Ann was capable of full participation. At other times, we struggled creatively to supply her with parallel activities so that she could still feel part of the group.

We also initiated the "facilitator of learning" role for each supporting adult on our classroom team. This means that their primary purpose was to assist Ann's integration; however, each team member was to support any child when not directly involved with Ann. In this way, the other children did not perceive Ann as having a special helper.

As I reflect on this past year, I know that Ann's life has been touched in many ways by her peers and teachers because she was afforded a free and public education in a regular classroom. Yet the integration process isn't easy. At times, it can become all-consuming. With no right answers, however, we cannot allow ourselves to be constrained by past practice. Don't be afraid to try. We can capitalize on mistakes and transform them into learning experiences and opportunities to creatively solve problems. My vision for education is students, parents, educators, and administrators working cooperatively to make learning positive and empowering for each student within a regular classroom.*

Mainstreaming has opened new learning opportunities for many students. In the past, students like Ann were segregated into a self-contained classroom with other students like herself. The realization that all students need to learn together in the least restrictive learning environment has been an important change in the classroom during this century. The public laws (e.g., P.L. 94–142), which created the groundwork for the mainstreaming of students into regular classrooms, have been at the forefront of creating the possibility of facilitative learning for all students.

Building Self-discipline through Freedom

What do all these vignettes have in common? They portray self-discipline as making choices, organizing time, setting goals and priorities, helping and caring, listening, constructing a social fabric, being peacemakers, trusting, and, perhaps most important, participating in free and open learning environments. The vignettes collectively give a picture of how freedom and responsibility are linked to developing self-discipline. Students and teach-

---

* Excerpt from Sherwood, Susan K. (1990). "A Circle of Friends in a First Grade Classroom," *Educational Leadership* 48,3. Reprinted with permission of the Association for Supervision and Curriculum Development. Copyright 1990 by ASCD. All rights reserved.

ers become partners in building a shared learning environment based on freedom of choice and freedom to make mistakes.

The freedom to learn requires a special understanding of what it takes to establish an open learning environment. Granting freedom is not a method, it's a philosophy. Unless you really believe that students can be trusted with responsibility, you won't be successful. But you can't build that philosophy out of thin air; you have to build it out of experience (3).

Self-discipline begins in small steps and grows with the individual. I shudder to think of a three-hour course on self-discipline being offered at a school or university. The course on self-discipline is the course of life, and schools and classrooms are part of our life experiences for eight hours a day. The movement from external discipline to self-discipline takes time. The freedom needed to nurture self-discipline will be a new experience for both teachers and students. There is always a risk in trying something new, and students who have been stifled in the past won't suddenly embrace new responsibility and freedom without support and encouragement.

Don't grab freedom if you are uneasy about it. It's better to have a little freedom that you can be easy with than to try to go all the way in giving your students responsibility for their learning and then get cold feet and try to pull it back to yourself. That can be disastrous. It's better to take small steps that you really mean and can stand by instead of giving freedom all at once. Giving students freedom means that they are going to make some mistakes in handling that responsibility. And that means a complete rethinking of the ordinary classroom procedure. Mistakes are the most valuable way of learning, provided the students are encouraged to examine what they do (3). The experience of responsibility combined with learning from one's mistakes is the foundation of new ideas. The earlier a child experiences both freedom and responsibility, the more natural the process.

THE PUBLIC'S VIEW OF DISCIPLINE

Unlike other institutions (church and the government), schools have been attended by 99 percent of the population. Public opinion polls about education conducted by the Gallup organization and Phi Delta Kappa show that discipline in schools has been a leading concern for more than thirty years. In 1971 a Gallup poll found discipline to be third behind finances and integration/segregation in a list of the biggest problems in public schools; in a 1982 poll, it ranked first. In 1992 a lack of discipline in schools again ranked third, behind school finance and drugs (4).

A comparative study of teacher concerns about discipline problems in the 1940s and the 1980s shows dramatically different concerns (Figure 12.1). In the 1990s the list would gain a new category: gangs. It is important to note that teacher concerns in the 1940s reflect issues that originated at the school, while teacher concerns of the 1980s reflect societal problems that have become part of everyday school life.

FIGURE 12.1
Discipline Problems Then and Now

1940s	1980s
Talking	Drug abuse
Chewing gum	Alcohol abuse
Making noise	Pregnancy
Running in the hallways	Rape
Getting out of place in line	Robbery
Wearing improper clothing	Assault
Not putting paper in wastebaskets	Burglary
	Arson
	Bombing

Dr. Harold L. Hodgkinson, *Discipline Problems Then and Now* (Washington, D.C.: Institute for Educational Leadership, Center for Demographic Policy). Used with permission.

Being Proactive

The list of teacher concerns reflects a society that has become disengaged with its young. When frustration leads to violence against property and people, we need to look at the root causes, not just its symptoms. I recall a meeting with teachers from West Virginia at a statewide teachers academy in the mid-1980s. We discussed the emergence of drugs in elementary schools as well as the gang violence and disorder in many urban schools. One teacher said, "Those problems won't happen here." A return visit five years later resulted in a very different response. "We have all those problems here," responded a middle school teacher. The other teachers nodded their heads in agreement. A fifth-grade teacher said, "We did nothing to prevent the problems, and now we spend large parts of our day responding and reacting to problems; many of us are worn out with 'management by crisis'." The cost in human lives and financial resources is much greater when problems are ignored and human interaction becomes a strategy of last resort. Preventing problems is clearly a better approach than trying to intervene.

Why Do Youth Join Gangs?

Since earliest times people have joined groups. Groups provide protection from the unknown; they provide a source of identity and linking with others, and they give a sense (often false) of control over one's environment. Primary and extended families are perhaps the most basic group, but there are other types: religious, school (such as band, chess, debate, and computer groups), sports, business, investment, and many others. Each group serves a function for the individual and collectively for the group as a whole.

Not all groups, however, are socially constructive. Since World War II, male youth gangs appeared in the late 1950s and early 1960s in the inner cities. They have reappeared in the 90s as a national problem. Why do students join gangs? There are a number of possible theories, including an observation that the lack of positive adult male role models in childhood leads to later changes in children's needs and personalities. Youth gangs of the 1950s may have been a result of the wartime absence of fathers during the formative years of their young sons during World War II and the Korean War. Today most male gang members come from fatherless homes or from homes where the father was also a gang member.

When students join gangs, they seek a source of identity. Almost all gangs have a name, a color, and an insignia to distinguish them from other gangs. Names such as Black Dragons, Black Disciples, Skinheads, Crypts, and Bloods give images of power and control, something that is missing from the lives of many of the youth who join these gangs. Gangs also provide a type of clanship, a support system that in the beginning is seductive. Members of a gang, in a distorted way, see the gang as a substitute for a family that, in most cases, is dysfunctional. Later, most gang members realize that joining a gang gives them no future, but often they are already stuck. "You can't just turn in your letter of resignation," quipped one gang member. Discipline is imposed through the threat of violence and, many times, death. "Trying to leave a gang without some help from the outside is suicide," explained a gang member.

Wes McBride, coauthor of *Understanding Street Gangs*, is an expert on gangs who works for the Los Angeles County Sheriff's Department. He indicates that membership in gangs and the resulting violence "is symptomatic of other root problems, like dysfunctional families, failure of schools, lack of jobs, despair, boredom and intense poverty." The lack of a vision for the future and the fact that "no one cares" are key reasons given by gang members for joining gangs (5, p. 6a).

But there is hope for these troubled students, and it begins with caring. Caring provides a degree of protection from the harshness of life outside of school. The theme of caring, described in chapter 1, was cited in every school interview with students who love school. If there is a factor that should be changed first in our classrooms and schools, it is that they become more caring places. With that step, many of the problems we face now and will continue to face in the future can be prevented.

WHAT DO WE KNOW ABOUT DISCIPLINE?

Discipline and classroom management are discussed extensively in books and articles on the subject. There are numerous lessons to be learned from the works of others about how person-centered classrooms and schools can be developed. The summaries that follow look at some of what we know about the kind of self-discipline that leads to person-centered schools and classrooms. Additional sources are listed at the end of the chapter.

Caring classrooms provide a better environment for learning and discipline. Eric Schaps and Daniel Solomon report on children's prosocial *development*: their kindness and the effects of the Child Development Project (CDP) on creating a caring community in seven elementary schools in two California districts. They found that schools can undermine a sense of a caring community when teachers focus on competition or working alone. The competitiveness of school guarantees that some students will succeed and others will fail. According to the authors, CDP schools focus on consideration and concern for others, interpersonal awareness and understanding, and the ability and inclination to balance consideration of one's own needs with consideration of others' needs (6, p. 39). Schaps and Solomon describe three key elements of the CDP program: (a) cooperative learning, (b) developmental discipline, and (c) literature-based approaches to reading. They followed a cohort of students from kindergarten through sixth grade and conducted classroom observations, interviews, and surveys with more than three hundred students during the six-year period.

The students work in non-competitive groups to learn. In literature-based approaches to learning, students read from complete book-length stories rather than from a reading textbook. Developmental discipline emphasizes the need for motivation that comes from the child rather than from external sources. Students receive neither rewards nor punishments as part of the discipline program; the emphasis is on self-discipline. Schaps and Solomon found a broad range of benefits for the students in classes using the CDP program:

> It helped them to improve social competence, interpersonal behavior . . . and understanding, endorsement of democratic values, and higher-level reading comprehension. They also reported themselves to be significantly less lonely in class and less socially anxious. Overall we believe the program is fostering a healthy balance between the tendencies to attend to their own needs and to attend to the needs and rights of others. (6, p. 40)

The authors also report, over a three-year period, that students perceived their classrooms to be more caring than did students in comparison classrooms. The development of a caring community was "measurably more effective at promoting all aspects of children's development—intellectual, social, and moral" (6, p. 42).

Students like school more when teachers are positive. The idea that you don't smile until Christmas is founded in folklore not research. Research synthesized by Vernon and Louise Jones indicates that a study by Bud Fredericks concluded that teachers who use more positive statements than negative ones, starting at the beginning of the year (September 20–27), have students who still like school more than fifteen weeks (January 22–24) into the school year. Conversely, the number of students who were interviewed during the third week of January who responded positively to the question "Do you like school?" dropped 48 percent in classrooms where teachers used *less* than 65 percent positive statements (7, pp. 42-43).

External rewards should be used sparingly, if at all.   A conclusion drawn from Walter Doyle's research on incentives for student learning in the *Handbook for Research on Teaching* suggests that "using rewards for desired behavior or academic performance can have deleterious effects on intrinsic motivation" (8, p. 423). Learning that is interesting and comes from the learner requires no external incentives. Learning that is boring and is externally determined seems to require enhanced external rewards to keep a minimal level of student engagement. If incentives are used, they should be of a temporary nature, with the goal of the learning environment being the primary incentive.

The degree of order in the classroom is relative to the types of learning activities in the classroom.   According to research conducted by Elizabeth Cohen at Stanford University on group learning, classroom order is a relative factor depending on the type of instruction in the classroom. For example, although the level of noise when students are working in small cooperative interactive groups is higher than in traditional classrooms, cooperative learning groups still function best when there is less direct teacher supervision. Cohen reports that she and her colleagues found that a teacher's direct instruction during group work inhibited the group's interactions and lowered student learning gains (9, p. 75). Conversely, they repeatedly found that "the larger the proportion of students talking and working together, the greater . . . the learning gains on standardized tests" (10, p. 9).

Student development of classroom norms reduces discipline referrals and increases student learning.   Students from five schools whose teachers attended professional development seminars in an instructional management program (Consistency Management) over a one-year period had fewer referrals for discipline and significantly higher achievement as measured both by criterion assessments and national achievement tests (11). Consistency Management is an instructional management program designed to create a positive and active learning environment for the students and a supportive working environment for the teachers and administrators. In one urban elementary school with six hundred students, discipline referral data, which covered a nine-year period (before and after the program began), showed a significant reduction in referrals: from ninety to three over a three-year period. Teachers found new ways to involve students, eliminating the need to send students to the principal's office. In a second urban elementary school, one with only 276 students, 109 students were referred to the office for discipline the year before the program began. During that same year, thirty-four students had suspension warning letters sent home, and twenty-four were actually suspended. One year later, there were nineteen referrals to the office for discipline, no suspensions, and only one warning letter (regarding an after-school altercation). Of the nineteen referrals to the office, nine were sent by substitute teachers (11). Parents from the five program schools evaluated their children's schools more positively in areas of safety, order, and learning climate than did parents from comparison schools. Observation data also indicated that students affected by the program (during the last year of data collection) enjoyed a more active learning environment. A source book on the program is listed at the end of this section.

Students like schools least when behavioristic discipline programs are used.   A study by Emmer and Aussiker investigated the effects of different management programs on discipline referrals, student attitudes toward school, and student learning. The researchers found that the more humanistic programs (for example, Teacher Effectiveness Training by Thomas Gordon and the Adlerian model by Rudolf Dreikurs) had a relationship to greater achievement, although none of the programs had a significant reduction in discipline referrals. They also found that students in schools that used Assertive Discipline, a behaviorist-oriented program, liked school less (12).

Perpetuating social class differences in secondary schools can create anger and discipline problems.   Ellen Brantlinger's research, which was reported in the *Journal of Classroom Interaction*, studied the social class struggle of forty low-income and thirty-four high-income students from two junior and two senior high schools in a medium-sized city in the Midwest (13). She found that student family income manifested itself in day-to-day interactions with teachers. The humiliation and anger expressed by the low-income students and the entitlements the high-income students enjoyed in their schooling experiences were in stark contrast to what many see as school's role as the great social equalizer (Figure 12.2). How schools are structured can lead to many of the discipline problems experienced by teachers. Brantlinger found that 57 percent of the misbehavior of low-income students was attributed to hostility and anger while only 8 percent of high-income students' misbehavior could be attributed to these causes.

Brantlinger describes a cycle that led low-income students in her study to fights and aggression. Initially, they felt more vulnerable and had greater sensitivity to comments and actions by others; and when provoked, they retaliated. Usually the students who retaliated received the more severe punishment. The students became angry with themselves and others. They began to see themselves as unworthy, which led to greater vulnerability. Low-income adolescents reported that public humiliation, academic failure, and favoritism toward others by teachers and administrators increased the level of misbehavior and conflict in the classroom. Brantlinger used the students' statements, drawn from interviews, to express their frustrations (13, p. 5):

FIGURE 12.2
*Causes of Anger and the Effects of Low-income Adolescents' Anger
within the Context of School*

Causes of Anger	Effects of Anger
Humiliation	Displacement of anger
	Friction among low-income peers
Derision (sassing, talking back)	Feeling threatened and vulnerable
	Friction with high-income schoolmates
Exclusion	Deliberate non-participation
	Passivity and withdrawal
Failure	Verbal conflict with teachers
	Feelings of unworthiness
Impotency (powerlessness)	Internalized anger
	Giving up
	Dropping out

Adapted from E. Brantlinger, "Adolescents' Interpretation of Social Class Influence on
Schooling," *Journal of Classroom Interaction* 28, no. 1 (1993): 1–12. Used by permission
of the *Journal of Classroom Interaction.* © 1993.

> ❦ *Most preps [high-income students] are snobs and care only
> about those that wear brand names. I try to fit with the styles but
> we're not in a condition where we can have brand name clothes.
> If people think you're really, really poor, then most of the time
> they try to avoid you or look down on you.*

Another student responded:

> ❦ *If a lower class kid sat next to them in the cafeteria they
> would get up and move. They have a real thing about grits.*

A third student stated:

> ❦ *The division of groups in the school bothered me. School
> closed off people I could have been friends with. There were invis-
> ible boundaries.*

Both high-income (57 percent) and low-income students (80 percent)
stated that discipline in the form of consequences was unfairly dispensed to
the low-income students. Affluent students were "talked to" or received
standard consequences for their infractions. However, "penalties of low
income adolescents involved expression of anger by school personnel,

public humiliation and ostracism (e.g., 'bawled out in front of the class,' 'made to sit in the hall,' 'shoved around,' 'yelled at for no reason')." A student who dropped out said:

> ✥ *I hated school. Teachers hassled me. Some was helpful. If you didn't understand they didn't treat you like trash. Mr. E. was a real cool teacher. He helped you if you had a problem. Miss B., she don't like me. The only thing she cared about was being on time. We argued a lot. I wouldn't understand. She'd get mad and say, "I showed you how to do it." She'd make you feel dumb. . . . Most teachers were hard on me. Mr. E. cared about me. Most didn't. (13, p. 6)*

Both groups of students felt the tracking system (college-bound and regular/vocational/special education) had an effect on them. Kim said, "The group [preps] felt proud, we—the lowest—stupid." Coping mechanisms by the low-income students typically involved nonparticipation, which included skipping class, being late, and ultimately dropping out of school. These passive activities were punctuated with outbursts of anger and a menacing personal style used as a defense against what was perceived by the students as a very hostile school environment.

Comments

Teachers and other educators do not create the economic and social conditions that students bring with them to school. However, Brantlinger's study indicates that schools perpetuate the separation of students based on social class and reinforce the perception that some students are unworthy of an education. The research and particularly the student comments are sobering. The level of teacher favoritism, unequal discipline, humiliation, labeling by teachers and students (for example, grits and preps), and the feelings of powerlessness felt by the low-income students, are a design for failure. The causes of anger reflected in Figure 12.2 portray a lack of caring and dignity on the part of teachers and others for all students in the schools. The social class problems reflected in this study are usually missed because individual students' thoughts and feelings are not explored.

But there are alternatives. At the High School for Performing and Visual Arts, for example, (as reported in chapter 1) seniors took the responsibility of diffusing cliques that had developed in the middle schools. Our schools need to show more caring. The low-income students in Brantlinger's study did have a few teachers who cared, but they seemed to be in the minority. The results of research highlight the depth of the problems faced by teachers and principals who want to make their schools and classrooms person-centered.

IS THERE ORDER IN PERSON-CENTERED CLASSROOMS?

Civilization may be viewed as humankind's need to create some order out of life's random events. In prehistoric times hunting and gathering were less predictable than growing one's own food. As basic needs for food, shelter, and safety were met, people had more time for other, more developed activities such as art, music, writing, and later reading. Day-to-day survival was a lesser concern, so people could turn their attention to the world around them. The concept of school evolved from this process of seeking to know more about one's world.

The word *school* can be traced to the Greek, meaning "leisure." During the time of the Greeks, a small class of people, through the labors of others, had the time or leisure to learn. In the same context, a *teacher* was a "guide" for the learner. The term *discipline*, used as a noun, comes from a Latin word meaning "teaching and learning."

Just as civilization thrives on some degree of order and stability, the classroom needs a certain level of order for all people to learn. Therefore, some day-to-day events should be established so that time is spent on learning rather than organizing. As human beings, we have different levels of needs that include the desire to belong; to be safe; to have food, clothing and shelter; to be seen as a person; and to maintain some form of stability and order to carry on our daily lives. These human needs do not change when the child enters the classroom. The interconnectedness of the modern world places a greater demand on us for predictable and consistent ways of doing things. So we establish routines to minimize our need to make a new decision for each and every event.

I recall reading an interview with Albert Einstein about his wardrobe. Einstein was known for having multiple sweaters, all the same color. When asked why he always wore the same clothes every day, he responded that deciding what to wear each day was not a decision he cared to make. He clearly had more important issues on his mind. In the same way, the students I interviewed in schools across the nation wanted a predictably warm, caring, orderly, and peaceful place to learn. Freedom has order, but the order is one that develops from the group, not one that is imposed. Once a compact is reached, however, breaking the compact should result in some degree of consequence.

Consequences for Actions

When a child touches a hot stove, there is a consequence: pain. When a child runs out into the street, there is also a potential consequence: being hit by a car. Adults need to provide safe environments for children to live and learn. Children can help in developing these safe environments along with adults. When consequences become imposed punishment, then the role of teacher as guide is changed to controller, and the role of student as learner becomes that of avoider.

Some school districts require teachers to follow certain discipline programs that focus on external systems of control. The use of punishment or consequence (words that seem to be used interchangeably) operates as if all students are the same, with identical needs and intent. I called these systems *fixed consequences*. Life does not have fixed consequences, but many classrooms operate as if "one size fits all."

Unlike fixed consequences, *rational consequences* have the student try to undo what has been done. If a student spills something, then he or she knows to clean it up. Placing a child's name on the board or adding a check does little to remedy the situation. Let's take another example: Two students who are in a fight are usually sent to the office. But an alternative, in less serious altercations, is to have the students sit down and cool off. Once their anger has abated, a teacher asks them to write a letter about what happened and what alternatives they could have used. I find it curious that an experience we all hope will be positive—schooling—is used as a punishment. Keeping students after school sends the wrong message. The rational consequence is one that reflects the deed.

I asked teachers who are also parents what their first reaction is when they get a call from their child's school. The unanimous response: "What's wrong?" It's unfortunate that the first contact between teacher and parent is so often based on a problem. Calling or visiting a parent to establish a connection at the beginning of the year is more effective than having the first call report a misdeed. Traditional classrooms are isolated classrooms. Parents and other adults are rarely invited to talk with the students about life in other settings. Person-centered classrooms encourage other adults to join in partnerships with the children to let them know they are not alone. The following example shows how parent interaction can help both students and teacher:

> ✑ *A second-grade teacher invited a veteran of the Desert Storm conflict to talk with her class at the beginning of the year. The twenty-five students, many from low-income families, listened intently as he talked with them about responsibilities and self-discipline. He talked with the children about his life, the rules he needs to follow, and the consequences he faces when he doesn't comply with certain rules. Students asked questions: "How did you learn to follow rules?" "Did you like school?" "What did you do when a teacher didn't like you?" After this discussion the students, with their teacher, developed a classroom constitution.*

Person-centered Classroom Management

Person-centered classroom management advances the facilitative conditions needed to encourage active participation in a cooperative learning environment. Classroom management has several facets, including caring, guidance, and cooperation as well as administration and oversight. Person-cen-

FIGURE 12.3

Discipline Compared in Teacher-centered and Person-centered Classrooms

Teacher-centered Classrooms	Person-centered Classrooms
Teacher is the sole leader.	Leadership is shared.
Management is a form of oversight.	Management is a form of guidance.
Teacher takes responsibility for all the paperwork and organization.	Students are facilitators for the operations of the classroom.
Discipline comes from the teacher.	Discipline comes from the self.
A few students are the teacher's helpers.	All students have the opportunity to become an integral part of the management of the classroom.
Teacher makes the rules and posts them for the students.	Rules are developed by the teacher and students in the form of a classroom constitution or compact.
Consequences are fixed for all students.	Consequences reflect individual differences.
Rewards are mostly extrinsic.	Rewards are mostly intrinsic.
Students are allowed limited responsibilities.	Students share in classroom responsibilities.
Few members of the community enter the classroom.	Partnerships are formed with business and community groups to enrich and broaden the learning opportunities for students.

tered classrooms emphasize caring, guidance, cooperation, and the building of self-discipline that is developmentally appropriate for all members of the classroom. Person-centered classrooms encourage students to think for themselves and help each other.

Figure 12.3 provides a balance point for the differences between teacher-centered and person-centered classrooms. Perhaps most important, in person-centered classrooms both the teacher and students benefit. Most classrooms are not totally on one side or the other, but there are clear differences between the two approaches.

MYTHS ABOUT DISCIPLINE

There are many myths and misconceptions about discipline, and they are very evident in the language used to describe philosophies about schools, children, and discipline:

"Spare the rod, spoil the child."

"This is going to hurt me more than it hurts you."

"No pain, no gain."

"A quiet school is a good school."

"She has good discipline."

"They are out of control."

Words typically used to describe discipline also come to mind: compliance, control, punishment, respect, authority, strict.

But a different language can describe person-centered discipline:

"They really care about kids here."

"I love this school."

"We don't need to fight here."

"Let's try it together."

"I did it myself—it feels great!"

"I needed the time to focus."

And words come to mind to describe person-centered discipline: sharing, helping, giving, cooperating, focusing, caring, respecting, freeing. Language connotes attitudes, values, and one's freeing philosophy.

We come back to the heart of the matter: Our philosophy about the nature of teaching, learning, and students determines the type of instruction and discipline included in schools and classrooms. We tend to teach the way we have been taught. We also tend to see discipline the way we have experienced it ourselves. These two experiences influence the course we take in facilitating a learning climate in classrooms and schools. New experiences in person-centered environments, both for teachers and students, will change the way instruction and discipline influence student learning.

THREE-DIMENSIONAL DISCIPLINE AND LEARNING

Discipline and instruction are not separate streams; they are interactive and have three dimensions: a teacher dimension (knowledge and structure derived from one source), a cooperative dimension (students and teacher working together), and a self-dimension (the individual who is learning independently from multiple sources). These three dimensions of discipline parallel the instructional continuum from teacher- to student-focused learning that we discussed in chapter 10.

The *teacher dimension* of discipline is the one with which we are most familiar. Discipline and knowledge are derived from the teacher; the student's role is to be the listener and defer to the teacher. Some conflict, particularly at the secondary level, is a function of student resistance to teacher demands that minimize consideration for the learner.

The *cooperative dimension* is a half-way point between external and self-directed discipline and instruction. Teachers and students work together at a rate based on the comfort levels of all persons in the classroom, moving away from the teacher as a source of all knowledge and discipline. Working in cooperative groups builds an experiential dimension necessary in many classrooms to guide teachers and students along a continuum toward self-directed discipline and learning. An analysis of Barbara Shiel's classroom (described in chapter 4) shows how she supported students at their own comfort levels, depending on whether they needed her to direct or facilitate their work. She was directive, cooperative, facilitative, and nondirective for her students, changing her approach according to their individual needs. We also saw in the vignettes presented earlier in this chapter that teachers and students can work together in constructing a classroom constitution and taking responsibility for specific jobs in organizing the classroom for learning.

The *self-dimension* of discipline indicates that teacher and students are working at very different planes of interaction. Students conduct their own research projects, work on learning contracts (see chapter 10), organize their own time, and report what they have learned by using a variety of media (from print and pictures to video). Schools that students love provide opportunities for self-directed learning and self-discipline. For example, at Clement McDonough City Magnet (grades K–8) in Lowell, Massachusetts, self-discipline comes in the form of a student court system where the laws and judging cases are decided by the students without a discipline system imposed from the outside (14). The New Orleans Free School, HSPVA, O'Farrell, Amy-6, and many other schools give students multiple opportunities every day for self-discipline through town meetings, projects, community service, and complex problem solving.

The three-dimensional discipline and learning continuum presented in Figure 12.4 shows the interrelationship between instruction and discipline (see the instructional continuum in chapter 10). Some teachers who have been teacher-focused for most of their lives will have difficulty moving from one end of the three-dimensional discipline and learning continuum to the other in a short period of time. Lasting change takes time as well as support from all sectors of the community. The continuum represents an extended repertoire of options for every facilitator of learning and every student. With support and opportunities to experience other approaches to discipline and instruction, movement over time from one end of the continuum to the other is both a realistic and attainable goal.

The teacher's role on the continuum changes with the type of instruction. Likewise, the student's role changes at the same time. Teacher and student become co-learners. Students, ultimately, are given the opportunity to learn from the entire continuum. Teachers and students who experience

FIGURE 12.4
Three-dimensional Discipline and Learning

Teacher-focused

Teacher dimension: Teacher directs and externally controls student behavior. **Teacher role is directive.**	• Lecture • Questioning • Drill and practice • Demonstration
Cooperative dimension: Teacher/students cooperate in designing a positive classroom learning environment. **Teacher role is semi-directive/facilitative.**	• Discussion • Cooperative groups • Guided discovery • Contracts • Role-play
Self-dimension: Students are internally self-disciplined and need minimal direct adult supervision. **Teacher role is non-directive/facilitative.**	• Projects • Inquiry • Self-assessment

Student-focused

more facilitative learning become part of a community of creative, self-disciplined learners. And self-disciplined learners are able to do more than acquire information; they are able to invent for the future and improve upon the past.

OTHER SOURCES

The subject of discipline has been examined from a different perspective in this chapter. Hundreds of books have been written on the subject of classroom management and discipline. The following small sampling may prove helpful to teachers eager to develop self-discipline in their classrooms:

Vernon Jones and Louise Jones, *Comprehensive Classroom Management*, 3d ed. (Boston: Allyn and Bacon, 1990).

H. Jerome Freiberg, *Consistency Management: Cooperative Strategies for Active Learning* (Houston: University of Houston, College of Education, National Center on Education in the Inner Cities, 1994).

H. Jerome Freiberg, "A School That Fosters Resilience in Inner-city Youth," *Journal of Negro Education, Yearbook Edition* 62, no. 3 (Washington, D.C.: Howard University Press, 1993).

Richard Curwin and Allen N. Mendler, *Discipline with Dignity* (Washington, D.C: Association of Supervision and Curriculum Development, 1988).

William Glasser, *The Quality School: Managing Students without Coercion* (New York: HarperCollins, 1992).

CONCLUDING COMMENTS

There are no marching bands or great honors for people who prevent problems—only the great satisfaction that something worth doing has been done. Creating caring classrooms and supportive schools will go a long way toward reducing the need for students to affiliate themselves with destructive gangs and cliques. Supporting youth in their search for a place that respects them, cares about them as individuals, offers them opportunities to select their own learning activities, and gives them the chance to solve complex problems today will make the future a much more hopeful place.

Freedom, order, and learning are not mutually exclusive. We don't need schools to be more like prisons. There is a move across the country to make punishment and control an answer to the escalating conflict and violence found in many schools. I hope this chapter shows that there are other more productive pathways for creating meaningful, safe, generative, and creative learning environments.

REFERENCES

1. H. Jerome Freiberg, *Consistency Management: Cooperative Strategies for Active Learning* (Houston: University of Houston, College of Education, National Center on Education in the Inner Cities, 1994).

2. S. Sherwood, "A Circle of Friends in a 1st Grade Classroom," *Educational Leadership* 48, no. 3 (1990): 41.

3. C. R. Rogers, Personal communications with H. Jerome Freiberg, 1984.

4. S. Elam, R. Lowell, and A. Gallup, *Phi Delta Kappa 24th Annual Poll Gallup/PDK Poll of the Public's Attitude Towards Public Schools* 74, no. 1 (1992): 41–55.

5. C. Horswell, "Sense of Belonging Is a Powerful Incentive to Join," *Houston Chronicle*, 20 May 1991, pp. 6a-7a.

6. E. Schaps and D. Solomon, "Schools and Classrooms as Caring Communities," *Educational Leadership* 48, no. 3 (1990): 38–42.

7. V. Jones and L. Jones, *Comprehensive Classroom Management: Motivating and Managing Students*, 3d ed. (Boston: Allyn and Bacon, 1990).

8. W. Doyle, "Classroom Organization and Management," in *Handbook of Research on Teaching*, 3d ed., ed. M. Wittrock (New York: Macmillan, 1986).

9. E. Cohen, R. Lotan, and L. Catanzarite, "Can Classrooms Learn?" *Sociology of Education* 62 (April 1989): 75–94.

10. E. Cohen, *Classroom Management and Complex Instruction* (Paper presented at the annual meeting of the American Educational Research Association, Chicago, April 1991).

11. H. J. Freiberg, N. Prokosch, E. Treister, and T. Stein, "A Study of Five At-risk Inner City Elementary Schools," *International Journal of School Effectiveness and School Improvement* 1, no. 1 (1990): 5–25.

12. E. Emmer and A. Aussiker, *School and Classroom Discipline Programs: How Well Do They Work?* (Paper presented at the national meeting of the American Educational Research Association, Washington, D.C., April 1987).

13. E. Brantlinger, "Adolescents' Interpretation of Social Class Influence on Schooling," *Journal of Classroom Interaction* 28, no. 1 (1993): 1–12.

14. D. Fadiman, *Why Do These Kids Love School?* (study guide). (Santa Monica, Calif.: Pyramid Film and Video, 1991).

Sources for S. Sherwood's "A Circle of Friends in a 1st Grade Classroom"

a. R. Perske, *Circles of Friends* (Nashville: Abingdon Press, 1988).

b. W. Stainbeck and S. Stainbeck, "Educating All Students in Regular Education, *The Association for Persons with Severe Handicaps Newsletter* 13, no. 14 (1987): 1, 7.

c. D. Donder and J. Nietupski, "Nonhandicapped Adolescents Teaching Playground Skills to Their Mentally Retarded Peers: Toward a Less Restrictive Middle School Environment," *Education and Training of the Mentally Retarded* 16 (1981): 270—76.

d. S. B. Stainbeck, W. C. Stainbeck, and C. W. Hatcher, "Nonhandicapped Peer Involvement in the Education of Severely Handicapped Students," *The Journal of the Association for Persons with Severe Handicaps* 8 (1983): 39–42.

CHAPTER 13

RESEARCHING PERSON-CENTERED ISSUES IN EDUCATION

◆

SHOW ME!

Despite the many accounts of significant outcomes from teaching in a facilitative way, we can report that the concepts presented in the preceding chapters have been successfully used not only in the classes and schools described, but also in the somewhat unlikely field of teaching human relations to officers in the Army, Navy, and Air Force, as well as in various contexts in Asia, Europe, and the United States. Nevertheless, such descriptions of the fruitful use of these concepts are often unconvincing to policymakers who themselves are removed and isolated from the day-to-day lives of children and youth. There is a tendency for people at the policy level to say, "Traditional schooling worked for me. Why can't kids today sit still and listen to the lecture?"

Skeptics might question if any of these ideas, philosophies, and concepts make a sustained difference where it counts: in the classroom, throughout the school, and, most important, with the learner. The answer is an unequivocal yes!

This is one of the most important chapters in the book for anyone interested in responding to cynics about the value of being human in the classroom. The major reason for the importance of this chapter is that it presents research, documented over time and in different contexts, that students learn more, attend school more often, are more creative, and are more capable of problem solving when the teacher provides the kind of human, facilitative climate that has been described thus far in this book. This chapter provides the additional facts and support you may need to build upon your own experiences as a source of documentation for success. It shows that a human approach is a fundamental precondition and foundation to learning and, in a great many basic ways, is more appropriate than traditional approaches to learning.

The reason, as we saw in chapter 2, is that the number of students who have been socialized to accept a passive approach to learning is dwindling. More important, the level of expertise needed for an adult in today's world is significantly more complex and demanding than it was just twenty years ago. Knowing is no longer enough; knowing *why* and *how* is of greater importance. It is also more important for students to develop their potential than to adjust to dysfunctional settings. This chapter provides another perspective on person-centered learning that can form the basis of transforming schools into places of meaningful endeavor.

The research presented here is drawn from several sources. Some of the data is based on tape recordings of thousands of hours of classroom interaction in eight countries. These represent all levels of education, many different ethnic and national groups, and a wide spread of geographical locations. Other research is drawn from longitudinal studies of caring schools and families. Some studies tackle the issue of how schools and others can foster resilience in high-risk students. Still other research reflects the synthesis of hundreds of studies on the differences between open and traditional learning.

You will come across some fascinating findings. What happens to school attendance when all the teachers in one school decide to increase the amount of direct interaction through eye contact they have with their students? What percentage of average classroom time is taken up by teacher talk: 20 percent? 40 percent? 60 percent? 80 percent? How often do students in elementary, middle, and high school select their own learning activities? What are the differences between open and traditional education on student learning, attitudes toward school, and creativity? What does research on the brain show about experiential learning and brain development in children and adults? What effect does cooperative grouping have on learning and self-esteem? What are adults like today who were raised in families that spared the rod with their children nearly forty years ago? Can schools foster resilience in youth who face a daily barrage of non-facilitative conditions? What proportion of student time involves actual thinking? More important, what percentage of teacher time is spent in thinking: 10 percent? 1 percent? or less? I hope you will come away from this chapter with ideas about altering your own way of being in the classroom.

The Importance of Research

Research is more than numbers; it includes the systematic collection of ideas and experiences to identify trends and test patterns and to develop directions upon which new learnings may be channeled. It's very necessary not simply to issue a statement about education, but to back your statements with research. Too many important educational experiences and ideas are being thrown out without careful consideration (1).

Change Takes Time

This chapter examines person-centered educational research findings, past and present. In recent years, I have been concerned that work on person-centered education is being ignored by policy makers, the general public, and the teaching profession. This is due, in part, to the fact that research in person-centered learning is a process first and an outcome second. Person-centered learning focuses on the whole person—individual values, beliefs, and attitudes—not a few skills or actions. When we focus on changing actions without providing opportunities for individuals to reflect on their values, beliefs, and attitudes, we run the risk of building our learning habitat on shifting sands.

The process of reflection takes time and most certainly precedes any changes in a person's actions. Our society, it seems, wants results now; however, the time it takes for ideas to be nurtured and for them to progress into meaningful person-centered programs requires patience and stay-with-itness. Given a window of opportunity and an avenue of support, people can achieve long-term benefits. The alternative is what we see today: a wave of mandated, top-down, fashionable programs that last a short time. When immediate results aren't realized, these programs are quickly scuttled and replaced by the next wave of fashionable programs. Many veteran teachers have become skeptics, quite weary of this revolving-door pattern, and they take the attitude "We can wait it out. This, too, will pass."

WHAT WORKS: DIRECT OR INDIRECT TEACHING?

If you examine much of the research conducted during the past twenty years on what works in teaching, you find a pattern that emulates what is currently the norm in schools and classrooms, not what could be or is the exception. The studies of existing schools and programs that are reported in most of the research literature reflect a direct approach to teaching (2).

In the classic direct teaching approach, the teacher presents information from the front of the room to a largely passive group of listeners. This direct instructional approach to teaching and learning has many advocates. Studies have, in fact, shown that some students who receive this type of instruction learn and do well on standardized tests. But many other students do not learn when this is the only model of instruction offered. The direct instructional model places the responsibility for achieving on the student while dramatically limiting the student's level of input and interaction. Figure 13.1 shows the impact of this approach on student opportunities to select learning activities.

The data in Figure 13.1 were collected during the 1991–92 school year by the National Center on Education in the Inner Cities and prepared as profiles for feedback to each of the schools that participated in the study (3). The data are based on observations of 512 randomly selected students in 128 classrooms in twelve schools in a large urban school district: four elementary schools (grades three and five), four middle schools (grades six and eight), and four high schools (grades nine and twelve). On average, four

FIGURE 13.1
Activity Selection and Settings of Elementary, Middle,
and High School Students

Activity Types			
	Elementary Schools	**Middle Schools**	**High Schools**
Variables	**Aggregated Mean (%)**	**Aggregated Mean(%)**	**Aggregated Mean (%)**
Teacher-assigned activity	99.85	97.96	99.07
Student-selected activity	0.14	2.03	0.93

Setting			
	Elementary Schools	**Middle Schools**	**High Schools**
Variables	**Aggregated Mean (%)**	**Aggregated Mean (%)**	**Aggregated Mean (%)**
Whole class	78.19	88.04	80.84
Small group	12.20	5.20	3.17
Individual	9.60	6.75	15.98

National Center on Education in the Inner Cities, *School Profiles* (Philadelphia: Temple University, Center for Research in Human Development and Education; Houston: National Center on Education in the Inner Cities, 1993). Composite profile adapted from H. J. Freiberg, S. Huang, W. C. Wang, and H. Waxman, 1993. The research reported herein is supported in part by the Office of Educational Research and Improvement (OERI) of the U.S. Department of Education through a grant to the National Center on Education in the Inner Cities (CEIC) at the Temple University Center for Research in Human Development and Education (CRHDE). The opinions expressed do not necessarily reflect the position of the supporting agencies, and no official endorsement should be inferred.

students at a time were observed from each classroom. The sample of four students was observed interacting with their teachers ten times in a fifty-minute period on two different days. Observers looked at the amount of time students spent selecting activities and the time teachers gave students activities to complete.

The results, similar to those of classroom studies in other urban schools, are startling: 99 percent of the activities were selected by the teacher at the high school level; nearly 98 percent at the middle school level; and, remarkably, nearly 100 percent at the elementary school level. Additionally, 78 percent of instruction in the elementary classrooms took place in whole- or large-group settings compared with 88 percent at middle schools and 81 percent at high schools. The high school classes had the lowest levels of small-group work: 3.17 percent; therefore, their lower levels of whole-group instruction could be explained by increased teacher-assigned independent seat work. The use of centers, cooperative learning groups, and independent learning activities were the exception, not the rule, in these classrooms.

BRAIN DEVELOPMENT AND RICH ENVIRONMENTS

The need for stimulus-rich and varied learning environments becomes more evident when we examine emerging brain research and the relationship between rich, interactive learning environments and brain development. Ronald Koutulak, a science reporter for the *Chicago Tribune*, recently summarized the research on learning and the brain in an article that speaks to the heart of person-centered learning. He interviewed the leaders in the field of brain research and asked them to discuss the implications of their work on learning (4).

Based on the current research summarized in Koutulak's article, it appears that a child goes through three initial stages of brain development. The first level occurs during fetal development. During this stage, brain cells are assigned specific tasks. Research neurobiologist Peter Huttenlocher at the University of Chicago discovered that at twenty-eight weeks of development, a fetus has 124 million connectors or synapses that link brain cells. Each one of these links is a potential learning path. The brain increases dramatically both in size and in number of connectors between birth and twelve months of age. The number of connections skyrockets from about fifty trillion to one thousand trillion, and then decreases. This number can easily increase or decrease by nearly 25 percent, according to his report.

The decrease in connections during infancy is related to the world around the child. The need to be stimulated through sight, sound, talking, movement, and visualization seems to determine the level of connectors or pathways and subsequent brain development. Connections not stimulated "shrink and perish. Left behind are brain cells that form 'maps'—a kind of biological integrated circuit—of those experiences" (4, p. 8b). Koutulak continues by describing the implications for the facilitation of learning:

> How the brain puts its early learning capacity to use to store words was discovered by psychologist Janellen Huttenlocher of the University of Chicago. In a pioneering study that struck down the old notion that some children learn words faster than others because of an inborn capacity, Huttenlocher showed that when socioeconomic factors are equal, babies whose mothers talked with them more had a larger vocabulary. (4, p. 8b)

Koutulak's report indicates that between the ages of four and ten, another change is taking place in the brain. According to neurologist Harry Chugani at the University of California at Los Angeles (UCLA), data collected from Positron Emission Tomography (PET), which measures the use of sugar that brain cells need to carry out their work, indicate a 225 percent increase in brain activity from age 4 to age 10 when compared to adult brain activity. It seems that after ten years of age, the "maps" of the brain become set; and new learnings require the building of new pathways and perhaps the atrophy of old ones. The process of building and losing pathways is an on-going process from life to death, but the most important opportunities for learning seem to occur during the first ten years of life. The increase or decrease in pathways are dependent "upon whether a child grows up in an enriched environment or in an impoverished one."

Koutulak reports on further developments:

> Scientists at UCLA recently found in autopsy patients that the brains of university graduates who remained mentally active had up to 40 percent more connections than the brains of high school dropouts. But education alone is no guarantee of a better brain, the UCLA scientists found. Unless the brain is continuously challenged, it loses some of the connections that grew out of college experience. The brains of university graduates who led mentally inactive lives had fewer connections than those of graduates who never stopped letting the light in. (4)

The implications of this emerging research on learning and the brain are both startling and exciting. These implications speak volumes about the need for enriched learning environments both at home and at the place called school. The data presented from the 128 classrooms in Figure 13.1 only reinforce this need for stimulus-rich learning environments. Students spend six to eight hours a day in school; opportunities for student input into the selection of learning activities are necessary if rich environments are to be created for all children regardless of their economic beginnings.

Children who grow up in poverty (who represent one out of every five children in the United States) face a lack of stimulation at home and an equally limited learning environment at school. You may ask, "What types of conditions are necessary to improve the richness of every child's learning, and is there research to support their effectiveness?" If you're looking for an answer, read on!

FACILITATORS CAN MAKE A DIFFERENCE

Flora Roebuck and David Aspy studied the effects of person-centered learnings on thousands of students and found significant improvements in student achievement and attitudes. Their important findings are summarized below.

Research Findings of David Aspy and Flora Roebuck

The Basic Question

❦ *The bottom line for many people is, "So what? What makes these classrooms with person-centered freedom any better than others?" The National Consortium for Humanizing Education (NCHE) has conducted research into that issue for seventeen years in forty-two states and seven foreign countries. The results of these investigations reveal that there are some very positive effects from applying person-centered principles to daily practice in schools.*

The NCHE findings can be briefly summarized in one statement: Students learn more and behave better when they receive high levels of understanding, caring, and genuineness than when they receive low levels of support. *It is important to treat students as sensitive and aware human beings (5).*

This statement is based upon almost two decades of research and training projects in which we have focused upon interpersonal relationships in classrooms (6). NCHE activities have included both research and training and have employed both subjective (phenomenological) and scientific procedures. Through a variety of approaches, we have examined relationships between Rogers's facilitative conditions (empathy, congruence, positive regard) and a variety of factors such as attitudes (toward self, school, others), discipline problems, physical health, attendance, learning changes, and cognitive growth. These investigations involved all levels of schools and included elementary, secondary, and college populations. In all, we have worked with more than two thousand teachers and twenty thousand students.

Facilitative Conditions and Student Learning

In a study involving six hundred teachers and ten thousand students from kindergarten to twelfth grade (6), Aspy and Roebuck compared students of teachers who were trained to offer high levels of facilitative conditions including empathy, congruence, and positive regard with students of teachers who did not offer high levels of these facilitative conditions. I've summarized those studies here, but additional research and procedures are also reported in Aspy and Roebuck's book *Kids Don't Learn from People They Don't Like* (6) and in previous editions of *Freedom to Learn*.

Their studies of students in classrooms of high facilitative teachers (when compared to low facilitative teachers) suggest the following:

1. *Students miss four fewer days of school during the year.* A study of 3,199 students with low-empathy teachers missed on average nine days per year, while 3,410 students with high facilitative teachers missed on average five days per year. The differences were statistically significant at the p<.005 level.

2. *Students have increased scores on self-concept measures, indicating a more positive self-regard.* Students in grades three through six and seven through twelve were given a "How I See Myself Test," which measures self-esteem in six areas. Students in grades three through six with high-empathy teachers had greater self-esteem about their teacher-school interactions, physical appearance, interpersonal adequacy, autonomy, academic adequacy, and their place within the total school environment. In grades seven through twelve, students had higher gains in self-esteem in all areas but teacher-school interactions. The size of the school may have had an influence on this area. All the gains were significant beyond the p<.05 level. Perhaps the most startling results were found in the comparison group of students who had teachers not trained in interpersonal development. Those students showed a decrease in student reporting of self-esteem in the areas of autonomy and physical appearance during the year.

3. *Students make greater gains on academic achievement measures, including both math and reading scores.* Students in grades one through three, four through six, seven through nine, and ten through twelve all had significantly higher reading gains. The lower the grade level, the greater the gain; but all were significant beyond the p<.05 levels. Students in grades four through six, seven through nine, and ten through twelve were tested in mathematics and English. Except for English achievement in grades ten through twelve, significant achievement gains were reported in all grades.

4. *Students in person-centered classrooms present fewer disciplinary problems and commit fewer acts of vandalism to school property.* In a study of eighty-eight classrooms in grades two through six, from 16 to 45 percent of the variance in disruptive student behavior and vandalism could be attributed to the teacher's level of interpersonal, person-centered aware-

ness. In their study Aspy and Roebuck found that "*more* disruptive behavior occurred in classes whose teachers were *low* in empathy, respect, praising, accepting student ideas, and asking for thinking" (7).

5. *Students are more spontaneous and use higher levels of thinking.* The characteristic of positive regard for pupils was significantly different for students in classrooms that were on the higher levels (2 through 6) of Bloom's Taxonomy of Cognitive Thinking when compared with classrooms that were at the lowest or recall level of the taxonomy. The upper ranges of Bloom's Taxonomy include analysis, synthesis, and evaluation. According to Aspy and Roebuck's research, "these benefits were cumulative; the more years in succession that students had a high functioning teacher, the greater the gains when compared with students of low functioning teachers" (6, p. 221).

While of great importance, numbers derived from research are only one of several significant pieces to making the case for changing the teaching and learning paradigm. The use of cases and case study examples included in chapters throughout this book place the statistics within a personal context and give added weight to the question: "How can we build a learning environment that meets the needs of every learner?" The moving narratives by students and teachers of empathy, congruence, realness, and unconditional positive regard document a foundation upon which a larger context for change can occur. While change needs to take place at several levels, the greatest change begins with us—the facilitators of learning.

The Interpersonal Skills of Teachers

In several studies Aspy and Roebuck assessed the levels of facilitative conditions that teachers offered to students, and they found that teachers who provided high levels of empathy were also characterized by a cluster of other behaviors (8, pp. 21–22; 9; 10). Their findings showed that teachers who created higher facilitative conditions tended to provide the following:

1. More response to student feeling
2. More use of student ideas in ongoing instructional interactions
3. More discussion with students (dialogue)
4. More praise of students
5. More congruent teacher talk (less ritualistic)
6. More tailoring of contents to the individual student's frame of reference (explanations created to fit the immediate needs of the learners)
7. More smiling with students

Furthermore, the classroom activities of these teachers who supported higher-order facilitative conditions in their classrooms tended to reflect similar general characteristics:

1. The learning goals were derived from cooperative planning between teacher and students.

2. The classroom was individualized for and by the present class to meet its needs. There were more projects and displays created by students. The room looked lived in.

3. There was more freedom from time limits. There were fewer deadlines and more flexible sequences of order.

4. The teacher placed more emphasis upon productivity and creativity than upon evaluation. Because it was more important to carry out a meaningful project than to make tests alone the criteria for success, there was less emphasis upon grades and tests.

The teachers and administrators at the New Orleans Free School, HSPVA in Houston, Amy-6 in Philadelphia, and many others discussed in earlier chapters, also exhibited these characteristics of congruence, empathy and positive regard.

The Importance of Eye Contact

In another study Aspy and Roebuck found that many teachers do not maintain eye contact with their students. The researchers concluded, "Some students never receive favorable eye contact from a teacher and receive negative eye contact only when they are being disruptive." When Aspy and Roebuck helped teachers develop more positive eye contact, student attendance increased significantly ($p < .01$) (11). As a result, the researchers and the faculty came to the decision that eye contact should be one of the school's humanizing goals.

Empathy, Congruence, and Positive Regard

In general, Aspy and Roebuck's findings about empathy, congruence, and positive regard can be summarized in seven points:

1. The mean level of empathy, congruence, and positive regard among teachers was about the same as that of the general population (2.0 on a 5.0 scale with 5.0 being the highest). A threshold level of 3.0 out of 5.0 is a good starting point for effective interpersonal response (12, p. 14).

2. The mean level of interpersonal skills among principals and counselors untrained in humanistic education was below 3.0 on the process scales (13, pp. 163–71).

3. The mean level of interpersonal skills among professors of teacher education who had not received interpersonal development was below the minimally facilitative (3.0) threshold (11, p. 15).

4. The distribution of naturally occurring (untrained) levels of interpersonal skills was not related to gender, race, years of experience in educational settings, or geographical location (14, pp. 9–14; 15, pp. 86–92).

5. The mean level of interpersonal skills among teachers in the United States was not significantly different from that in seven foreign countries (13, pp. 163–71).

6. There was a deterioration in the course of the school year (from September to May) in the level of facilitative conditions offered to students by their teachers (16).

Research Findings of David Aspy and Flora Roebuck

Increasing the Interpersonal Skills of Teachers

🦋 *The early work by the NCHE indicated that most classroom teachers were not concerned deeply about maintaining facilitative interpersonal behaviors in their classroom as an end in itself. However, they were interested in those things that affect their students' immediate schooling behaviors—learning, discipline, and attendance. Thus, we wanted to close the gap between researchers and practitioners by depicting the relationship between facilitative interpersonal behaviors and outcomes the teachers valued.*

The human relations specialist tends to view the person first and the content as secondary; the classroom teacher, particularly at the high-school level, views substantive content as primary and human relations as secondary. Our studies revealed that for enhancing learning outcomes the teacher was the most important interpersonal factor in the classroom; it was essential to present interpersonal faculty development as an adjunct to effective instruction.

After a three-year study on the effects of training educational personnel to offer higher levels of empathy, congruence, and positive regard to their students, NCHE came up with the following results (16):

1. Teachers, principals, and counselors were successfully trained to function above the minimally effective threshold (3.0 on the scales for empathy, congruence, and positive regard) through training programs.

2. There was no systematic differential response to this training by subgroups of teachers differentiated according to characteristics of race, sex, years of teaching experience, or geographical location.

3. In general, in order to reach the 3.0 level of facilitative functioning, secondary teachers required training programs of longer duration or greater intensity than did elementary teachers.

4. The teachers learned more effectively in programs that (a) combined training in interpersonal processes with training in applying those skills to learning interactions; (b) provided periodic feedback about the teachers' level of functioning in the classroom; and (c) were conducted by instructors who were themselves functioning above the 3.0 level of empathy, congruence, and positive regard.

5. When principals and school-system administrators supported the training program by providing incentives for teacher involvement in the training, greater gains in skills and the gains in levels of empathy, congruence, and positive regard were more frequently put into practice in the classroom.

6. When principals were trained to use higher levels of interpersonal and interactional skills with their faculties, the teachers (a) used higher levels of skills with their students, (b) reported that their working environment and instructional tasks were more attractive, and (c) had decreased turnover rates and absence rates.

7. The teachers' level of *empathy* was the single most frequently recurring predictor of other teacher and student behavior in the classroom as well as of outcome behaviors in terms of student growth on self-concept, achievement measures and attendance, and less disruptive behavior.

Interpersonal Skills and Physical Fitness

Several investigations of the physical fitness dimension supported a relationship between that factor and the interpersonal skills dimension. Findings from these studies included the following (5, 17, 18, 19):

1. In case studies of school administrators, 93 percent of high-functioning principals were involved in some regular physical exercise program; 60 percent of these person-centered principals (aged forty-five and older) were able to run two miles in less than fifteen minutes.

2. In general, teacher responsiveness toward students declines within each week from Monday morning to Friday afternoon and recovers on the following Monday.

3. When only the data from the high physical fitness group are examined, the pattern is different from that described in 2)—the highest peak of responsiveness is reached on Friday afternoon, at the time students need it most.

4. Physical fitness was a significant predictor of gain both in immediate skills learning and in subsequent classroom performance of teachers who participated in in-service training workshops designed to increase constructive responsiveness to students.

5. Teachers' hearts beat approximately twelve times more per minute when teaching than when engaged in physically equivalent nonteaching activity. That is, there is some real physical wear and tear in the teaching process.

6. When teachers are responding to students, they have significantly ($p < .02$) faster pulse rates than when they are initiating structure.

7. However, this finding for number 6, above, does not hold true for physically fit teachers.

8. The teacher's level of physical fitness was significantly ($p < .001$) correlated with the frequency with which the teacher made eye contact with students and the number of times the teacher smiled while teaching.

9. Physical fitness was a better predictor of practicum performance of student teachers and student nurses than grade point average.

10. Student teachers with higher levels of physical fitness accepted their students' ideas more often and criticized their students less often than did student teachers with lower levels of physical fitness ($R^2 = 0.483$; $p < .002$).

Aspy and Roebuck came to this conclusion:

> ❦ *Fatigue, poor nutrition, and lack of physical exercise are deterrents to positive interpersonal relationships. The data from subsequent work suggest strongly that physical fitness is necessary for sustaining constructive interpersonal relationships across long periods of time. It seems that all teachers who understand constructive human relationships can be humane for a short period of time, but their levels of physical fitness determine the durability of their interpersonal facilitation.*
>
> *. . . Physical fitness is not the only factor in constructive interpersonal behavior; that is, a person may be quite fit physically and be inept interpersonally. Physical fitness seems to be a necessary, but not a sufficient, condition for sustaining high levels of interpersonal functioning. Also, we cannot say that all of those teachers who provide good interpersonal facilitation are physically fit. It seems that we can say that our levels of physical fitness determine the length of time we can employ our highest interpersonal skills. Of course, if our skills are very limited, then high levels of physical fitness would not enhance them.*

. . . Many school practices do not encourage physical fitness for either students or teachers. For instance, few schools provide exercise facilities for teachers, and lunch periods are often very short and associated with stressful conditions of noise, responsibility for student behavior, isolation from adult peers, and so on. In the light of the data relating physical fitness and interpersonal functioning, there is little wonder that teachers often provide low levels of interpersonal facilitation.

If we were to summarize the bits and pieces of our work, it would be something like this: Physical fitness seems to be the foundation out of which interpersonal skills can develop, and they, in turn, lay the basis for intellectual growth. *This is not a new set of formulations. It is a reaffirmation of some things we have under-supported for a long time in our schools.*

OTHER STUDIES THAT SUPPORT PERSON-CENTERED LEARNING

The work of Aspy and Roebuck was corroborated by Reinhard and Anne-Marie Tausch and colleagues in Germany. While Aspy and Roebuck focused on skill development in changing the way teachers and students interact, the Tausches used human relations groups to bring about similar results (20). Their research indicated that only 10 percent of the teachers in their German studies "approach their classes from a person-centered way" (21, 22, 23). The studies conducted by Aspy and Roebuck and Anne-Marie and Reinhard Tausch, while conducted in the 1970s, are still highly relevant today as parents, teachers, and other concerned citizens seek to improve the quality and conditions of learning for our nation's youth.

In addition to the studies already reported in this chapter, I would like to summarize a series of more recent studies to provide additional research perspectives on other person-centered philosophies to learning. It is not surprising that the results of more than twenty years of research reaches remarkably similar conclusions: higher social and cognitive outcomes are significantly more likely where the teachers rate high on the facilitative conditions. They are genuine persons in class; they respect the uniqueness of each student; they let students know that their feelings and the meaning that the school experience has for them is understood. Without positive interpersonal interactions, what is supposedly learned is quickly forgotten; worse still, barriers are erected that inhibit future learnings. What happens when the system of learning is freed and opened to the students' need for active involvement?

How Effective Is Open Education?*

Many of the examples in this book and the research on interpersonal development in the classroom done thus far could be classified under the term *open teaching and learning*, which has been well defined as:

> an open approach to the teaching-learning process which recognizes the valid wish of every student to be involved in some way in the direction of his own learning. It respects children's natural impulse to learn and understands the ways they gain and create knowledge. Of special concern, it changes the function of a teacher from 'telling information' to one of providing choice and facilitating inquiry activity. (24, p. 3)

Open education has been evaluated in many research investigations. Horwitz (25) and Walberg (26), in two separate reviews of 102 such studies, came to similar conclusions; Walberg states: "Open education, authentically implemented, consistently reaches its goals in creativity, self-concept, school attitudes, curiosity and independence" (27, p. 102). Horwitz tabulated the studies in a way that illustrates this conclusion even more dramatically, as Table 13.1 shows.

Open education is a trend usually associated with open-space classrooms or schools without walls that flourished in the late 1960s and early 1970s. But even though open education operates in only about 10 percent of classrooms today, that number is growing. Studies conducted in the 1980s to synthesize the research on open education concluded that it has a significant effect on the broad goals of education, including "cooperation, critical thinking, self-reliance, constructive attitudes, and lifelong learning" without diminishing the more specific achievement gains of students (26, p. 226).

The need for creativity, student-centered learning, critical thinking, cooperative learning, and positive self-concept were concepts expressed by Ravens (28), Samson (29), and others as providing the framework for future success and satisfaction. In a synthesis of studies on open education, Walberg (26) reviewed the works of researchers who themselves reviewed hundreds of studies on open education. Horwitz (25) summarized 200 studies; Peterson (30) reviewed 45 studies; and Hedges, Giaconia, and Gage (31) analyzed 153 studies. The conclusions of each of the studies and the subsequent reanalysis by Giaconia and Hedges (32) indicate that on standardized tests, students in open education and those in traditional education scored about the same. Some achievement differences, however, were

---

* A portion of this section is adapted from H. Jerome Freiberg, "Carl Rogers's Philosophy and Current Educational Research Findings," *Person-centered Review* 3, no. 1 (1988): 30–40.

TABLE 13.1
Overview of Results Between Open and Traditional Classrooms*

Variable and Number of Studies	Results (percent of studies)			
	Open Better	Traditional Better	Mixed Results	No Significant Differences
Academic achievements (102)	14%	12%	28%	46%
Self-concept (61)	25%	3%	25%	47%
Attitude toward school (57)	40%	4%	25%	32%
Creativity (33)	36%	0%	30%	33%
Independence and conformity (23)	78%	4%	9%	9%
Curiosity (14)	43%	0%	36%	21%
Anxiety and adjustment (39)	26%	13%	31%	31%
Locus of control (24)	25%	4%	17%	54%
Cooperation (9)	67%	0%	11%	22%
Overall Average	**39%**	**4%**	**24%**	**33%**

* Results are reported based on percent of studies. Numbers in parentheses represent the total number of studies.

Source: R. A. Horwitz, "Psychological Effects of the 'Open Classroom'." *Review of Educational Research* 49 (1979): 71–85. ° 1979 by the American Educational Research Association. Reprinted by permission of the publisher.

observed in students from open education programs who had limited experience with standardized tests. For example, in the areas of self-concept, attitudes toward school, creativity, independence, curiosity, and cooperation, students from open education environments showed greater gains, according to the research reviews.

It was found that success in open education is not contingent upon the actual facilities but rather on the philosophy of the teachers and staff. Giaconia and Hedges found in their meta-analysis (synthesis of studies) on open education that

> open education programs can produce greater self-concept, creativity, and positive attitude toward school. The open education programs that produced superior effects on nonachievement outcomes are characterized by the four features that we have described as: the role of the child in learning, diagnostic evaluation, manipulative materials, and individualized instruction. Although these four features are often central to theoretical conceptions of open education, researchers have sometimes focused on more concrete features such as open space architecture of multiage grouping. Our results suggest that multiage grouping, open space, and team teaching do

not distinguish more effective open education programs from less effective programs. (32, p. 600)

Only in the last few years have results from longitudinal studies begun to appear in the research literature. The findings reported in this chapter support the contention that open education is a viable and needed educational program.

Early Experiential Learning

Early childhood education is an area in which the philosophy of open education is growing dramatically, as shown by the increased interest of parents in Montessori and other active approaches to learning. Maria Montessori started a revolution in preschool and early elementary education in 1912 with her book *The Montessori Method.* Her method is based on the philosophy that children should educate themselves rather than be taught by a teacher in the traditional sense. The teacher in a Montessori class creates an environment for learning by providing a rich variety of materials and activities, while the child is allowed to explore and discover relationships and meaning through interaction with the materials, teacher, and other children. Montessori envisioned structure and order in the classroom only as a means to provide children with the opportunity for freedom. According to her philosophy, the needs of the child rather than the teacher, school, or bureaucracy are of primary importance. This is evident when Montessori states: "The school should become the place where the child may live in freedom" (33, p. 142); and "the new school, indeed, must not be created for the service of science, but for the service of living humanity; and teachers will be able to rejoice in the contemplation of lives unfolding under their eyes"(33, p. 127).

The research reviews by Jane Stallings and Deborah Stipek (34) on several early intervention programs for low-income minority preschool students indicate that the boys who attended preschool Montessori programs scored higher on standardized tests than did boys in traditional classes, both at the end of kindergarten and ten years later. Tenth-grade inner-city boys who were in Montessori preschools operated above national norms academically. The importance of structured yet experiential learning for low-socioeconomic-status minority boys produced measurable learning gains for their entire schooling experience, according to Miller and Bizzell (35).

It is important to note that inner-city girls did not benefit academically (as measured by standardized achievement tests), as the boys did in the Montessori program. Stallings and Stipek indicate that

boys are typically less mature than girls at age four, and it may be that they were more susceptible to the effects of this individually paced structured program than were the girls. . . . Perhaps there are teachable moments when children are more likely to learn through the sensory experiences that Montessori believed were so closely related to the development of a child's mind. (34, p. 734)

Another explanation may be found in the research on resilience of high-risk children. The studies of Emmy Werner (36) and others indicate that boys are more vulnerable than girls during their first ten years to caregiver deficits. This trend, however, reverses itself when girls enter adolescence. The Montessori approach may have provided protective factors for the boys in areas of greater need.

Research can be supported by other indicators. Inner-city parents who could not afford to send their children to private Montessori schools camped out with sleeping bags for days in front of inner-city public elementary schools in Houston and New Orleans to enroll their children into public school Montessori programs. (Houston, in recent years, has used a lottery system to eliminate the lines.) Many parents who were interviewed by the local media indicated that older siblings in the Montessori program had gained from the hands-on experience provided by the teachers. Freedom to choose and explore the natural environment is a necessary ingredient for effective and fulfilling learning in these parents' eyes.

But any one program will not meet all the needs of every child. The Montessori approach may be too structured or too unstructured for certain children. In addition, the degree of authentic implementation in the classroom may be a factor in the success of the Montessori program as well as other open education programs.

It is perhaps a twist of fate and a touch of irony that a program originally designed by Maria Montessori for children from poverty is the choice of so many affluent parents, and out of the reach of many poor children. These inequities must be changed if our nation is to grow. Schools in a democracy should be the great meeting place of ideas, cultures, and people. Once in school, however, where and how do children have the opportunities to meet together and share ideas in order to learn to understand and care for each other?

Cooperative Learning

We bring students together to learn in schools, yet we isolate them from each other. We expect school to act as a socializer for society, yet we seldom encourage dialogue and interchange among students. We assume that higher-level and critical thinking skills will emerge from academic rigor and are mystified when our students are unable to make decisions for themselves. The natural order of business, industry, families, religion, military, and society is cooperation. Only in schools, it seems, is cooperation unnatural. Recently, research and experience have shown that cooperative learning can produce powerful social and academic results. How can we tap in our schools what seems to be so natural in most of society?

Each student brings to the classroom a wealth of knowledge and experience that must be channeled through the teacher before it can be shared with others in the classroom. It is little wonder that students begin school with great enthusiasm and then gradually lose their motivation to learn. After classroom management, the next greatest concern of teachers and parents is student motivation, which so often exhibits its negative side through apathy, drug abuse, dropping out, and suicide. Learning in most schools is a lonely, solitary experience. Students must sit quietly and listen to others speak without the opportunity for meaningful dialogue and interaction.

Studies by David Aspy and Flora Roebuck (6), John Goodlad (37), Jere Brophy and Tom Good (38), and Ned Flanders (39) have all reached similar conclusions about classroom interaction: Between 70 and 80 percent of the talk in the classroom is done by the teacher. During the past ten years, researchers and educators have begun to look at cooperative learning as a means of providing instructional variability and higher degrees of interaction for learning. In cooperative settings, the role of the teacher is one of facilitator of learning rather than imparter of information, as is the case in direct instruction models. Cooperative learning creates an opportunity for students to work together in groups of differing sizes to help each other learn. The goal of cooperative learning is to enable students to develop positive interdependence with each other, face-to-face interaction, individual as well as group learning, and interpersonal and small-group skills (40).

The results of this student-centered approach have been generally impressive. The research reported by David Johnson and Roger Johnson and associates at the University of Minnesota (40) and Robert Slavin at Johns Hopkins University (41) indicates that when the teacher takes the role of facilitator and the classroom norms are changed from individual to cooperative learning, gains are made in achievement. More important, according to Lyn Corno and Richard Snow, the greatest and most consistent gains, when compared to traditional classrooms, have been achieved in the area of student motivation, "such as peer support, self-esteem, and self-attributions" (42, p. 622). The opportunity to learn from each other in the classroom is becoming recognized as a viable approach to increasing student motivation and learning. Cooperative grouping also provides the opportunity for students to learn and practice interpersonal skills, including cross-cultural communication necessary for them to function in a larger society.

The importance of interpersonal skills has long been recognized by the business community, which spends enormous resources each year training its employees. Much of the money is spent on preparing people to work together in groups to maximize interpersonal relations. The business community realizes what too many school policymakers have failed to understand: People working together make the difference.

CARING: A PROTECTIVE SHIELD

When students say they love school, they also say that people in their schools care. Caring is a theme that echoed from students who were interviewed for this book from across the nation. From Amy-6 in Philadelphia, to HSPVA and Milby High School in Houston, to O'Farrell Community School in San Diego, to the Dett* and Montefiore schools in Chicago, to the New Orleans Free School in New Orleans, people care about each other.

Schools can either provide protective factors for children or they can diminish them. In a longitudinal study from birth to thirty-two years of age, Emmy Werner studied the data on 698 infants born in 1955 on the island of Kauai, Hawaii. Beginning in the prenatal stage and continuing for thirty-two years, the longitudinal study monitored children born into poverty and other high-risk situations (for example, dysfunctional families or those suffering from alcoholism or mental illness). Werner made some remarkable findings about the importance of protective factors for children who are at high risk for emulating the life they were born into—a life of poverty (36). Many of the children showed resilience despite their high-risk beginnings, and Werner examined some of the reasons for their progression beyond vulnerability. One important factor was that the resilient children in this study sought out caring and helpful people during their school-age years. Werner notes:

> The [resiliant] boys and girls also found emotional support outside their own families. They tended to have at least one and usually several close friends, especially the girls. They relied on an informal network of kin and neighbors, peers and elders, for council and support in times of crisis. Some had a favorite teacher who became a role model, friend and confidant for them. (36, p. 74)

As stressful life situations increased in the study participants, there was a need for parallel development in protective factors. Developmental stages

---

* The Dett School (K–8) is located next to one of Chicago's infamous high-rise housing projects. The outside of the school is bleak and looks like the set from a futuristic movie. Inside the school, the place exudes color, warmth, and caring. As an eighth grader said during an interview in 1991, "They [the teachers] bring out the best in you, they don't put you down, they have confidence in you, they care." The school is going through a restructuring effort, and we will visit with members of the school community in chapter 17.

of life (infancy, adolescence, and adulthood) as well as gender differences changed the life situations of the people in the study. Boys were more vulnerable during the first ten years of life while girls tended to be more vulnerable during adolescence.

A study recently reported by Dr. Bonnie Benard at the Northwest Regional Educational Laboratory (43), *Fostering Resiliency in Kids: Protective Factors in the Family, School and Community*, found that children who overcome adversity in their surroundings have four basic protective traits: social competence, strong problem-solving skills, autonomy, and a sense of purpose for the future. The researcher concludes that family, school, and community can foster these protective traits in children. She states:

> Individuals who have succeeded in spite of adverse environmental conditions in their families, school, and/or communities have often done so because of the presence of environmental support in the form of one family member, one teacher, one school, one community person that encouraged their success and welcomed their participation. (43, pp. 18–19)

Benard indicates in her study that communities that establish literacy programs, teen-sponsored day care for younger children, elder care, tutoring, and other community support programs can assist children by providing a foundation for resilience.

Carol Franz, David McClelland, and Joel Weinberger (44) conducted a follow-up study to one initiated in 1951 by Sears, Maccoby, and Levin (45) into the child-rearing practices of 379 mothers and their five-year-old children in the Boston area. The thirty-six year (1951–87) prospective study examined "the long-term influence of parental warmth on adult social skills" (44, p. 587), and it provided important insights into the roles mothers and fathers can play in the well-being and resilience of their children—which, according to the study, lasts through adulthood.

A follow-up study of ninety-four subjects was conducted from the original sample of 379 five-year-olds when they reached forty-one years of age. Combining this follow-up with interviews over a thirty-six-year period, the researchers found that children had higher self-esteem at age twelve (46), an improved cooperative interpersonal style at age twenty-three (47), and higher adult social accomplishment at age forty-one (44) when either parent had shown warmth through hugs, kisses, holding, and cuddling (as opposed to strictness) when the subject was five years old (45). The midlife differences in children who came from either a warm mother or father, as compared to those children who did not, was demonstrated in their ability "to sustain long and relatively happy marriages, raise children, and be involved with friends outside their marriage at mid-life" (44, p. 592). Antithetically, parental coldness was associated in the study with five-year-olds who had "feeding problems, bed-wetting, greater aggression, and slower conscience development" (44, p. 586). Contrary to what had been predicted by some researchers, parental harmony was not associated with adult social accomplishment in this study.

In a review of the literature about the role that schools play in the alienation of high-risk students, Dr. Dona Kagan found that the most frequent and consistent perception of students in at-risk situations is that their teachers do not care about them (48). Dr. Alfie Kohn, in an article entitled "Caring Kids: The Role of the Schools," describes in detail how schools play a pivotal role in facilitating the conditions of caring for each other (49). He cites a study by Nancy Berg-Eisenberg and Cynthia Neal who studied the free-play characteristics of four and five year olds (50). Of seventy-seven children, sixty-seven "shared with, helped, or comforted another child" during a forty-minute observation period (50, p. 499). When the researcher asked the children individually about their reasons, the usual response was that another child needed their help. As demonstrated by both of these studies, schools can build on the natural inclination of children to be helpful and caring for others.

The research of Nel Noddings, professor of education at Stanford University, discusses a "Crisis of Caring" in schools (51).

> 🦋 *Some years ago, . . . educators came up with the idea that middle schools should be created to attend to the developmental needs of adolescents. But what still has not occurred to most people is that isolating a particular group may not be the best way to address its developmental needs. . . . They [middle-school children] should be in schools where there are younger children to be helped, and it should be part of their education—an important part—to learn how to provide that help. . . .*
>
> *At a time when the traditional structures of caring have deteriorated, schools must become places where teachers and students live together, talk with each other, take delight in each other's company. My guess is that when schools focus on what really matters in life, the cognitive ends we now pursue so painfully and artificially will be achieved somewhat more naturally.*
>
> *Schools cannot end the crisis of caring in our society, but they can help young people to learn how to care and be cared for, and those people may eventually make this crisis a phenomenon of the past. (51, p. 32)*

Noddings's statement rings true: we need a different way of looking at schools and the conditions necessary to create a caring habitat for learning. Many students interviewed for this book, including those at the New Orleans Free School and Dett School (both of them K–8), had younger children at the school and talked about the opportunities available to help others, be it working with the homeless or in a children's museum, tutoring or playing ball with a younger student. As facilitators of learning, we have both the responsibility and the opportunity to create facilitative conditions for caring learning communities.

CONCLUDING REMARKS

To a Nigerian, a zebra is a black animal with white stripes; to a European, a zebra is a white animal with black stripes. In the coldest parts of Alaska, hell, in the Eskimos's culture, is portrayed as a place of ice and cold, not extreme heat. In much of the temperate Western world, however, hell is portrayed as fire and brimstone. How can all four of these perspectives be right? The answer is that a person's experiences confirm that person's beliefs. When person-centered teachers, programs, and schools are developed and studied, they prove to be a significant benefit to both students and teachers.

It is of interest to me that the improved facilitative attitudes and conditions, as reported in several disparate studies in this chapter, took different approaches to learning. However, these research studies had one common thread that linked their findings: They were person-centered. Such an approach to building protective factors can provide a counterbalance to the risk factors with which many children begin their lives today. The research clearly validates the importance of teachers as a source of resilience for many children. Schools in which principals and teachers exhibit high levels of empathy, congruence, and positive regard can increase the richness of every child's learning and life. Schools with these facilitative conditions are places where everyone enjoys being; there is less teacher turnover and student absenteeism as well as higher morale. The whole school becomes a place for learners.

The research on person-centered education is bimodal, much like the humps of a camel: We saw person-centered studies in the late 1960s and early 1970s and again on a smaller scale in the mid-1980s and early 1990s. The lack of federal funding and a view that person-centered education represented a liberal agenda helped it fall into disfavor during much of the 1980s—the height of the back-to-basics movement. This resulted in a paucity of new research and limited dissemination of existing studies. The difficulty faced by person-centered researchers in the past has been the limited concentration of student-centered programs and schools to study. This problem seems to be improving in the current movement toward student-centered learning.

There remain many gaps in the research that need to be addressed. For example, what do teaching-learning interactions look like when schools function with high levels of facilitative conditions? How can person-centered schools become the standard rather than the exception? What federal, state, and district level policies need to change in order for facilitative conditions to be implemented? How can schools and teachers create the facilitative conditions needed to provide protective factors for all students? It is becoming increasingly evident that the 1990s will see a resurgence of research on the facilitative conditions of learning and on studies of the person.

There are many challenges ahead. Perhaps the greatest is changing perceptions of how people learn and what it will take to significantly move us in new directions. (Some of these new directions will be discussed in chapter 17. The chapter presents a vision of transforming schools, from a person-centered perspective.) Teachers, principals, students, and parents need to become integral parts of research teams who design, study, and document the processes of learning and the facilitative conditions necessary for every child to succeed. It is my hope that you will become one of the many people who get involved in documenting the efforts and results of person-centered learning through cases and other forms of research. Our most precious resources—our children—rest in the balance.

REFERENCES

1. C. R. Rogers, Personal communications with Jerome Freiberg, 1984.

2. M. Wittrock, ed., *Handbook of Research on Teaching*, 3d ed. (New York: Macmillan, 1986).

3. National Center on Education in the Inner Cities, *School Profiles* (Philadelphia: Temple University Center for Research in Human Development and Education, 1993).

4. R. Koutulak, "Human Brain Teaches Science a Thing or Two," *Houston Chronicle*, 10 May 1993, p. 8b. Originally published in the *Chicago Tribune*, © copyrighted date of publication, Chicago Tribune Company, all rights reserved, used with permission.

5. D. N. Aspy and F. N. Roebuck, *Client Centered Therapy in the Educational Process* (Paper presented at the proceedings of the European Conference on Client Centered Therapy, Wurtzburg, Germany; Wurtzburg: University of Wurtzburg Press, 1975).

6. D. N. Aspy and F. N. Roebuck, *Kids Don't Learn from People They Don't Like* (Amherst, Mass.: Human Resource Development Press, 1977).

7. F. N. Roebuck, *Cognitive and Affective Goals of Education: Towards a Clarification Plan* (Paper presented at the annual meeting of the Association for Supervision and Curriculum Development, Atlanta, March 1980).

8. D. N. Aspy and F. N. Roebuck, "The Relationship of Teacher-offered Conditions of Meaning to Behaviors Described by Flanders' Interaction Analysis," *Education* 95 (Spring 1975): 216–22.

9. F. N. Roebuck, *Polynomial Representation of Teacher Behavior* (Address presented at American Educational Research Association, National Convention, Washington, D.C., 31 March 1975; abstracted in *Resources in Education* [October 1975], ERIC document ED106718).

10. F. N. Roebuck and D. N. Aspy, *Response Surface Analysis*, Interim report no. 3 for NIMH grant no. 5 PO I MH 19871 (Monroe, La: Northeast Louisiana University, 1974; abstracted in *Resources in Education* [October 1975], ERIC document ED106732).

11. D. N. Aspy and F. N. Roebuck, *The National Consortium for Humanizing Education: An Update of Research Results* (Paper presented to the annual meeting of the American Educational Research Association, San Francisco, 12 April 1979).

12. F. N. Roebuck et al., *Maintaining Reliability*, Interim report no. 1 for NIMH grant no. 5 PO I MH 19871 (Monroe, La: Northeast Louisiana University, 1974; abstracted in *Resources in Education* [October 1975], ERIC document ED106730).

13. D. N. Aspy and F. N. Roebuck, "From Humane Ideas to Humane Technology and Back Again Many Times," *Education* 92 (Winter 1974): 163–71.

14. F. N. Roebuck, "Human Thoughts and Humane Procedures/Effective Behavior," *Peabody Journal of Education* (October 1975): 9–14.

15. F. N. Roebuck and D. N. Aspy, "Grade-level Contributions to the Variance of Flanders' Interaction Categories," *The Journal of Experimental Education* (Spring 1974): 86–92.

16. D. N. Aspy and F. N. Roebuck, *Research Summary: Effects of Training in Interpersonal Skills*, Interim report no. 4 for NIMH grant no. 5 PO I MH 19871 (Monroe, La.: Northeast Louisiana University, 1974; abstracted in *Resources in Education* [October, 1975], ERIC document ED106733).

17. D. N. Aspy and F. N. Roebuck, *A Lever Long Enough* (Dallas: The National Consortium for Humanizing Education, 1976).

18. J. H. Buhler and D. N. Aspy, *Physical Health for Educators: A Book of Readings* (Denton, Tex.: North Texas State University Press, 1975).

19. F. N. Roebuck and J. H. Buhler, "The Relationship between Physical Fitness of a Selected Sample of Student Teachers and Their Performance on the Flanders' Verbal Interaction Scale," in *Physical Health for Educators: A Book of Readings*, ed. J. H. Buhler and D. N. Aspy (Denton, Tex.: North Texas State University Press, 1975).

20. A. Tausch, O. Wittern, and J. Albus, "Erzieher-Kind-Interaktionen in einer Vorschul-Lernsituation im Kindergarten," *Psychol. in Erz. u. Unterricht* 23 (1976).

21. J. Hoder, R. Tausch, and A. Weber, *Forderliche Dimensionen des Lehrerverhaltens und ihr Zusammenhang mit der Qualitat der Unterrichtsbeitrage der Schuler* (Manuscript, 1976).

22. H. Joost, "Forderliche Dimensionen des Lehrerverhaltens in Zusammenhang mit emotionalen und kognitiven Prozessen bei Schuler," in *Psychol. in Erz. u. Unterricht* 25 (1978): 69–94.

23. P. Klyne, *Dimensionen des Lehrerverhaltens in ihrem Zusammenhang mit Vorgangen der Schuler* (Manuscript, 1976).

24. M. L. Silberman, J. S. Allender, and J. M. Vannoff, eds., *The Psychology of Open Teaching and Learning: An Inquiry Approach* (Boston: Little, Brown, 1972).

25. R. A. Horwitz, "Psychological Effects of the Open Classroom," *Review of Educational Research* 49 (1979): 71–85.

26. H. Walberg, "Synthesis of Research on Teaching," in *Handbook of research on teaching*, 3d ed., ed. M. Wittrock (New York: Macmillan, 1986).

27. H. Walberg, D. Schiller, and G. D. Haertel, "The Quiet Revolution in Educational Research," *Phi Beta Kappan* 61 (1979): 179–83.

28. J. Ravens, "The Most Important Problem in Education Is to Come to Terms with Values," *Oxford Review of Education* 7 (1981): 253–72.

29. G. Samson, M. E. Graue, T. Weinstein, and H. J. Walberg, *Academic and Occupational Performance: A Quantitative Synthesis* (Chicago: University of Illinois, Office of Evaluation Research, 1982).

30. P. L. Peterson, "Direct Instruction Reconsidered," in *Research on Teaching*, ed. P. L. Peterson and H. J. Walberg (Berkeley, Calif.: McCutchan, 1979).

31. L. V. Hedges, R. M. Giaconia, and N. L. Gage, *Meta-analysis of the Effect of Open and Traditional Instruction* (Stanford: Stanford University, Program on Teaching Effectiveness, 1981).

32. R. Giaconia and L. Hedges, "Identifying Features of Effective Open Education," *Review of Educational Research* 52, no. 4 (1982): 579–602.

33. M. Montessori, *Spontaneous Activity in Education: The Advanced Montessori Method* (New York: Schocken, 1965).

34. J. Stallings and D. Stipek, "Research on Early Childhood and Elementary School Teaching Programs," in *Handbook of Research on Teaching*, 3d ed., ed. M. Wittrock (New York: Macmillan, 1986).

35. L. Miller and R. Bizzell, *Long-term Effects of Four Preschool Programs: Ninth and Tenth Grade Results* (Louisville: University of Louisville, 1983).

36. E. E. Werner, "High-risk Children in Young Adulthood: A Longitudinal Study from Birth to Thirty-two Years," *American Journal of Orthopsychiatry* 59, no. 1 (1989): 72–81.

37. J. Goodlad, *A Place Called School: Perspectives for the Future* (New York: McGraw Hill, 1983).

38. J. Brophy and T. Good, "Teacher Behavior and Student Achievement," in *Handbook of Research on Teaching*, 3d ed., ed. M. Wittrock (New York: Macmillan, 1986).

39. N. A. Flanders, *Teacher Influence on Pupil Attitudes and Achievement*, U.S. Department of Health, Education, and Welfare, Cooperative Research Monograph No. 12 (Washington, D.C.: Government Printing Office, 1965).

40. D. W. Johnson, R. G. Johnson, and E. J. Holubec, *Circles of Learning: Cooperation in the Classroom* (Edina, Minn: Interaction, 1986).

41. R. Slavin, *Cooperative Learning* (New York: Longman, 1983).

42. L. Corno and R. Snow, "Adapting Teaching to Individual Differences Among Learners," in *Handbook of Research on Teaching*, 3d ed., ed. M. Wittrock (New York: Macmillan, 1986).

43. B. Benard, *Fostering Resiliency in Kids: Protective Factors in the Family, School and Community* (Portland, Or.: Western Regional Center for Drug Free Schools and Communities, Far West Laboratory Monograph, 1991).

44. C. Franz, D. McClelland, and J. Weinberger, "Childhood Antecedents of Conventional Social Accomplishment in Midlife Adults: A Thirty-six Year Prospective Study," *Journal of Personality and Social Psychology* 60, no. 4 (1991): 586–93.

45. R. R. Sears, E. E. Maccoby, and H. Levin, *Patterns of Child-rearing* (Evanston, Ill.: Row, Peterson, 1957).

46. R. R. Sears, "Relation of Early Socialization Experiences to Self-concepts and Gender Role in Middle Childhood," *Child Development* 41 (1970): 267–89.

47. C. N. Edwards, "Interactive Styles and Social Interaction," *Genetic Psychology Monographs* 87 (1973): 123–74.

48. D. M. Kagan, "How Schools Alienate Students at Risk: A Model for Examining Proximal Classroom Variables," *Educational Psychologists* 25, no. 2 (1990): 105–20.

49. A. Kohn, "Caring Kids: The Role of the Schools," *Phi Delta Kappan* (1991): 496–506.

50. N. Berg-Eisenberg and C. Neal, "Children's Moral Reasoning About Their Own Spontaneous Prosocial Behavior," *Developmental Psychology* 15 (1979): 228—29.

51. N. Noddings, "Schools Face 'Crisis in Caring,'" *Education Week* vol. 32, 7 December 1988, p. 32.

THE PHILOSOPHICAL AND
VALUE RAMIFICATIONS

CHAPTER 14

A MODERN APPROACH TO THE VALUING PROCESS

◆

The work of the teacher and educator, like that of the therapist, is inextricably involved in the problem of values. The school has always been seen as one of the means by which the culture transmits its values from one generation to the next. But now this process is in upheaval, with many of our young people declaring themselves "dropouts" from the confused and hypocritical value system that they see operating in the world. How are educators—how are citizens—to orient themselves in relation to this complex and perplexing issue?

While on vacation in Jamaica many years ago, watching the abundant sea life through my snorkel and the equally fascinating development of three of our grandchildren, I attempted an essay on this problem based largely on my experience in psychotherapy.*

When I finished, I felt quite dissatisfied with it; but it has, for me, stood the test of time, and I now feel good about its venturesome quality. I feel in

---

* A condensed version of this chapter was first published by Carl Rogers as "Toward a Modern Approach to Values," *Journal of Abnormal and Social Psychology* 68 (1964): 160–67. © 1964 by the American Psychological Association. Adapted by permission of the publisher and the author.

regard to it, as with a small number of other papers, that I was writing more than I consciously "knew," and that it took my intellect some time to catch up with what I had written. I have also found that it has had significant meaning for many other people. I did not at that time foresee the tremendous shift in values that would so markedly change our culture, yet in a profound way I believe I did see something of the process by which that change would come about.

Social researcher Daniel Yankelovich, studying a great mass of data from national polls in the early 1980s, has tried to picture something of that shift. He writes, "Americans show unmistakably that the search for new meanings is an outpouring of popular sentiment and experimentation," involving perhaps 80 percent of all adults. "It is as if tens of millions of people [have] . . . decided simultaneously to conduct risky experiments in living, using the only materials at hand—their own lives" (1). I will let it speak for itself. A picture of the way in which this shift in values has come about, and some of the outcomes that have come to be culturally accepted will be found in this.

There is a great deal of concern today with the problem of values. Youth, in almost every country, is deeply uncertain of its value orientation; the values associated with various religions have lost much of their influence; sophisticated individuals in every culture seem unsure and troubled about the goals they hold in esteem. One does not have to look far to find the reasons. The world culture, in all its aspects, seems increasingly scientific and relativistic; and the rigid, absolute views on values that come to us from the past appear anachronistic. Even more important, perhaps, is the fact that the modern individual is assailed from every angle by divergent and contradictory value claims. It is no longer possible, as it was in the not too distant historical past, to settle comfortably into the value system of one's forebears or one's community or one's religion and live out one's life without ever examining the nature and the assumptions of that system.

In this situation it is not surprising that value orientations from the past appear to be in a state of disintegration or collapse. People question whether there are, or can be, any universal values. It is often felt that we may have lost, in our modern world, all possibility of any general or cross-cultural basis for values. One natural result of this uncertainty and confusion is that there is an increasing concern about, interest in, and search for a sound or meaningful value approach that can hold its own in today's world.

I share this general concern. I have also experienced the more specific value issues that arise in my own field, and I should like to attempt a modest approach to this whole problem. I have observed changes in the approach to values as the individual grows from infancy to adulthood. I have observed further changes when, if an individual is fortunate, she continues to grow toward true psychological maturity. Many of these observations grow out of my experience as an educator and therapist, where I have had the rare opportunity of seeing the ways in which individuals move toward a richer life. From these observations I believe I see some directional threads emerging that might offer a new concept of the valuing process that are more tenable in the modern world. I have made a beginning by presenting some of these ideas partially in previous writings (2, 3); I would like now to voice them more clearly and more fully. I would like to stress that my vantage point for making these observations is not that of the scholar or philosopher: I am speaking from my experience as a functioning human being who sees growth, change, and development.

SOME DEFINITIONS OF VALUES

Before I present some of these observations, perhaps I should try to clarify what I mean by values. Many definitions have been used, but I have found helpful some distinctions made by Charles Morris (4). He points out that value is a term we employ in different ways. We use it to refer to the tendency of living beings to show preference, by their actions, for one kind of object or objective rather than another. Morris calls this preferential behavior *operative values*. It need not involve any cognitive or conceptual thinking. It is simply the value choice that is indicated behaviorally when the organism selects one object, rejects another. When the earthworm, placed in a simple *Y* maze, chooses the smooth arm of the *Y* instead of the path that is paved with sandpaper, it is indicating an operative value.

A second distinction might be called *conceived values*. This is the preference of the individual for a symbolized object. Usually in such a choice, an individual shows anticipation or foresight about the outcome of behavior directed toward such a symbolized object. A preference for "honesty is the best policy" is such a conceived value.

A final distinction might be called *objective values*. People use the word in this way when they wish to speak of what is objectively preferable—whether or not it is, in fact, sensed or conceived of as desirable. What I have to say in this chapter scarcely touches on this last definition. I am, instead, more concerned with operative values and conceived values.

THE INFANT'S WAY OF VALUING

Let me first speak about the infant. The living human being has, at the outset, a clear approach to values. She prefers some things and experiences and rejects others. We can infer from studying her behavior that she prefers those experiences that maintain, enhance, or actualize her organism, and rejects those that do not serve this end. Watch her for a moment:

❦ *Hunger is negatively valued. Her expression of this often comes through loud and clear.*

Food is positively valued. But when she is satisfied, food is negatively valued: The same milk she responded to so eagerly is now spit out, or the breast that seemed so satisfying is now rejected as she turns her head away from the nipple with an amusing facial expression of disgust and revulsion.

She values security and the holding and caressing that seem to communicate security.

She values new experience for its own sake, and we observe this in her obvious pleasure in discovering her toes, in her searching movements, and in her endless curiosity.

She shows a clear negative valuing of pain, bitter tastes, and sudden loud sounds.

All of this is commonplace, but let us look at these facts in terms of what they tell us about the infant's approach to values. That approach is, first of all, a flexible, changing, valuing *process*, not a fixed system. She likes food and dislikes the same food. She values security and rest, and rejects it for new experience. Her approach seems best described as a self-valuing process, in which each element, each moment of what she is experiencing, is somehow weighed and selected or rejected, depending on whether, at that moment, it tends to actualize the self or not. This complicated weighing of experience is clearly an organismic function, not a conscious or symbolic one. These are operative, not conceived values. But this process can nonetheless deal with complex value problems. I would like to remind you of an experiment in which young infants had twenty or more dishes of natural (that is, unflavored) foods spread in front of them. Over a period of time they clearly tended to value the foods that enhanced their own survival, growth, and development. If, for a time, a child gorged herself on starches, this would soon be balanced by a protein binge. If, at times, she chose a diet deficient in some vitamin, she would later seek out foods rich in this very vitamin. She was using the wisdom of the body in her value choices; or, perhaps more accurately, the physiological wisdom of her body guided her behavioral movements, resulting in what we think of as objectively sound value choices.

Another aspect of the infant's approach to value is that the source or locus of the evaluating process is clearly within herself. Unlike many of us, she *knows* what she likes and dislikes, and the origin of these value choices lies strictly within herself. She is the center of the valuing process, the evidence for her choices being supplied by her own senses. She is not at this point influenced by what her parents think she should prefer or by what the church says or by the opinion of the latest expert in the field or by the persuasive talents of an advertising firm. It is from within her own experiencing that her organism is saying in nonverbal terms, "This is good for me,"

"That is bad for me," "I like this," "I strongly dislike that." She would laugh at our concern over values, if she could understand it. How could anyone fail to know what she liked and disliked, what was good for her and what was not, and what was important and what was trivial?

THE CHANGE IN THE VALUING PROCESS

What happens to this highly efficient, soundly based valuing process? By what sequence of events do we exchange it for the more rigid, uncertain, inefficient approach to values that characterizes most of us as adults? Let me try to state briefly one of the major ways in which I think this happens.

The infant needs love, wants it, tends to behave in ways that will bring a repetition of this wanted experience. But this brings complications. A boy pulls his baby sister's hair and finds it satisfying to hear her wails and protests. He then hears that he is "a naughty, bad boy," which may be reinforced by a slap on the hand. He is cut off from affection. As this experience is repeated, and many, many others like it, he gradually learns that what feels good to him is often bad in the eyes of others. Then the next step occurs, in which he comes to take the same attitude toward himself that others significant in his life have taken. Now, as he pulls his sister's hair, he solemnly intones, "Bad, bad boy." He is introjecting the value judgment of another, gradually taking it as his own. To that degree he loses touch with his own self-valuing process. He has deserted the wisdom of his organism, giving up the locus of evaluation, and is trying to behave in terms of values set by another in order to hold love.

Or take another example at an older level. A boy senses, though perhaps not consciously, that he is more loved and prized by his parents when he thinks of being a doctor than when he thinks of being an artist. Gradually, he introjects the values attached to being a doctor. He comes to want, above all, to be a doctor. Then in college he is baffled by the fact that he repeatedly fails in chemistry, which is absolutely necessary to becoming a physician, in spite of the fact that the guidance counselor assures him he has the ability to pass the course. Only in counseling interviews does he begin to realize how completely he has lost touch with his organismic reactions, how out of touch he is with his own valuing process. The same missive would apply to a young girl who is given the message that being an artist is better than being a doctor, when she herself truly wants to be a doctor.

Let me give another instance from a class of mine, a group of prospective teachers. I asked them at the beginning of the course, "Please list for me the two or three values that you would most wish to pass on to the children with whom you will work." They turned in many value goals, and I was surprised by some of the items. Several listed such things as "to speak correctly," "to use good English," "not to use words like *ain't*." Others mentioned neatness, such as "to do things according to instructions"; and one expressed her hope that "when I tell them to write their names in the upper right-hand corner with the date under it, I want them to do it *that way*, not in some other form."

I confess I was somewhat appalled. For some of these young teachers, the most important values to be passed on to pupils were to avoid bad grammar or to follow the teacher's instructions meticulously. I felt baffled. Certainly these behaviors had not been experienced as the most satisfying and meaningful elements in their own lives. Listing such values could only be accounted for by the fact that these behaviors had gained approval—and thus had been introjected as deeply important.

The previous illustrations show that in an attempt to gain or hold love, approval, or esteem, the individual relinquishes the locus of evaluation that was hers in infancy and places it in others. The infant learns to have a basic distrust for his or her own experiencing as a guide to behavior. Children learn from others a large number of conceived values and adopt them as their own, even though they may be widely discrepant from what is actually experienced. Because these concepts are not based on a child's own valuing, they tend to be fixed and rigid rather than fluid and changing. In this fashion, I believe, most of us accumulate the introjected value patterns by which we live.

Some Introjected Patterns

Introject is a psychological term that best describes the internalization of another's characteristics without a conscious effort. In today's fantastically complex culture, the patterns we introject as desirable or undesirable come from a variety of sources and are often highly contradictory in their meanings. Let me list a few commonly held introjections:

- *Sexual desires and behaviors are mostly bad.*   The sources of this construct are many: parents, church, teachers. The lack of sexual understanding and a locus of evaluation has led many teens to go in the opposite direction, resulting in more than a million teen pregnancies each year.

- *Disobedience is bad.*   Here parents and teachers combine with the military to emphasize this concept: to obey is good. To obey without question is even better. The holocausts of the world have been carried out by ordinary people following orders without thinking.

- *Making money is the highest good.*   The sources of this conceived value derive from valuing things more than people.

- *Learning an accumulation of scholarly facts is highly desirable.*   This comes from a time when only the elite had books and knowledge was a commodity to be kept from others.

- *Browsing and aimless exploratory reading for fun is undesirable.* The source of these last two concepts is apt to be the school, the educational system.

- *Style and fashion are important.* Here the people we regard as sophisticated and as performers are the originators of the value.

- *Dictatorships are utterly bad, except when they support our goals.* Here the government is a major source.

- *To love thy neighbor is the highest good.* This concept comes from the church and perhaps from parents.

- *Competition is preferable to teamwork and cooperation.* Here businesses and corporations are an important source.

- *Cheating is clever and desirable.* The peer group and some adults are the origin.

- *Coca-Cola, MTV, chewing gum, video games, American jeans, and automobiles are utterly desirable.* This conception comes not only from advertisements but is reinforced by people all over the world. From Jamaica to Japan, from Copenhagen to Kowloon, the Coca-Cola culture has come to be regarded as the acme of desirability.

This is a small diversified sample of the myriad of conceived values that individuals often introject and hold as their own. It seems, all too often, that an individual is not encouraged to give credence to his or her own inner feelings and beliefs, but to rely on those imposed upon the individual by outside influence.

Common Characteristics of Adult Valuing

I believe it is clear from the foregoing examples that the usual adult—I feel I am speaking for most of us—has an approach to values with the following characteristics:

- Most of our values are introjected from other individuals or groups significant to us, but the values are regarded by many as our own.

- The source or locus of evaluation on most matters lies outside the self.

- The criterion by which values are set is the degree to which they cause us to be loved or accepted.

- These conceived preferences are either not related at all, or not clearly related, to our own process of experiencing.

- Often there is a wide and unrecognized discrepancy between the evidence supplied by our own experience and these conceived values.

◆ Because these conceptions are not open to the test of experience, we must hold them in a rigid and unchanging fashion. The alternative would be a collapse of our values. Hence, they are "right": Like the law of the Medes and the Persians, they changeth not.

◆ Because they are untestable, there is no ready way of solving contradictions. If we have absorbed from others the concept that money is *summum bonum* and from the church the concept that loving one's neighbor is the highest value, then we have no way of discovering which concept has more value for us. Hence, a common aspect of modern life is living with absolutely contradictory values. We calmly discuss the possibility of dropping bombs on a country we regard as our enemy or we step over the body of a homeless person, but then we find tears in our eyes when we read headlines about the suffering of one small child.

◆ Because we have relinquished the locus of evaluation to others and have lost touch with our own valuing process, we feel profoundly insecure and easily threatened in our values. If some of these conceptions are destroyed, what will take their place? This threatening possibility makes us hold our value conceptions more rigidly or more confusedly, or both. The crisis facing us today is not based on a loss of values but on a contradiction of values with experience.

THE FUNDAMENTAL DISCREPANCY

I believe that this picture of the individual, with values mostly introjected, held as fixed concepts that are rarely examined or tested, is the picture of most of us. By taking over the conceptions of others as our own, we lose contact with the potential wisdom of our own functioning and lose confidence in ourselves. Because these value constructs are often sharply at variance with what is going on in our own experiencing, we have, in a very basic way, divorced ourselves from ourselves; and this accounts for much modern strain and insecurity. The fundamental discrepancy between our individual concepts and what we are actually experiencing, between the intellectual structure of our values and the valuing process going unrecognized within this, is a part of the fundamental estrangement of the modern person from his or herself. This is a major problem for those in the helping professions: teachers, social workers, and therapists.

Restoring Contact with Experience

Some individuals are fortunate. They are able to go beyond the picture I have just given, developing further in the direction of psychological maturity. We see this happen in psychotherapy, where we endeavor to provide a climate favorable to the growth of the person. We also see it happen in life, whenever life provides a supportive climate for the individual. Let me concentrate on the further maturing of a value approach, as I have seen it.

In the first place, let me say somewhat parenthetically that the helping relationships are *not* devoid of values. Quite the contrary. When helping relationships are most effective, it seems to me, they are marked by one primary value: namely, that this person has worth and is valued in his or her separateness and uniqueness. When we sense and realize that we are prized as persons, we can slowly begin to value the different aspects of ourselves. Most important, we can begin, with much difficulty at first, to sense and to feel what is going on within us: What are we are feeling, experiencing? How are we reacting? We use our experiencing as a direct referent to which we can turn in forming accurate conceptualizations and take as a guide to our behavior. Gendlin has elaborated the way in which this occurs (5, 6). As our experiencing becomes more and more open to us, as we become able to live more freely in the process of our feelings, then significant changes begin to occur in our approach to values. Our approach begins to assume many of the characteristics it had in infancy.

In the classroom, teachers who want students to use appropriate language may be directly conflicting with the language used in students' other (and usually more important) worlds. I listened as a sixth-grade middle school teacher responded to several students who were swearing in the classroom. He sat at the edge of the desk and said:

> *Class, I realize that we use language in many ways and we say things to one person that we wouldn't say to another person. There is language you use with your friends, with your family, perhaps at church and in school and work. I feel uncomfortable when you swear in class. The language used in other places may not always be best for school.*

The class then had a discussion about the meaning of language and what is communicated to others. It was a very different approach to what students valued. Compare it with another classroom in which students were swearing. That teacher yelled, "Shut your mouths." Respecting students' values and letting them see that what a person values is fluid can build a much stronger sense of values. The students respected the approach that didn't diminish their "other world" values. That approach also gave them a sense of context, which illustrated how different situations require different perspectives. Perhaps not unexpectedly, the students in the class began to value their teacher at a different level.

VALUING IN THE MATURE PERSON

The valuing process that seems to develop in a more mature person is in some ways very much like that in the infant, and in some ways quite different. It is fluid and flexible, based on a particular moment and the degree to which this moment is experienced as enhancing and actualizing. Values are not held rigidly but are continually changing. The painting that last year seemed meaningful now appears uninteresting; the way of working with individuals that was formerly experienced as good now seems inadequate; the belief that then seemed true is now experienced as only partly true or perhaps false.

Another characteristic of the way this more mature person values experience is to understand that it is highly differentiated or, as the semanticists would say, extensional. As the members of my class of prospective teachers learned, general principles are not as useful as sensitively discriminating reactions. One student said, "With this little boy, I just felt I should be very firm, and he seemed to welcome that, and I felt good that I had been. But I'm not that way at all with the other children most of the time." She relied on her experiencing of the relationship with each child to guide her behavior. Before we begin to ask others to reflect on their values, we must begin with ourselves. This process allows us to realize how much more differentiated are the individual's reactions to what were previously rather solid, monolithic, introjected values.

In another way the mature individual's approach is like an infant's. The locus of evaluation is again established firmly within the person; our own personal experience provides the value information or feedback. This does not mean that we are not open to all the evidence that can be obtained from other sources. But it means that this is taken for what it is—outside evidence—and is not as significant as our own reactions. Thus, we may be told by a friend that a new book is very disappointing after she reads two unfavorable reviews of the book. Her tentative hypothesis is that she will not value the book. Yet if she reads the book, her valuing will be based upon the reactions it stirs in her, not on what she has been told by others.

Letting oneself down into the immediacy of what one is experiencing is also involved in this valuing process—endeavoring to sense and to clarify all the complex meanings of these feelings. I think of a client, who toward the close of therapy, when he was puzzled about an issue, would put his head in his hands and say, "Now what is it that I'm feeling? I want to get next to it. I want to learn what it is." Then he would wait, quietly and patiently, trying to listen to himself until he could discern the exact flavor of the feelings he was experiencing. He, like others, was trying to get close to himself.

For the mature person, getting close to what is going on within is a much more complex process than it is in the infant. In the mature person, it has much more scope and sweep; for there is involved in the present moment of experiencing the memory traces of all the relevant learnings from the past. This moment has not only its immediate sensory impact, but it has meaning growing out of similar experiences in the past. It has both the new and the old in it. So when I experience a painting or a person, my experiencing contains within it the learnings I have accumulated from past meetings with paintings or persons, as well as the new impact of this particular encounter. Likewise, the moment of experiencing contains, for the mature adult, hypotheses about consequences: "I feel now that I would enjoy a third drink, but past learnings indicate that I may regret it in the morning." "It is not pleasant to express forthrightly my negative feelings to this person, but past experience indicates that in a continuing relationship it will be helpful in the long run." Past and future are both in this moment and enter into the valuing.

I find that in a mature person (and here again we see a similarity to the infant), the criterion of the valuing process is the degree to which the object of the experience actualizes the individual: "Does it make me a richer, more complete, more fully developed person?" This may sound as though it were a selfish or unsocial criterion, but it does not prove to be so because deep and helpful relationships with others are experienced as actualizing. Like the infant, too, we as psychologically mature adults trust and use the wisdom of our organism, with the difference that we are able to do so knowingly. We realize that if we can trust ourselves, our feelings and intuitions may be wiser than our mind, that as a total person we can be more sensitive and accurate than our thoughts alone. Hence, we are not afraid to say, "I feel that this experience (or this thing or this direction) is good. Later I will probably know *why* I feel it is good." We trust the totality of ourselves.

It should be evident from what I have been saying that this valuing process in the mature individual is not an easy or simple thing. The process is complex, the choices often very perplexing and difficult, and there is no guarantee that the choice that is made will in fact prove to be self-actualizing. But because whatever evidence exists is available to the individual, and because we are open to our experiencing, errors are correctable. If this chosen course of action is not self-enhancing, this will be sensed and we can make an adjustment or revision. We thrive on a maximum feedback interchange and thus, like the gyroscopic compass on a ship, can continually correct the course toward the true goal of self-fulfillment.

SOME PROPOSITIONS REGARDING THE VALUING PROCESS

Let me sharpen the meaning of what I have been saying by stating two propositions that contain the essential elements of this viewpoint. It may not be possible to devise empirical tests of each proposition in its entirety, yet each is to some degree capable of being tested through the methods of science. I would also state that though the following propositions are stated firmly in order to give them clarity, I am actually advancing them as decidedly tentative hypotheses.

I.   *There is a living base for an organized valuing process within the human individual.*   It is hypothesized that this base is something that human beings share with the rest of the animate world. It is part of the functioning life process of any healthy organism. It is the capacity for receiving feedback information that enables the organism continually to adjust its behavior and reactions so as to achieve the maximum possible self-enhancement.

II.   *This valuing process in the human being is effective in achieving self-enhancement to the degree that the individual is open to the experiencing that is going on within.*   I have tried to give two examples of individuals who are close to their own experiencing: the tiny infant who has not yet learned to deny in her awareness the processes going on within, and the psychologically mature person who has relearned the advantages of this open state. There is a corollary to this second proposition that might be put in the following terms. One way of assisting individuals to move toward openness to experience is through a relationship in which we are prized as a separate person, in which the experiencing going on within is empathically understood and valued, and in which we are given the freedom to experience our own feelings and those of others without being threatened by doing so. This corollary obviously grows out of therapeutic experience. It is a brief statement of the essential qualities in any growth-promoting relationship. There are empirical studies that give support to such a statement.

PROPOSITIONS REGARDING THE OUTCOMES OF THE VALUING PROCESS

I come now to the nub of any theory of values or valuing. What are its consequences? I should like to move into this new ground by stating bluntly two propositions about the qualities of behavior that emerge from this valuing process. I shall then give some of the evidence from my own experience as a therapist in support of these propositions.

I.   *In persons who are moving toward greater openness to their experiencing, there is a living commonality of value directions.*

II.   *These common value directions are of such kinds as to enhance the development of the individual, of others in the community, and to contribute to the survival and evolution of humankind.*

It has been a striking fact of my experience that in therapy, where individuals are valued and where there is greater freedom to feel and to be, certain value directions seem to emerge. These are not chaotic directions but instead have a surprising commonality. This commonality is not dependent on the personality of the therapist, for I have seen these trends emerge in the clients of therapists sharply different in personality. It does not seem to be due to the influences of any one culture, for I have found evidence of these directions in cultures as divergent as those of the United States, Holland, France, and Japan. I like to think this commonality of value directions is due to the fact that we all belong to the same species—that just as a human infant tends, individually, to select a diet similar to that selected by other human infants, so a client in therapy tends, individually, to choose value directions similar to those chosen by other clients. As a species, we may share certain elements of experience that tend to make for inner development and that would be chosen by all individuals if they were genuinely free to choose.

Let me indicate a few of these value directions as I have seen them in my clients in their move toward personal growth and maturity.

- They tend to move away from facades. Pretense, defensiveness, and putting up a front tend to be negatively valued.

- They tend to move away from "oughts." The compelling feeling of "I ought to do or be this particular way" is negatively valued. The client moves away from being what "I ought to be," no matter who has set the imperative.

- They tend to move away from meeting the expectations of others. Pleasing others, as a goal in itself, is negatively valued.

- Being real is positively valued. The client tends to move toward being her or himself, being his real feelings, being what she is. This seems to be a very deep preference.

- Self-direction is positively valued. The client discovers an increasing pride and confidence in making her own choices, guiding her own life.

- Oneself, one's own feelings come to be positively valued. Instead of looking upon himself with contempt and despair, the client comes to value himself and his reactions as being worthwhile.

- Being a process is positively valued. From desiring some fixed goal, clients come to prefer the excitement of being a process of potentialities being born.

- Perhaps more than anything else, the client comes to value an openness to all inner and outer experiences. To be open and sensitive to individual inner reactions and feelings, the reactions and feelings of others, and the realities of the objective world—this is a direction that the person clearly prefers. Openness becomes the client's most valued resource.

◆ Sensitivity to others and acceptance of others is positively valued. The client comes to appreciate others for what they are, just as she has come to appreciate herself for what she is.

◆ Finally, deep relationships are positively valued. To achieve a close, intimate, real, fully communicative relationship with another person seems to meet a deep need in every individual and is very highly valued.

These, then, are some of the preferred directions that I have observed in individuals moving toward personal maturity. Though I am sure that the list I have given is inadequate and perhaps to some degree inaccurate, it holds for me exciting possibilities. Let me try to explain why. I find it significant that when individuals are prized as persons, the values they select do not run the full gamut of possibilities. I do not find, in such a climate of freedom, that one person comes to value fraud and murder and thievery, while another values a life of self-sacrifice and another values only money. Instead there seems to be a deep and underlying thread of commonality. I dare to believe that when human beings are inwardly free to choose whatever they deeply value, they tend to value those objects, experiences, and goals that contribute to and enhance their own survival, growth, and development and contribute to the survival and development of others. I hypothesize that it is characteristic of the human organism to prefer such actualizing and socialized goals when we are exposed to a growth-promoting climate.

A corollary of what I have been saying is that in any culture, given a climate of respect and freedom in which the person is valued as a person, the mature individual would tend to choose and prefer these same value directions. This is a highly significant hypothesis that could be tested. It means that although the individual would not have a consistent or even a stable system of conceived values, the valuing process within that person would lead to emerging value directions that would be constant across cultures and across time.

Another implication I see is that individuals who exhibit the fluid valuing process I have tried to describe, whose value directions are generally those I have listed, are highly effective in the ongoing process of human evolution. If the human species is to survive at all on this globe, human beings must become more readily adaptive to new problems and situations, must be able to select that which is valuable for development and survival out of new and complex situations, must be accurate in the appreciation of reality if we are to make such selections. The psychologically mature person I have described here has, I believe, the qualities that would cause us to value those experiences that would facilitate the survival and enhancement of the human race. This individual and many others would be worthy participants and guides in the process of human evolution.

Finally, it appears that we have returned to the issue of the universality of values, but by a different route. Instead of universal values out there or a universal value system imposed by philosophers, rulers, or priests, we have the possibility of universal human value directions emerging from the experiencing of the human being. Evidence from therapy indicates that both personal and social values emerge as natural, and experienced, when the individual is close to her own organismic valuing process. The tentative conclusion is that even though modern humans no longer trust religion or science or philosophy or any system of beliefs to give them their values, they can find an organismic valuing base deep within themselves, which, if they can learn to be in touch with it, will prove to be an organized, adaptive, and social approach to the perplexing value issues that face all of us.

VALUES AND THE CO-LEARNER

Does what I have presented here have any relevance or meaning for teachers and students? I think it does. It appears to me that the process of developing a locus of evaluation, which may come through therapy as an adult, comes through a series of meaningful and supportive experiences in other learning environments. But if schools remain as they are, the next generation of adults will need extensive assistance in finding meaning in their lives. The world is changing at such a rapid rate that the fifteen thousand hours most children spend in school need to be reshaped if young adults are to flourish in a complex and interdependent world.

Students, teachers, administrators, parents, and the learning environments in which they all work have a remarkable set of common values. Descriptions of schools that kids love (as discussed in chapter 1) show that children want to be valued as people and given opportunities to share their ideas as well as to learn from others. The students in the examples you have read view teachers as resources and sometimes as referees, but always as people who care and "know me as a person." Schools are places where they love to go because life is fun and filled with stimulating hard work; learning is "an adventure in trust" and discovery. The values people live in those schools are not rigid but flexible; reason as well as actions are part of a discussion of consequences for student behavior. Freedom is not license: it carries equal measures of responsibility and participation. Healthy values nurture a healthy climate for learning, and encourage healthy children.

SUMMARY

I have tried to present some observations, growing out of my experience in psychotherapy, that are relevant to humankind's search for some satisfying basis to an approach to values and the implications of this search for members of facilitating professions. I have described the human infant entering directly into an evaluating transaction with her world, appreciating or rejecting her experiences as they have meaning for her own actualization, using all the wisdom of her tiny but complex organism. I have said that we seem to lose this capacity for direct evaluation and come to behave in those ways and to act in terms of those values that will bring us social approval, affection, esteem. To buy love, we relinquish the valuing process. Because the center of our lives now lies in others, we are fearful and insecure and must cling rigidly to the values we have introjected.

But if life or therapy gives us favorable conditions for continuing our psychological growth, we move on in something of a spiral, developing an approach to values that partakes of the infant's directness and fluidity but goes far beyond in its richness. In our transactions with experience, we are again the locus or source of valuing; we prefer those experiences that in the long run are enhancing; we partake in all the richness of our cognitive learning and functioning, but at the same time we trust the wisdom of our organism. I have pointed out that these observations lead to certain basic statements. Humans have within themselves an organismic basis for valuing. To the extent that we can be freely in touch with this valuing process in ourselves, we behave in ways that are self-enhancing. We even know some of the conditions that enable us to be in touch with our own experiencing process. In therapy, such openness to experience leads to emerging value directions that appear to be common among individuals and perhaps even across cultures. Stated in older terms, individuals who are thus in touch with their experiencing come to value such directions as sincerity, independence, self-direction, self-knowledge, social responsivity, social responsibility, and loving interpersonal relationships.

I have concluded that a new kind of emergent universality of value directions becomes possible when individuals move in the direction of psychological maturity or, more accurately, move in the direction of becoming open to their experiencing. Such a value base appears to make for the enhancement of self and others and to promote a positive evolutionary process.

REFERENCES

1. D. Yankelovich, "New Rules in American Life: Searching for Self-fulfillment in a World Turned Upside Down," *Psychology Today* 15 (1981): 39.

2. Carl R. Rogers, *Client-centered Therapy* (Boston: Houghton Mifflin, 1951).

3. Carl R. Rogers, "A Theory of Therapy, Personality and Interpersonal Relationships," in *Psychology: A Study of a Science*, vol. 3, ed. S.

Koch, pp. 185–256; *Formulations of the Person and the Social Context* (New York: McGraw-Hill, 1959), pp. 185–256.

4. Charles W. Morris, *Varieties of Human Value* (Chicago: University of Chicago Press, 1956).

5. E. T. Gendlin, *Experiencing and the Creation of Meaning* (New York: Macmillan, The Free Press, 1962).

6. E. T. Gendlin, *Focusing* (New York: Everest House, 1978).

CHAPTER 15

FREEDOM AND COMMITMENT

◆

Freedom to learn or choose; self-directed learning: these are completely untenable concepts in the minds of many behavioral scientists, who believe that humans are simply the inevitable products of their conditioning. Yet they are terms that I have used freely in this book, as though they have real meaning. I endeavored to face this discrepancy squarely in a talk I gave at the time I was honored as "Humanist of the Year" by the American Humanist Association. I do not pretend that I resolved the age-old problem of freedom and determinism, but I have, for myself, formulated a way of living with it. I hope my statement will be clarifying to those who are perplexed by differences between the mechanistic-behaviorist point of view in education and the humanistic approach to learning.

One of the deepest issues in modern life is the question as to whether the concept of personal freedom has any meaning whatsoever in our present-day scientific world. The growing ability of the behavioral scientist to predict and to control behavior has brought the issue sharply to the fore. If we accept the logical positivism and strictly behavioristic emphases that are predominant in the American educational scene, there is not even room for discussion. But if we step outside the narrowness of the behavioral sciences, this question is not only an issue; it is one of the primary issues that define the modern person. Friedman in his book *The Problematic Rebel* makes his topic "the problematic of modern man—the alienation, the divided nature, the unresolved tension between personal freedom and psychological compulsion which follows 'on the death of God'" (1, p. 251). The issues of personal freedom and personal commitment have become very sharp indeed in a world in which the individual feels the division between awareness and those elements of dynamic functioning of which an individual is unaware. If we are to wrest any meaning from the universe, which for all we know may be indifferent, we must arrive at some stance that we can hold in regard to these timeless uncertainties.

One might ask, "Why do teachers and other educators need to know these things?" If we take a mechanical view of teaching, then one skilled teacher is the same as any other skilled teacher. When a teacher leaves, we replace her with another person called "teacher," and all is well. In fact, this perspective has led to the system we currently have in place in many of our schools. In this system, teachers are interchangeable parts. A case in point is the response when there is a shortage of teachers. In other professions, including medicine, law, accounting, and engineering, a shortage usually leads to higher salaries, better working conditions, and efforts to give the professional some control, and ultimately freedom, over his or her destiny. In teaching when there is a shortage, the opposite occurs. Salaries in real terms have gone down since 1970, while standards have been changed—some say lowered—to allow more people into the classrooms. Curriculum has been prepackaged to make it teacherproof; and teachers are evaluated, monitored, tested, and paperworked to death with a system that acts as if the person in the classroom is a liability rather than a valued gift to be cherished. With all this top-down management of the teaching profession during the last decade, the state of schools and learning, by most perspectives, is in dire need. In response to these conditions and to the lack of valuing for the individual, a majority of teachers leave the classroom within the first five years. They are tired of being controlled.

While behaviorism has diminished in its importance for most psychologists, it continues to rule the educational system in this country. The examples are numerous. From the way students are disciplined to the way teachers are evaluated, the method is one of control, reward, and punishment. So writing both as a behavioral scientist and as one profoundly concerned with the human, the personal, the phenomenological, and the intangible, I should like to contribute what I can to this continuing dialogue regarding the meaning of and the possibility of freedom. For if we see teaching as a facilitative process in which the individual is valued, then the words *freedom* and *commitment* take on very vital meanings.

THE INDIVIDUAL IS UNFREE

Let me explain, first of all, that to most psychologists and workers in the behavioral sciences, the title of this chapter must seem very strange indeed. In the minds of most behavioral scientists, humans are not free; nor can they as free humans commit themselves to some purpose, for they are controlled by factors outside of themselves. Therefore, neither freedom nor commitment is even a possible concept to modern behavioral science as it is usually understood.

To show that I am not exaggerating, let me quote a statement from the late B. F. Skinner of Harvard, who was one of the most consistent advocates of a strictly behavioristic psychology. The use of behavior modification in schools is based on his theories. He says,

> The hypothesis that man is not free is essential to the application of scientific method to the study of human behavior. The free inner man who is held responsible for his behavior is only a prescientific substitute for the kinds of causes which are discovered in the course of scientific analysis. All these alternative causes lie outside the individual. (2, p. 477)

This view is shared by some psychologists, educators, and others who feel, as did Dr. Skinner, that all the effective causes of behavior lie outside of the individual and that it is only through the external stimulus that behavior takes place. The scientific description of behavior avoids anything that partakes in any way of freedom. For example, Dr. Skinner described an experiment in which a pigeon was conditioned to turn in a clockwise direction (3, pp. 90–91). The behavior of the pigeon was "shaped up" by rewarding any movement that approximated a clockwise turn until, increasingly, the bird was turning round and round in a steady movement. This is what is known as *operant conditioning*.

Students who watched the demonstration were asked to write an account of what they had seen. Their responses included the following ideas: The pigeon was conditioned to *expect* reinforcement for the right kind of behavior; the pigeon *hoped* that something would bring the food back again; the pigeon *observed* that a certain behavior seemed to produce a particular result; the pigeon *felt* that food would be given to it because of its action; the bird came to *associate* its action with the click of the food dispenser. Skinner ridicules these statements because they all go beyond the observed behavior by using such words as *expect, hoped, observed, felt,* and *associate.* The whole explanation from his point of view is that the bird was reinforced when it emitted a given kind of behavior; the pigeon walked around until the food container again appeared; a certain behavior produced a given result; food was given to the pigeon when it acted in a particular way; and the click of the food dispenser was related in time to the bird's action. These statements describe the pigeon's behavior from a scientific point of view.

Skinner goes on to point out that the students were undoubtedly reporting what they would have expected, felt, and hoped under similar circumstances. But he then makes the case that there is no more reality to such ideas in the human being than there is in the pigeon, that it is only because such words have been reinforced by the verbal community in which the individual has developed that such terms are used. He discusses the fact that the verbal community that conditioned them to use such terms saw no more of their behavior than they had seen of the pigeon's. In other words, the internal events, if they indeed exist, have no scientific significance.

As to the methods used for changing the behavior of the pigeon, many people besides Dr. Skinner feel that through such positive reinforcement human behavior as well as animal behavior can be shaped up and controlled. In his book, *Walden Two*, Skinner says,

> Now that we know how positive reinforcement works and how negative doesn't, we can be more deliberate and hence more successful in our cultural design. We can achieve a sort of control under which the controlled, though they are following a code much more scrupulously than was ever the case under the old system, nevertheless *feel free.* They are doing what they want to do, not what they are forced to do. That's the source of the tremendous power of positive reinforcement—there is no restraint and no revolt. By a careful cultural design we control not the final behavior but the inclination to behave—the motives, the desires, the wishes. The curious thing is that in that case the question of freedom never arises. (4, p. 218)

Another psychological experiment, this one by Dr. Richard Crutchfield at the University of California at Berkeley, again illustrates a way in which behavior may be controlled and in which it again appears that the individual is unfree (5). In this experiment five subjects at a time are seated side by side, each in an individual booth screened from one another. Each booth has a panel with various switches and lights. The subject can use the switches to signal his judgments about items that are projected on the wall in front of the group. The lights are signals that indicate what judgments the other four members are giving to the items. The subjects are told that they will be given the identifying letters *A, B, C, D,* and *E* and are instructed to respond one at a time in that order. However, when they enter the cubicles, each discovers that he is letter E. They are not permitted to talk during the session.

Actually the lights in each booth are controlled by the experimenter and do not express the judgments of the other four members. Thus, on those critical items where the experimenter wishes to impose group pressure, he can make it appear that all four members, A through D, agree on an answer that is clearly at variance with the correct answer. In this way each subject is confronted with a conflict between her own judgment and what she believes to be the consensus of the group. Thus, for example, the question may be, "Which of these two irregular figures is larger, X or Y?" The individual sees clearly that X is larger than Y, yet one after another the lights flash on indicating that all of the other four members regard Y as the larger figure. Now it is her turn to decide. How will she respond? Which switch will be pressed? Crutchfield has shown that given the right conditions, most people will desert the evidence of their senses or their own honest opinion and conform to the seeming consensus of the group. For example, some high-level mathematicians yielded to the false group consensus on some fairly easy arithmetic problems, giving wrong answers that they would never have given under normal circumstances.

Here again there would seem to be evidence that the behavior of the individual is shaped by the outside stimulus, in this case a social stimulus, and that there is no such thing as freedom in choosing one's behavior. It helps to explain how Skinner in *Walden Two* can have his hero say:

> "Well, what do you say to the design of personalities? Would that interest you? The control of temperaments? Give me the specifications and I'll give you the man! What do you say to the control of motivation, building the interests which will make men most productive and most successful? Does that seem to you fantastic? Yet some of the techniques are available and more can be worked out experimentally. Think of the possibilities. . . . Let us control the lives of our children and see what we can make of them." (4, p. 243)

An experience I had some time ago in a university on the West Coast further illustrates the *unfreedom* of the person. Some psychologists were studying the ways in which individual patterns of behavior in a group can be changed. Four male subjects are seated around a table. Each has in front of him a shielded light bulb invisible to the others. They are given a topic on which to talk. Notice is taken of the individual who seems least dominant in the group, who never takes a leadership role. Then for the second part of the experiment, this individual is given a paper in which he is told that the discussion is being listened to and observed by experts and that when these experts think he is contributing usefully to the group process, his light will blink. He will have to judge for himself what he is doing that is helpful. The other, more dominant three are given similar sheets of instructions, except that each is told that his light will blink when he is not contributing helpfully. They are then given another question to discuss, with the instruction that by the end of the half hour they are to try to arrive at conclusions in regard to this problem. Now, every time the *shrinking violet* speaks, his light blinks. And whenever the others speak their lights also blink, but with the opposite meaning: that they are not contributing. After half an hour of such conditioning, the shy member is nearly always the perceived leader of the group. Furthermore, this pattern seems to carry over through an additional half hour in which no use is made of lights. The story is told of three mature scientists and one young graduate student who were put through this procedure. In the first session, the young student took almost no part. In the session with the blinking lights, he became so dominant that at the end when the group was asked for a summary of what had gone on, the older men turned to him and said, "Why don't you summarize it? You're the one best able to do that." Here again it seems as though behavior is extremely manipulable and that there is no such thing as freedom. The members of the group are behaving like puppets on a string at the whim of the experimenters.

One more example of the degree of control that scientists have been able to achieve involves an experiment with rats. Years ago, Dr. James Olds found that he could implant tiny electrodes in the septal area of the brain of laboratory rats (6). When one of these animals presses a bar in his cage, it causes a minute current to pass through these electrodes. When the electrode has penetrated just the right area of brain tissue, this appears to be such a rewarding experience that the animal goes into an orgy of bar pressing, often until it is exhausted. However, the subjective nature of the experience seems to be so satisfying that the animal prefers it to any other activity. Even after exhaustion, with a brief rest and a small bit of food and water, the rat returns to its orgy of pleasure. In one experiment, rats went on in this fashion for twenty-four hours a day for three weeks straight. Curiously enough, there seemed to be no physical or mental damage to the rats then or later. One can only speculate what this procedure might bring forth if applied fully to human beings. For not only are there experiments of this sort with animals, but there are also beginning to be situations in which such electronic stimulation of the human brain is used for a number of medical purposes. Obviously researchers cannot experiment with human beings to the degree they can with animals. Yet already we know that these tiny electronic currents passing through minute portions of the brain elicit feelings of happiness, rage, or terror and even depress feelings of extreme pain.

I think it is clear from all of this that humans are a machine—a complex machine, to be sure, but one that is increasingly subject to behavioral control. Whether behavior will be managed through operant conditioning as in *Walden Two*, or whether we will be shaped up by the unplanned forms of conditioning implied in social pressure, or whether we will be controlled by electrodes in the brain, it seems quite clear that science is making us into objects and that the purpose of such science is not only understanding and prediction but *control*. Thus, it would seem to be quite clear that there can be no concept so foreign to the facts as the concept that people are free. We are machines; we are unfree; we cannot commit ourselves in any meaningful sense. We are simply controlled by planned or unplanned forces outside of ourselves.

THE INDIVIDUAL IS FREE

I am impressed by the scientific advances illustrated in the examples I have given. I regard them as a great tribute to the ingenuity, insight, and persistence of the individuals making the investigations. They have added enormously to our knowledge. Yet for me they leave something very important unsaid. Let me try to illustrate this, first from my experience in therapy and then from the classroom.

I think of a young man classed as schizophrenic with whom I had been working for a long time in a state hospital. He was a very inarticulate man, and during one hour he made only a few remarks about individuals who had recently left the hospital; then he remained silent for almost forty minutes. When he got up to go, he mumbled almost under his breath, "If some of *them* can do it, maybe I can too." That was all—not a dramatic statement, not uttered with force and vigor, yet a statement of choice by this young man to work toward his own improvement and eventual release from the hospital. It is not too surprising that about eight months after that statement he was out of the hospital. I believe this experience of responsible choice is one of the deepest aspects of psychotherapy and one of the elements that most solidly underlies personality change.

I think of another young person, this time a young female graduate student who was deeply disturbed and on the borderline of a psychotic break. Yet after a number of interviews in which she talked very critically about all of the people who had failed to give her what she needed, she finally concluded: "Well, with that sort of a foundation, it's really up to me. I mean it seems to be really apparent to me that I can't depend on someone else to give me an education." And then she added very softly, "I'll really have to get it myself." She went on to explore this experience of important and responsible choice. She found it a frightening experience, and yet one that gave her a feeling of strength. A force seemed to surge up within her that was big and strong, and yet she also felt very much alone and sort of cut off from support. She added, "I am going to begin to do more things that I know I should do." And she did.

I could add many other examples. A young fellow, talking about the way in which his whole life had been distorted and spoiled by his parents, finally came to this conclusion: "Maybe now that I see that, it's up to me." Or perhaps I could somehow communicate best the significance of free and responsible choice by quoting one sentence from a confused, bitter, psychotic individual who had been in a state hospital for three admissions, the last admission having lasted two and a half years at the time I began working with him. I think the changes that gradually took place were based on and epitomized by one sentence in an interview when he was feeling particularly confused. He said, "I don't know what I'm gonna do; but I'm gonna do it." For me, that speaks volumes.

The film *David and Lisa*, made a number of years ago, illustrates exactly what I have been discussing. David, the adolescent schizophrenic, goes into a panic if he is touched by anyone. He feels that "touching kills," and he is deathly afraid of it and afraid of the closeness in human relationships that touching implies. Yet toward the close of the film he makes a bold and positive choice of the kind I have been describing. He has been trying to help Lisa, the girl who is out of touch with reality. He tries to help at first in an intellectually contemptuous way, then increasingly in a warmer and more personal way. Finally, in a highly dramatic moment, he says to her, "Lisa, take my hand." He chooses, with obvious conflict and fear, to leave behind the safety of his untouchableness and to venture into the world of real human relationships where he is literally and figuratively in touch with another. You are an unusual person if you don't grow a bit misty at this point of the film. Perhaps a behaviorist could try to account for David's reaching out of his hand by saying that it was the result of intermittent reinforcement of partial movements. I find such an explanation both inaccurate and inadequate. It is the *meaning* of the decision that is essential to understanding the act.

The need to have choices in the classroom is just as important in the evolution of healthy individuals. If all parts of a child's life are controlled, then control becomes the driving force in decisions about teaching and learning. What is taught and how it will be taught become controlling issues. After the child's learning life is controlled for thirteen years in school, suddenly at age eighteen he or she is free to choose. The newfound freedom comes with little or no prior experience. If experience is the best teacher, then choosing and freedom are alien experiences for too many students in our schools.

A colleague shared an experience about a talk he had with a clinical psychologist who works with students in a public school district. The psychologist was attending one of a series of workshops that was being offered to improve the learning climate of middle-school students. The sixth-grade teachers talked and shared examples about the way they were involving students in classroom decisions and creating avenues for young adolescents to develop outlets for their feelings. They also talked about the importance of choices in the classroom. Teachers discussed how students select from a range of projects to work, and their sharing of the operations of the classroom with the students. For example, students working in teams prepared mini-lessons based on subject areas they had been studying and presented them to the class using visual aids and demonstrations. The discussion by the teachers about their newfound partners in learning was animated and exciting. At the conclusion of the session, a school psychologist who asked to sit in on the session said that the discussion was important for him because he usually only hears about problems and the lack of choices given to students. He commented, "Usually, they give me a student and say, 'He has a problem; fix it.'" He also realized the potential for teachers working together with students to create healthy learning environments, which could prevent the need for him to see some of the students he is currently counseling. Teachers usually do not receive education in counseling, but a supportive and caring learning environment can go a long way in reducing the numbers of students who need specialized counseling services. This would allow time for psychologists to work with those students with the greatest needs.

Let me spell out a trifle more fully the way such choosings occur in the classroom. A student, Dexter, was retained a second time in sixth grade; he had failed all his subjects due to excessive absences. He was placed in a different sixth-grade classroom with a teacher new to the school. After only a week it became clear that Dexter was very bright and capable but also a disruptive factor in the classroom. After several talks, the student explained that he was ashamed about not being with his peers in the next grade and didn't want to be in sixth grade for another year. The teacher asked Dexter if he would be willing to work independently in the library, in school, and at home to make up the learning he had missed. He said, "I need to move on; I can't stay here any longer." With that statement, the teacher developed a learning contract detailing what Dexter needed to move to seventh grade. The contract was approved by the principal and signed by the teacher and Dexter. Dexter completed his work in seven weeks. He moved to seventh grade where some tutoring was provided. Follow-ups with Dexter and his teachers showed he was doing well and was helping other students with their work. He took responsibility for his actions and was able to turn around a situation that would most likely have led him to drop out physically from a situation he had already mentally distanced himself from in the past.

In previous chapters of this book you read about students who had choice and freedom in school. But many students choose to be free earlier, a choice the educational establishment calls *dropping out*. In many cases it's the only way a young adult can express his or her need to choose. Not all students have Dexter's option.

I am trying to suggest in these examples that I would be at a loss to explain the positive change that can occur in psychotherapy or in education if I had to omit the importance of the sense of free and responsible choice on the part of clients, teachers, and students in schools. I believe that the freedom to choose is one of the deepest elements underlying change.

THE MEANING OF FREEDOM

Considering the scientific advantages that I have mentioned, how can we even speak of freedom? In what sense is a client, teacher, or student free?

In what sense are any of us free? What possible definition of freedom can there be in the modern world?

Let me attempt such a definition. In the first place, the freedom that I am talking about is essentially an inner element, something that exists in the living person quite aside from any of the outward choices of alternatives that we so often think of as constituting freedom. I am speaking of the kind of freedom that Viktor Frankl vividly describes in his experience of the concentration camp, when everything—possessions, status, identity—was taken from the victim. But even months and years in such an environment showed only "that everything can be taken from a man but one thing: the last of the human freedoms—to choose one's own attitude in any given set of circumstances, to choose one's own way" (7). It is this inner, subjective, existential freedom that I have observed. It is the realization that "I can live myself, here and now, by my own choice." It is the quality of courage that enables a person to step into the uncertainty of the unknown as she chooses herself. It is the discovery of meaning from within oneself, meaning that comes from listening sensitively and openly to the complexities of what one is experiencing. It is the burden of being responsible for the self one chooses to be. It is a person's recognition that she is an emerging process, not a static end product. The individual who is thus deeply and courageously thinking her own thoughts, becoming her own uniqueness, responsibly choosing herself may be fortunate in having hundreds of objective outer alternatives from which to choose, or she may be unfortunate in having none. But her freedom exists regardless. So we are first of all speaking of something that exists within the individual, something phenomenological rather than external, but nonetheless to be prized.

The second point in defining this experience of freedom is that it exists not as a contradiction of the picture of the psychological universe as a sequence of cause and effect, but as a complement to such a universe. Freedom rightly understood is a fulfillment by the person of the ordered sequence of her life. The free person moves out voluntarily, freely, responsibly to play her significant part in a world whose determined events move through her spontaneous choice and will.

I see this freedom of which I am speaking, then, as existing in a different dimension than the determined sequence of cause and effect. I regard it as a freedom that exists in the subjective person, a freedom that she courageously uses to live her potentialities. The fact that this type of freedom seems completely irreconcilable with the behaviorist's picture of our being is something that I will discuss a bit later.

Freedom Makes a Difference

Curiously enough, there is scientific evidence about the importance of this sense of freedom. For example, in the study done by Crutchfield (5), which I mentioned earlier, I stated that under especially extreme circumstances, nearly everyone yielded in some degree to group pressure. Yet there were sharp individual differences, and these are found to be definitely correlated with personality characteristics. For example, the individuals who tended to yield, agree, conform—the ones who could be controlled—gave general evidence of an incapacity to cope effectively with stress, while the nonconformists did not tend to panic when placed under pressure of conflicting forces. The conformists also tended to have pronounced feelings of personal inferiority and inadequacy, while those who did not yield to pressure had a sense of competence and personal adequacy. They were more self-contained and autonomous in their thinking. They were also better judges of the attitudes of other people.

Most important of all for our purposes is the fact that those who yielded, the conformists, tended to show a lack of openness and freedom in emotional processes. They were emotionally restricted, lacking in spontaneity, tending to repress their own impulses. The nonconformists, those who made their own choices, were, on the other hand, much more open, free, and spontaneous. They were expressive and natural, free from pretense and unaffected. Where the conformist tended to lack insight into her own motives and behavior, the independent person had a good understanding of herself.

What is the meaning of this aspect of Crutchfield's study? It seems to imply that the person who is free within herself, who is open to her experience, who has a sense of her own freedom and responsible choice is not nearly so likely to be controlled by her environment as is the person who lacks these qualities.

Another story from research in this field, a study with which I was closely connected, had a very decided impact on me in the years following the experience. Many years ago a student doing his graduate work under my supervision chose to study the factors that would predict the behavior of adolescent male delinquents. He made careful objective ratings of the psychological environment in the family, the educational experiences, the neighborhood and cultural influences, the social experiences, the health history, and the hereditary background of each delinquent. These external factors were rated as to their favorableness for normal development, using a continuum that moved from elements destructive to the child's welfare and inimical to healthy development to elements highly conducive to healthy development. Almost as an afterthought, a rating was also made of the degree of self-understanding since it was felt that although this was not one of the primary determining factors, it might play some part in predicting future behavior. This was essentially a rating of the degree to which the individual was open and realistic regarding himself and his situation, a judgment about whether he was emotionally acceptant of the facts in himself and his environment.

These ratings on seventy-five delinquents were compared with ratings of their behavior and adjustment two to three years after the initial study. It was expected that the ratings on family environment and social experience with peers would be the best predictors of later behavior. To our amazement the degree of self-understanding was much the best predictor, correlating with later behavior, while quality of social experience correlated .55 and family environment .36. We were simply not prepared to believe these findings and laid the study on the shelf until it could be replicated. Later it was replicated on a new group of seventy-six individuals; and all the essential findings were confirmed, although not quite so strikingly. Furthermore, the findings stood up even in detailed analysis. When we examined only the delinquents who came from the most unfavorable homes and who remained in those homes, it was still true that their future behavior was best predicted, not by the unfavorable conditioning they were receiving in their home environment, but by the degree of realistic understanding of themselves and their environment that they possessed (8).

The significance of this study was only slowly driven home to me. I began to see the significance of inner autonomy. The individual who sees himself and his situation clearly and who freely takes responsibility for that self and for that situation is a very different person from the one who is simply in the grip of outside circumstances. This difference shows up clearly in important aspects of his behavior.

THE EMERGENCE OF COMMITMENT

I have spoken thus far primarily about freedom. What about commitment? Certainly the disease of our age is lack of purpose, lack of meaning, lack of commitment on the part of individuals. Is there anything that I can say in regard to this?

It is clear to me that in therapy and in other learning settings, as indicated in the examples that I have given, commitment to purpose and to meaning in life is one of the significant elements of change. It is only when the person decides, "I am someone; I am someone worth being; I am committed to being myself," that change becomes possible.

At a very interesting symposium at Rice University, Dr. Sigmund Koch sketched the revolution that is taking place in science, literature, and the arts, in which a sense of commitment is again becoming evident after a long period in which that emphasis has been absent. Part of what he meant by an emerging sense of commitment may be illustrated by talking about Dr. Michael Polanyi, a philosopher of science, formerly a physicist, who has presented his notions about what science basically is. In his book *Personal Knowledge,* Polanyi makes it clear that even scientific knowledge is personal knowledge, committed knowledge. We cannot rest comfortably on the belief that scientific knowledge is impersonal and "out there," that it has nothing to do with the individual who has discovered it. Instead, every aspect of science is pervaded by disciplined personal commitment, and Polanyi makes the case very persuasively that the whole attempt to divorce science from the person is a completely unrealistic one. I think I am stating his belief correctly when I say that in his judgment logical positivism and all the current structure of science cannot save us from the fact that all knowing is uncertain, involves risk, and is grasped and comprehended only through the deep, personal commitment of a disciplined search.

Perhaps a brief quotation will give something of the flavor of his thinking. Speaking of great scientists, he says:

> So we see that both Kepler and Einstein approached nature with intellectual passions and with beliefs inherent in these passions, which led them to their triumphs and misguided them to their errors. These passions and beliefs were theirs, personally, even though they held them in the conviction that they were valid, universally. I believe that they were competent to follow these impulses, even though they risked being misled by them. And again, what I accept of their work today, I accept personally, guided by passions and beliefs similar to theirs, holding in my turn that my impulses are valid, universally, even though I must admit the possibility that they may be mistaken. (9)

Thus, we see that a modern philosopher of science believes that deep personal commitment is the only possible basis on which science can firmly stand. This is a far cry indeed from the logical positivism of forty years ago, which placed knowledge far out in impersonal space.

Let me say a bit more about what I mean by commitment in the psychological sense. I think it is easy to give this word a much too shallow meaning, indicating that the individual has, simply by conscious choice, committed himself to one course of action or another. I think the meaning goes far deeper than that. Commitment is a total organismic direction involving not only the conscious mind but the whole direction of the organism as well.

In my judgment, commitment is something that one discovers within oneself. It is a trust of one's total reaction rather than one's mind only. It has much to do with creativity. Einstein's explanation of how he moved toward his formulation of relativity without any clear knowledge of his goal is an excellent example of what I mean by the sense of commitment based on a total organismic reaction. Wertheimer quotes Einstein as saying:

> During all those years there was a feeling of direction, of going straight toward something concrete. It is, of course, very hard to express that feeling in words but it was decidedly the case and clearly to be distinguished from later considerations about the rational form of the solution. (10, pp. 183–84)

Thus, commitment is more than a decision. It is the functioning of an individual who is searching for the directions that are emerging within himself. Kierkegaard has said, "The truth exists only in the process of becoming, in the process of appropriation" (11, p. 72). It is this individual creation of a tentative personal truth through action that is the essence of commitment.

Persons are most successful in such a commitment when they are functioning as integrated, whole, unified individuals. The more that they are functioning in this total manner, the more confidence they have in the directions that they unconsciously choose. They feel a trust in their experiencing, of which, even if they are fortunate, they have only partial glimpses in their awareness.

If we think about it in the way I am describing, it becomes clear that commitment is an achievement. It is the kind of purposeful and meaningful direction that is only gradually achieved by individuals who have come increasingly to live closely in relationship with their own experiencing—a relationship in which their unconscious tendencies are as much respected as their conscious choices. This is the kind of commitment toward which I believe individuals can move. It is an important aspect of living in a fully functioning way.

THE IRRECONCILABLE CONTRADICTION

I trust it will be very clear that I have given two sharply divergent and irreconcilably contradictory points of view. On the one hand, modern psychological science, and many other forces in modern life as well, hold the view that the person is unfree, that she is controlled, that words such as *purpose, choice, commitment* have no significant meaning, that the individual is nothing but an object that we can more fully understand and more fully control. Enormous strides have been and are being made in implementing this perspective. It would seem heretical indeed to question this view.

Yet as Polanyi has pointed out in another of his writings, the dogmas of science can be in error (12). He says:

> In the days when an idea could be silenced by showing that it was contrary to religion, theology was the greatest single source of fallacies. Today, when any human thought can be discredited by branding it as unscientific, the power previously exercised by theology has passed over to science; hence science has become in its turn the greatest single source of error.

So I am emboldened to say that over against this view of the individual as unfree, as an object, is the evidence from therapy, from the schoolhouse, from subjective living, and from objective research as well that personal freedom and responsibility have a crucial significance, that one cannot live a complete life without such personal freedom and responsibility, and that self-understanding and responsible choice make a sharp and measurable difference in the behavior of the individual. In this context, commitment does have meaning. Commitment is the emerging and changing total direction of the individual based on a close and acceptant relationship between the person and all of the trends of his or her life, conscious and unconscious. Unless as individuals and as a society we can make constructive use of this capacity for freedom and commitment, humans are, it seems to me, set on a collision course with fate.

What is the answer to the contradiction I have described? For myself, I am content to think of it as a deep and lasting paradox. While paradoxes are often frustrating, they can still be very fruitful. In physics, there is the paradox that light is a form of wave motion and at the same time can be shown to exist in quanta—the contradiction between the wave theory and the corpuscular theory of light. This paradox has been irreconcilable; and yet on the basis of it, physics has made important advances.

The philosopher Friedman believes that much the same point of view is necessary when we face the philosophical issue of meaning. He says, "Today, meaning can be found, if at all, only through the attitude of the man who is willing to *live* with the absurd, to remain open to the mystery which he can never hope to pin down" (1, p. 468). I share this conviction that we must live openly with mystery, with the absurd. Let me put the whole theme of my discussion into the form of a contradiction. A part of modern living is to face the paradox that when viewed from one perspective, we are a complex machine. Every day researchers are moving toward a more precise understanding and a more precise control of this objective mechanism that we call *Homo sapiens*. On the other hand, in another significant dimension of our existence, we are subjectively free; our personal choices and responsibility account for the shape of our lives; we are, in fact, the architect of ourselves. A truly crucial part of our existence is the discovery of our own meaningful commitment to life with all of our being.

If in response to this you say, "But these views cannot both be true," my answer is, "This is a deep paradox with which we must learn to live."

An Update on the Paradox

Since those words were written, scientists have moved a long way in recognizing the deficiencies of a mechanistic world view and the inadequacy of the linear cause-effect science on which behaviorism rests. The universe is far more mysterious than it once seemed, and we find prominent physicists likening this view of the cosmos to that of a fluid puzzle—always in a state of flux. As to the issues I have discussed in this chapter, I will include here some quotations by Fritjof Capra, a theoretical physicist, although the same ideas have been expressed by other scientists and philosophers of science.

I'll mention Capra's discussion of the modern world view, including his ideas on the disappearance of a narrow cause-effect science:

The universe is thus experienced as a dynamic, inseparable whole which always includes the observer in an essential way. In this experience the traditional concepts of space and time, of isolated objects, and of cause and effect lose their meaning. Such an experience, however, is very similar to that of the Eastern mystics. (13, p. 81)

Capra also considers the question of choice: "A living organism is a self-organizing system, which means that its order in structure and function is not imposed by the environment, but is established by the system itself. . . ." Living systems interact with the environment continually, "but this interaction does not determine their organization." Capra continues:

The relative autonomy of self-organizing systems sheds new light on the age-old philosophical question of free will. From the systems point of view, both determinism and freedom are relative concepts. To the extent that a system is autonomous from its environment it is free; to the extent that it depends on it through continuous interaction its activity will be shaped by environmental influences. The relative autonomy of organisms usually increases with their complexity, and it reaches its culmination in human beings.

This relative concept of free will seems to be consistent with the view of mystical traditions that exhort their followers to transcend the notion of an isolated self and become aware that we are inseparable parts of the cosmos in which we are embedded. The goal of these traditions is to shed all ego sensations completely and, in mystical experience, merge with the totality of the cosmos. Once such a state is reached, the question of free will seems to lose its meaning. If I am the universe, there can be no "outside" influences and all my actions will be spontaneous and free. (14, pp. 269–70)

Stephen Hawking, physicist and author of *A Brief History of Time*, says that current theory holds that there are either many universes or that there is one large universe with many shapes. The universe based on the best case evidence is chaotic and irregular rather than smooth. Yet we see our part of the universe as smooth. If only the smooth part of the universe can support life then, "we see the universe the way it is because it exists" (15, p. 124). Perhaps as we see more about ourselves, the paradox of freedom will become less chaotic and more "smooth."

I look back to my statement earlier in this chapter: "The free person moves out voluntarily, freely, responsibly to play her significant part in a world whose determined events move through her spontaneous choice and will." For me these words acquire an added meaning and a new richness in light of Capra's and Hawking's statements. It is a confirming thing to find that views based primarily on experience in psychotherapy are paralleled by the thinking of theoretical physicists, which is based on experimentation and mathematics. The paradoxical quality of our freedom is still there, but it is a paradox with its roots in the nature of the universe.

REFERENCES

1. M. Friedman, *The Problematic Rebel* (New York: Random House, 1963).

2. B. F. Skinner, *Science and Human Behavior* (New York: Macmillan, 1953).

3. B. F. Skinner, "Behaviorism at Fifty," in *Behaviorism and Phenomenology: Contrasting Bases for Modern Psychology*, ed. T. W. Wann (Chicago: University of Chicago Press, 1964).

4. B. F. Skinner, *Walden Two* (New York: Macmillan, 1948).

5. Richard S. Crutchfield, "Conformity and Character," *American Psychologist* 10 (1955): 191–98.

6. James Olds, "A Physiological Study of Reward," in *Studies in Motivation*, ed. D. C. McClelland (New York: Appleton-Century Crofts, 1955).

7. V. E. Frankl, *From Death Camp to Existentialism* (Boston: Beacon Press, 1959).

8. C. R. Rogers, B. L. Kell, and Helen McNeil, "The Role of Self-understanding in the Prediction of Behavior," *Journal of Consulting Psychology* 12 (1948): 174–86.

9. M. Polanyi, *Personal Knowledge* (Chicago: University of Chicago Press, 1958).

10. M. Wertheimer, *Productive Thinking* (New York: Harper, 1945).

11. S. Kierkegaard, *Concluding Unscientific Postscript,* ed. Walter Lowre (Princeton: Princeton University Press, 1941).

12. M. Polanyi, "Scientific Outlook: Its Sickness and Cure," *Science* 125 (1957): 480–84.

13. Fritjof Capra, *The Tao of Physics* (Boulder, Colo.: Shambala Press, 1975).

14. Fritjof Capra, *The Turning Point* (New York: Simon and Schuster, 1982).

15. Stephen Hawking, *A Brief History of Time* (New York: Bantam Books, 1990).

CHAPTER 16

THE GOAL: THE FULLY FUNCTIONING PERSON

◆

What are we striving for? Why is it that we desire the *best* (however we define that term) in family life, in the school, in the university, in the community? It is, I believe, because we hope to develop the *best* of human beings. But rarely do we give explicit thought to the exact meaning of this goal. What sort of human being do we wish to grow?*

A number of years ago, I tried to state my personal answer to this question (1). I make no apology for the fact that this chapter is cast in the framework of therapy. To my mind the best of education would produce a person very similar to the one produced by the best of therapy. In therapy some psychologists will help you build a key to open your own doors to understanding. Some psychologists will give you a key to open your own doors, and some will lecture you about the importance of opening doors. Like education, the role and philosophy of the facilitator is the key to creating a fully functioning person. Indeed, it may be of help to teachers and educators to think about this issue in a setting outside the school. It may make it easier

_____

* Gender is being switched from *she* to *he* to provide balance in our discussion of person-centered therapy.

for them to see, in sharper focus, those points where they agree with the picture I paint and those points where they disagree.

I suspect that each one of us, from time to time, speculates on the general characteristics of the optimal person. If education were as completely successful as we could wish it to be in promoting personal growth and development, what sort of person would emerge? Or, speaking from the field in which I have had the most experience, suppose psychotherapy were completed in optimal fashion, what sort of person would have developed? What is the hypothetical end point, the ultimate psychological growth and development? I wish to discuss this question from the point of view of therapy, but I believe the tentative answers that I formulate are equally applicable to education or to the family or to any other situation that has as its aim the constructive development of persons.

I am really raising the issue: What is the goal? What is the optimal person? I have often asked myself these questions and have felt an increasing dissatisfaction with the kind of answers that are current. They seem too slippery, too relativistic to have much value in a developing science of personality. They often contain, too, I believe, a concealed bias that makes them unsatisfactory. I think of the commonly held notion that the person who has completed therapy or is fully mature is now adjusted to society. But what society? Any society, no matter what its characteristics? I cannot accept this. I think of the concept, implicit in much psychological writing, that *successful therapy* means that a person will have moved from a diagnostic category considered pathological to one considered normal. But the evidence is accumulating that there is so little agreement on diagnostic categories as to make them become practically meaningless as scientific concepts. And even if a person becomes normal, is that a suitable outcome of therapy? Furthermore, the experience of recent years has made me wonder whether the term *psychopathology* may not be simply a convenient basket for all those aspects of personality that diagnosticians as a group are most afraid of in themselves. For these and other reasons, change in diagnosis is not a description of therapeutic outcome that is satisfying to me.

I turn now to another prevailing concept in the field: *mental health*. The person whose psychological growth is optimal is said to have achieved positive mental health. But who defines mental health? I suspect that the Menninger Clinic and the Center for Studies of the Person would define it rather differently. I am sure that the totalitarian states would have still another definition.

Pushed about by questions such as these, I find myself speculating about the characteristics of the person who comes out of therapy, if therapy is maximally successful. I should like to share with you some of these tentative personal speculations. What I wish to do is to formulate a theoretical concept of the optimal end point of therapy or, indeed, of education. I hope that I can state it in terms that are free from some of the criticisms I have mentioned, terms that might eventually be given operational definition and objective test.

THE BACKGROUND FROM WHICH
THE PROBLEM IS APPROACHED

I have to make it clear at the outset that I am speaking from a background of client-centered or person-centered therapy. Quite possibly all successful psychotherapy has a similar personality outcome, but I am less sure of that than formerly; hence, I wish to narrow my field of consideration. So I shall assume that this hypothetical person whom I describe has had an intensive and extensive experience in client-centered therapy and that the therapy has been as completely successful as is theoretically possible. This would mean that the therapist has been able to enter into an intensely personal and sub-jective relationship with this client relating not as a scientist to an object of study, not as a physician expecting to diagnose and cure, but as a person to a person. It means that the therapist feels this client to be a person of unconditional *self-worth*, a person of value no matter what his condition, his behavior, or his feelings. It means that the therapist is able to let himself go in understanding this client, that no inner barriers keep him from sens-ing what it feels like to be the client at each moment of the relationship, and that he can convey something of his empathic understanding to the client. It means that the therapist has been comfortable in entering this relationship fully, even without knowing cognitively where it will lead; satisfied with pro-viding a climate that will free the client to become himself.

For the client, this optimal therapy means an exploration of increasingly strange and unknown and dangerous feelings in himself; the exploration is proving possible only because he is gradually realizing that he is accepted unconditionally. Thus he becomes acquainted with elements of his experi-ence that have in the past been denied to his awareness as too threatening, too damaging to the structure of the self. He finds himself experiencing these feelings fully, completely in the relationship, so that for the moment he *is* his fear, or his anger, or his tenderness, or his strength. And as he lives these widely varied feelings, in all their degrees of intensity, he discov-ers that he has experienced himself, that he *is* all these feelings. He finds his behavior changing in constructive fashion in accordance with his newly experienced self. He approaches the realization that he no longer needs to fear what experience may hold but can welcome it freely as a part of his changing and developing self.

This is a thumbnail sketch of what client-centered therapy might be at its optimum. I give it here simply as an introduction to my main concern: What personality characteristics would develop in the client as a result of this kind of experience?

THE CHARACTERISTICS OF THE
PERSON AFTER THERAPY

What, then, is the end point of optimal psychotherapy, of maximal psychological growth? I shall try to answer this question for myself, basing my thinking upon the knowledge we have gained from clinical experience and research but pushing this to the limit in order to see better the kind of person who would emerge if therapy were most effective. As I have puzzled over the answer, the description seems to me quite unitary; but for clarity of presentation I shall break it down into three facets.

1. *This person would be open to his or her experience.*   This is a phrase that has come to have increasingly definite meaning for me. It is the polar opposite of *defensiveness*, which is described as being the organism's response to experiences that are perceived or anticipated as incongruent with the structure of the self. In order to maintain the self-structure, such experiences are given a distorted symbolization in awareness, which reduces the incongruity. Thus, the individual defends against any threat of alteration in the concept of self.

In the person who is open to personal experiences, however, every stimulus, whether originating within the organism or in the environment, would be freely relayed through the nervous system without being distorted by a defensive mechanism. There would be no need for the mechanism of *subception*, whereby the organism is forewarned of any experience threatening to the self. On the contrary, whether the stimulus was the impact of a configuration of form, color, or sound in the environment on the sensory nerves, or a memory trace from the past, or a visceral sensation of fear or pleasure or disgust, the person would be living it, would have it completely available to awareness.

Perhaps I can give this concept more vivid meaning if I illustrate it with a recorded interview. In the following example, a young professional man reports in his forty-eighth interview the way in which he has become more open to some of his bodily sensations as well as to other feelings.

Client   It doesn't seem to me that it would be possible for anybody to relate all the changes that I feel. But I certainly have felt recently that I have more respect for, more objectivity toward my physical makeup. I mean I don't expect too much of myself. This is how it works out: It feels to me that in the past I used to fight a certain tiredness that I felt after supper. Well now I feel pretty sure that I really am *tired*—that I am not making myself tired—that I am just physiologically lower. It seemed that I was just constantly criticizing my tiredness.

Therapist   So you can let yourself *be* tired, instead of feeling along with it a kind of criticism of it.

Client   Yes, that I *shouldn't* be tired or something. And it seems in a way to be pretty profound that I can just not fight this tiredness, and along with it goes a real feeling of I've got to slow down, too, so that being tired isn't such an awful thing. I think I can also kind of pick up a thread here of why I should be that way in the way my father is and the way he looks at some of these things. For instance, say that I was sick, and I would report this, and it would seem that overtly he would want to do something about it but he would also communicate, "Oh, my gosh, more trouble." You know, something like that.

Therapist   As though there were something quite annoying, really, about being physically ill.

Client   Yeah, I am sure that my father has the same disrespect for his own physiology that I have had. Now last summer I twisted my back, I wrenched it, I heard it snap and everything. There was real pain there all the time at first, real sharp. And I had the doctor look at it and he said it wasn't serious, it should heal by itself as long as I didn't bend too much. Well, this was months ago—and I have been noticing recently that—hell, this is a real pain and it's still there and it's not my fault, I mean it's—

Therapist   It doesn't prove something bad about you—

Client   No—and one of the reasons I seem to get more tired than I should maybe is because of this constant strain and so on. I have already made an appointment with one of the doctors at the hospital that he would look at it and take an X ray or something. In a way I guess you could say that I am just more accurately sensitive—or objectively sensitive to this kind of thing. I can say with certainty that this has also spread to what I eat and how much I eat. And this is really a profound change, as I say. And of course, my relationship with my wife and the two children is—well, you just wouldn't recognize it if you could see me inside—as you have—I mean—there just doesn't seem to be anything more wonderful than really and genuinely—really *feeling* love for your own child and at the same time *receiving* it. I don't know how to put this. We have such an increased respect—both of us—for Judy and we've noticed just—as we participated in this—we have noticed such a tremendous change in her—it seems to be a pretty deep kind of thing.

Therapist   It seems to me you are saying that you can listen more accurately to yourself. If your body says it's tired, you listen to it and believe it, instead of criticizing it; if it's in pain you can listen to that; if the feeling is really loving your wife or child, you can *feel* that, and it seems to show up in the differences in them too.

Here, in a relatively minor but symbolically important excerpt, can be seen much of what I have been trying to say about openness to experience. Formerly the client could not freely feel pain or illness because being ill meant being unacceptable. Neither could he feel tenderness and love for his child because such feelings meant being weak, and he had to maintain his facade of being strong. But now he can be genuinely open to the experience of his self: He can be tired when he is tired, he can feel pain when he is in pain, he can freely experience the love he feels for his daughter, and he can also feel and express annoyance toward her, as he went on to say in the next portion of the interview. He can fully live the experiences of his total being rather than shutting them out of awareness.

I have used this concept of availability to awareness to try to make clear what I mean by openness to experience. This concept might be understood. I do not mean that this individual would be self-consciously aware of all that was going on within himself, like the centipede who has become aware of all of his legs. On the contrary, he would be free to live a feeling subjectively as well as be aware of it. He might experience love or pain or fear by living in this attitude subjectively. Or he might abstract himself from this subjectivity and realize in awareness, "I am in pain," "I am afraid," "I do love." The crucial point is that there would be no barriers, no inhibitions that would prevent the full experiencing of whatever was present within him; and availability to awareness is a good measure of this absence of barriers.

2. *This person would live in an existential fashion.*   I believe it would be evident that for the person who was fully open to his experience and completely without defensiveness, each moment would be new. The complex configuration of inner and outer stimuli that exists in this moment has never existed before in just this fashion. Consequently, our hypothetical person would realize, "What I will be in the next moment, and what I will do, grows out of that moment and cannot be predicted in advance either by me or by others." Not infrequently we find clients expressing this sort of feeling. One client, at the end of therapy, said in a rather puzzled fashion,

> ❦ *I haven't finished the job of integrating and reorganizing myself, but that's only confusing, not discouraging, now that I realize this is a continuing process. . . . It is exciting, sometimes upsetting, but deeply encouraging to feel yourself in action and apparently knowing where you are going even though you don't always consciously know where that is.*

One way of expressing the fluidity that would be present in such existential living is to say that the self and personality would emerge from experience rather than experience being translated or twisted to fit a preconceived self-structure. It means that one becomes a participant in and an observer of the ongoing process of self-experience rather than being in control of it. In the following passage, I have tried to describe how this type of living seems to me:

> ❦ *This whole train of experiencing, and the meaning that I have thus discovered in it, seems to have launched me on a process that is both fascinating and at times a little frightening. It seems to mean letting my experience carry me on, in a direction which appears to be forward, toward goals that I can but dimly define, as I try to understand at least the current meaning of that experience. The sensation is that of floating with a complex stream of experience, with the fascinating possibility of trying to comprehend its ever-changing complexity.*

Such living in the moment, then, means an absence of rigidity, of tight organization, of the imposition of structure on experience. It means instead a maximum of adaptability, a discovery of structure in experience, a flowing, changing organization of self and personality. The personality and the self are continually in flux, the only stable elements being the physiological capacities and limitations of the organism: the continuing or recurrent needs for survival, enhancement, food, affection, sex, and the like. The most stable personality traits are openness to experience and the flexible resolution of the existing needs in the existing environment.

3. *This person would find his being a trustworthy means of arriving at the most satisfying behavior in each existential situation.* He would do what felt right in this immediate moment, and he would find this in general to be a competent and trustworthy guide to his behavior.

If this seems strange, let me explain the reasoning behind it. Since he would be open to his experience, he would have access to all of the available information in the situation on which to base his behavior: the social demands, his own complex and possibly conflicting needs, his memories of similar situations, his perception of the uniqueness of this situation, and so on. The dynamic aspects of each situation would be very complex indeed. But he could permit his total organism, his consciousness participating, to consider each stimulus, need, and demand, its relative intensity and importance; and out of this complex weighing and balancing, he could discover the course of action that would come closest to satisfying all his needs in the situation.

An analogy that might come close to a description would be to compare this person to a learning network. Because he would be open to his experience, all of the information from his sense impressions, from his memory, from previous learning, from his visceral and internal states would become a sum greater than its parts. The person takes all of these multitudinous pulls and forces that have been fed in as information and quickly determines the course of action that would be the most economical avenue of need satisfaction in this existential situation. This is the behavior of our hypothetical person.

Recent interviews with successful corporate leaders found that many of their decisions were more intuitive than based on numbers alone. They expressed a sense of "gut feelings" and reactions to finding solutions to complex problems. Annette Watson, the principal at HSPVA in Houston, talked in chapter 6 about listening to yourself:

> ❦ *If you would take time to sit down and get very quiet and look inward and say, "What is the right thing to do?" There's an inner voice that tells me if it's right or wrong, and if you go against your inner voice, you pay the price every time, because sometimes you let your mentality override your intuition. You have to trust yourself.*

The defects that in most of us make this process untrustworthy are the inclusion of nonexistential material or the absence of data. It is when memories and previous learnings are fed into the computation as if they were *this* reality and not memories and learnings, that erroneous behavioral answers arise. Or when certain threatening experiences are inhibited from awareness, and hence are withheld from the computation or fed into it in distorted form, this, too, produces error. But our hypothetical person would find her organism thoroughly trustworthy because all the available data would be used, and it would be present in accurate rather than distorted form. Hence, her behavior would come as close as possible to satisfying all the person's needs—for enhancement, for affiliation with others, and the like.

In this weighing, balancing, and synthesizing, the organism would not by any means be infallible. It would always give the best possible answer for the available information, but sometimes data would be missing. Because of the element of openness to experience, however, any errors, any following of behavior that was not satisfying would be quickly corrected. The estimating, as it were, would always be in the process of being corrected because they would be continually checked in behavior.

Let me put the abstract into more personal terms. The client I previously quoted found himself expressing annoyance to his daughter when he "felt like it," as well as affection. Yet he found himself expressing his feelings in a way that not only released tension in himself, but that freed his small daughter to voice her annoyances. In the following example, he describes the differences between communicating his angry annoyance or imposing it on her:

> ❦ *Because it just doesn't feel like I'm imposing my feelings on her, and it seems to me I must show it on my face. Maybe she sees it as "Yes, Daddy is angry, but I don't have to cower." Because she never does cower. This in itself is a topic for a novel, it just feels that good.*

In this instance, being open to his experience, he selects, with astonishing, intuitive skill, a subtly guided course of behavior that meets his need for the release of his angry tension, but also satisfies his need to be a good father and his need to find satisfaction in his daughter's healthy development. Yet he achieves all this by simply doing the thing that feels right to him.

On quite another level, this same kind of complex organismic selection seems to determine the behavior of the creative person. She finds herself moving in a certain direction long before she can give any completely conscious and rational basis for it. During this period, whether she is moving toward a new type of artistic expression, a new literary style, a new theory in the field of science, or a new approach in the classroom, she is simply trusting her total organismic reaction. She feels an assurance that she is on her way, even though she cannot describe the end point of that journey. This is the type of behavior that is, I believe, also characteristic of the person who has gained greatly from therapy or of the person whose educational experience has enabled him or her to learn how to learn.

THE FULLY FUNCTIONING PERSON

I should like to pull together these three threads—*the person being open to experience, existential living,* and *trusting self*—into one more unified descriptive strand. It appears that the person who emerges from a theoretically optimal experience of personal growth, whether through client-centered therapy or some other experience of learning and development, is then a fully functioning person. This person is able to live fully in and with each and all of his or her feelings and reactions. The individual is making use of all the organic equipment to sense, as accurately as possible, the existential situation within and without. The person is using all of the information the nervous system can supply, using it in awareness, but recognizing that the total organism may be, and often is, wiser than one's awareness. The person is able to permit the total self to function in all its complexity in selecting, from the multitude of possibilities, the behavior that in this moment of time will be most generally and genuinely satisfying.

The individual is able to trust the self in this functioning, not because it is infallible but because she can be fully open to the consequences of each of her actions and correct them if they prove to be less than satisfying. She is able to experience all of her feelings and is afraid of none of them; she is her own sifter of evidence but is open to evidence from all sources; she is completely engaged in the process of being and becoming herself and thus discovers that she is soundly and realistically social; she lives completely in this moment but learns that this is the soundest living for all times. She is a fully functioning organism; and because of the awareness of herself that flows freely in and through her experiences, she is a fully functioning person.

Some Implications of This Description

This, then, is my tentative definition of the hypothetical end point of therapy, my description of the ultimate picture that our actual clients approach but never fully reach—the picture of the person who is continually learning how to learn. I have come to like this description, both because I believe it is rooted in and is true of my clinical and educational experience and also because I believe it has significant clinical, scientific, and philosophical implications. I should like to present some of these ramifications and implications as I see them.

A.   *Appropriate to Clinical Experience.* In the first place, my description appears to contain a basis for the phenomena of clinical experience in successful therapy. We have noted the fact that the client develops a locus of evaluation within herself; this is consistent with the concept of the trustworthiness of the organism. We have commented on the client's satisfaction at being and becoming herself, a satisfaction associated with functioning fully. We find that clients tolerate a much wider range and variety of feelings, including feelings that were formerly anxiety producing, and that these feelings are usefully integrated into their more flexibly organized personalities. In short, the concepts I have stated appear to be sufficiently broad to contain the positive outcomes of therapy as we know it.

B.   *Leads toward Operational Hypotheses.* While the formulation as given is admittedly speculative, it leads, I believe, in the direction of hypotheses that may be stated in rigorous and operational terms. Such hypotheses would be culture-free or universal, I trust, rather than being different for each culture. It is obvious that the concepts given are not easily tested or measured; but with our growing research sophistication in this area, their measurability is not an unreasonable hope.

C.   *Explains a Paradox of Personal Growth.* We have found, in several research studies in psychotherapy, some perplexing differences in the analyses of before-and-after personality tests by different outside experts. In clients whose personal gain in therapy is amply supported by other evidence, we have found contradictions among the experts in the interpretation of their personality tests. Briefly, psychologists who are oriented strictly toward personality *diagnosis*—in other words, those who are comparing the individual with general norms—tend to be concerned about what they see as a lack of personality defenses or a degree of disorganization at the conclusion of therapy. They may be concerned that the person is "falling apart." The psychologist who is therapeutically oriented tends to see the same evidence as indicative of fluidity, openness to experience—an existential rather than a rigid personality organization. To me it seems possible that the looseness, the openness of the person who is undergoing marked personal growth may be seen, in terms of population norms, as deviating from these norms, as "not normal." But these same qualities may indicate that all personal growth is marked by a certain degree of disorganization followed by reorganization. The pain of new understandings, of acceptance of new facets of oneself; the feeling of uncertainty, vacillation, and even turmoil within oneself are all an integral part of the pleasure and satisfaction of being more of oneself, more fully oneself, more fully functioning. This, to me, is a meaningful explanation of what would otherwise be a puzzling paradox.

D.   Creativity As an Outcome.   One of the elements that pleases me in the theoretical formulation I have given is that this fully functioning individual is a creative person. This person at the hypothetical end point of therapy could well be one of Abraham Maslow's "self-actualizing people." With his sensitive openness to the world, his trust of his own ability to form new relationships with our environment, he would be the type of person from whom creative products and creative living emerge. He would not necessarily be adjusted to his culture, and he would almost certainly not be a conformist. But at any time and in any culture he would live constructively, in as much harmony with his culture as a balanced satisfaction of needs demanded. In certain cultural situations, he might in some ways be very unhappy; but he would continue to be himself and to behave in such a way as to provide the maximum possible satisfaction of his deepest needs. Such a person would, I believe, be recognized by the student of evolution as the type most likely to adapt and survive under changing environmental conditions. He would be able creatively to make sound adjustments to new as well as old conditions. He would be a fit vanguard of human evolution.

E.   Builds on Trustworthiness of Human Nature.   It will have been evident that one implication of the view I have been presenting is that the basic nature of the human being, when functioning freely, is constructive and trustworthy. For me this is an inescapable conclusion from more than forty years of experience in psychotherapy. When we are able to free the individual from defensiveness, so that he is open to a wide range of his own needs as well as the wide range of environmental and social demands, his reactions may be trusted to be positive, forward-moving, and constructive. We do not need to ask who will socialize him, for one of his own deepest needs is for affiliation and communication with others. When he is fully himself, he cannot help but be realistically socialized. We do not need to ask who will control his aggressive impulses; for when he is open to all of his impulses, his need to be liked by others and his tendency to give affection are as strong as his impulses to strike out or to seize for himself. He will be aggressive in situations in which aggression is realistically appropriate, but there will be no runaway need for aggression. His total behavior, in these and other areas, when he is open to all his experience, is balanced and realistic, behavior that is appropriate to the survival and enhancement of a highly social animal.

I have little sympathy with the rather prevalent concept that persons are basically irrational and that their impulses, if not controlled, would lead to destruction of others and self. Our behavior is exquisitely rational, moving with subtle and ordered complexity toward the goals the organism is endeavoring to achieve. The tragedy for most of us is that our defenses keep us from being aware of this rationality, so that consciously we are moving in one direction while organismically we are moving in another. But in our hypothetical person there would be no such barriers, and he would be a participant in the rationality of his organism. The only control of impulses that would exist or that would prove necessary is the natural and internal balancing of one need against another and the discovery of behaviors that follow the avenue most closely approximating the satisfaction of all needs. The experience of extreme satisfaction of one need (for example, aggression or sex) in such a way as to do violence to the satisfaction of other needs (such as companionship or a tender relationship), an experience very common in the defensively organized person, would simply be unknown in our hypothetical individual. He would participate in the vastly complex self-regulatory activities of his organism—the psychological as well as physiological thermostatic controls—in such a fashion as to live harmoniously with himself and with others.

F. Behavior Dependable but Not Predictable.

There are certain implications of this view of the optimum human being that have to do with predictability, which I find fascinating to contemplate. It should be clear from the theoretical picture I have sketched that the particular configuration of inner and outer stimuli in which the person lives at this moment has never existed in precisely this fashion before; and also that his behavior is a realistic reaction to an accurate apprehension of all this internalized evidence. It should, therefore, be clear that this person will see himself as dependable but not specifically predictable. If he is entering a new situation with an authority figure, for example, he cannot predict what his behavior will be. This person's own behavior is contingent upon the behavior of the authority figure and his own immediate internal reactions, desires, and so on. He can feel confident that he will behave appropriately, but he has no knowledge in advance of *exactly* what he will do. I find this point of view often expressed by clients, and I believe it is profoundly important.

But what I have been saying about the client himself would be equally true of the scientist studying his behavior. The scientist would find this person's behavior lawful and would find it possible to postdict it, but could not forecast or predict the specific behavior of this individual. The reasons are these: if the behavior of our hypothetical person is determined by the accurate sensing of all of the complex evidence that exists in this moment of time, and by that evidence only, then the data necessary for prediction are clear. It would be necessary to have instruments available to measure every one of the multitudinous stimuli of the input, and a supercomputer to calculate the most economical vector of reaction. While this computation is going on, our hypothetical person would have already made this complex summation and appraisal within himself and have acted. Science, if it could eventually collect all this data with sufficient accuracy, should theoretically be able to analyze it, come to the same conclusion, and thus postdict his behavior. But it is doubtful that science could ever collect and analyze the data instantaneously, and this would be necessary if it were to predict the behavior before it occurred.

It may clarify this if I point out that it is the maladjusted person whose behavior can be specifically predicted, and some loss of predictability should be evident in every increase in openness to experience and existential living. In the maladjusted person, behavior is predictable precisely because it is rigidly patterned. If such a person has learned a pattern of hostile reaction to authority and if this "badness of authority" is part of his conception of himself in relation to authority, and if because of this he denies or distorts any experience that should supply contradictory evidence, then his behavior is specifically predictable. It can be said with assurance that when he enters a new situation with an authority figure, he will be hostile to this authority figure. But the more that therapy or any growth-promoting relationship increases the openness to experience of this individual, the less predictable his behavior will be. This idea receives some crude confirmation from a Michigan study attempting to predict success in clinical psychology (2). The predictions for the men who were in therapy during the period of investigation were definitely less accurate than those for the group as a whole.

What I am saying here has a bearing on the common statement that the long-range purpose of psychology as a science is "the prediction and control of human behavior," a phrase that for me has had disturbing philosophical implications. I am suggesting that as the individual approaches this optimum of complete functioning, his behavior, though always lawful and determined, becomes more difficult to predict; and though always dependable and appropriate, more difficult to control. This would mean that the science of psychology, at its highest levels, would perhaps be more of a science of understanding than a science of prediction, an analysis of the lawfulness of that which has occurred rather than primarily a control of what is about to occur.

In general this line of thought is confirmed by our clients, who feel confident that what they will do in a situation will be appropriate and comprehensible and sound, but who cannot predict in advance exactly how they will behave. It is also confirmed by our experience as therapists, where we form a relationship in which we can be sure individuals will discover themselves, become themselves, and learn to function more freely, but where we cannot forecast the specific content of the next statement, of the next phase of therapy, or of the behavioral solution the client will find to a given problem. The general direction is dependable, and we can rest assured it will be appropriate; but its specific content is unpredictable.

G.   *Relates Freedom and Determinism.*   I should like to give one final philosophical implication that has meaning for me. For some time I have been perplexed over the living paradox that exists in psychotherapy between freedom and determinism, as I have indicated in the preceding chapter. I would like to add one more thought on that topic. In the therapeutic relationship some of the most compelling subjective experiences are those in which the client feels within himself the power of naked choice. He is *free*— to become himself or to hide behind a facade, to move forward or to retrogress, to behave in ways that are destructive of self and others or in ways that are enhancing—quite literally free to live or die, in both the physiological and psychological meanings of those terms. Yet as we enter this field of psychotherapy with objective research methods, we are, like other scientists, committed to a complete determinism. From this point of view, every thought, feeling, and action of the client is determined by what precedes it. The dilemma I am trying to describe is no different from that found in other fields; it is simply brought to sharper focus. I tried to bring this out in a paper written some time ago contrasting these two views. The following passage from that paper refers to the field of psychotherapy:

> Here is the maximizing of all that is subjective, inward, personal;
> here a relationship is lived, not examined, and a person, not an
> object, emerges, a person who feels, chooses, believes, acts, not as
> an automaton, but as a person. And here too is the ultimate in sci-
> ence—the objective exploration of the most subjective aspects of life;
> the reduction to hypotheses, and eventually to theorems, of all that
> has been regarded as most personal, most completely inward, most
> thoroughly a private world. (3, pp. 267–68)

In terms of the definition I have given of the fully functioning person, the relationship between freedom and determinism can, I believe, be seen in a fresh perspective. We could say that in the optimum of therapy, the person rightfully experiences the most complete and absolute freedom. He wills or chooses to follow the course of action that is the most economical vector in relation to all the internal and external stimuli because that behavior will be most deeply satisfying. But this is the same course of action that from another vantage point may be said to be determined by all the factors in the existential situation.

Let us contrast this with the picture of the person who is defensively organized. He wills or chooses to follow a given course of action, but finds that he *cannot* behave in the fashion that he chooses. He is determined by the factors in the existential situation, but these factors include his defensiveness, his denial or distortion of some of the relevant data. Hence it is certain that his behavior will be less than fully satisfying. His behavior is determined, but he is not free to make an effective choice. The fully functioning person, on the other hand, not only experiences, but utilizes, the most absolute freedom when he spontaneously, freely, and voluntarily chooses and wills that which is absolutely determined.

I am quite aware that this is not a new idea to the philosopher, but it has been refreshing to come upon it from a totally unexpected angle: analyzing a concept in personality theory. For me it provides the rationale for the subjective reality of absolute freedom of choice, which is so profoundly important in therapy, and at the same time the rationale for the complete determinism that is the foundation stone of present-day science. With this framework I can enter subjectively the experience of naked choice that the client is experiencing; I can also as a scientist study his behavior as being absolutely determined.

CONCLUSION

Here, then, is my theoretical model of the person who emerges from therapy or from the best of education, the individual who has experienced optimal psychological growth: a person functioning freely in all the fullness of all the organismic potentialities; a person who is dependable in being realistic, self-enhancing, socialized, and appropriate in behavior; a creative person, whose specific formings of behavior are not easily predictable; a person who is ever changing, ever developing, always discovering the newness in each succeeding moment of time. Let me stress, however, that what I describe is a person who does not exist. The person is the theoretical goal, the end point of personal growth. We see persons moving *in this direction* from the best of experiences in education, from the best of experiences in therapy, from the best of family and group relationships. But what we observe is the imperfect person moving toward this goal. What I have described is my version of the goal in its *pure* form.

I have written this chapter partly to clarify my own ideas. What sort of person tends to come from my classes, from my groups, from my therapy? But of more importance, I have written it to try to encourage all of us to think much more deeply about our own goals. The assumption has been prevalent for so long that we all know what constitutes an *educated person*, and the fact that this comfortable definition is now completely irrelevant to modern society is almost never faced. So this chapter constitutes a challenge to educators at all levels. If my concept of the fully functioning person is abhorrent to you as the goal of education, then give *your* definition of the person who should emerge from modern-day education and publish it for all to see. We need many such definitions so that there can be a really significant modern dialogue about what constitutes our optimum, our ideal citizen of today. I hope this chapter makes a small contribution toward that dialogue.

REFERENCES

1. Carl R. Rogers, "The Concept of the Fully Functioning Person," *Psychotherapy: Theory, Research, and Practice* 1 (1963): 17–26.

2. E. L. Kelley and Donald W. Fiske, *The Prediction of Performance in Clinical Psychology* (Ann Arbor: University of Michigan Press, 1951).

3. Carl R. Rogers, "Persons or Science: A Philosophical Question," *American Psychologist* 10 (1955): 267–78.

A MORATORIUM
ON SCHOOLING?

CHAPTER 17

TRANSFORMING SCHOOLS: A PERSON-CENTERED PERSPECTIVE

◆

We don't know what problems the future will have. . . . So the best way of preparation for the future is to learn to solve complex problems today. (1)

Our Nation is at risk. Our once unchallenged preeminence in commerce, industry, science, and technological innovation is being overtaken by competitors throughout the world. . . . If an unfriendly foreign power had attempted to impose on America the mediocre educational performance that exists today, we might well have viewed it as an act of war. As it stands we have allowed this to happen to ourselves. (2, p. 5)

All the King's horses and all the King's men

Couldn't put Humpty Dumpty together again.

Each of these quotations—an observation on learning, a federal commission report on schools, and a children's nursery rhyme—reflects the problems we face in transforming our schools into true communities of learning and joy. If we do not engage our youth at a very early age in the experience of solving complex problems, we will fail to prepare a generation for its future. By solving problems together today we can prevent other problems tomorrow.

The report *A Nation at Risk: National Commission on Excellence in Education* was the result of a twenty-month study by an eighteen-member national commission on excellence in education. The federal report was written in 1983. It has now been over a decade since the alarm was raised by the commission, and billions of dollars have subsequently been spent on efforts to improve schooling. Countless reports, task forces, and commissions have followed *A Nation at Risk*; all have found someone to blame for the conditions of school, offering prescriptions from their own perspective on how schools must change. Sadly, there have been too few discernable results. Looking at the educational landscape now, I would say our nation is at greater risk today of failing to provide meaningful learning opportunities for all students than it was a decade ago.

During the past decade, proposed changes in schools have come from the federal government, state governors, state and local legislative bodies, business leaders, national and regional school and teacher accreditation agencies, teacher unions, private foundations, higher education and individual academics. The efforts of these different groups have resulted in a swirl of activity from teacher career ladders (to improve competition), to the development of a national standards board for teacher certification, to greater controls on what and how teachers teach, to teacher evaluations based on prescribed measures and teacher testing—just to list a few. With so much effort directed at improving schools during the past decade, why haven't they changed?

TRANSFORMING THE BOX

In the cities along the East Coast and throughout the Midwest and across the United States, schools, factories, and prisons look remarkably alike and often function in the same way. They were built out of the same materials at the turn of the century and served the purpose of responding to the industrial development of the country. Like their factory and prison counterparts, most schools appear as large boxes subdivided by many smaller boxes—the classroom. Pollution, noise, crowding, disease, child labor, and sweatshops were the norm for the working-class poor rather than the exception. The public school became an oasis from a very oppressive environment for many children. While few children stayed in school beyond the sixth grade, the time spent in school was time not spent in twelve-hour factory shifts. The affluent, on the other hand, lived a very different life, not only with much better sanitary and living conditions, but with private schools, summer vacations, and trips abroad. The public school schedule was adapted to the needs of the work environment, not the learner. The influences of an agrarian society were felt in the urban schoolhouse at the turn of the century, with nine months of schooling and summers off. While their rural cousins helped with the crops, urban children worked in factories during the summers or roamed the streets.

That time is long gone, but the patterns of schooling established a hundred years ago remain with us today. While learning could be a year-round experience, we still operate on an agrarian calendar. This may be useful for some students; but for many urban children, summer experiences detract rather than add to their learning (e.g., extensive television watching and idle time). Although modern architecture and engineering could create schools on a human scale, schools continue to be built today like boxes—only much larger and more impersonal versions of their earlier counterparts. A new elementary school was recently built in the southwestern United States for twelve hundred students, and a new high school was also built in the same area for three thousand students. Schools still operate like factories, with changes in shifts. In many secondary schools this takes the form of twelve hundred students entering the hallways every forty-two minutes between regimented classroom structures, where "learning" is dispensed in premeasured blocks of time. How many adults can complete any important activities such as writing, thinking, or discussing in forty-two minutes?

Schools are unnecessarily stressful places. From the public address system, which beckons the few but disturbs the many, to the school cafeteria—which creates stress for most who eat there—schools operate without real thought for creating positive and peaceful environments. Take, for example, school cafeterias: they are designed for mass food production, not relaxed dining. Lunchtime is guaranteed to increase stress levels because of overcrowding and deafening noise levels. School cafeterias were not designed for normal conversations. Few adults would willingly eat under these conditions, but students must endure them for at least 180 days each year. Even if they don't eat in the cafeteria, most teachers dread after-lunch classes.

The factory-like atmosphere is also very difficult for teachers. At times teachers are like ticket agents at a busy bus terminal, giving slips for students who are coming or going to class. Teachers feel like police—conducting hall sweeps, breaking up fights, and *standing guard* outside their doors during change of classes.

The list of factory examples could go on for an entire book. But my intent is not to show how factory-like our schools remain; this is already well documented. The issue is, How do we move from this antiquated model of the box to the present and on to a more productive future?

MASS-PRODUCED LEARNING

I realize that this model of mass-produced learning worked for millions of people during this century. So why change now? Steel-hulled, steam-powered ships brought millions of immigrants to the shores of the United

States. The locomotive opened the West and allowed for unprecedented growth in our nation. But how many people today take the train from Los Angeles to New York, or take the boat to England? Schools and the greater society can't close their doors to change. Unless we want to return to the factory era, we must move forward to allow places of learning to become responsive to the needs of students in a new century.

Based on the most recent information about the well-being of our children, the need for change is greater today than in any time in the last fifty years. Education remains the primary opportunity for success and well-being in life. There is growing evidence that high school and college graduates live longer and have a better quality of life than their counterparts who never finish school. However, our nation is headed in two directions: one toward poverty and one toward wealth. The disparity is becoming more evident with each new round of statistics. Nearly one child in four is poor, with children under five years of age representing the greatest level of poverty. One teenager in five also lives in poverty. The institutions with which these children have contact—family, community, and school—do not function as supportive and protective agents; rather, they are in themselves risk factors for many children (3).

There have been many programs and activities intended to improve the quality of schools, but they seem to have limited short-term impact. However, one should not confuse activity with real change. The school reforms of the past decade have done little to respond to the most fundamental questions: (a) How do we radically and permanently change the patterns of interactions between students and teachers to improve the capacity and joy of a child's learning? (b) What support efforts are needed to create meaningful learning communities? (c) How does the box known as school become transformed to respond to the needs of the person?

MORATORIUM ON SCHOOLING

The nursery rhyme "Humpty Dumpty" describes the frustration of trying to fix something that is irrevocably broken. As we have illustrated in earlier chapters, not all schools are in this situation. Some schools are meeting the needs of children and their parents and should receive continued support for their efforts. However, others are beyond repair and need to be transformed into a new type of learning community. There is a need for a moratorium on these schools because they can't be fixed while school is in session. *Presently, these dysfunctional schools are a hazard to the intellectual and social-emotional health of children and other people who work there.*

But what will happen to the students while the schools are being transformed? Perhaps lessons could be gleaned from the bombings of London during World War II. Nearly a million children were sent out of the city to the countryside to live and learn. Five years later British parents found that their children had gained, both academically and socially from the experience. Within our own context today, students in schools that are being transformed could learn at community learning centers, work in business apprenticeships, study at museum and library centers (which are under-utilized during the day), learn at local community colleges and universities, and attend other schools. If the transformation process is phased in over time (two to three years), the larger community will be able to respond to the changes. In many cases these new arrangements may become semi-permanent elements in a larger learning community. Teachers and administrators from the schools could work with other educators and community leaders in rethinking education. They could have opportunities to visit, work, and learn in schools that are person-centered during this moratorium on schooling.

MORATORIUM ON THE BUREAUCRACY

Other schools inhibited by the bureaucracy need to be given the life space to breathe. State, district, and school-level policies and procedures should be transformed to allow and encourage schools to flourish instead of being stifled. In Texas, for example, each school district is required to complete eighty-four separate reports required by state or federal agencies, which must then be read by thousands of bureaucrats. The cost of these imposed regulations is enormous—a total of $1.5 billion a year for all schools in the state of Texas (4). When multiplied by fifty states, the resource requirements are staggering. Some regulations protect children, but many others simply impede the ability of schools and districts to meet the unique needs of their students. All rules and regulations need to be *sunseted* and rethought: that is, be reviewed to see if the regulation really protects or inhibits the people they are supposed to benefit. The bureaucracy needs to be reformed to allow principals, teachers, parents, and students to change the way schools function from the inside.

Schools have become boxed in by forces that allow little room for real and lasting change. When school boards, superintendents, or federal and state legislatures expect *compliance* rather than creative solutions, the rippling effect has its greatest impact in the classroom. Schools that have become trapped in cycles of failure need to be transformed. These schools require our greatest efforts and discussion. Many are in our inner cities, but others are in rural and suburban America. For real change to occur in these schools, the learning environment needs to be rethought and reconfigured physically, emotionally, and educationally. Safeguards in the form of regulations and laws need to be driven by the needs of the child, and his or her facilitators, rather than others far removed from schools. The focus must be on the needs of all persons. The reshaping of the box begins with the school but does not end there. Schools need to become energizers of the community, bringing both near and far communities together to help build dynamic learning communities that foster resilience in children.

REFORMING FROM THE INSIDE OUT

It is abundantly clear from a decade of efforts to reform schools that change must come from the inside out. Mandates from above have not improved the quality of learning, the satisfaction of the learner, or the lives of teachers. A 1993 report from the Center on Organization and Restructuring of Schools at the Wisconsin Center for Educational Research, entitled *Estimating the Extent of School Restructuring,* concludes that

> in spite of plentiful rhetoric and extensive initiative by districts, states, and national organizations, the restructuring movement has yet to touch the mass of American schools in any significant way. (5, p. 4)

Teachers are constantly asked to respond to external demands, sapping the energy required to rethink what needs to go on inside schools and classrooms. Teachers are asked to do more with fewer resources. It takes time to plan and learn new ways, and this must be part of the transformation process. Currently, American elementary school teachers spend more than thirty hours a week teaching, while their counterparts in Japan and Germany teach from seventeen to twenty-one hours a week.

Person-centered schools have found creative ways to meet state guidelines for the number of hours a child must attend school each day. For example, they may start school ten minutes earlier each day to allow one or two days a month for teachers to meet, discuss, and learn. It is difficult to be creative when you are exhausted. Adding more to an impacted schedule and curriculum will not lead to healthier children, teachers, or schools. We simply cannot add more to the box without its sides exploding. The amount of time allocated for learning has remained remarkably constant for the last one hundred years, but the curriculum or what is mandated to be taught has mushroomed. The box of schooling, educating, teaching, and learning needs to take on a shape that is no longer four-sided. Teachers and students can only become *co-learners* in the journey that begins at an early age and continues for a lifetime if the nature of the interaction between them becomes more balanced and the conceptual shape of the box is transformed.

REAL CHANGE

Since *A Nation at Risk* was first published, much of the school reform efforts have been directed at the periphery of change: site-based management, national testing and accreditation, different school organizations, community councils, and the like. While having the potential to transform learning, reform efforts only work to the extent that the basic relationship between student and teacher changes from giver of information to facilitator of learning and the learning environment changes from school building to learning community.

As a starting point for discussing the process of transforming school buildings into learning communities, I would like to turn to the paths we have in terms of childhood learning. In our efforts to reform and transform education, we tend to miss the most important part of our reform efforts—the child.

The Miracle of Childhood

I get flashes: pictures of the young children I have known and observed, children before they have been exposed to school. These are children I have observed on the streets, in homes, and in supermarkets with their parents. These are the youngsters I have seen in China and Japan, in Brazil, in Austria, and in England—children all over the world. I see a small girl pounding nail after nail after nail into a large wooden box until it is studded with the metal heads. I see a little boy insisting stubbornly that he will wear only the pants he has chosen, not the ones selected by his mother. I see a child in a supermarket trying to feel every can, box, and bunch of vegetables—stopped only temporarily by a mother's desist. I see a three-year-old very carefully take a cup filled with milk and pour it on the floor and ask, "Why didn't it stay in the cup?" I see a group of children playing with clay, laughing at the forms they create. I see youngsters learning to thwart parental rules, manipulating parental behavior. I hear a child asking over and over, "What letter is that? And what letter is that?" I see the homeless street children of Brazil, unloved and unwanted, roaming the streets—stealing, searching for bread in trash cans, deceiving and manipulating adults, struggling to survive. I see children on the beach building sand castles, carrying buckets of water to and fro. I see children counting out nickels for a candy bar. I see and hear a small child kicking an empty can along a city street. I hear the ever-repeated questions, "Why?" "How?" "Why does water run downhill?" "How does the baby get inside the mother?" "Why is he talking so loud?" "How do you make it go?"

The questions are ceaseless; the curiosity endless. Young children are eager to find out; they want to do, to shape, to create. They are soaking up information through eyes, ears, nose, mouth, fingers. They are moving, restless, spontaneous, determined. They are assimilating knowledge, perceiving patterns, acquiring a language, and improving skills. They are learning, learning, learning—probably at a rate they will never again equal.

And then their "education" begins. Off they go to school. What will they find? The possibilities are almost endless, but I will sketch two of the extremes, recognizing that there are many schools whose methods, attitudes, and procedures would fall between these two extremes.

One Pathway to Education.   A small boy enters school, his first day. He is eager to go because it is a step toward being grown up. He has watched as the big boys and girls go to school each morning and return again each afternoon. But he is also frightened. It is a strange new situation full of fearsome possibilities. He has heard stories about school—about punishments, about exciting times, about report cards, about teachers, friendly and unfriendly. It is a scary uncertainty.

He is directed to his room. His teacher is businesslike. Here is his desk and chair, one in a straight row of desks and chairs. Here are his books and pencils. The teacher greets the group with a smile, but it seems forced. Then come the rules. He cannot leave his seat, even to go to the toilet, without first raising his hand and receiving permission. He is not to whisper or talk to his neighbors. He is to speak only when called upon. No one is to make unnecessary noise. He thinks of yesterday. He was continually on the move, making as much noise as he pleased, shouting to his friends. School is so very different.

Then classes begin—the reading book, letters and words on the board. The teacher talks. One child is called upon and is praised for a correct response. He is called on. He makes a mistake. "Wrong! Who can give Johnny the right answer?" Hands go up, and he is soon corrected. He feels stupid. He leans over to tell his neighbor how he happened to make the mistake. He is reprimanded for talking. The teacher comes and stands by his seat to make clear that she is watching him, that he must abide by the rules.

Recess is fun—much shouting, running, some games—but it's all too short. Then school begins again. His body squirms, his mind wanders, finally lunch. Not until the students are all lined up in a perfectly straight row are they permitted to walk silently to the lunchroom.

The child's educational career has commenced. He has already learned a great deal, though he could not put it into words. He has learned that:

- There is no place for his restless physical energy in the schoolroom.
- One conforms or takes the unpleasant consequences.
- Submission to rules is very important.
- Making a mistake is very bad.
- The punishment for a mistake is humiliation.
- Spontaneous interest does not belong in school.
- Teacher and disciplinarian are synonymous.
- School is, on the whole, an unpleasant experience.

At the end of the day, he asks his parents, "How long do I have to go?" Gradually, he will learn that he has been sentenced to a very long term.

As the days, months, years roll by, he learns other things:

- Most textbooks are boring.
- It is not safe to differ with a teacher.
- There are many ways to get by without studying or learning.
- It is okay to cheat as long as you don't get caught.
- Daydreams, doodling, and fantasy can make the day pass more quickly.
- To study hard and get good grades is behavior scorned by your peers.
- Most of the learning relevant to life takes place outside of school.
- Original ideas have no place in school.
- Exams and grades are the most important aspects of education.
- Some teachers are impersonal and boring in class.

Small wonder that the child looks forward to vacations as being the time when he really lives. Graduation becomes desirable as a release from boredom, constriction, and coercion.

This is one pathway, one type of school experience. I believe, based on observations and current research, that it is a pathway experienced by millions of children and young people. Have I painted it in terms that are too gloomy? Listen to some student comments and decide for yourself.

The humiliation and degradation of students from low-income families, as reported by Ellen Brantlinger (see chapter 12), punctuate the comments made by other students from an inner-city elementary school in northern California. They were asked, "What would you like to change about your school and community?" The list was shared with me by Barbara Levin, a teacher for more than seventeen years who recently completed her doctorate in education at the University of California at Berkeley (6). The list was given to her by a teacher at the school.

Things We Would Like to Change about Our School and Community

1. We need more cooperation. "There are too many fights," and "it is hard for kids to learn" with so much conflict.

2. There are problems with kids in gangs. "The police, the governor, the president and vice-president, and the mayor all need to give help to kids before there is a problem." "Kids join gangs to have a family and to feel safe." "Kids in gangs want to be loved, and to belong, and to follow friends."

3. We are worried about kids who use drugs and alcohol. "Peer pressure is a problem." "Media pressure is bad; [it] gives kids

messages that it is okay to use." TV, radio, rappers, and street signs are all part of a problem. "Media could be good and help us."

4. [There is too much] sexual harassment of girls.

5. [We need] more after school activities.

6. There [are] . . . no after-school sports for girls.

7. [There is a] culture clash. Kids talk about each other in different languages.

8. We want language classes.

9. Some kids are scared to walk home because of drug dealers and people who harass them.

10. [We need] clean bathrooms! Give [us] supplies. This [lack of supplies] makes us feel that we are not important.

11. Our school is dirty!!! "Put money into painting and cleaning up the school." "When important people come, they think bad things about our school because of litter and graffiti and dirty walls." "We feel judged by others because of what our school looks like; they think this is a bad school and that we are bad."

12. We want a real education. "My sister is in the fourth grade and is still doing subtraction." "Some teachers don't know how to teach; they just have us work out of books and handouts." "Teachers need tutoring!" "Teachers need to listen to kids."

13. Some teachers are prejudiced. "My teacher favors Cambodian kids in class and thinks that Black kids are bad."

14. Teachers need to learn to respect [other] teachers—no put downs.

Comments

When I first read the list, I thought the comments were from high school students. I was stunned to find out that they were from girls in the sixth grade who had met with a teacher in a support group. You can feel their anger and despair, but you can also feel the hope that things can change. I also sense that they would be willing to help resolve many of the problems with some positive encouragement.

The students' comments also speak volumes about their need to be respected and treated fairly and to learn in a clean, safe, and caring environment. I believe their statements express the feelings of many as we observe some of the tragic realities of inner-city and many other schools. The people who work in these schools are as much victims as the students. It is not a pretty picture, but it is one that can be transformed.

A Second Way to Learning.   We have seen in the preceding chapters that there is another path, another way. Let me sketch that picture very briefly.

A small girl goes to school for the first time. The atmosphere is friendly and informal. Part of her fear and anxiety disappears as the teacher greets her warmly and introduces her to some of the other children. When it is time for school to begin, the students sit in a circle with the teacher. She asks the children to tell about one thing in which they are interested, one thing they like to do. The teacher's interest in each youngster is evident, and the little girl relaxes even more. This may be fun. There are all kinds of interesting things in the room—books, maps, pictures, building blocks, crayons and paper, some toys—and soon the children are investigating their environment. Our small girl looks at a picture book of children in another country.

When the teacher calls the class together again, she asks the girl if she can tell a little story. Our youngster starts to tell about going to the zoo with her mother. The teacher prints part of the story on the board and points out the words and letters. And so the day has begun.

What has this small girl learned? She has learned that:

◆   Her curiosity is welcomed and prized.

◆   The teacher is friendly and caring.

◆   She can learn new things, both on her own and with the teacher's help.

◆   There is room for spontaneity here.

◆   She can contribute to the group learning.

◆   She is valued as a person.

We don't need to follow her school career further because it has all been described in earlier chapters. But in this humanistically oriented school, we will find various elements as she continues through the years:

◆   She has a part in choosing what she wishes and needs to learn.

◆   She learns reading and mathematics more rapidly than her friends do in other schools.

◆   She finds an outlet for her creativity.

◆   She becomes more expressive of both her feelings and thoughts.

◆   She develops confidence in and a liking for herself.

◆   She discovers that learning is fun.

◆   She looks forward to going to school.

◆   She likes and respects her teachers and knows that they, in turn, like and respect her.

◆   She finds a place in school for all of her many and expanding interests.

◆ She develops a knowledge of resources—ways of finding out what she wants to know.

◆ She reads about, thinks about, and discusses the crucial social issues of her time.

◆ She finds some things very difficult to learn, requiring effort, concentration, and self-discipline.

◆ She finds such learning very rewarding.

◆ She learns to attack tasks cooperatively, working with others to achieve a goal.

◆ She is on her way to becoming an educated person, one who is learning how to learn.

WHAT WE KNOW

We have already discovered, as we have journeyed through this book, the elements that make this second school possible.

◆ We know with some precision the attitudes, the ways of being that create a learning climate.

◆ We have found that prospective teachers can be helped to develop in these ways as facilitators of learning.

◆ It is also possible to help teachers on the job develop such attitudes and ways in relatively short, intensive experiences.

◆ We have found that these facilitative ways are learned most rapidly in schools where the administrator maintains a facilitative environment for the teachers.

◆ Research and experience show that more learning, more problem solving, more creativity is found in classrooms that have such a climate.

◆ We have seen teachers, from elementary classrooms to graduate school seminars, find ingenious ways to help students learn and choose and grow.

◆ We have watched students develop in responsibility, in self-discipline, in the ability to work.

◆ We know, in short, that it is possible for any teacher to move in the direction of becoming more real, more sensitively understanding, more caring in relation to his or her students.

◆ We have learned that it is possible in such a climate for students to become reliably self-directing, to choose and bear the responsibility of the consequences of their choice, to learn more than in the traditional classroom, and to do so with enthusiasm.

So the logical conclusion from this is that every school would wish to become more of a center for freedom to learn, more of a place where human qualities in teacher and student are prized. Such is not the case. Great sections of our educational system seem wedded to a traditional mode of education and are incredibly resistant to change. Other institutions in our culture—industry, government, marriage, the family—have all changed greatly in recent decades to meet modern conditions. But schools, by and large, have shown much less change. Why is this?

NO FEEDBACK

I believe the main reason for this monolithic opposition to any change can be summed up in two words: no feedback! What I mean by this cryptic phrase is that the school has an almost complete lack of evidence about the eventual effect of its work.

Obtaining Information from the Learner

It is not difficult for schools to obtain learner feedback, as evidenced by student responses reported earlier in this chapter to the question, "What would you like to change about your school and community?" The students gave very specific feedback on how their school could be improved. I believe the study of this type of information would lead to markedly improved qualities of teaching and administration. The process would not need to be elaborate. Student reactions could be obtained at the end of the elementary, secondary, and college experience, and again three to five years later. A great deal could be learned from a simple, anonymous questionnaire. The items might include such queries as the following:

- Describe two or more ways in which this school experience has met your needs.
- Name two or more ways in which the school has failed to meet your needs.
- List briefly some of the experiences—courses, teachers, students, projects, events—from which you have learned the most.
- What experiences, classes, and procedures have you felt were irrelevant or a waste of time?
- To what degree do you find that this school experience has prepared you for the next step in your life? Excellently__ Well__ Moderately__ Poorly__ Very poorly__ Explain your response.
- Are there any changes you believe would make this school a better place for learning?

A questionnaire could also be devised for parents and members of the community. For example, Houston schools have been asking parent and community members to give feedback for the past three years. In addition to questionnaires, an outside interviewer might be employed to ask these same questions of a representative sample of community members, students, and parents. Such interviews would have more depth and would help to uncover areas of satisfaction or dissatisfaction that had not been anticipated. This same person might then be asked, as an objective outsider, to tabulate and summarize all the findings from the questionnaires and the interviews—giving names, courses, and administrators where the frequency of mention justifies it. This summary could then be distributed to all the faculty and administrators and used as data when planning for the next year.

The National Center on Education in the Inner Cities has been providing educators and parents with School Profiles, which measure the academic and social well-being of the school. The profiles are based on student feedback on learning environments, teacher and parent perceptions of school climate, and classroom observations of teacher and student interactions. Part of a School Profile was reported in chapter 13 (Figure 13.1). A section of the observation data reports on the degree of choices students have in selecting learning activities. The profiles are provided in confidence to the staff at each school, and responses to the profiles have been very positive. The faculty, administration, and parents have used the profile information to redirect their efforts to improve the quality of learning in their schools. The LISAM self-assessment instrument (discussed in chapter 6), where teachers use audiotapes of their classes, is another tool for improving the quality of feedback in the schools.

I am well aware that such self-analysis may contain material very painful to contemplate, as well as very rewarding information. I imagine many schools would be frightened at the thought of inaugurating such a process. Yet a refusal would mean that we do not wish to know whether our students are learning in our schools or how they are learning. Certainly, responsible educators would want to take the risk because the advantages would be enormous. We invest huge amounts of effort and money in teachers, textbooks, equipment, and furnishings for our schools. Feedback would begin to let us know the extent to which this learning environment and its curricular content is being received and integrated into the life of the student. It would also bring the students alive because they would realize that they had some opportunity to participate in shaping the educational process. The cost would be very small in relation to the valuable information obtained. It is obvious that student reactions should not be the sole criteria in evaluating the school and its teachers, administrators, and curriculum. Nevertheless, those reactions would be a vast improvement over the present situation. For example, we now have no idea whether the high school years promote significant and useful learning in an individual student or whether they stifle it.

Let me give you an example of how feedback worked in one county in West Virginia that needed to consolidate its small high schools into a larger regional high school.

Asking for Feedback about Student and Parent Concerns

🦋 *Large organizations can be person-centered, but it takes more planning and time to be sure all members become part of a learning community. In West Virginia, due to serious financial problems, small rural town high schools of 150–300 students were required to close and bus their children to a much larger regional or consolidated high school. The closing and consolidations created serious conflicts.*

Small towns in such a situation don't just lose a school; they lose part of their local history, traditions, and identity. Students feel less important or lost in the shuffle when they are placed in a facility with over a thousand other students from different parts of the county. In addition, a number of teachers lose their jobs.

When consolidation occurred in West Virginia in the 1970s, adults responded with violence in the form of threats, bombings, and shootings. However, in the 1990s when consolidation had to occur again due to dwindling state resources to support small (200–300 student) high schools, one county avoided the violence. What was the difference?

The county educators brought together a team of parents, teachers, and students to plan the opening of the new consolidated high school. In an effort to humanize the consolidation process (which few educators or parents wanted), the team decided that it was important that personal contact be made with each student and parent prior to the opening of school. Through a grant from a local hospital, the team developed a program of home visits during the summer and an advisory program throughout the year for all students. Every teacher, administrator, and staff member who had any contact with students joined the visitation team. A team member would make an appointment and meet with families and students at their homes. The students' schedules, descriptions of the advisory sessions, and discussions of student and family interests were also part of the meeting. In addition to the visits, the school conducted a survey of student concerns and needs. A videotaped interview of students from different towns talking about their concerns entering the new high school was also produced. The tape was shown to teachers and team members who received specialized staff development training for the visits. Staff development meetings were also held in order to develop ideas for the first few advisory group meetings.

A student survey was given to all incoming students from the town high schools. Their concerns included the following:

- *60 percent were worried or very worried about* giving presentations in front of others.
- *45 percent were worried or very worried about* taking tests.
- *44 percent were worried or very worried about* failure in school.
- *40 percent were worried or very worried about* drugs, homework assignments, and keeping up with assignments.
- *38 percent were worried or very worried about* getting lost.
- *27 percent were worried or very worried about* unkind people.
- *24 percent were worried or very worried about* being picked on.
- *23 percent were worried or very worried about* having an adult who listens (7).

A clear pattern of interpersonal as well as cognitive concerns begins to emerge from the survey.

The teachers were asked to complete the same survey form during a week of summer staff development to prepare for the opening of school. They were asked to answer the survey from the students' perspective. There were very few overlaps in what the teachers thought and what the students answered.

In a separate survey, teachers were asked to list their own concerns about the opening of the new school. The first concern was discipline, and the second was home visits. Prior to looking at the student survey responses, teachers joked about how the students were going to have an easy time while teachers were going to have a hard time. The student survey responses refocused the faculty on student concerns and what they needed to do to respond to their students. The teachers spent the next few days developing strategies for meeting student needs. For example, instead of asking students to present before the entire class, teachers would ask students to make presentations in small groups. As students began to feel comfortable, they would have the option to present before the entire class or continue in small groups. Follow-up discussions indicated that both students and teachers thought the strategy was very effective in alleviating this concern.

Strategies were also developed for the other student concerns. Many teacher concerns were also addressed in the process. The efforts began during the summer with the home visits and continued with an advisory program. A second videotape, this one of graduating seniors, was produced at the end of the school year as feedback for the high school teachers. The advisory program and the home visits continued for a third year. And now each year the school asks for feedback from the middle-school students coming into the high school and from the seniors leaving the high school.

When you're focusing on the needs of parents and students, you're putting the emphasis on the real consumers of education. This is a factor that is missing in many schools. But some private schools focus specifically on consumer needs and have a clear advantage over public schools in this area.

The Need for Conformists

The pressure to produce conformists is another factor that makes schools resistant to change. But does our society, oriented as it is toward industrial, technological, and military goals, need vast numbers of conformists to make it operate successfully? I think you will find few people who openly argue that this is our need. Yet I believe that at an unconscious or unverbalized level, society wants the products of our schools to be good, obedient followers who are willing to be led. Those who are independent, who think for themselves, tend to rock the boat. It is easier to manage an industry or an army with men and women who have learned to conform to the rules.

Actually, in our present critical situation, this is a very short-sighted view. Our industrial production is slowly passing into the hands of less developed countries. Our technology is overreaching itself and becoming the cause of enormous pollution and waste. Our military, with the end of the Cold War, is reducing its scope and closing hundreds of bases. We are in dire need of individuals capable of critical independent thinking and creative problem solving if we are to remain a viable culture. We need precisely the kind of learners who develop in a person-centered school.

A Reluctance to Share Power

Another element that makes it difficult for many educators to change is the reluctance of those in power to share that power with the group for which they are responsible. Administrators pull away from sharing power with teachers; teachers are fearful of sharing power with their students. It seems too risky. It is easier to stay with the conventional authority structure—the hierarchical order—that is so prevalent in our society. At a deeper level this means that we are fearful of adopting a genuinely democratic philosophy. The belief that in the long run the best decisions are made by the people is a concept we rarely utilize in practice. The fact that our country was founded on the belief that those affected by a decision have a right to participate in making the decision is all too easily forgotten. Many American presidents have reiterated this point; John F. Kennedy may have said it best:

We are not afraid to entrust the American people with unpleasant facts, foreign ideas, alien philosophies and competitive values. For a nation that is afraid to let its people judge the truth and falsehood in an open market is a nation that is afraid of its people. (8)

We do not recognize that a slogan from the time when our nation was not yet independent—"no taxation without representation"—conveys a meaning that is relevant to every institution in our country. In our schools today it should be translated as "no curriculum without student participation; no educational policies without representation of those affected by the policies." This book upholds the conviction that the democratic way, based on a fundamental trust in persons, is applicable and effective in education. What this means—as exemplified by the many educators who have presented their experiences in these pages—is that for a democratic philosophy to be carried out in our schools, an educator must take the risk of empowering the student to participate actively in his or her own educational process. There is ample evidence that in our society, especially at this time, putting a democratic philosophy into action in the classroom is a very important thing to do. We can see the future by looking into the faces of today's children. The leadership of tomorrow is in our classrooms today. What future do we want?

AN OVERRIDING ISSUE: DO WE KEEP THE STATUS QUO OR CHANGE?

Here, then, is the challenge of this book. What do we, the people, want from our schools? What do we hope for in the students who emerge? What sort of young citizens do we need and want in our society?

We have shown that very diverse individuals, working at various educational levels with different intellectual interests, can bring into being a learning environment in which there is responsible freedom. These facilitators of learning create a humane climate in which, being themselves real persons, they also respect the personhood of the student. In this climate there is understanding, caring, and stimulation. And we have seen students respond with an avid interest in learning, with a growing confidence in self, with independence, with creative energy.

We have made available the evidence, gleaned from research and decades of experience, which shows that more effective learning takes place in person-centered classrooms than in traditional classes. It is also clear that a host of other desirable outcomes—more regular attendance, better morale, less vandalism—follow when the teacher personifies a facilitative approach. We have endeavored to make it clear that the philosophy underlying such a person-centered approach is one that is consistent with the values, the goals, the ideals that have historically been the spirit of our democracy.

We have set forth openly the risks, the difficulties of adopting such an approach, and the obstacles society places in its way. To be fully human, to trust in persons, to grant freedom with responsibility—these are not easy goals to achieve. The way we have presented is a challenge. It involves changes in our thinking, in our way of being, in our relationships with our students. It involves a difficult commitment to a democratic ideal.

It all comes down to two questions we must ask both individually and collectively: can we continue in our current state? And what are the first steps toward change?

TRANSFORMATION

The monarch butterfly is one of nature's most remarkable and beautiful creations, but its beginnings are less than beautiful. The transformation from caterpillar to butterfly is a process our schools will need to make if we are to emerge as a society from the current educational bleakness to a transformed work of beauty. This transformation will have many stages; and like the butterfly, each stage will gain its strength from the previous stages. There is no one best model or school. It would be contrary to the core of being person-centered if I tried to create a template through which all students, teachers, and educators would fit. There are, however, some necessary and sufficient conditions for this metamorphosis to occur.

There is a need for *Congruence* where the learning experiences are made real to the learner, and the facilitators of learning are real people without pretense or facade. Other needs are *Unconditional Positive Regard* for the learner that is without preconditions; *Empathic Understanding,* or seeing the world through the eyes of the learner; *Reflection,* the ability of the facilitator to reflect thoughtfully on the conditions at hand and respond appropriately in the best interest of the learner; and finally, *Awareness* is the ability of the learner to seek out congruence, acceptance, empathy, and reflection in the learning environment. It is not enough for the conditions to exist; they must also be communicated to and understood by the learner.

A LEARNING COMMUNITY

Taking the necessary conditions as a starting point, what would be the elements of a person-centered community of learners? There are at least four responses to this question. I am sure you can think of others, but the following list represents a starting point for facilitating an authentic and congruent learning environment.

1. *Partnerships and Networks* that include parents, teachers, administrators at all levels, and other adults who have a direct and indirect investment in the learning process

2. *Caring Communities* that focuses on the needs of all its members—learners and facilitators alike

3. *Active Communities* that solves complex problems today and builds from what we know to what we need to know

4. *Just-in-time Learning* that changes where and how facts are accessed. Information will be acquired from multiple sources, not just teachers and books

I want to examine each of these elements in more detail to see how they might work together to benefit a community of learners.

Partnerships and Networks

Interpersonally, we have become an island nation—the young isolated from the old, the school from the community, children from their parents. The growing isolation felt by many in society is reflected in our schools. Few adults, including parents, spend much time in schools, and schools rarely reach out in positive ways to encourage support from parents or other community members.

If we are to encourage healthy schools and children, then we need to invest more than property taxes in something called public education; we need to invest ourselves. Schools need to do more than hold an open house or contact parents when something is wrong. Teachers and administrators need to reach out and bring together all the human and financial resources necessary to support children and youth in their learning. We need to separate the novelty of doing something high profile and trendy from the long-term commitment needed to achieve the goal of improving the quality of life for all children.

Near Community.   I would like to broaden the commonly held view of the school community as being primarily that of parents, of students, and a few others in the neighborhood. Schools have geographic communities that are both near and far. The near community is best represented by people living in the neighborhood surrounding a school. The near community, therefore, is more than parents and their children; it is all the adults who have a stake in the education of youngsters living in the neighborhood. Historically, many neighborhood schools have served the needs of more than their students and parents. Schools during the last one hundred years have served as the centerpiece of their communities, offering multiple services including night classes for new immigrants and social and community-based programs that kept the schools open into the evenings and on weekends (9). Many schools today serve a broader clientele cutting across neighborhoods and communities. Magnet schools draw from across a city; regional rural and suburban schools draw students from across the county. The concept of school community as being in one's own neighborhood is changing.

Far Community. The concept of a far community begins where the near community ends. The larger city, county, or the nation as a whole represents this broader community. With mega-corporations becoming the norm, the local gas station, movie theater, or convenience store is most likely owned and operated by a corporation far removed from the neighborhood. Decisions are also removed from the local site. This detachment of local services and decision making can add to the isolation of a community and its schools.

Schools today must reach out to establish partnerships and networks with people, organizations, corporations, and agencies that can become shareholders in the learning process. Inner-city schools that work for their students have three times the number of near and far business and community partners working with them when compared to other schools in the same districts (10). Participation by businesses in schools far removed from corporate headquarters may reflect the realization that skilled and well-educated (rather than just trained) workers will not be available in the next twenty years if current school practices and detachment continues. Partnerships with businesses and networks with other people is an essential element in bringing the outside in and breaking the isolation of schools, teachers, and students. Active involvement of business leaders from the far community through school business partnerships will encourage the corporate store to respond to the school and near community as if it were owned by a neighbor. This will enable mega-corporations who are geographically removed to become partners with schools and communities. Partnerships can become another source of support for students, teachers, administrators, and parents (3).

Caring Community

Caring must be experienced to be real. Most schools are not physically designed to be caring places. In almost every interview I have conducted with students, caring teachers and others make a positive difference for students. In the factory-like, pigeonholed box school designs of the past one hundred years, one-to-one human interactions were not a high priority.

A caring community needs to be small enough for each person to know the name of everyone in the school. Few of our high schools have less than a thousand students. Many average-sized high schools have between fifteen hundred and twenty-five hundred students. Schools of three thousand to four thousand students reflect a philosophy that bigger is better. Too often bigger is only cheaper. What may be gained initially in lower building costs in these mega-schools is lost in the long term with alienated, apathetic, and joyless students and teachers. Personal well-being most surely suffers in the process of reaping short-term financial gains.

Redesigning School Organizations. Students are often strangers to each other and their teachers, even though they go to the same school each day. I have had high school teachers tell me, "I don't know the names of my students yet; it's still early in the year"—a comment made to me in November, three months after the start of the school year. It is unrealistic to expect that existing schools will be physically demolished and replaced by new small-designed schools. However, a number of school districts are rethinking their existing designs and establishing "families" of teachers and students. This is the case in the San Diego school district where O'Farrell Community School, serving thirteen hundred students, divided an old building into nine *educational families.* The school secured additional resources by eliminating counselor and assistant principal positions and placing those resources where they were needed—in the classroom. The Dett School in Chicago and the New Orleans Free School also function without an administrative staff. You will recall reading about the New Orleans Free School in chapter 6. Bob Ferris was a teacher there for several years before the district required the school to have a principal or close its doors. The Dett School used its assistant principal position to hire more part-time teachers from the community to provide additional expertise and to give students more resources in the classroom. This strategy of reallocating resources is possible when a school begins to move away from the factory model of supervision and progress toward the person-centered model of facilitating learning. Learning communities can be much more self-disciplined and self-sufficient than traditional school organizations.

Personal Attributes of Caring. There are several personal attributes of a caring school: people listen to each other; humor is spontaneous and supportive, not hurtful; people help each other and celebrate each other's successes; visitors are greeted with smiles; people respect each other's views, although they may not agree with them; and caring is authentic, not contrived. At the Amy-6 School in Philadelphia I was greeted by a parent. She said, "hello" and asked if I needed directions to the office. I later discovered from the students that parents were hired at a minimal wage to be there for the students. Each parent acted in the role of a security guard, but when needed, the parent quickly became a shoulder to cry on and an ear to talk to.

At Amy-6, which is a public school in inner-city Philadelphia, teachers give students hugs. During a time of great sensitivity toward personal contact with students, the teachers "give good greetings," said one tough-looking seventh grader. He continued by saying, "It makes you feel like you are welcome to that classroom." Another student agrees, "Yeah and you are doing something to deserve that hug. You must be doing something good; it makes you feel important."

Caring Schools Listen. The schools discussed in this book have many ways to listen to their students. At HSPVA, Amy-6, New Orleans Free

School, Dett, Montefiore, and O'Farrell, the students and staff meet regularly to discuss issues, solve problems, and celebrate important moments in the lives of their members. Each of the principals has an open-door policy for students and staff alike. Modeling openness for all members of the learning school has a ripple effect. It is clearly more important to do what one believes than to just talk about it.

Mistakes Are Lessons Learned.   Caring schools have curriculum that allow mistakes to become part of the learning process. Mistakes are not blots on one's character but opportunities to see what could have been done differently. Most of the schools described in this book use tests as self-measuring tools. Students may retake tests as long as they improve each time.

The traditional process of testing in its current state is viewed by many in these schools as a sorting and sifting function, which in the end dooms a large percentage of students to failure. Most person-centered schools use a portfolio system for reviewing student efforts. At HSPVA, the students meet with *all* their teachers twice a year to get feedback on their portfolios and discuss how they are doing. At the New Orleans Free School no grades are given, only feedback in the form of portfolios and narratives. Both schools have successfully used these feedback approaches for over two decades.

If testing is not a requirement of the greater society, then let's stop the game of spending weeks—sometimes months—preparing for state and national standardized tests. Mary Lee Smith, professor of education at Arizona State University, studied the effects of testing on teaching and learning in elementary schools. She concludes:

> From classroom observations it was concluded that testing programs substantially reduce the time available for instruction, narrow curricular offerings and modes of instruction, and potentially reduce the capacities of teachers to teach content and the use of methods and materials that are incompatible with standardized testing formats. (11, p. 8)

The best way to avoid wasting golden opportunities for learning is to randomly select a few students at an unannounced point in time to be tested. No one would know when the test would be given or which students would be tested. The test would not be noted on any student's file, but it could be used by the school community as one of many sources of data.

Comments

When developing partnerships, networks, and caring communities, the emphasis is on improving both the quality of life and the persons involved in the learning communities of the schools. Teachers *want* to be at the schools, and there are often waiting lists of teachers and many times students seeking to learn there. The vision or mission of the schools may be varied, but the process of reaching the mission is shared by all school members. This shared process requires active participation of every member.

Active Learning Community

To meet the growing challenge of today's learner, we should consider a redefinition of community and the ways in which schools function within the community. Apple Computer's invention of *Newton*, a handheld computer that has the capacity to recognize written instructions on a notepad-sized screen, is only one example of the potential in this area. Eventually computers like *Newton* will be able to recognize voice instructions.

Intergenerational Centers.   Within the learning community, Intergenerational centers are places where the young and old work together. For the most part, these two groups of people have been artificially separated. But the learning community can offer classes on language, arts, and computers. A day-care facility for young and old may also be part of Intergenerational centers. For example, Capital High School in Charleston, West Virginia, has a day-care facility in the high school for infants whose parents are students in the school. Senior citizens volunteer, along with the mothers and fathers of the children who attend school. Intergenerational centers can also house a literacy center for members of the near community. Older students may tutor younger students at the center. The Houston Read Commission, for example, currently has twenty-one such literacy programs operating in schools, businesses, and libraries.

The Academy.   The term *school* carries a great deal of negative baggage, both for many students today and for parents who were less than successful in school. A learning community can change those attitudes. The *Academy* is a term that refers to the portion of the learning community where students meet with each other and their facilitators. The Academy would have both flexibility and structure; it would have freedom. The factory-like operations of today's secondary schools would change. Gone would be the bells, P.A. systems, fixed forty-two-minute classes, barren eating areas, and hall sweeps. The Academy would establish a compact between all of its members relating to its operations. All persons in the Academy would participate, including the custodians, cooks, and cleaning people as well as students and facilitators (aka teachers and administrators).

Extended Family.   A core of facilitators would join with a learning group of students to form houses, or families of learners. To this primary family, an extended family of facilitators may also be added. HSPVA has forty such extended family members. They conduct workshops, hold seminars, observe the students work, and give feedback. The additional cost at HSPVA comes to about $150 per student per year. Other facilitators of learning add a new dimension to the Academy: expertise evolved from practice. These extended family members provide renewal for the teacher as well as new perspectives for the students. A wealth of knowledge and experience waits outside the classroom; it just needs to be *invited* in.

Time Spent.   The time one spends at the Academy may vary. Learning contracts and mission statements would be established with each student, and regular meetings between the student and all his or her facilitators would be an ongoing occurrence. (HSPVA is an example.) Assessments would focus on self-assessment and portfolio assessments. High-risk standardized tests (if required) would be administered to a few students on a random basis. Thus, students would become shareholders in their learning, and the Academy would facilitate rather than impede student responsibility. A governance plan would be established that calls for cooperative management of the Academy as part of the larger learning community. The energies that traditional schools direct toward cheerleading, proms, and competitive sports would be redirected toward service to others. In many different ways, the Academy and the community would join together for the common good of both.

An active community of learners is one that has both an internal and external locus of energy. The Academy would be a portal to near and far communities, becoming the centerpiece of the community and providing protective support for all its members. Older students could be tutors for both younger students and adults. Parents would learn alongside their children in specially designed classes. The possibilities are limitless. Yale psychologist James Comer has included mental health facilities in schools he has been working with for many years. The Hogg Foundation has funded in-house mental health centers for students at their schools. These learning communities are not unique ideas. They exist in schools throughout the nation, but there are too few of these schools.

The school calendar, class periods, school size, and curriculum would become a function of current and future needs and interests of the learner. Flexibility and responsiveness would be the framework around which an active learning environment should evolve. The work of Harvard psychologist Howard Gardner on multiple intelligences proposes the use of individual and group projects that more accurately reflect what people do outside of school and the range of intelligences exhibited in the classroom. The continued development of technology can be used as a tool to reduce dependence on the textbook or teacher as the primary source of facts and information.

Just-in-time Learning

If the role of teacher is to change, then the fundamental need to dispense facts will also have to change (12). Consider this analogy. Henry Ford developed the assembly line for the production of automobiles, using a method of stockpiling parts to feed long lines of assemblers. When the cost of parts and labor was low, this seemed like a reasonable way to ensure adequate supplies when they were needed. However, it became increasingly expensive to maintain an inventory when it was not used for several months or years. American industry saw the inventory issue as a problem that could be solved with more controls and better management and technology. They didn't see it as a problem of philosophy but rather: why do we need to waste valuable resources on something we aren't using now?

In the late 1970s, when Japanese car makers began looking at ways to build better cars for less money, stockpiling of parts was an area of immediate savings. But how could they get parts to the assembly lines if the parts were not stockpiled? The answer to that question has been referred to by many in the auto and other manufacturing industries as a *just-in-time response* (13, 14, 15). It works something like this. Suppliers agree to send their parts within two days from the time they are needed by the factory rather than operate within a several-month window, as had been the case before. The just-in-time response allows the auto industry to save warehouse space and costs, time, and the need to use resources before they are required. It is a philosophy as well as a procedure to reduce waste in the production of new goods.

Some of the leaders in the field talk about this philosophy:

> ❦ *Just-in-Time is not a quick fix nor is it a system to be brought in overnight by top management. . . . Just-in-Time . . . requires the commitment and leadership of top management and, at the same time, the understanding and full dedication of every individual in the process. (15, p. 21)*

> ❦ *Begin with people. No matter how automated the equipment, improvement begins with people, and those who transform their companies regard the physical changes as manifestation of success with the workers and managers. (13, p. 81)*

> ❦ *In a Just-in-Time system, the necessary materials are brought to the necessary place to build the necessary product at the exact time when they are required. . . . [It] will only succeed when management, workers, and suppliers make a strong commitment to work together in solving problems. (14, p. 6)*

I am usually not enamored with business approaches to education because they usually focus on the outcomes without looking at the human being. The concept of a just-in-time response is intriguing, however, if you think of parts as facts. Rather than trying to stockpile facts in the minds of children until they are needed at some later date, facts can be used on a timely basis. Facts are quickly forgotten if they are not applied to real problems, and in many instances students only learn them for tests. This is easily documented. According to Gary M. Galles, professor of economics at Pepperdine University, in his article entitled "Our Graduates Soon Purge What They Learned," he reaches the same conclusion:

> In considering useful education reforms, we must remember that . . . if they [students] believe what they are taught isn't worth remembering, no content reforms can stem 'the rising tide of mediocracy.' . . . Having decided that much they are being taught does not merit retention, they do what it takes to look good on their transcripts without cluttering their minds with all the 'useless' things they learned in the process.

> . . .Students are interested in learning, but are unwilling to remember every word the teachers say simply because they say it. That is good for education, not bad. After all, questioning the value of what is being taught reflects the sort of intellectual development that is the goal of education. (16, p. 13a)

If facts are not stockpiled, then how can students learn? They can retrieve facts just in time for learning. The facts or information about a topic are tapped when the student needs them to seek solutions. Thus, teaching truly becomes a facilitative process, providing opportunities for learning through simulations, research projects, cooperative-learning groups, guest interactors, inquiry and discovery challenges. The teacher becomes an orchestrator of resources and has assistance from the students to create a dynamic learning environment.

For the last one hundred years, facts have been driven by teachers and textbooks. The problem with facts in today's world is their half-life factor: the usefulness and accuracy of the information has diminished rapidly. By some estimates the half-life factor of useful facts has gone from twenty years to ten years to five years or less in many disciplines. In 1970 a professor of chemistry who received his degree from Oxford University in England concluded that nearly half of what he learned as "facts" was incorrect or outdated (17).

Technology As a Tool. We may be wowed by technology, but past experiences indicate that the human being is the most important element in learning. In the learning community, however, the teacher's role is metamorphosed to the role of a facilitator. The real potential of learning is realized when teachers are freed from the burden of being the sole source of expert knowledge. Technology can be a tool used to develop solutions to today's problems and create simulations of problems that have yet to be defined. While computers seem to be the logical solution to the problem of updating and retrieving information, they have been less than successful in changing the ways students learn. The current problem with computers in schools today is the lack of accessibility. Most schools have a computer lab where students work on the computers perhaps once a week if the schedule permits.

The use of handheld computers could revolutionize the retrieval of information or facts; and the costs and accessibility will be within reach of most schools in the next five years. When each student has his or her own portal to the world's knowledge, the role of teacher as giver of information will forever change. It is not a matter of *if* but *when* this transformation will occur.

We don't need to wait for individual computers to capture just-in-time learning. Each classroom, in addition to relying on the resources of "extended family members," should have a range of rich resources including books, tapes, magazines, and newspapers from around the world, which students and teachers can tap to gain immediate information for projects or other needs.

There may be attempts to diminish the role of teacher as the job of information-giver becomes obsolete. Indeed, teachers who hold fast to their traditional role in the next decade may find that the world has truly changed. There will be fewer "teaching" positions and more "facilitator" positions opening during the next twenty years. The potential for freeing the learning environment will be exhilarating. People who become facilitators of learning will have a greater role in the development of the whole person, allowing the beauty and potential of learning to emerge from its cocoon. Building (a) Partnerships and Networks, (b) Caring Communities, (c) Active Communities, and (d) Just-in-time Learning will be a starting point for a dialogue on how these changes will occur in places of learning across our nation.

THE CHALLENGE: A NATIONAL DIALOGUE

We need a sustained national dialogue on the future of education in America. The dialogue should be person-to-person both in town meetings and across the nation. I challenge people in cities and towns, small and large, to come together to develop a *dialogue on learning* and a plan that meets the needs of the individual while shaping a direction for the nation. We can no longer pick up and move away from the problems of our cities or communities.

The media can assist in this dialogue through a series of newspaper and magazine articles, through television programs and movies about some of the issues raised in this book and other sources. As Buckminster Fuller proposed in the 1950s, some meetings may be held electronically. But I would prefer that thousands of smaller meetings be held in schools, community centers, colleges, and universities to discuss the issues of education that are facing us. I also hope that these meetings would be held throughout the nation and that people who have facilitated and learned in schools that meet the needs of all children and youth would add to the discussion. You may want to give some thought to the issues and questions that would be part of such a national dialogue. I will propose a few questions and issues in the final chapter of the book for you to consider.

From dialogue, I believe, will come direction. The answers are within us. We need to listen and talk with each other to build a consensus and support system for learning.

CONCLUDING COMMENTS

Although some would say, "We can't reform one school at a time; it would take too long," I say this is the only way to get lasting change. Mass-produced school reform hasn't worked in the past, and there is no reason to think it will work now. In education, one size does *not* fit all.

As a nation, we can reasonably expect our schools to serve as the great equalizer, a meeting place for democratic values to emerge. This remains, I believe, a viable goal for education. An active learning community will not set restrictions on the sources of learning. It will continually challenge what and how it learns, even though it may be on the cutting edge of change.

As a nation, and as a democratic people, we must begin talking with and listening to each other again. The isolation experienced by many of our people will continue without some reflection and dialogue about the important things in our lives and the lives of future generations. The reduction of America's budget deficit is important because of the legacy of a financial burden it will leave future generations. We have an educational deficit that will leave an even greater burden on future generations if we do not respond to the needs of our children today. The time for transforming the caterpillar to the butterfly has arrived. Such opportunities do not always occur when we want, so we must take the chance and make the changes needed to revitalize the present in order to have a more vibrant and hopeful future.

REFERENCES

1. C. Rogers, Personal communication with H. J. Freiberg, 1984.

2. National Commission on Educational Excellence, *A Nation at Risk: The Imperative of Educational Reform* (Washington, D.C.: Government Printing Office, 1983).

3. H. J. Freiberg, "Understanding Resilience: Implications for Inner-city Schools and Their Near and Far Communities," in *Educational Resilience in Inner-city America: Challenges and Prospects*, ed. M. Wang and E. Gordon (Hillsdale, N.J.: Erlbaum, 1994).

4. C. Rugley, "Schools Seek to Drop Costly Bureaucratic Burdens," *Houston Chronicle*, 28 March 1993, p. 1d.

5. Center on Organizing and Restructuring of Schools, "Estimating the Extent of School Restructuring," Wisconsin Center for Educational Research, Brief no. 4 (Fall 1992): p. 4.

6. B. Levin, Personal communications about student interviews, 1993.

7. "Preston County Teachers' Institute Needs Assessment" (Preston County, West Virginia, Summer 1992).

8. J. F. Kennedy, Comments made on the Twentieth Anniversary of the Voice of America (Health, Education, and Welfare Building Auditorium, 25 February 1962).

9. A. Perry, *The Management of a City School* (New York: Macmillan, 1914).

10. H. J. Freiberg, "Schools That Foster Resilience in Inner-city Youth," *Journal of Negro Education*, yearbook edition, 62, no. 3 (1993): 364–376.

11. M. L. Smith, "Put to the Test: The Effects of External Testing on Teachers," *Educational Researcher* 20, no. 5 (1991): 8–11.

12. Thanks to Professor Jerry Willis at the University of Houston for directing me to this topic.

13. R. Hall, *Attaining Manufacturing Excellence* (Homewood, Ill.: Dow Jones-Irwin, 1987).

14. A. Hernandez, *Just-in-time Manufacturing: A Practical Approach* (Englewood Cliffs, N.J.: Prentice-Hall, 1989).

15. M. Sepehri, *Just-in-Time, Not Just in Japan* (Falls Church, Vir.: The American Production and Inventory Control Society, 1986).

16. G. Galles. "Our Graduates Soon Purge What They Learned," *Houston Chronicle*, 24 May 1993, p. 13a.

17. A. Toffler. *Future Shock* (New York: Random House, 1970).

A JOURNEY BEGUN

CHAPTER *18*

SOME REFLECTIONS

◆

But how is one to realize this Truth. . . . By single-minded devotion. . . .
however, of such devotion, what may appear as truth to one person
will often appear as untruth to another person. . . . there is nothing wrong
in everyone following Truth according to one's lights. Indeed it is
one's duty to do so. Then if there is a mistake on the part of any one so
following the Truth, it will automatically be set right. (1, p. 57)
Mahatma Gandhi

Vision is the ability to see what is unseen, realize what has yet to be, and act upon one's beliefs in the face of uncertainty. Truth, according to Mahatma Gandhi, a person who changed a continent through his teachings of nonviolent confrontation, reflects the importance of setting a path and following it. A vision of education that benefits the well-being of all children and youth is the foundation of *Freedom to Learn.* We have seen what is, what should be, and what could be both in reality and in the potential for learning in our schools. The pathway toward person-centered learning communities is strewn with challenges; this is a given. However, challenges can be opportunities missed or gained.

CHALLENGES ABOUND

Every endeavor has its challenges; transforming schools into person-centered environments certainly has its share. It is my hope that the challenges we undertake lead in a direction that will benefit millions of students, parents, teachers, and their communities.

Creating a Dialogue

The first challenge is to establish a national dialogue on learning as a nation and as a democratic people, as proposed in chapter 17. This should be pursued with vigor and urgency. It may begin with letters to the editor or to elected representatives at local, state, and federal levels. It may start with a class project to create a dialogue on learning within a college, university, or school district. However you decide to begin, it cannot be left to someone else. If the other person is responsible, then no one is responsible. It must begin with you.

Listed here are a few questions that could get the dialogue started. I hope you thought about your list of questions. Do we have some overlap?

1. How can all children receive equal opportunities to learn when funding for education is unequal?
2. Should the investment in a child's public education be solely supported by property taxes?
3. How can our peacemaking rather than violence be the goal of schools and society?
4. Can the definitions of successful schools be expanded to go beyond test scores, grades, and athletics?
5. Should there be a moratorium on schools that are unhealthy for the academic or emotional well-being of students?
6. How can the cycle of youth's being either a witness, victim, or perpetrator of violence be broken?
7. Should resources be shifted from intervention to prevention for supporting children and families?
8. How can schools become more person-centered?
9. How can resources be directed away from the bureaucracy and into the classroom to benefit student learning?
10. What commitments will it take to make the nation's children the focus of our support?

As you can see, we have much to talk about. The list is only a beginning. Some of the issues are discussed in this book, but the dialogue needs to be broadened and sustained. There are reasonable solutions to most issues, but our nation is running out of time. It will require each of us to make education and the well-being of our youth our number one priority. The future of the nation and the leadership that will govern us in our twilight years are in our classrooms today. Based on the resources we have provided, what kind of world will they be able to build?

The dialogue between parents, teachers, students, and members of near and far communities should focus on what is right with schools that meet the needs of students. If we only look at what's wrong with learning, then we are in a constant state of repair rather than in a state of transformation. Positive examples of the Academy described by students, teachers, parents, administrators, and other citizens should be part of the dialogue.

If a moratorium is deemed necessary, and some schools close during their transformation, the process should be discussed in light of the opportunities that could be created for the staff as well as students. It is not enough to discuss the changes that are required. Those involved in the restructuring must experience the changes firsthand. They must truly understand that not only do these ideas work in theory and in print, but they also work in the real world—in schools that are actually implementing the concepts. Teachers and administrators in a restructured school should be allocated the time to visit person-centered schools—spending days, perhaps weeks, talking with and participating in the day-to-day workings of several person-centered learning environments.

The O'Farrell Community School, a public inner-city school in San Diego whose transformation was described in chapter 9, is a good example of how the process could occur. The developers of a new school within an old building began with a dream, a vision of a place that "promotes excellence by providing all middle level students . . . [with] an academically enriched curriculum within a multiethnic, student-centered environment . . . . [And it hopes] to attend to the social, intellectual, psychological, and physical needs of middle level youth so they will become responsible, literate, thinking, and contributing citizens" (2, p. 12).

The key to student success at O'Farrell has been a sustaining dialogue about what's important for members of its learning community. This dialogue has been built over time. It began in 1989 with a need to know about the experiences of others in transforming schools. The faculty who formed O'Farrell Community School were given opportunities to visit other restructuring programs and schools that had successfully met the challenges of developing learner-centered schools. The O'Farrell design, while incorporating ideas that have worked for others (for example, teachers and students learning in family teams, social services at the school, and the reallocation of administrative resources to the classroom), designed a program that is unique to O'Farrell's learning community. This design changed after the first year when the student population grew from 450 students in one grade level to 1,350 students in three grade levels. Retreats were held to build a dream and vision of what could be for students who in the past had been poorly served by the educational system. All members of Team O'Farrell, as they call themselves, including parents, teachers, office staff, and others who have a direct or indirect role in the well-being of the lives of children at O'Farrell, were in attendance. The retreats and intensive group meetings began during the planning stages and have been ongoing each year since 1989.

The need for continuous dialogue and interaction facilitated the dream and has helped in the realization of a vision of a school that works for all its members. The learning schedule at O'Farrell is designed around the needs of students and teachers. Time is provided every day for dialogue between the team members, students, and parents. In addition to daily contact among team members, the staff at O'Farrell meets throughout the year in retreat settings to reconnect with one another and revitalize their dialogue. At one retreat the members were asked by a facilitator to read Langston Hughes's poem "Harlem" and talk about dreams deferred. One team member said, "As a backpacker I can appreciate a heavy load, but as the journey goes on the load gets lighter and lighter. And you know that you can't ever get to high places without the load, so you must get stronger to carry it." "That's right," said another, "and in the old way of teaching you had to carry the load alone. At O'Farrell we share the load" (3, p. 27).

Renewal through dialogue, working in teams, and meeting and learning together combine to create a path many teachers desire but too few teachers experience. Teachers who stay in the same place, doing the same things every day with little or no interaction with others can become desensitized to the needs of children. An international study coordinated by Professor Theo Wubbels of the Netherlands looked at teachers' interactions with students in several countries (the United States, the Netherlands, Australia, Israel, and Finland). The study showed that after ten years in the classroom, teachers have significantly lower affective (cooperative) interactions with their students (4).

Apprenticeships

Changing the patterns from teacher-directed to student-centered learning is perhaps the greatest challenge. If lasting change is to occur in schools across the nation, apprenticeships by teachers in person-centered learning environments need to take place. This is particularly true for those teachers in schools that are undergoing transformation. We learn best by doing; and if change is to be sustained, then apprenticeships need to be offered by schools with an ongoing record of meeting the needs of students. People need to see that what has been discussed in this book really does occur and is a reasonable, practical, and more enjoyable way of being.

Apprenticeships could be part of each new facilitator's entry to the profession. Functioning in ways that go beyond student teaching, apprenticeships could help new members of the profession, along with university faculty, become part of one or more learning communities. These changes will take a rethinking of the philosophy of teaching and learning. They will also take a reallocation within universities and colleges to place resources in learning communities where new members of the profession work in apprenticeships with veteran members.

Resources

Resources are another challenge, both in terms of people and money. There is an assumption that we have enough resources to do what is needed. This may be the case in some schools, but it is clearly not the case in many urban and rural schools. I spoke with a principal who recently moved from an urban high school in the southwestern part of the United States to a suburban high school near Chicago. He had $3,728 per student in his urban high school and $10,540 per student in his suburban high school. He told me how much more was taking place in his newly assigned school because of the resources. In his new assignment, technology was available for every student rather than rationed. The facilities were bright and cheerful; all the systems, from heating to air-conditioning, worked. There was flexible space to meet the needs of students as they developed their learning projects. The principal's previous high school was terribly overcrowded, with little or no space for creative activities. The inequality of educational funding for students across the nation is a serious barrier to better education and one that needs to be part of any national dialogue.

In addition to resources for students, there is a need to see teachers as assets to our future, not liabilities. The transformation of O'Farrell Community School required resources both in terms of people and money. The need to sustain dialogue required time during the day for people to talk and plan, and it also required money to allow people to leave the school building and visit other sites and meet with each other during planned retreats. Some of the funds came from the district; other funding came from foundations and local businesses. O'Farrell was the first school in San Diego to completely restructure, so resources were available. But what will happen when twenty, forty, or all the schools in San Diego seek to follow O'Farrell's example? It becomes very clear that we need to rethink the level of resources that schools actually require to meet the learning and social-emotional needs of students.

In a two-part series on myths about education, David Berliner, professor at Arizona State University, examined data from UNESCO (a United Nations educational organization) on educational expenditures. Berliner concluded from the data that the United States spends more on all forms of education, from preschool through college, than do most other nations, with the exception of Sweden. (Canada and the Netherlands spend about the same amount.) However, when the intervals between preschool and high school are considered, Berliner found that we spend 14 percent less than Germany, 30 percent less than Japan, and 51 percent less than Switzerland

(5, pp. 12–3). When you add to these findings the deterioration of the family and the desperation exhibited by teenagers resulting in the world's highest rates of youth suicide and murder, you have a situation crying for an immediate and sustaining response.

Great changes can be made with a few clearly directed ideas. I would like to review a few of these additional challenges and propose some possible directions one could take when seeing them as opportunities gained. We have seen throughout the book how educators have taken small steps to gain significant results. But lasting change will not occur overnight. It takes persistence and time, but most of all a mission and a vision. Having a mission or direction that focuses on the best interests of students allows for multiple approaches. Those best interests need to be constantly checked to be sure that student needs continue to be met.

Chapter 1 illustrated the impact on students when their needs *are* met: they love school. Motivation, which is a natural part of each of us, is sustained in person-centered learning communities. We have also seen what happens when students' needs are ignored. Therefore, it is far better to begin by moving along the continuum from teacher-focused to student-focused at a pace that is reflective of both student and teacher needs. Take your time; if you teach in a high school, begin with one or two of your classes rather than all at once.

I recall a teacher's telling me after she began cooperative learning groups that it wasn't working well. "The students were floundering," she explained. When I spoke to the students, they said, "The teacher went from lecture every period to us working in groups, and we don't know what to do." Two points seem clear here: First, the pace of change was too quick for the students; and second, the teacher spent little time helping her students learn how to work together. But the teacher did not receive any feedback from her students on how they were doing in their learning groups. In further conversations with me, the students were very specific about their need to spend more time with the teacher discussing issues that were bothering them. Moving from one approach to the other is a process, not a race. Some students needed more time to make the adjustment. Feedback from students and reflecting on what has occurred are two important qualities of a successful change process.

Many Paths to the Same Goal

Another challenge is that there can never be a codifiable pattern for the operation of a person-centered institution. By empowering the members of the group, we guarantee that each situation will be unique and must be dealt with by the group in its own special way. In another book, *Carl Rogers on Personal Power*, I discuss my firsthand experience at the University of Chicago. Here is an excerpt from that book:

🦋 *I first recognized this at the University of Chicago. In the eyes of the university I was the responsible person in charge of the Counseling Center. I handled that responsibility by empowering all the staff, myself included, to operate the organization. I have written about that period.*

I learned many strange things from the experience at the Counseling Center. It was quite dismaying to me at first that we never seemed to be able to find the right way of operating the Center. First, all decisions were made by consensus. That was too burdensome. We delegated decision-making to a small group. That proved slow. We chose a coordinator, and agreed to abide by his/her decisions, though like a prime minister he/she could be given a vote of no confidence. Only gradually did I realize that there is no right way. The life and vitality and growth of the Center was closely bound up with its lack of rigidity, with its continually surprising capacity to change its collective mind, and to utilize a new mode of operation.

I found that when power was distributed, it was no big thing to be the coordinator or chairman of the budget committee or whatever. Consequently administrative tasks were very often sought by the newest members of the staff, because it was an avenue of becoming acquainted with the workings of the operation. An intern might chair a group making up next year's budget. The newest staff member might head a planning group, or a group to pass on membership or promotions. Senior members of the group were freed to spend more time on research and therapy, knowing that if the various administrative task groups failed accurately to represent the sentiment of the members, their decisions would be rejected by the staff as a whole.

I found the enormous importance of personal feelings in administrative matters. Often the staff would spend hours (or so it seemed) in arguing some trivial issue, until a perceptive member would see and state the feelings underlying the issue—a personal animosity, a feeling of insecurity, a competition between two would-be leaders, or just the resentment of someone who had never really been heard. Once the feelings were out in the open, the issue which had seemed so important became a nothing. On the other hand when the staff was in open communication with one another, heavy issues such as the allocation of the budget for the following year, the election of a coordinator, the adoption of an important policy might take only minutes to decide. (6, pp. 94–95)

Creeping Bureaucracy

Another challenge is how to minimize the growth of bureaucracies in the decision process. For example, many businesses, as they grow, find that what were once creative working groups have evolved into gatekeepers presenting formidable barriers to needed change. P. R. Fairfield's *Person-centered Graduate Education* has an excellent chapter pointing out the tendency of every organization to develop routinized, bureaucratic ways of operation (7, chap. 5). He says:

> Anybody who has been involved in developing an institution—public school, private hiking club, business, church, or whatever—knows that it is easy to apply some kind of rational system to persuade others to conform to recommended viewpoints, codes, or rules. Hence, it seems probable that any institution advocating a liberal, radical, or freedom-seeking end is virtually bound to reinvent autocratic reasons for not acting in accordance with its own goals. (7, p. 100)

Anything can become an imposed rule—even freedom. There is more than a modicum of truth in the old cartoon of the child in a *progressive* school saying plaintively, "Do I have to do what I want to do?" In the structureless freedom of an encounter group, participants frequently discover norms to which they are expected to conform. So the accumulation of customary procedures all too easily slides into the codification of rules for required procedures.

There is another element involved in bureaucracy: the tendency to act as if an organization should be continued just because it has been formed. Temporary committees become permanent. We say that the organization tends to perpetuate itself. It would be more accurate to say that the persons in the organization find themselves striving to maintain the status quo rather than seeking to achieve their original goals. Elected officials have realized the problems associated with committees that seem to last forever. Many state legislative bodies have started a "sunset" policy that limits the time span for each committee. After a set period, usually three to five years, the committee must be reviewed to determine if it is serving its original goals.

This approach would also be useful in our public schools. School groups could form temporary committees that usually focus on a practical goal involving the solution of some specific problem. These temporary committees would be composed of those whose interests were involved (including parents, students, teachers, and administrators). Once the problem was solved—or proven insolvable—the temporary committee would disappear. These two ways of working, both in educational and administrative areas, could be highly useful models for slowing the development of dehumanizing and rule-bound procedures. They would ensure the continuation of a human approach.

The Lure of "Power Over"

The need for power is perhaps one reason that explains why committee members refuse to examine their own usefulness. There is one final element that may account for the relatively short life of most institutions aiming to respect the dignity, worth, and capacity of the individual. The lure of power can best be illuminated by examining a significant case history from the business world.

🦋 *I know a man who has, for fifteen years, been a consultant for a very large industrial firm. The business of this firm is diversified, but for the most part its units of manufacture are small and widely used.*

This man has, by his way of being, by his training approach, and through cognitive methods, brought into being in this organization a person-centered way of management—not with the whole organization, but with a sizable number of middle- and upper-management personnel.

So highly has he been regarded, and so effective are the managers who had trained with him, that a number of years ago he was permitted to set up an "experiment." Three factories were set aside as experimental manufacturing plants, where the consultant had trained, and continued to work with, management and nonmanagement personnel. Three other plants were designated as control units. It should be stressed that this is a very modern industrial giant, with generally good labor relations, a high level of efficiency compared with other firms manufacturing the same types of items, and of course a rigorous cost-accounting system. Hence both the control and experimental plants started the experiment as "well-run" systems.

During the past nine years the people in the experimental plants have become more and more deeply involved with a person-centered philosophy. Employees tend to be trusted by those in charge, rather than having their work closely supervised, inspected, and scrutinized. Likewise, employees tend to trust each other. The degree of mutual regard among the employees is unusually high, as is their respect for each other's capabilities. The emphasis of the consultant and of the plant personnel has been upon building up good interpersonal relations, vertical and horizontal two-way communication, and a dispersion of responsibility, choice, and decision-making.

Now the results are clearly apparent. In the experimental plants the average cost of a particular unit is about 22¢. In the control plants the average cost of the same item is 70¢! In the experimental plants there are now three to five managers. In the control units of comparable size there are seventeen to twenty-three managers! In the experimental units workers and supervisors come sauntering in from the parking lots in earnest conversation, generally about their work. In the control plants they come in quickly, mostly singly, to punch the time clock. (6, pp. 101–2)

This is a truly remarkable success story. Surely the conclusion should be that these person-centered ways are now being fostered throughout the corporation. But that is not the way it has turned out. Later I talked with this consultant. He told me that while the experimental plants continue to do extremely well, and he feels pride in the work he has done with them, he regards his work with the corporation as a failure. The top management, though appreciative of the increased profits and good morale of the experimental plants, has not moved to follow this model in their other plants, even though it appears evident that overall profits would be increased. "Why not?" I inquired. His answer was most thought provoking: "When managers from other plants look closely at what we are doing, they gradually realize how much of their power they would have to give away, have to share with their employees. And they are not willing to give up that power." When I stated that it appeared that power over people was even more important than profits—which are supposed to be the all-important goal in industry—he agreed.

An interesting footnote to this story is that when managers in the three experimental plants were offered promotions that would move them out of the experimental factories, many declined and sought higher-level positions in organizations where there was understanding of their human way of facilitating production. Companies who followed a policy of allowing power over others to rule the workplace were in for a real shock a few years down the road. Many of these companies saw their profits dwindle, their markets disappear, and their workers leave.

The same may be true today in education. Administrators of educational institutions may place a higher value on power over people than on the enhancement of learning. Everyone begins to horde power. Administrators don't want to share their power with teachers for fear of losing some of it; and teachers, in turn, don't want to pass on their power to students for fear of losing control. Students see the importance of power and begin using it in the same way with each other as well as with their teachers. Passive as well as violent behaviors sometimes result. This pattern of power hording requires even greater control to sustain power from the top. The need for control is so great that some schools become prisonlike while others stifle all forms of creativity.

National Control

The need for a national dialogue becomes more urgent with each passing day. The actions of different groups intent on improving education become contradictory and counterproductive. The movement toward national standards, while well intentioned, has the potential to be another controlling mechanism from above and afar. Teachers and students will spend enormous amounts of time and energy either trying to meet or subvert the standards. This debate is just beginning; but the following response, which appeared in a recent issue of *Educational Leadership*, shows a teacher's perspective on the issue of imposed standards.

A Teacher Talks to the Standards Bearers

by Andrew Dunn*

❦ *The movement to create national standards is well under way. Soon the standards set by three large groups—the National Council of Teachers of English, the International Reading Association, and the Center for the Study of Reading—will affect every language arts teacher in the nation.*

Average classroom teachers have one main concern about national standards: once standards are established and assessments of the standards are in place, will teachers and the children they teach be better off?

If experience with standardized tests and statewide proficiency assessments [is] . . . indicative, the answer is no. This is what will happen. First, comparisons will be drawn among the assessment scores of districts, counties, and states. The results will tell us what we already know: some schools are having a hard time educating students. Nonetheless, the bad news will be trumpeted in countless bureaucratic reports, political speeches, and media commentaries.

Second, district officials will try mightily to raise scores, all the better to reduce political heat or garner some good publicity. They will "align" curriculum to the new assessments and then the manufacturers of newly "aligned" textbooks will make their entrance, glossy packets in hand.

Third, money will be pumped into lagging systems, but little of it will be used on initiatives like reducing class size or giving teachers more time to work with children. Resources will be soaked up hiring a specialist (my colleague's name for a specialist is "a clipboard and a coffee cup"), on central office reports, and on photocopiers that will be off-limits to teachers.

Fourth, standards will become standardized. How nice. A third grader who moves in midyear from state to state will never miss a beat, since all schools will be on the same page.

. . . Setting national standards will be worthwhile only if it improves what happens between teachers and students, and that will only happen if national tests are eliminated and standards are allowed to function as models rather than fixed rules.

Further, resources must be put into helping districts meet the standards. . . .

National testing, now called "assessment" in the Newspeak idiom, will do nothing to improve the genius of the teacher, students' prospects in life, or the opportunities in the immediate surroundings of the school. Nor will assessment alleviate a bitter reality: regular classroom teachers today do not get the support that they need to pursue, adapt, and meet world-class standards. Teachers get no time, for example, to reflect upon learning theories, write and publish scholarly articles, or pursue grant money. Even as I write this, I wonder how many teachers will read it. Who has time?

Begrudging teachers adequate resources is serious.

. . . If America really wants to educate its children better, we cannot substitute assessment for proper support of the classroom teacher. (8, p. 78)

Comments

The lack of a dialogue on what's important in education places facilitators of learning such as Andrew Dunn, an English teacher at Northern Highlands Regional High School in Allendale, New Jersey, in a defensive position. He tries to fend off another wave of requirements from above without the opportunity for input into decisions that will impact him and his students for years to come.

A JOURNEY BEGUN

The conclusion of a book can be seen as an ending or as a beginning. I hope, as you turn these last pages, you see yourself at the beginning of a journey that will lead to a lifetime of exploration and sharing with others.

A journey is much like a river, beginning with individual droplets of water that link with each other and feed into streams that eventually become great rivers and oceans. Without these small droplets, the rivers would run dry and the oceans vanish. We are much like droplets of water: The paths we take both individually and collectively will influence others and change the future.

Educational change, like a river, will take time to reshape the landscape. Meaningful change seems to become less daunting when we look at one child, one classroom, and one school at a time. As with droplets of rain, it is the linking together that brings about a significant reshaping.

I trust your journey through the pages of this book—with its themes of hope, caring, trusting, sharing, and, most of all, facilitating freedom so that others may learn—reflects a starting point. At its best, life is a changing process, never determined in advance. It is my hope you will join with others to form a river of change. The beneficiaries are others who want and need to learn in caring communities with caring people. This change should not be prescribed by others but rather designed by yourself. Not all journeys are trouble-free. There are times when we pass through the darkness to get to the light. But the process alone makes us a bit wiser. Gaining wisdom comes not from time or age, but from living the challenges of life, learning from mistakes, and building on experiences. The disequilibrium created through new experiences is, in the truest sense, learning.

We must trust our feelings and risk the challenges of new experiences. Let's rededicate ourselves to provide learning communities that kids love and that are so rewarding for adults. To accomplish that goal, we must step back and trust our students and ourselves, and give us all the *freedom to learn.*

REFERENCES

1. M. Gandhi, *Selected Writings.* Cited in R. Arnett, *Dialogic Education: Conversation about Ideas and between Persons* (Carbondale: Southern Illinois University Press, 1992).

2. P. Gordon and K. Bachofer, *Restructuring: An Inside Look: The Evolution of the O'Farrell Community School: Center for Advanced Academic Studies* (San Diego: San Diego Unified School District; Planning, Research, and Evaluation Division, 1990).

3. K. Bachofer and William Borton, *Restructuring: A View From the Trenches: The Continuing Evolution of O'Farrell Community School: Center for Advanced Academic Studies* (San Diego: San Diego Unified School District; Planning, Research, and Evaluation Division, 1992).

4. T. Wubbels, "Special Issue: Guest Editor's Notes," *Journal of Classroom Interaction* 27, no. 1 (1992): v–38.

5. D. Berliner, "Are Our Schools Really Failing?: Twelve Years of Myths Debunked," *NJEA Review* 66, no. 5 (1993): 12–19.

6. C. R. Rogers, *Carl Rogers on Personal Power* (New York: Delacorte Press, 1977).

7. P. R. Fairfield, *Person-centered Graduate Education.* (Buffalo, N.Y.: Prometheus, 1977).

8. A. Dunn, "A Teacher Talks to the Standards Bearers," *Educational Leadership* 50, no. 8 (1993): 78.

APPENDIX

RESOURCES FOR CHANGE:
A LEARNING COMMUNITY

◆

This section is included to give you a network of people, programs, and materials for extending the ideas presented in *Freedom to Learn* to develop a learning community. Change takes time and support. Think of this section as community support for helping you in your efforts to change the way schools and classrooms develop person-centered learning.

We are indebted to the editors of the *Holistic Education Review* (P.O. Box 328, Brandon, VT 05733) and Ron Miller in particular for providing sections of their *Guide to Resources in Holistic Education* for inclusion in the book.

Your comments about *Freedom to Learn* are welcome and encouraged. Please send any correspondence to:

H. Jerome Freiberg, Professor of Education
Farish Hall, Room 350
University of Houston
Houston TX 77204–5872
Telephone: (713) 743–4953

NETWORKS AND ORGANIZATIONS

Alliance for Parental Involvement in Education (ALLPIE)

P.O. Box 59, East Chatham NY 12060–0059

A nonprofit organization to encourage and assist parental involvement in education in public and private schools and at home. ALLPIE offers pamphlets, a book catalog, a newsletter, referral services, conferences, workshops, and seminars on parental rights and involvement in education.

Association for Childhood Education International

11501 Georgia Avenue, Suite 315, Wheaton MD 20902

A professional association that advocates developmentally appropriate curricular materials. Offers a variety of publications on educational topics, including *Learning Opportunities Beyond the School*, a comprehensive resource guide for parents, teachers, and other care givers that contains practical ideas for facilitating learning in multiple settings.

Association for Play Therapy

c/o California School of Professional Psychology, 1350 M Street, Fresno CA 93721

An interdisciplinary and international society dedicated to play therapy and child-centered approaches to learning. Play is viewed as an integral component of healing and learning. Members include teachers, counselors, health care workers, and child life specialists. Sponsors newsletters and conferences.

Center for Integrative Learning

315 University Street, Healdsburg CA 95448

Promoting whole-brain learning, the use of imagery, multimodal learning, brain-compatible learning processes, and integrative curriculum design, as inspired by the work of the late Beverly-Colleen Galyean. Sponsors institutes and conferences, publishes relevant writings, and develops curriculum materials. Offers consulting, networking, and a "creative think tank process."

Center for the Study of Learning and Teaching Styles

Learning Styles Network, St. John's University, Grand Central Parkway, Jamaica NY 11439

Supports the application of learning style research in educational settings. Encourages teachers to become familiar with the different learning styles of individual students, as well as their own teaching styles. Publishes newsletter, research guide, software, and other materials. Sponsors conferences.

Center for Teaching and Learning

Box 7189, University of North Dakota, Grand Forks ND 58202–7189

Publishes journals on progressive and open classroom approaches, as well as a series of research papers.

Cooperative Learning Center

200 Pattee Hall, University of Minnesota, Minneapolis MN 55455

Disseminates research and sponsors teacher training in cooperative educational methods as developed by David Johnson and Roger Johnson.

Educational Kinesiology Foundation

P.O. Box 3396, Ventura CA 93006–3396

Educational Kinesiology (also known as EduKinesthetics or Edu-K) is a biologically based approach for integrating whole-brain and body learning. The Foundation publishes *Brain Gym Magazine,* books and other materials, and sponsors classes in Edu-K principles and techniques around the U.S.

FairTest

342 Broadway, Cambridge MA 02139

The National Center for Fair and Open Testing explores the problems and inequities inherent in standardized testing of both students and teachers. Publications include the quarterly *FairTest Examiner,* biannual updates on various issues, as well as several investigative reports, such as "Sex Bias in College Admissions Tests: Why Women Lose Out" and "None of the Above: Behind the Myth of Scholastic Aptitude."

Folk Education Association of America

4112 38th Street NW, Washington DC 20016

Promotes the Scandinavian folk high school model; these "schools for life" aim to prepare young people for "creative, perceptive, and active living." Folk education is student-centered, cooperative, and holistic, with an emphasis on personal development as well as responsible citizenship. Adult education and "study circles" are also emphasized. Association publishes a journal and newsletter and sponsors an annual conference.

Global Alliance for Transforming Education (GATE)

P. O. Box 21, Grafton VT 05146

GATE is a worldwide network of holistic educators working together to proclaim and promote a vision of education that fosters personal empowerment, social justice, peace, and a sustainable environment. Its activities include revisioning processes for local schools and communities as well as annual conferences on holistic teaching and teacher education.

Individual Education International (IEI)

c/o Bill Kiskaddon, 4404 242nd Place SW, Mountlake Terrace WA 98043

A network of educators who are involved or interested in the Corsini 4R method. Individual Education is based on the principles of Alfred Adler's Individual Psychology and seeks an education that is more democratic and more respectful of students. Membership in IEI includes a subscription to the *Individual Education Bulletin.*

Institute for Democracy in Education

1241 McCracken Hall, Ohio University, Athens OH 45701–2979

Brings together educators and parents to explore how education can prepare students to become democratic citizens through democratic methods of teaching. A grassroots organization with no political affiliation. Publishes the quarterly journal *Democracy and Education*, a newsletter, and other publications; sponsors workshops and institutes, resource center, speakers' bureau, and bookstore.

Institute for Learning and Teaching

449 Desnoyer, St. Paul MN 55104

Provides training in brain-compatible education methods, assists schools and districts with staff development, and publishes the newsletter *The Brain-based Education Networker*.

International Affiliation of Alternative School Associations and Personnel

c/o Dr. Raymond Morley, Office of Education Services for Children, Families, and Communities, Department of Education, Grimes State Office Building, Des Moines IA 50319–0146

A communication network among alternative education associations, educators, and parents. Assists states and local groups in developing alternative schools, programs, and services. Advocates for all facets of alternative education.

International Alliance for Invitational Education

c/o School of Education, University of North Carolina, Greensboro NC 27412

Invitational Education is a humanistic approach based in large part on the work of William Purkey. It encourages the development of human potentials through a cooperative, inviting educational approach that nurtures self-esteem and personal growth. The Alliance offers a newsletter, books, and other publications as well as networking, workshops, and special activities.

International Association for the Study of Cooperation in Education

P. O. Box 1582, Santa Cruz CA 95061

Promotes the study and practice of cooperative methods, where students work together in learning teams and where educators support each other as well. A newsletter, *Cooperation in Education*, has insightful articles and resource listings. Conflict resolution and peace education are also addressed. Also publishes the journal *Cooperative Learning*, a comprehensive resource and forum in the area of cooperative education.

National Association for Core Curriculum, Inc.

404 White Hall, Kent State University, Kent OH 44242–0001

Promotes interdisciplinary, unified, integrated, "block-time" studies in K–12 and college curriculum. Workshops, publications, and consultations.

National Association for the Education of Young Children

1509 Sixteenth Street NW, Washington DC 20036

A network of people committed to fostering the healthy growth and development of children from birth through age eight. Advocates developmentally appropriate educational methods for young children. Publishes journal, books, brochures; sponsors conferences, local groups, and information service.

National Association for Mediation in Education

205 Hampshire House, University of Massachusetts, Amherst MA 01003

Promotes the teaching of conflict resolution skills and programs for peer mediation. A national clearinghouse for publications, curriculum guides, and information on conflict resolution programs already in action. Publishes bibliography and directory, newsletter, and reports.

National Association for Student-Centered Learning (NASCL)

c/o David Jackson, 2 Church View, Norton-sub-Hamdon, Somerset, England, TA14 6SG

Founded in 1990, NASCL is a network of educators who believe that learners learn best when they are at the center of the learning process. Publishes a newsletter and other publications, and sponsors conferences and meetings. Source for two books by Donna Brandes and Paul Ginnis: *A Guide to Student-centered Learning* and *The Student-centered School*, published in the UK by Basil Blackwell.

National Coalition of Alternative Community Schools

P. O. Box 15036, Santa Fe NM 87506

A network of parent cooperatives, free schools, and home schoolers. Facilitates student exchanges and travel. Sponsors annual and regional conferences, a journal (*Skole*), and a newsletter. Has published a directory of member schools with a resource listing.

Network of Progressive Educators

P. O. Box 6028, Evanston IL 60204

An organization for educators from public and private alternative, open, and progressive schools. Aims to bring together all those who identify with progressive ideas, with a focus on teachers and children's learning.

New Horizons for Learning

P. O. Box 15329, Seattle WA 98115–0329

Publishes *On the Beam,* which describes the latest research in learning and thinking skills; also a clearinghouse for seminars, workshops, and ideas for applying these findings. Sponsors extraordinary conferences. Will publish electronic newsletter.

The Person-centered Expressive Therapy Institute

c/o Natalie Rogers, P. O. Box 6518, Santa Rosa CA 95406

The Institute, founded by Natalie Rogers, provides books, videotapes, workshops, and other resources for creativity and consciousness. She has recently authored *The Creative Connection: Expressive Arts as Healing,* published by Science & Behavior (Palo Alto, Calif.: 1993).

Renaissance Educational Associates

4817 North County Road 29, Loveland CO 80537

An international membership association of educators and parents who know that their example of creative living invites others into meaningful and purposeful lives. Publishes *The Renaissance Educator* quarterly, sponsors an annual membership conference, hosts local activities in thirty places around the world, and offers a professional leadership institute each summer.

Teachers' Research Network

c/o Dr. John Chattin-McNichols, Seattle University, Seattle WA 98122

Encourages teachers to be observers of children's development and of the results of innovative educational practices. Focuses on Montessori education; seeks to make connections between Montessori and other early childhood practitioners.

Wholistic Special Interest Group

American Educational Research Association, 1230 Seventeenth Street NW, Washington DC 20036–3078

> Brings together researchers from around the world who meet at the annual meeting of the American Educational Research Association to report on research findings and discuss issues related to affective education.

PUBLICATIONS FOR EDUCATORS

AERO-Gram

Alternative Education Resource Organization, 417 Roslyn Road, Roslyn Heights NY 11577

> Newsletter containing inside, up-to-date information on alternative schools and communities throughout the U.S. and around the world. Edited by Jerry Mintz, who has been actively involved in alternative education for over twenty years. (He is also an independent consultant assisting parents and others wanting to start new alternative schools.)

Childhood—The Waldorf Perspective

c/o Nancy Aldrich, P. O. Box 39, Westford VT 05494

> Explores holistic and spiritual alternatives in parenting, schooling, and home schooling with a focus on the Waldorf view of child development. Discusses family life, cooperative initiatives, curriculum, imaginative play, the wonder of the natural world, storytelling, music, artwork, handwork, handicrafts, festivals, reviews, resources, networking.

Consortium for Whole Brain Learning

461 Ohio Street, St. Paul MN 55107

> A small newsletter, published four times during the school year, with ideas and resources for addressing various learning styles.

Early Education and Development

39 Pearl Street, Brandon VT 05733–1007

> A quarterly professional journal for those involved in educational and preschool services to children and their families. Emphasizes the implications of current research on child development for early education and day-care programs, special needs programs, and other practical educational problems.

Green Teacher

95 Robert Street, Toronto, Canada, M5S 2K5

Published five times per year, this North American magazine helps elementary/secondary teachers and parents promote global and environmental awareness with young people. Articles to rethink education, classroom-ready activities, review of new resources on varied themes (such as native peoples' perspectives, international development, marine education, conflict resolution, and energy education) all find room in its pages.

Holistic Education Review

P.O. Box 328, Brandon VT 05733-0328

Joyful Child

P.O. Box 5506, Scottsdale AZ 85261

A magazine designed to awaken self-esteem, love, peace, and joy in children as well as adults. Emphasizes that joy is the true essence of humanity but needs to be cultivated more carefully in this society. To this end, *Joyful Child* has leadership training classes for facilitating Joyful Child parenting classes. It also distributes books and other products and puts on a symposium.

Limbic Plus

Jenzen Kelly Associates, Inc., 32260 88th Avenue, Lawton MI 49065

A bimonthly newsletter about the educational implications of recent research on the brain, consciousness, and learning. Includes features on lifelong learning, educational resources, exemplary teachers, and more.

Pollen: Journal of BioRegional Education

Sunrock Farm, 103 Gibson Lane, Wilder KY 41076

Promotes a bioregional perspective in education—the recognition that "humans must establish a new respectful relationship with nature and recover a sense of place." This ecological approach emphasizes diversity and decentralization, relevant to both the content and process of education. *Pollen* is connected to the work of the North American Bioregional Conferences.

Rethinking Schools

1001 East Keefe Avenue, Milwaukee WI 53212

An independent educational journal/newspaper published by educators in Milwaukee area public schools. Examines a wide scope of problems in today's education, including urban social problems, standardized testing, reading methods, and many issues of interest to parents as well as educators.

PEACE AND GLOBAL EDUCATION

American Friends Service Committee

1501 Cherry Street, Philadelphia PA 19102

Offers the publication *Peace Education Resources* and other materials.

Canadian Peace Educators' Network

c/o The Pembina Institute, P.O. Box 7558, Drayton Valley, Alberta, Canada, TOE 0M0

An information and resource exchange network. Publishes a national directory and a quarterly newsletter that explore peace education issues on an international scale and include an extensive resource listing.

Center for Cross-cultural Education

College of Education, Georgia State University, Atlanta GA 30303–3083

Has published eight volumes on educational issues from an international perspective. The most recent volumes examine educational reform movements and teacher training in several countries, including the U.S. and the former Soviet Union.

Children Around the World Resource Center

P.O. Box 40657, Bellevue WA 98015

Assists teachers and schools (grades one through nine) in making connections with their peers in other countries for the exchange of letters and artwork. Also currently developing International Packets that include slides, songs, and stories from various cultures. The newsletter *Courier* gives ideas and news from around the world.

Children's Creative Response to Conflict

522 North Broadway, Nyack NY 10960–0271

Offers activities, publications, workshops, and courses to help teachers as well as children learn skills of cooperation, communication, affirmation, conflict resolution, bias, and mediation. A holistic, experiential approach dealing with the roots of conflict. Affiliated with the Fellowship of Reconciliation, it has twenty-seven branches worldwide.

Educators for Social Responsibility

23 Garden Street, Cambridge MA 02138

Curricular materials on nuclear and other global issues, conflict resolution, critical thinking. Sponsors teacher workshops.

Global Education Associates

475 Riverside Drive, Suite 1848, New York NY 10115

Produces an extensive list of books, monographs (*The Whole Earth Papers*), filmstrips, audiocassetes and videotapes as well as the excellent magazine *Breakthrough*. Explores alternative solutions to international conflicts and advocates crosscultural understanding.

International Association of Educators for World Peace

Box 3282, Huntsville AL 35810

Aims to build a global community where all people live together in harmony, prosperity, and peace. Promotes cooperative international ventures (focusing on space exploration) as a way of eliminating fear and mistrust. Publishes *Peace Education* and other publications. Has chapters in fifty countries.

Legacy International

Route 4, Box 265, Bedford VA 24523

Provides training and action programs in three major areas: dialogue and conflict resolution, environment and sustainable development, and crosscultural communication. In seminars, workshops, work projects, curriculum-development programs, consultations, conferences, and grassroots action and education campaigns, emphasis is placed on intercultural understanding as a key to creating solutions for the issues of the world today and in the coming decades.

Martin Luther King, Jr., Center for Nonviolent Social Change, Inc.

449 Auburn Avenue, Atlanta GA 30312

Curricular materials for students in primary grades through high school are available. Write for a catalog.

Nuclear Age Peace Foundation

1187 Coast Village Road, Suite 123, Santa Barbara CA 93108

Publishes a series of booklets on waging peace that covers a broad range of important issues, which are written by leading thinkers in peace studies, as well as a new book, *Waging Peace*. Also sponsors a high school essay contest.

Parents and Teachers for Social Responsibility

Box 517, Moretown VT 05660

Publications, conferences, and special projects to promote a safer, saner world for all children. Publications include *What About the Children?* and *The Monkey's Dilemma*. A major international congress for educators will be sponsored in 1995.

Peace Education Program

Box 171, Teachers College, Columbia University, New York NY 10027

Publisher of books (*Comprehensive Peace Education, Educating for Global Responsibility*, and others) and other materials. Sponsors international institutes and seminars.

Peace Links

747 Eighth Street SE, Washington DC 20003

Dedicated to public education about peace and nuclear issues. Has put together information and resource kits for parents, educators, and young people entitled *Celebrate Peace, Reach for Peace*, and *Global Awareness*. Publishes *Student Action Update* and *Connection* newsletters. Sponsors exchanges and other programs.

Peace of Our Minds

R.D. l-H, Box 171, West Edmeston NY 13485

A forum by kids, for kids. Encourages young people (ages eight to eighteen) to explore their role as peacemakers. They write about cultural, ethnic, and familial differences as well as challenges of physical disabilities. "Kid-to-Kid" column is a question-and-answer forum for kids to explore issues of concern.

Skipping Stones

80574 Hazelton Road, Cottage Grove OR 97424

This multi-ethnic children's forum truly brings global education to life. Gathers together poetry, articles, stories, art, photos, and pen pal requests from around the world to promote cooperative on celebration of cultural diversity and awareness. Regular noteworthy news, networking book reviews, and rhymes.

HOLISTIC EDUCATIONAL THEORY

Thomas Armstrong, *The Radiant Child* (Wheaton, Ill.: Quest Books, Theosophical Publishing House, 1985); *In Their Own Way* (Los Angeles: Tarcher, 1987).

John P. Miller, *The Holistic Curriculum* (Toronto: Ontario Institute for Studies in Education Press, 1988).

Ron Miller, *What Are Schools For? Holistic Education in American Culture* (Brandon, Vt.: Holistic Education Press, 1992).

Maria Montessori, *The Secret of Childhood* (New York: Ballantine, 1972).

Margaret Naumburg, *The Child and the World* (New York: Harcourt Brace, 1928).

Donald W. Oliver and Kathleen Gershman, *Education, Modernity, and Fractured Meaning: Toward a Process Theory of Teaching and Learning* (Albany: State University of New York Press, 1989).

Joseph Chilton Pearce, *Magical Child* (New York: Dutton, 1977); *Magical Child Matures* (New York: Dutton, 1985).

David E. Purpel, *The Moral and Spiritual Crisis in Education* (Granby, Mass.: Bergen and Garvey, 1989).

Mary C. Richards, *Toward Wholeness: Rudolf Steiner Education in America* (Middletown, Conn.: Wesleyan University Press, 1980).

Thomas B. Roberts, ed., *Four Psychologies Applied to Education* (Cambridge, Mass.: Schenkman, 1975).

Douglas Sloan, *Insight-Imagination: The Emancipation of Thought and the Modern World* (Westport, Conn.: Greenwood, 1983).

ADDITIONAL READINGS

M. J. Adler, *The Paideia Proposal: An Educational Manifesto* (New York: Macmillan, 1982).

E. Anderson, *StreetWise* (Chicago: The University of Chicago Press, 1990).

D. Aspy and F. Roebuck, *Kids Don't Learn from People They Don't Like* (Amherst, Mass.: Human Resource Development Press, 1977).

R. Barth, *Improving Schools from Within* (San Francisco: Jossey-Bass, 1990).

A Bayer, *Collaborative-Apprenticeship Learning* (Mountain View, Calif.: Mayfield, 1990).

W. Bechtol and J. Sorenson, *Restructuring School for Individual Students* (Needham Heights, Mass.: Allyn and Bacon, 1993).

W. Bennis, *Why Leaders Can't Lead: The Unconscious Conspiracy Continues* (San Francisco: Jossey-Bass, 1989).

G. Caine and R. Caine, *Making Connections* (Alexandria, Vir.: Association for Supervision and Curriculum Development, 1991).

M. Cohn and R. Kottkamp, *Teaching the Missing Voice in Education* (Albany: State University of New York Press, 1993).

R. Elmore, *Restructuring Schools* (San Francisco: Jossey-Bass, 1990).

H. Fisher Darrow, *Independent Activities for Creative Learning* (New York: Teachers College Press, 1986).

W. Glasser, *The Quality School* (New York: Harper Perennial, 1992).

J. I. Goodlad, *A Place Called School: Prospects for the Future* (New York: McGraw-Hill, 1984).

L. Hergert, J. Phlegar, and M. Perez-Selles, *Kindle the Spark* (Andover, Mass.: The Regional Laboratory, 1991).

J. Herman, P. Aschbacher, and L. Winter, *A Practical Guide to Alternative Assessment* (Alexandria, Vir.: Association for Supervision and Curriculum Development, 1992).

G. A. Hess, *School Restructuring, Chicago Style* (Newbury Park, Calif.: Corwin Press, 1991).

R. Hunter and E. Scheirer, *The Organic Curriculum* (New York: Falmer Press, 1988).

D. Johnson, *Reaching Out*, 5th ed. (Needham Heights, Mass.: Allyn and Bacon, 1993).

B. Joyce and B. Shower, *Student Achievement Through Staff Development* (White Plains, N.Y.: Longman, 1987).

E. Lawler, B. Markovsky, C. Ridgeway, and H. Walker, *Advances in Group Processes* (Greenwich, Conn.: JAI Press, 1992).

G. Morrow, *The Compassionate School* (Englewood Cliffs, N.J.: Prentice-Hall, 1987).

J. Murphy, *Restructuring Schools* (New York: Teachers College Press, 1991).

V. Richardson, Casanova, U., Placier, P., and Guilfoyle, K., *School Children At-Risk* (New York: Falmer Press, 1989).

P. Schlechty, *School for the Twenty-first Century* (San Francisco: Jossey-Bass, 1990).

T. Sizer, *Horace's Compromise: The Dilemma of the American High School* (Boston: Houghton Mifflin, 1984).

E. Stone, *Quality Teaching* (London: Routledge, 1992).

C. Teddlie and S. Stringfield, *Schools Make a Difference* (New York: Teachers College Press, 1993).

G. Wehlage et al., *Reducing the Risk* (New York: Falmer Press, 1989).

J. Wertsch, *Vygotsky and the Social Formation of Mind.* (Cambridge: Harvard University Press, 1985).

VIDEO SOURCE

"...And Learning for All" A seven-part video series developed by McREL and Dr. Barbara McCombs, 2550 S. Parker Rd., Suite 500, Aurora, CO 80014. The 1993 video series shares dramatic stories about educational programs that work, of communities committed to quality and of people who care. The video programs are approximately 25 minutes in length.

END NOTES

◆

The Table of Contents is repeated here to identify the types of changes that occurred in the book. Chapters in the text that are newly developed by Jerome Freiberg for the third edition are indicated by an asterisk (*). Chapters that have been largely retained from the second edition of *Freedom to Learn* are indicated by two asterisks (**). Chapters that have been revised from the second edition and include new examples, cases, and updated research are indicated by the following symbol (†).

INDEX

AUTHOR PROFILE

CARL ROGERS

◆

Carl Rogers (1902–1987) is the most influential psychologist in American history. His influence in the fields of education, counseling, psychotherapy, conflict resolution, and peace is similarly outstanding. A founder of humanistic psychology, he has impacted the world through his empathic presence, his rigorous research, and his authorship of sixteen books and more than 200 professional articles. His best known books are: *On Becoming a Person, Client Centered Therapy, Freedom to Learn for the 80's, A Way of Being, Carl Rogers on Personal Power, Carl Rogers on Encounter Groups,* and *Becoming Partners: Marriage and Its Alternatives.*

His lifetime of research and experimental work focused on demonstrating the psychological conditions for allowing open communication and empowering individuals to achieve their full potential. He pioneered the move away from traditional psychoanalysis, and developed client-centered psychotherapy, which recognizes that "each client has within him or herself the vast resources for self-understanding, for altering his or her self-concept, attitudes, and self-directed behavior—and that these resources can be tapped—by providing a definable climate of facilitative attitudes."

Rogers' last decade was devoted to applying his theories in areas of social conflict within nations, and he traveled worldwide to accomplish this. In Belfast, Ireland, Rogers brought together influential Protestants and Catholics, in South Africa, blacks and whites, in the United States, consumers and providers in the health field.

Recognition of his work has come through dozens of honorary awards and degrees bestowed on him from throughout the world, among them the American Psychology Association's Distinguished Scientific Contribution Award the first year it was given. A few years later he also received its Distinguished Professional Contribution Award. The day he died, February 4, 1987, also happened to be the day he was nominated for the Nobel Peace Prize. The nomination stated, ". . .your work in Central America, South Africa, Northern Ireland is truly deserving of consideration for the Nobel Peace Prize."

Two of his books have been published posthumously: *The Carl Rogers' Reader*, a collection of his most influential writings, and *Carl Rogers' Dialogues*, which features his interchanges with such other giants in the field as Paul Tillich, B. F. Skinner, Gregory Bateson, and Rollo May.

Most importantly, Carl Rogers modeled the compassion and democratic ideals which he voiced.

AUTHOR PROFILE

H. JEROME FREIBERG

◆

H. Jerome Freiberg is a professor of education in the College of Education at the University of Houston and is Senior Research Associate at Temple University for the National Center on Education in the Inner Cities. He is also the Director at Houston for the National Center on Education in the Inner Cities. He has devoted most of the last twenty years to improving the quality of life for children, teachers, and administrators in the inner city.

He has published nearly 100 scholarly works including articles in national and international journals, chapters, and books. He is the Editor of the *Journal of Classroom Interaction*, an international journal with subscribers in over 50 nations. Two recent books include *Universal Teaching Strategies* with Amy Driscoll, and *Touch the Future: Teach?* with Robert Houston, Renée Clift, and Allen Warner. Dr. Freiberg has received the 1988-89 University of Houston's Teaching Excellence Award and the College of Education Award for Teaching Excellence.

He developed the first Teachers' Academy and Institute in Preston County, West Virginia. He founded the Providence Free School for Teachers. Dr. Freiberg also directed Teacher Corps in Houston, Texas. His efforts in schools emphasize creating person-centered learning environments including the ways school and classroom management work for the benefit of students and teachers. Dr. Freiberg was the Director of the Institute for Research on Urban Schooling, Chair of the College of Education faculty, and Associate Chair for the Department of Curriculum and Instruction at the University of Houston.

He taught grades 6–12 as a teacher and long-term substitute and is certified as a high school American History/Social Studies teacher. He also was a volunteer teacher at a maximum security prison. He has served as principal investigator and researcher for numerous state and federal projects, including the Houston Read Commission Learning Center. He is the developer of the "Read Along Project" for parents and students in six Houston ISD schools.

Dr. Freiberg has also worked with the Department of Defense Overseas Schools and with the ministries of education in Italy and Israel on improving school climate. He has worked with educators from Italy, Spain, England, Canary Islands, Azores, Portugal, Israel, Canada, and Mexico. He has also consulted with State Departments of Education, colleges and universities and school districts throughout the United States.